Fundamentals of SUPPLY CHAIN MANAGEMENT

A Practitioner's Perspective

William McLaury
Eugene Spiegle

Kendall Hunt
publishing company

Definitions throughout the chapters used with permission. Copyright 2016 APICS.

Cover, section, and chapter opener images © Shutterstock.com

Kendall Hunt
publishing company

www.kendallhunt.com
Send all inquiries to:
4050 Westmark Drive
Dubuque, IA 52004-1840

Contents

PLAN

CHAPTER 1 - Introduction to Supply Chain Management   3
CHAPTER 2 - Forecasting and Demand Planning   35
CHAPTER 3 - Supply Chain Planning   63
CHAPTER 4 - Inventory Management   95

SOURCE

CHAPTER 5 - Purchasing Management   139
CHAPTER 6 - Strategic Sourcing   165
CHAPTER 7 - Supplier Relationship Management   187

MAKE

CHAPTER 8 - Operations Management with LEAN and Six Sigma   213

DELIVER AND RETURN

CHAPTER 9 - Logistics: Warehousing, Transportation, and Reverse Logistics   251
CHAPTER 10 - Global Logistics and International Trade   305
CHAPTER 11 - Customer Relationship Management   331
CHAPTER 12 - Supply Chain Management in the Service Industry   355

ENABLE

CHAPTER 13 - Project Management   381

The authors would like to recognize Haiyan Liu and Zachary Riffell for their contributions to the completion of this manuscript.

PLAN

Chapter 1

Introduction to Supply Chain Management

CHAPTER OUTLINE

Introduction

What Is Supply Chain Management?

Supply Chain Management versus Logistics

Your Role in a Supply Chain

Supply Chain Flow

Supply Chain Management in the Service Industry

Origins and Evolution of Supply Chain Management

The Future of Supply Chain Management

Foundation of Supply Chain Management

Supply Chain Capabilities Models

Managing the Supply Chain through Defined Tasks

The Challenge of Supply Chain Management

Supply Chain Planning and Execution

Benefits of Supply Chain Management

Current Trends in Supply Chain Management

Summary

INTRODUCTION ....

The discipline of supply chain management is dynamic and evolving. Innovation, technology, the internet, and the escalation of globalization, among other things, have contributed to the ongoing and rapid evolution of the field. In addition, pressure is being applied to supply chains by fluctuating demand, changing customer expectations, reduced product lifecycles, speed to market, and increased complexity. All of these factors intensify the need to understand and examine how we manage our supply chains. This text will explore supply chains and the fundamentals of how supply chains are managed in an effort to improve our understanding.

The American Production and Inventory Control Society (APICS), the premier professional association for supply chain and operations management, defines a **supply chain** as "the global network used to deliver products and services from raw materials to customers through an engineered flow of information, physical distribution, and cash."[1] In simpler terms, a supply chain is everything that happens to a product on the journey from "concept to consumer."

There are different ways to set up and operate a supply chain depending on the type of product or service a company provides. A company may even operate multiple supply chain setups simultaneously if the company's product portfolio is broad or complex. Regardless of the specific setup, supply chains are generally described as spanning from end to end (i.e., from your supplier's suppliers, to your suppliers on one end, through your organization's operations, and out to your customers, and to your customer's customers, on the opposite end). Most supply chains follow the basic Supply Chain Operations Research (SCOR) model shown in figure 1.1.

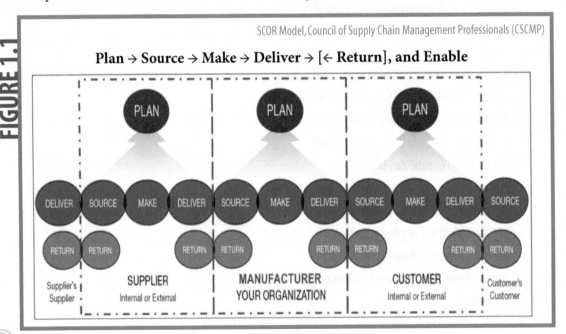

FIGURE 1.1

SCOR Model, Council of Supply Chain Management Professionals (CSCMP)

Plan → Source → Make → Deliver → [← Return], and Enable

The model depicts the relationships and linkages between the trading partners that form a supply chain. Companies <u>plan</u> what they make, <u>source</u> the materials, <u>make</u> the products, and <u>deliver</u> them to the marketplace. Companies may also have to handle <u>return</u> of products back through the supply chain. Whether you are a supplier, a manufacturer, or a customer, you're likely doing each of these activities. If you are a manufacturer, as shown in the middle of figure 1.1, you have suppliers on one side that must make the products or materials that you need, and they likely have sources of raw materials to support their production. Similarly, you as the manufacturer are a supplier to your customers. You make the products that your customers want. If your customers are not the end consumers of the product, they are also suppliers to their customers who will ultimately consume the product. Suppliers and customers can be internal (i.e., part of your organization) or external to your organization, and many companies have both internal and external suppliers and customers. In addition to the functions of plan, source, make, deliver, and (potentially) return, which each of the trading partners must execute, supply chains are also typically <u>enabled</u> through various types of processes and technologies (e.g., systems software and hardware).

This text will use the SCOR model as an outline to describe all of the functions, processes, and activities involved in managing a supply chain. To better understand this model, following is a description and quick overview of each major function.

PLAN: The first phase of the model is "Plan." Planning establishes the parameters within which the supply chain will operate. Companies need a strategy for managing all of the resources necessary to address how a product or service will be created and delivered to meet the needs of their customers. Planning includes the determination of marketing and distribution channels, promotions, quantities, timing, inventory and replenishment policies, and production policies. Part of supply chain planning is developing metrics to monitor the supply chain so that it is efficient and cost effective and also delivers high quality and value to the customers it serves.

SOURCE: The next phase of the model is "Source." Sourcing is the process of identifying the suppliers that provide the products/materials and services needed for the supply chain to deliver the finished product(s) desired by the customer(s). This phase involves not only identifying reliable suppliers but also building a strong relationship with those suppliers. Supply chain managers must also develop pricing, shipping, delivery, and payment processes with suppliers and create metrics for monitoring and improving the performance of the buying process over time and potentially supplier performance as well.

MAKE: The third phase of the model is "Make." Make or manufacturing is the series of operations performed to convert materials into a finished product. This is the step where the finished product is manufactured, tested, packaged, and scheduled for delivery. Quality management is an important aspect of the manufacturing process. Aspects such as LEAN Manufacturing and Six Sigma are introduced in the "Make" process. This is the most metric-intensive portion of the supply chain, where companies are able to measure quality levels, production output, and worker productivity.

DELIVER: The fourth phase of the model is "Deliver." Also known as the logistics phase, this is the part of supply chain management that oversees the planning and execution of both the forward and reverse flow of goods and related information between various points in the supply chain to meet customer requirements. During the deliver phase, companies coordinate the receipt of orders from customers, develop a network of warehouses, pick carriers to transport products to customers, and set up an invoicing system to receive payments, among other aspects.

RETURN: The fifth phase of the model is "Return." Also known as reverse logistics, this is the part of supply chain management that deals with planning and controlling the process of moving goods specifically from the point of consumption back to the point of origin for repair, reclamation, re-manufacture, recycling, or disposal. As this process quite literally goes against the normal outbound flow of products to the market, this can be a problematic part of the supply chain for many companies. Supply chain managers have to create a responsive and flexible network for receiving defective and excess products back from their customers and supporting customers who have questions and problems with delivered products. It is often an unwanted part of the supply chain and is frequently outsourced to a third party to handle for the company.

ENABLE: An additional aspect of the model is "Enable." Enabling processes facilitate a company's ability to manage the supply chain. Enabling processes include elements such as supply chain systems and network operations, systems configuration control, interfaces, gateways, database administration, electronic data interchange (EDI), telecommunications services, performance measurement, contract management, business rules, standards, and training and education, to name just a few. The processes associated with this component of the SCOR model are spread throughout every stage. In other words, we want to enable our capabilities as we plan, source, make, and deliver (and return). This is not a stage that occurs sequentially after all of the others.

WHAT IS SUPPLY CHAIN MANAGEMENT? ....

In order to define what supply chain management is, we should start by dispelling some common misconceptions. Supply chain management is NOT just a chain of businesses, it is NOT just a new name for purchasing or operations management, and it is NOT just a synonym for logistics. People may think of supply chain management as simply controlling the sequence of steps involved in the production of a product, that you obtain some materials and manufacture or assemble them step by step into a product that you then sell to a customer, but supply chain management is really **the coordination of a network of independent organizations** (i.e., trading partners) **involved in creating a desired product or service, where the partners function together as one seamless organization.** APICS defines supply chain management as "the design, planning, execution, control, and monitoring of supply chain activities, with the objective of creating net value, building a competitive infrastructure, leveraging worldwide logistics, synchronizing supply with demand, and measuring performance globally."[1] Supply chain management is not just the production of products; it's about how people, process, technology, equipment, infrastructure, money, and information all integrate efficiently and effectively to facilitate the flow of products and services from the raw material stage to finished product manufacturing, out into wholesale and distribution channels, and ultimately to retailers and consumers, to the benefit of everyone in the supply chain.

The principle mission of supply chain management is to ensure that demand is met. Supply chain management delivers value by managing the processes of all of those otherwise independent trading partners so that they collaborate with one another in an efficient, effective, and cost-conscious way. The goals are to improve customer service while simultaneously reducing both inventory investment and operating expenses. By reaching these goals, companies will make significant progress toward achieving world-class supply chain management. In line with these goals, the two main reasons that firms implement supply chain management are to achieve cost savings and to better coordinate their resources.

Because these individual goals can be diametrically opposed to one another, they can be very hard to achieve. Companies that want to improve their customer service have a tendency to do it by increasing their inventory in an effort to always have enough product available to supply any potential demand and to offset any deficiencies in their ability to maintain a continuity of supply. This may be the easiest and fastest way to improve customer service in terms of availability; however, increasing inventory in turn increases operating expenses and ties up capital that could otherwise be used for activities such as research and development, marketing and sales, new product launches, salary increases, shareholder dividends, and more. We will detail more on the trade-offs between customer service, inventory investment, and operating expenses throughout this text.

SUPPLY CHAIN MANAGEMENT VERSUS LOGISTICS ....

There are those who confuse supply chain management with logistics. The concept of **logistics** refers to "the art and science of obtaining, producing, and distributing material and product in the proper place and in proper quantities."[1] On the surface this sounds very similar to supply chain management. Whereas supply chain management refers to a network of independent companies that work together and coordinate their actions to deliver a product(s) or service(s) to market for the benefit of all companies in the supply chain, **logistics is more inwardly focused on your own organization's operations,** encompassing activities specific to inventory management, warehousing (i.e., material handling and storage), distribution (i.e., order fulfillment, pick, pack and ship), and transportation (i.e., the movement of inventories into and out of an organization). These internal processes are often aligned functionally but operated independently, creating inefficiencies due to a lack of coordination. **This lack of cohesion is where supply chain management goes beyond logistics by recognizing the need for integration of these functions and by promoting collaboration between internal and external members of a supply chain**. Supply chain management extends beyond the four walls of your organization and incorporates your supply chain partners on both the supplier side and the customer side, bringing them into a collaborative process with you to the **benefit of all participants in the supply chain**. Supply chain management incorporates all of those traditional logistics activities as well as aspects of activities such as forecasting and demand management, procurement, supplier relationship management, planning and scheduling, new product development, finance, and customer relationship management—all of which will be covered in this text.

YOUR ROLE IN A SUPPLY CHAIN...

Any organization that offers a product or a service has a supply chain. Supply chains can be **very simple** or **very complex**. At first glance, the supply chain for bottled water looks very simple, but it is more complex than you may think. There are suppliers of the bottles, caps, labels, corrugated boxes, clear shrink wrapping, energy/utilities, maintenance supplies, office supplies, warehousing, distribution, transportation services, insurance, etc., and of course, a source of supply for the water itself. However, this supply chain is certainly not as complex as the supply chains for producing automobiles or airplanes which may involve hundreds if not thousands of suppliers and trading partners.

Both **large** and **small organizations** have supply chains, from major corporations that can have multiple supply chains for their products located all over the world, down to even the small mom-and-pop operation on the local corner, which also has a supply chain for whatever products or services that they are providing. **Public** or **private organizations** whether they are **for-profit** or **nonprofit** all have supply chains. Organizations such as Johnson & Johnson, Walmart, and General Motors are publicly traded major for-profit corporations with extensive and complex supply chain operations. Nonprofit organizations such as American Red Cross, Doctors without Borders, and Habitat for Humanity also have supply chains for the products and services that each provides. You don't need to be a large company or have significant revenue to realize the need to manage your supply chain. All businesses need resources, materials, and services, whether they are large or small, public or private, for-profit or nonprofit. They all have a supply chain.

You are part of multiple supply chains whether you are aware of it or not. You are on the supply side if you work for a company that provides a product or a service. You are most certainly on the demand side of many supply chains as a consumer of products and services. We all consume food, use fuel and utilities, and take advantage of numerous services such as banking, insurance, hotels, dry cleaning, and car repair. On the demand side, companies make and ship products to customers, either directly or through intermediaries, based on customer demand. Customer demand may be in the form of actual orders, or part of a forecast model based on knowledge of what consumers want. Companies use forecast information to develop plans to produce the products and services they determine their customers want, so almost everyone is part of multiple supply chains.

SUPPLY CHAIN FLOW

To fully understand your supply chain, you need to understand the flow. It may help to see what your supply chain looks like, which means that you may need to actually draw it, at least at a macroscopic level. To facilitate this task, it may help to ask and answer the following questions: Who are my suppliers? Where do they get their materials? Who is manufacturing the product or service that I'm selling? How is it being distributed? Who are my customers and where are they? Do I sell direct to consumers or to wholesalers or distributors? How are the products actually transported: by truck, by ocean, by rail, etc.?

Figure 1.2 is a generic supply chain showing the linear flow of supply from left to right as indicated by the **Product & Service Flow** arrow.

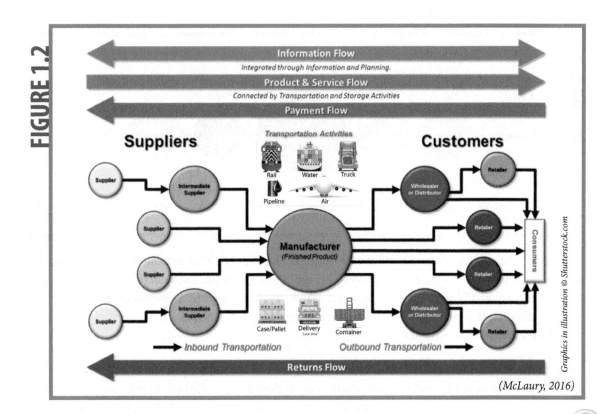

FIGURE 1.2

Graphics in illustration © Shutterstock.com

(McLaury, 2016)

For illustrative purposes, let's assume we are the manufacturer in the middle of the diagram producing a finished product. Beginning on the left side, we see **links** or **nodes** (the circles) for our suppliers and intermediate suppliers, who are providers of materials and services that we as the manufacturer will need in order to produce the product(s) that our customers want. Some suppliers provide products or services to us <u>indirectly</u> through intermediate suppliers while other suppliers provide products or services to us <u>directly</u>. Referring to figure 1.3, any company that delivers to us directly is a Tier 1 supplier. A supplier that supplies products we need to our Tier 1 supplier is our Tier 2 supplier. The tiers continue to grow as we move through more and more entities (Tier 3, Tier 4, etc.). In other words, Tier 1 is our direct supplier, and Tier 2, Tier 3, and so forth, are our indirect suppliers. It is also possible for a supplier to occupy multiple tiers. We might buy a component from one supplier directly but another product from that same supplier through an intermediate supplier. In this case, this supplier is a Tier 1 supplier for the first component and Tier 2 supplier for the second component. Just as our suppliers occupy different tiers, our customers occupy different tiers as well. To the right of the manufacturer are the customers, including wholesalers and distributors, retailers, and consumers. Wholesalers, distributors, and retailers are generally intermediaries in the supply chain who facilitate the transfer of products from manufacturers to the consumer (i.e., the entity who is actually going to use the finished product). Anyone we ship directly to is our Tier 1 customer. As manufacturers we might provide our products to wholesalers and/or distributors, retailers, or consumers. Our Tier 2 customers are any customers who receive our product(s) or service(s) through a Tier 1 customer. Customers can occupy multiple tiers simultaneously just as suppliers can.

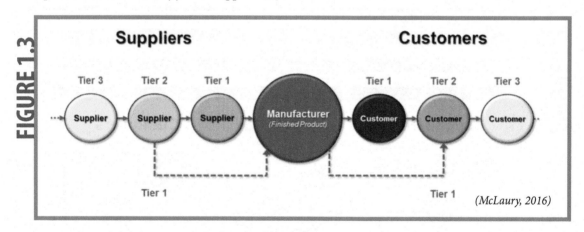

FIGURE 1.3

(McLaury, 2016)

The arrows connecting each of the links or nodes in the supply chain indicate **transportation** activities, both inbound to the manufacturer and outbound from the manufacturer. Transportation modes can vary widely and include rail, water, truck, air, and pipeline. Using more than one mode of transportation to make a single shipment is referred to as intermodal. Transportation will be explored in more detail in Chapter 9.

To facilitate the physical flow of products and materials along the supply chain, information such as forecasts, orders, confirmations, and invoices must flow in both directions as shown by the double-sided **Information Flow** arrow at the top of figure 1.2. Information is vital for planning all of the activities in the supply chain, and for allocating and managing all of the resources necessary to execute the plan once developed.

The **Payment Flow** arrow indicates the flow of funds or money paid to members in the supply chain for product and services rendered.

While products generally flow from left to right, there may be the need for some reverse logistics (i.e., right to left flow) to accommodate returns, recycling, rejected products, and so forth, as depicted by the **Returns Flow** arrow. Companies need to invest in managing both their outbound flow of products to the marketplace and their reverse flow, handling customer issues and problems that might occur in the field with the products that have already been sold and distributed.

The following are examples of supply chains from various industries.

Example #1: Fresh Produce

The example depicted in figure 1.4 is for fresh produce such as strawberries or peaches, which may come from South America to the United States. From the orchards in South America, the produce

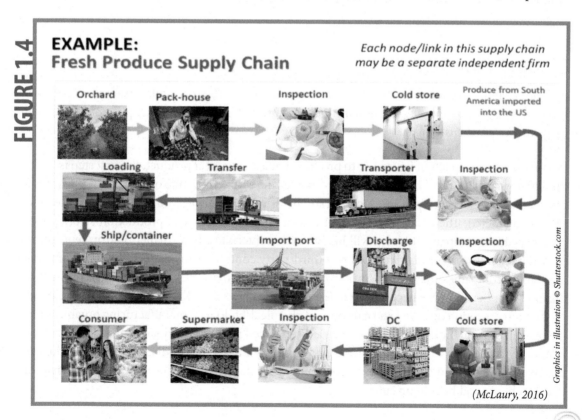

FIGURE 1.4

EXAMPLE: Fresh Produce Supply Chain

Each node/link in this supply chain may be a separate independent firm

Orchard — Pack-house — Inspection — Cold store — Produce from South America imported into the US

Loading — Transfer — Transporter — Inspection

Ship/container — Import port — Discharge — Inspection

Consumer — Supermarket — Inspection — DC — Cold store

Graphics in illustration © Shutterstock.com

(McLaury, 2016)

is picked and then moved to a pack-house. In the pack-house, the produce is inspected for quality and then packed for shipment. To preserve freshness and shelf life, most produce is cold stored (i.e., refrigerated). An extra inspection may be needed before transportation to make sure the quality has been maintained through the picking and packing process. The produce is then loaded onto a truck and transported to the port for export to the United States. At the port, the produce is transferred from the truck into a refrigerated container and then the container is loaded onto a cargo ship that travels from South America to the United States. When the ship arrives in the United States, the produce goes through an import process and inspection. It is then discharged or offloaded from the cargo ship into the port. There is another inspection to make sure the produce is still good. The produce will likely then go back into cold storage temporarily until the produce is actually released by U.S. Customs and Border Protection and any other government agencies involved in the import process, such as the U.S. Agricultural Department. Once released, the produce is removed from the port and transported to the distribution center where it is likely put back into cold storage. Before the produce is shipped out from the distribution center to the retail outlet (e.g., supermarket), there is yet another inspection to make sure the produce is still good. Finally, the produce is shipped out to a supermarket where we as consumers are able to select and buy the produce off the shelf. Each one of these separate activities may be performed by a different legal entity. In this simple example of supplying produce from South America to U.S. consumers, there are numerous steps and multiple parties involved in delivering the product from one stage to the next throughout the entire supply chain.

Example #2: Pharmaceuticals

Another example comes from the pharmaceutical industry. This particular example is laid out in three swim lanes or groupings: external suppliers, internal operations of the pharmaceutical company, and external customers.

Starting from the top left of figure 1.5, to produce a pharmaceutical product, the first step is to make the active pharmaceutical ingredient (API)—that is, the actual molecule of the drug itself. You must complete this step before you can incorporate the drug into a dosage form (tablet, capsule, injectable, inhaler, etc.). The creation of the API is a chemical or biological production step. In a large pharmaceutical company, this step will likely be done internally. In a smaller pharmaceutical company the formulation may be provided to a third-party contractor to produce the API. Some pharmaceutical companies may use both internal and external manufacturing. To make the API, raw material suppliers ship the necessary starting materials in to either the internal chemical/biological production operation or to an external contract chemical/biological manufacturing organization. In the pharmaceutical industry, APIs are generally produced in a large campaign/production run (e.g., maybe a years' worth of inventory at a time), as the synthesis for producing a drug product may involve many steps and take months to complete. Once the API is produced, it is likely transported to a warehouse and held in inventory.

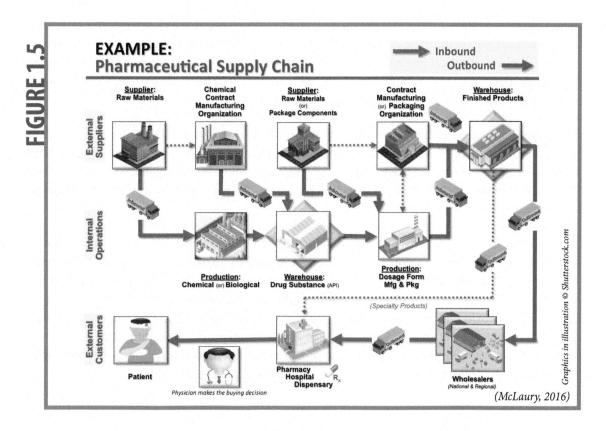

FIGURE 1.5

EXAMPLE:
Pharmaceutical Supply Chain

Inbound →
Outbound →

Supplier: Raw Materials

Chemical Contract Manufacturing Organization

Supplier: Raw Materials (or) Package Components

Contract Manufacturing (or) Packaging Organization

Warehouse: Finished Products

External Suppliers

Internal Operations

Production: Chemical (or) Biological

Warehouse: Drug Substance (API)

Production: Dosage Form Mfg & Pkg

(Specialty Products)

External Customers

Patient

Physician makes the buying decision

Pharmacy Hospital Dispensary Rx

Wholesalers (National & Regional)

Graphics in illustration © Shutterstock.com

(McLaury, 2016)

The API will then be used in the manufacture of different dosage forms—not only tablets, capsules, inhalers, injectables, and the like, but also different strengths/concentrations (100 milligram, 50 milligram, 25 milligram, etc.) for each dosage form type. From the drug substance/API warehouse, the API is transported to either an internal pharmaceutical dosage form production site, an external contract manufacturing organization, or a combination of both, where the API will be converted into a finished dosage form.

To produce the finished dosage form, in addition to the API, you may also need raw materials such as starch, lactose, and other excipients from external suppliers to bind with the API to make a tablet. Other external suppliers may provide materials to package the product such as capsule shells, bottles and caps, blister foils and plastics, an inhaler device, an injectable syringe, labeling, corrugated boxes, or pallets. All of these materials are provided by external suppliers to the internal or external manufacturing and packaging operations.

Once the packaged finished product is completed, it will be shipped to an internal or external finished product warehouse for storage until it is ordered by a customer.

When customers place orders, the finished product will be picked/selected from the warehouse and packed for shipment to the customers by an external freight carrier (e.g., motor carrier/truck). Almost all pharmaceutical product in the United States is sold through wholesalers. Wholesalers buy the product from the manufacturer and sell it to pharmaceutical dispensing outlets such as pharmacies, hospitals, mail-order outlets, and institutions.

The dispensing outlets order the product from the wholesaler who then ship the product out to the dispensing outlets where consumers/patients like you and I go to get our prescriptions filled. Dispensing outlets like pharmacies hold a very small amount of inventory due to cost, space, and shelf life issues; therefore, they need frequent replenishments (e.g., daily) from wholesalers to avoid running out of stock/inventory.

An interesting aspect of the pharmaceutical industry is that the customer (i.e., the patient) is not actually making the buying decision and also may not be directly paying for the product. Consumers/patients are not deciding which prescription pharmaceutical to buy. Their physician actually makes the buying decision by determining which product the patient needs for his or her particular health situation and providing the patient with a prescription accordingly. Physician prescribing preferences have a huge impact on demand for these pharmaceutical products. Additionally, the payment for the product may come from an insurance company that also influences demand for pharmaceutical products by deciding which products they will and will not cover/reimburse.

Example: Craft Beer Industry

The craft beer supply chain requires suppliers and asset management, beer production, inventory control, transportation, and distribution. Craft breweries must also carefully balance their supply and demand to maximize their annual profit and lower their costs while keeping their doors open and their customers happy. Figure 1.6 provides a look at the supply chain in the craft beer industry from the acquisition of grains to the pouring of growlers.

FIGURE 1.6

SUPPLY CHAIN MANAGEMENT IN THE SERVICE INDUSTRY ···········

Up to this point we have been mainly discussing supply chains that produce a physical product, but supply chains exist in the service industry as well. Service firms offer intangible products, meaning products that cannot be physically touched. What customers are actually paying for in the service industry is the labor and the intellectual property of the service provider. While the service itself is not tangible, it likely involves use of or work on a tangible item. For example, we do not pay a dry cleaner for a shirt; instead, we provide our own shirt and pay the dry cleaner for the service of cleaning the shirt. Service products include such things as insurance, healthcare, entertainment, finance/banking, training/education, transportation, warehousing, and business consulting, to name a few.

Because the nature of service products is so significantly different from physical products, the supply chain models for service products operate differently from those of physical products. Service products cannot generally be produced in advance or inventoried, and frequently the customer of a service provides the tangible item that will receive the service (e.g., a car for automotive repair, hair for a haircut, carpets for cleaning). Customers play a vital and more involved role in the delivery aspect of the service supply chain than they do in the supply chain for a physical/tangible product. Customers supply clothes to the dry cleaner to be cleaned, their refrigerator to the appliance repair shop to be serviced, and themselves to the healthcare provider to receive checkups and treatment. These types of services are said to provide *state utility*, meaning that the service is performed on something that is owned by the customer. In this context, without the customer also being a supplier in the service supply chain, the service could not be delivered. **Consequently, in the service supply chain, it is much more about managing the relationships between the trading partners than it is about managing the chain of supply**.

Some services require tangible items but do not provide state utility because the customer does not provide the item. Customers do not provide their own hotel room, for example. It is important to note, however, that a customer does not pay a hotel for the room; instead, a customer pays the hotel for use of the room. Similarly, we do not pay a rental car company for the car; rather, we pay the company for use of the car. In these cases, the service is predicated on the existence of a facilitating good. Facilitating goods, contrary to the services themselves, can be made and inventoried ahead of time. Some facilitating goods are far less obvious than the preceding examples. A glass is a facilitating good for a glass of ice tea in a restaurant. Customers do not pay for the glass; instead, customers are paying for the tea that is simply served in the glass. **Facilitating goods** will be discussed in more detail in Chapter 12.

ORIGINS AND EVOLUTION OF SUPPLY CHAIN MANAGEMENT ....

1950S AND 1960S: The basic concept of supply chain management goes back to the 1950s. In these early years, the discipline was limited to **materials management** and **logistics**. In the 1950s and 1960s, the entire focus was on how to produce as much product as possible at the lowest possible cost. Policies and practices were established to maintain large material inventories to keep production running. Manufacturers were internally focused: They looked primarily at maximizing their own internal operations, asking and answering one question: How can we be the most efficient with our resources? External collaboration and partnerships were virtually nonexistent. The focus of materials management and logistics was on the material flow cycle: purchasing the necessary materials, managing the work-in-process, storage/warehousing, shipping/transportation, and the downstream distribution of the finished product to customers. Advantages brought forward through this period included higher output and more productivity, reduced cycle times, and lower work-in-process inventories. The drawbacks included high investment in facilities and infrastructure, the overall cycle time was limited by the slowest operation, and a breakdown of one machine could stop an entire production line.

1960S AND 1970S: Computer technology was introduced in the 1960s and 1970s, and concepts such as material requirements planning (MRP) and manufacturing resource planning (MRP II) were developed and propagated throughout industry along with related software applications. The managing of the supply chain was still internally focused but evolving to a higher level of sophistication. MRP was introduced as a fundamental method of determining what materials were needed and when they were needed to support the production plan and to coordinate inventory management. MRP II was developed to improve internal communication and operations. Manufacturers extended their processes to include their own finance, marketing, sales, research and development, etc. functions to bring all their expertise into the process. As an example, manufacturers began using the expertise from internal marketing and sales functions to improve their forecasts since these were the individuals who were interacting with the customers directly. They would have the best information about how much and when the customer would buy. They would also have known what competitors were doing.

1980S, 1990S, AND 2000S: In the early 1980s, the term *supply chain management* was coined by Dr. Wolfgang Partsch and his team at Booz, Allen & Hamilton, and the concept began to come into its own. Instead of focusing only internally, companies started to look beyond their four walls and incorporate their supply chain partners into their planning activities. Global competition was intensifying throughout the 1980s to 2000s, and this intense global competition led U.S. manufacturers to adopt new practices such as just in time (JIT) management, total quality management (TQM), and business process reengineering (BPR) to remain competitive.

> **JUST IN TIME MANAGEMENT** is a philosophy of manufacturing based on the planned elimination of all waste and continuous productivity improvement.[1]

TOTAL QUALITY MANAGEMENT is a management approach to long-term success through customer satisfaction based on the participation of all members of an organization in improving processes, goods, services, and the culture in which they work.[1] Everyone in the organization has to take ownership for quality.

BUSINESS PROCESS REENGINEERING is a procedure that involves the fundamental rethinking and radical redesign of business processes to achieve dramatic organizational improvements in such critical measures of performance as cost, quality, service, and speed.[1]

THE FUTURE OF SUPPLY CHAIN MANAGEMENT..............................

The old supply chain paradigm involved companies that were seeking to integrate vertically. They subscribed to the idea of doing as much for themselves as possible in an effort to maintain ultimate control. If they were in control of all aspects of the supply chain, they did not have to rely on anyone else who could possibly let them down. A company gained synergy as a vertically integrated firm encompassing the ownership and coordination of several supply chain activities. In addition to manufacturing the product, they performed their own warehousing, distribution, transportation, etc. These organizations focused on the short term and on their own company's performance.

In the new supply chain paradigm, a company in a supply chain focuses activities in its area of specialization and enters into voluntary, trust-based relationships with suppliers and customers. Companies actively and increasingly look at outsourcing their non-core competencies to external partners based on a two-part question: What is it that I do well, and what is it that an external trading partner can do better than I can? By transferring responsibility for non-core competencies to trusted trading partners who have those functions or activities as their core competencies, businesses can accomplish two things. First, they can focus on what they do well and use their resources more efficiently. As a result, companies may need fewer resources or can focus more of their resources on doing what they do well: their core competencies. Second, companies can develop these partnerships and use their partners' expertise potentially to improve their own product. Their partners may be able to deliver innovation through their expertise/core competencies for an advantage that would not otherwise be available to the original company. This can be done on either end of the supply chain, with suppliers and with customers. **Focusing on core competencies, outsourcing those things are not core competencies, using the expertise of trading partners, and strengthening those relationships are the key components of a successful supply chain.** All participants in the supply chain benefit from individual focus on core competencies.

Establishing supplier and customer partnerships is not without risk. A chain is only as strong as its weakest link. You will want to perform a **risk assessment** and potentially take some **risk mitigation** steps. Many companies will qualify backup sources of supply for critical materials and services and/ or carry some select additional inventory for critical materials as a measure of risk protection.

Companies are focusing on **sustainability** at the behest of customers from every market. Issues of sustainability will only increase in importance in the future. Bottled water makes use of plastic bottles and caps. What happens to that plastic after the product is consumed? Will it end up in a landfill and degrade over many years? Will it end up floating around in the ocean? Is there a program to collect those plastic bottles and caps and recycle them, reuse them, or convert them into some other product? Companies are looking at the sustainability of their supply chain, making a commitment to environmental responsibility. How can we be more efficient, and less wasteful with our supply chain resources? We ask such questions as: Can we use less materials? Can we use materials with less environmental impact? Can we use less energy, burn less fossil fuel? There are potential cost savings, the benefit to the environment, and public goodwill for companies that can establish and achieve sustainability goals.

Companies are also focusing on **corporate social responsibility:** a commitment by a company's management not only to behave ethically but also to contribute to community development (e.g., establishing a policy of not buying from suppliers in countries where they have unfair labor practices or use child labor or establishing a program to provide training, education, and job opportunities to underprivileged populations).

FOUNDATION OF SUPPLY CHAIN MANAGEMENT ....

The underlying foundation of supply chain management consists of four functional, elemental areas: operations management, supply management, logistics management, and integration.

Operations Management

The operations management area involves managing internal resources: How am I determining my demand? How am I planning my supply? How am I running my operations? What equipment and people do I have? What is the level of quality I am producing? The major elements of operations management include forecasting and demand planning, planning systems, inventory management, and process management. In the SCOR model, the entire area of Make, where materials are converted into finished product, is part of the operations management area. Processes such MRP, MRP II, LEAN manufacturing, and Six Sigma are integral to managing operations efficiently and effectively. LEAN is an operating philosophy that focuses on eliminating wastes and improving efficiency. Six Sigma is an operating philosophy that focuses on reducing both defects and process variations. These are processes that complement one another. LEAN and Six Sigma will be discussed in Chapter 8.

Supply Management

The supply management area involves all of the supplies and suppliers that you need to run your business. What materials do you need? How much of those materials do you need at a given time period in your operation? Who are your suppliers? What capabilities do they have? How well are they performing? The major elements of supply management include purchasing management, strategic sourcing, and supplier relationship management. You need to have great suppliers who can meet your requirements not only today, but also as your company grows and evolves in the future. What priority is your company in their business? How important are you as a customer to them? You must evaluate your suppliers, their capabilities, reputation, quality, pricing, and current customers. You may want to create a strategic partnership with them and qualify them as a certified supplier to your organization. Managing your suppliers is not only managing the physical supply but the entire supplier relationship, too.

Logistics Management

The logistics management area involves all of the movement and storage of products and materials within the supply chain, whether the flow is forward or reverse. It is the planning and coordination of the physical movement aspects of a firm's operations such that a flow of raw materials, parts, and finished goods is achieved in a manner that minimizes total costs for the levels of service desired. The major elements of logistics management include warehousing, distribution, transportation, international trade management, and customer relationship management.

Integration

The integration area involves all of the enabling systems, software packages, processes, policies, procedures, performance standards and measures, information, and risk management necessary to facilitate the complete integration of the operations, supply, and logistics functions outlined above. Integration also involves collaborating with your trading partners to maximize total supply chain profits. Companies must integrate internally as well as externally to create a more efficient and cost-effective supply chain. Performance measurement is a critical element to determine if the supply chain is achieving its goals and delivering desired benefits. Performance measurement can also be used to identify areas for improvement and further integration.

SUPPLY CHAIN CAPABILITIES MODELS ·····················

Efficient versus Responsive Model

There are two different supply chain capability models. In order to determine which model is best suited for your organization, you first need to understand what type of product(s) you are producing: functional or innovative. You also need to understand your customers' requirements and expectations as well as the competitive market. What do your customers want? Do they want the product immediately? Do they want product they can customize? Is comparable product to yours readily available from multiple sources? What are your core capabilities? What do you do well and how can you use what you do well to satisfy your customer? What supply chain capabilities do you need to develop to be able to meet your customers' expectations if you don't possess them already? Once all those questions are answered, you can determine whether you need to establish an efficient supply chain model or a responsive supply chain model.

An **efficient** supply chain model is designed to minimize cost and to maximize capacity utilization. It is generally the appropriate strategy for functional products. **Functional products** are low margin and have stable demand, high inventory turnover, high volume, and are readily available from multiple sources (e.g., home, school, and office supplies). Consumers have many choices. Manufacturers producing these types of products want to produce and distribute mass quantities as efficiently and effectively, and as cost conscientiously, as they can in order to be competitive.

A **responsive** supply chain model is designed to respond quickly to market demand with minimal stockouts. Flexibility in capacity is necessary to meet fluctuating demand so there is normally an inventory of parts and materials readily available and production lead times are minimized. The responsive supply chain model is generally the appropriate strategy for innovative products. **Innovative products** are newly developed products with high margins, volatile demand, short product lifecycles, and relatively less competition than functional products. Computers and smartphones are examples of innovative products. Unlike the efficient model, the responsive model is designed for customization where customers want some flexibility. A good example is a laptop computer. Computer companies such as Dell have a base model for which they offer all kinds of different features customers can specify. Customers can choose different amounts of RAM and hard drive capacity, different graphics models and interfaces, different size screens, and so forth. Companies such as Dell provide responsiveness/flexibility by buying and holding quantities of the various component parts and <u>not</u> holding large inventories of finished laptops in stock. When a consumer places an order, Dell will assemble exactly what the consumer wants and deliver it very quickly (this is known as an assemble-to-order manufacturing strategy). This approach is wholly dedicated to being responsive to customer demand. It's allowing some customization, some flexibility, but still trying to get the product to the customer when and where he or she wants it. These types of innovative products have a short lifecycle as there is always a new innovation coming out.

Push Model versus Pull Model

The vast majority of businesses today follow the **push** business model (figure 1.7).

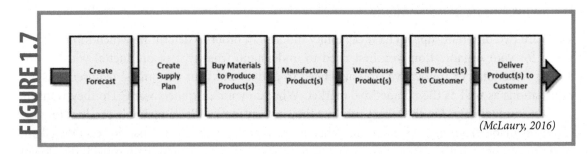

FIGURE 1.7

Create Forecast → Create Supply Plan → Buy Materials to Produce Product(s) → Manufacture Product(s) → Warehouse Product(s) → Sell Product(s) to Customer → Deliver Product(s) to Customer

(McLaury, 2016)

In this model, manufacturers create a sales forecast, create a supply plan based on that forecast, buy the materials necessary to satisfy the supply plan, manufacture the product(s) accordingly, and then store the product(s) in a warehouse until they receive a customer order for the product(s). This production strategy is known as plan-to-stock or make-to-stock, where products are finished <u>before</u> receipt of a customer order, and then these orders are typically filled from the existing stock. New production orders are used to replenish the depleted warehouse stocks. The product is pushed through the supply chain toward the customer based on anticipated need.

- The major <u>advantages</u> of this model are that if the manufacturer creates a good forecast and supply plan, the product is immediately available to ship to the customer on demand from the existing finished product inventory in the warehouse. Manufacturers also have the opportunity to plan resources better or with more flexibility, and can maximize the utilization of resources at the lowest cost.

- The major <u>disadvantages</u> are high inventories (and capital tied up in inventory), long lead times, dependency on forecasting, and forecasting errors that create nonvalue by adding time, inefficiencies, obsolescence, shortages, and additional cost.

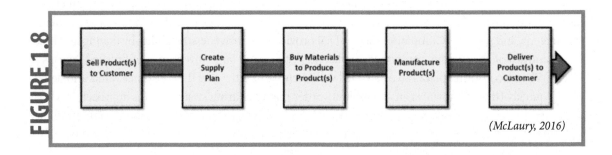

FIGURE 1.8

Sell Product(s) to Customer → Create Supply Plan → Buy Materials to Produce Product(s) → Manufacture Product(s) → Deliver Product(s) to Customer

(McLaury, 2016)

Only a small percentage of businesses today follow the **pull** business model (figure 1.8).

In this model, manufacturers sell the product(s) first, then they create the supply plan, buy the materials, manufacture the product(s), and deliver the finished product. This production strategy is known as make-to-order, where the manufacturer is actually waiting for the customer to pull production of the product through operations, triggered by the customer order.

- The major <u>advantages</u> are high levels of customer service through responsiveness and flexibility to meet uncertain customer demand. Pull models have short lead times, reduce dependency on forecasting, use short and flexible production runs, store very low inventories, reduce waste, provide opportunities for customization, and improve cash flow.

- The major <u>disadvantages</u> are that every order is a rush order, and any problems will lead to customer dissatisfaction. Pull models are highly dependent on customer relationships. This model inherently has a reduced ability to take advantage of economies of scale. Fast, responsive, flexible, robust, and integrated systems and processes are a must for this model to work. Resource issues will have a significant and immediate impact on throughput and customer satisfaction.

MANAGING THE SUPPLY CHAIN THROUGH DEFINED TASKS ....

In order to manage all these activities efficiently and effectively, you will need to have a formal, step-wise, and robust process in place so that you are able to consistently deliver your products when and where your customers want them.

Figure 1.9 shows the major processes that companies must plan and execute on a regular schedule/cycle to manage their supply chain. We will introduce each of these processes in more detail later in the text: however, it is important to note that to be efficient and effective, all of these activities should be fully integrated and as seamless as possible, not only in your internal operation, but also with your suppliers and your customers. In order to be successful, companies must **bring key suppliers and key customers into their processes** and work with them to identify what primary processes they have and who their suppliers and customers are. Companies must determine how they can work with their suppliers and customers to make the collective operations more efficient. Companies must establish a collaborative relationship with their key supply chain partners and share critical supply planning information such as forecasts, production plans, and inventory levels with them. If they can look beyond the four walls of their company and include trading partners on either end of the supply chain in planning activities, these companies will be collectively much more efficient as a supply chain.

FIGURE 1.9

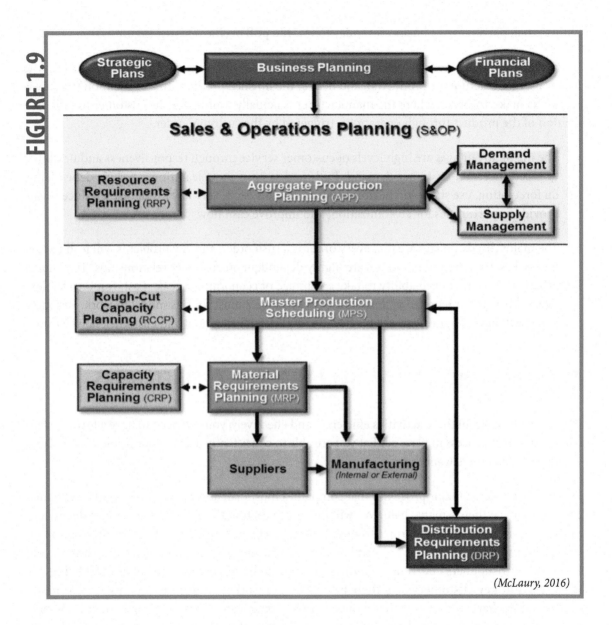

(McLaury, 2016)

THE CHALLENGE OF SUPPLY CHAIN MANAGEMENT ....

One of the key challenges in supply chain management is managing or balancing demand versus supply. There are potentially many different demands that place a burden on a company's resources. There are also potentially many different resources that companies use to create supply capabilities. The aim of supply chain management is to balance all of the demands against all available supplies on a continuous basis.

DEMAND (as shown in figure 1.10) includes trade requirements. This is the demand that most people think of: the finished product(s) that companies sell. However, there are other types of demand that impact a company's resources and supply as well. The need to do maintenance on equipment and facilities, the need to do training and development of personnel, and the need to do research and development work on new products are all examples of activities that demand time from these various supply resources, which takes away from the time available to produce product. Even the decision to maintain safety stock as a buffer against unexpected demand is a demand in and of itself as the safety stock has to be produced.

SUPPLY (as shown in figure 1.10) includes equipment and facilities, labor, suppliers and materials, lead time, warehousing and transportation, and even money/capital—all of the resources that a company amasses to be able to support its anticipated demand.

The ideal situation would be for demand and supply to be in balance (i.e., just the right amount of supply to support demand, not more and not less). The function of supply chain management is to

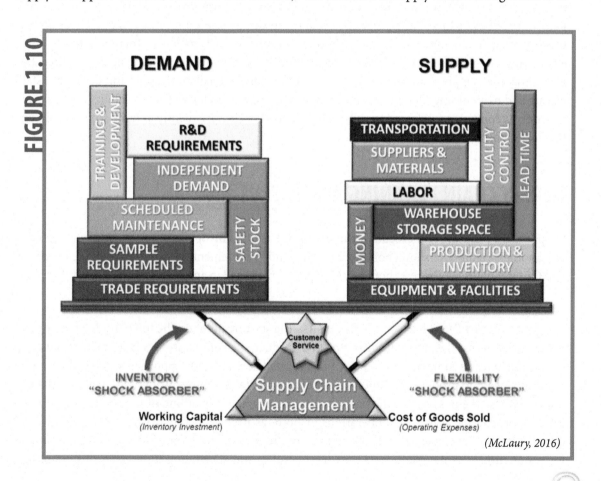

(McLaury, 2016)

maintain this ideal balance in an effort to deliver exceptional customer service (the fulcrum in figure 1.10), with the minimal amount of inventory investment and the lowest possible operating costs.

In order to assist in balancing demand and supply and to deliver against these customer service goals, a robust supply chain management process has some built-in *shock absorbers* that allow an organization to withstand some variability in demand and in supply.

INVENTORY acts as a shock absorber for both demand and supply variability. For example, we don't always know exactly what our demands will be and we may actually sell more than we projected. Having additional inventory may help to meet this unanticipated demand and maintain customer service. If our planned supply is not available as expected due to late deliveries, product rejections, and so forth, having additional inventory may also help to meet demand in the face of this potential supply shortage.

FLEXIBILITY acts as another shock absorber for both demand and supply variability. Flexibility might mean having extra capacity (i.e., capacity beyond what was projected and needed). If a company does sell more than was projected, having the flexibility to produce more may allow us to meet this unanticipated demand. On the supply side, if a supplier delivers late or there is a quality issue, a company can use this same flexibility to buffer for that variability by ramping up production. This is one way that supply chain management tries to manage and balance supply and demand. Establishing and maintaining these shock absorbers costs money. Obviously, less variability in the system is better, as companies will need to utilize shock absorbers less frequently and the supply chain will be more efficient.

SUPPLY CHAIN PLANNING AND EXECUTION ··································

Supply chain planning and execution can be viewed as two mirror image processes complementing one another. Figure 1.11 shows both the Planning and Procurement Process (top) and the Execution and Order Fulfillment Process (bottom). Companies make a plan and then execute against that plan.

PLANNING AND PROCUREMENT PROCESS: The starting point on the top left side of figure 1.11 is the sales forecast (i.e., the volume of finished product[s] a company expects to sell to its customers). From here the company determines its aggregated demand and supply plans, determining what it actually needs to produce to support the sales forecast, taking into consideration what inventories it already has. The next step is the production planning and scheduling of the product(s) through internal or external production operations or both, as needed to support demand. This involves establishing the specific quantities of product and the specific time frame and necessary resources for production. The company then uses the planning and scheduling information to establish a

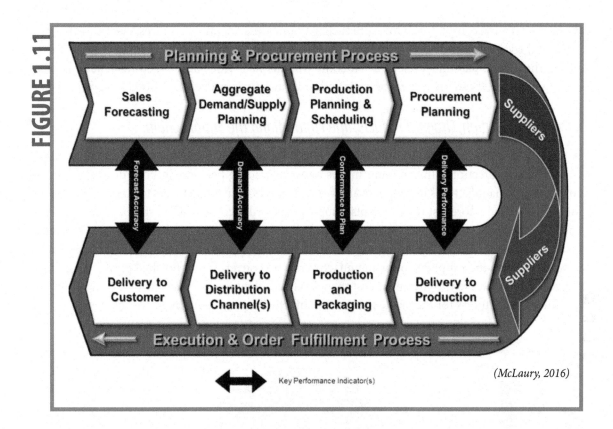

FIGURE 1.11

Planning & Procurement Process

Sales Forecasting | Aggregate Demand/Supply Planning | Production Planning & Scheduling | Procurement Planning

Suppliers

Forecast Accuracy | Demand Accuracy | Conformance to Plan | Delivery Performance

Delivery to Customer | Delivery to Distribution Channel(s) | Production and Packaging | Delivery to Production

Suppliers

Execution & Order Fulfillment Process

↔ Key Performance Indicator(s)

(McLaury, 2016)

purchasing (procurement) plan to buy all of the required materials and services to support production. The purchase plan is then negotiated with the company's suppliers and confirmed through the issuance of purchase orders.

EXECUTION AND ORDER FULFILLMENT PROCESS: The execution and order fulfillment process proceeds in reverse of the planning and procurement process. It starts with the suppliers delivering the materials and services which were ordered, to the company's internal or external production operations, or both. Production and packaging activities can then be executed according to the plan. These activities are followed by delivering the finished product(s), including any necessary additional quantities from inventory, out into the various distribution channels and ultimately to the end customer.

KEY PERFORMANCE INDICATORS: At each major point along the continuum, a measurement can be established and checked to determine if what was planned was executed as planned. Delivery Performance: What did the company plan to buy versus what was actually delivered? Conformance to Plan: What did the company plan to produce versus what was actually produced? Forecast Accuracy: What did the company forecast in terms of product sales versus what was actually ordered by the customer? The company can measure each major process, identify variances, determine the root cause of the variance, and develop and implement an improvement plan. If a company can do this as part of the regular planning cycle, it can identify whether its performance is getting better, worse, or staying the same. It can identify focus areas and continuously improve its supply chain performance.

Flow of Information, Orders, Products, and Funds along the Supply Chain

Figure 1.12 depicts the flow of all the various types of information and materials along the supply chain in both directions. Information moves between trading partners in both directions—from customers to manufactures to suppliers and from suppliers to manufacturers to customers. This information includes forecast requirements, supply plans, order confirmation, shipping notifications, and invoices. Purchase orders flow from the customers to the manufacturers and from the manufacturers to the suppliers. The physical material flows in the opposite direction of the purchase order flow, going from the suppliers to the manufacturers who convert it into finished products and then deliver the products to the customer. Last there is a funds flow. Based on the invoices, the customers pay the manufacturers for the products, and manufacturers pay the suppliers for the materials.

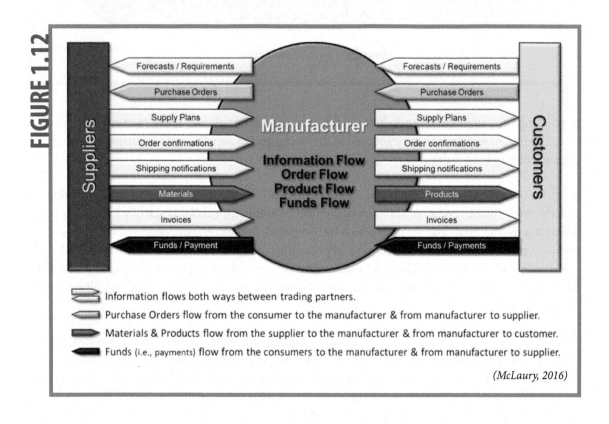

(McLaury, 2016)

BENEFITS OF SUPPLY CHAIN MANAGEMENT ································

Supply chain management provides value for both internal and external customers. Some of the major benefits are improving customer service, increasing revenues, lowering costs, providing a better utilization of assets, reducing uncertainty, and the elimination of rush activities. The better companies plan, the less they will have to react to the unexpected. Companies will be able to minimize delays, establish shorter lead times, and have lower inventory levels throughout the extended supply chain both for the company and their supply chain partners. An improvement in customer service can enhance customer value, and retain more customers, particularly when competitors don't manage their supply chain as well. Supply chain management can be a competitive advantage by creating the ability to respond to disruptions and conflicts effectively. Companies with well-run supply chain processes might be positioned better to satisfy their own customers during a crisis and also potentially gain customers from their competitors.

Who benefits the most from implementing supply chain management processes? Obviously, companies that have a large and or complex supply chain benefit the most. They have large inventories, large numbers of suppliers, and large purchasing budgets. They have the most to lose, but they also have the most to gain. The obvious benefit to large companies doesn't mean that a small company can't also benefit. Small companies may actually be in a more precarious situation. A supply chain issue could be enterprise threatening for a smaller company, causing them to go out of business, so implementing supply chain management can be just as important for smaller companies as it is for larger companies.

CURRENT TRENDS IN SUPPLY CHAIN MANAGEMENT ····················

GLOBALIZATION: One of the trends in supply chain management is globalization. Companies are doing business in an ever-expanding marketplace and technological advancements are making the world smaller. Even the small mom-and-pop operation on the corner can now source materials and sell products internationally through the internet. Many companies large and small are now competing in a global marketplace whether they are ready for it or not. Companies can expect the complexity of their supply chains to grow significantly in the coming years in terms of new customers, locations, markets, products and variants, and demand volatility.

There are two aspects of globalization: breadth and depth. Breadth involves companies having foreign suppliers and foreign customers. Global business often requires some foreign manufacturing and foreign offices taking orders, providing customer service, and distributing products. Depth involves companies having not only foreign first-tier suppliers and customers but second- and third-tier suppliers and customers in foreign markets as well.

Globalization is a major driving force for acquiring supply chain talent. Companies of all sizes in all industries all over the world need professionals with significant supply chain training and education to run their operations in a global environment. This demand is a significant contributor to the current supply chain talent shortage.

DEMAND VOLATILITY AND FORECAST INACCURACY are creating major challenges to supply chain management. Globalization, technology, and other factors have provided customers with increased competitive choices that allow them to make more and easier decisions to switch between alternatives. The lack of flexibility in a company's supply chain to manage these demand changes has become an increasing problem which could be further magnified by the **bullwhip effect**, which will be discussed in more detail in Chapter 2.

The best approach to deal with this trend is to develop more flexible capacity throughout the supply chain in order to be more responsible to forecast inaccuracy. Best performing companies tend to improve supply chain responsiveness through improving visibility across all supply chain partners. Companies can also focus more effort on collaboration with key customers to reduce or eliminate unanticipated changes.

SUPPLY CHAIN COST OPTIMIZATION is essential for continued economic growth for companies. Improvements in gross margins over the next couple of years will not likely come from price increases; rather, gross margin improvements will come from reductions in supply chain costs. The recent trend of outsourcing non-core competencies and specific functions is critical for controlling supply chain costs. Many companies are taking advantage of lower costs in emerging markets and increasing the flexibility of their own supply chain operations. However, process and management costs could be on the rise as supply chains become more global. Companies are embracing the concept of managing total supply chain cost across all supply chain functions and interfaces. Rigorous cost optimization across the end-to-end supply chain is a critical success factor in an increasingly competitive and global marketplace.

RISK MANAGEMENT has become an increasingly critical challenge across the entire global supply chain. Dealing with cost pressures, many companies have started shifting supply chain risks (i.e., holding inventory) upstream to their suppliers. Companies are also shipping finished products to customers immediately after production. However, these approaches only shift risk from one part of the supply chain to another and do not reduce risk for the overall end-to-end supply chain. Supply chain risks can only be effectively mitigated by taking the approach of managing risk at each node of the supply chain. To keep the supply chain as lean as possible, companies are taking a more active role in demand planning, ensuring they order only the amount of material needed to fill firm orders.

SUSTAINABILITY AND GREENING THE SUPPLY CHAIN is an increasingly prominent trend, with companies actively trying to be more socially and environmentally responsible. They are paying attention to their carbon footprint. They want to have less of an impact on the environment. If a company can be more efficient with its production, it will potentially also have a lower negative impact on the environment, using fewer utilities and resources. If companies are able to manage their supply chain better, they can actually reduce their carbon footprint. For example, if a company ships products in full truckload quantities, the products not only cost less per unit to ship but the company can ship the same total volume of product on fewer trucks than if they are partially empty, less-than-truckload shipments. Less fossil fuel is consumed, simultaneously lessening transportation's impact on the environment and reducing costs.

Poland Spring bottled water provides a great example of greening the supply chain. The company reduced the amount of plastic in its bottle and cap by approximately 25%. This percentage doesn't seem like a whole lot when considering an individual bottle, but given the number of bottles of water the company sells, that change will result in a significant cost savings for the company and also in tons of plastic that do not end up in a landfill or as litter somewhere else. A redesigned product like the newer Poland Spring bottle and cap is also lighter, so they add less weight in transportation, potentially burning less fuel to transport.

Surveys have shown that most consumers, given a choice between two different supply chains, will pick a product that is more socially responsible, more sustainable, and greener. They will pick companies that have recycling programs and have a positive attitude toward the environment over companies and supply chains that do not, so there is a competitive advantage in sustainability and greening the supply chain.

SUMMARY

- A supply chain is the global network used to deliver products and services from raw materials to customers through an engineered flow of information, physical products, and cash. There are different ways to set up and operate a supply chain depending on the type of product or service a company provides. Most supply chains follow the basic Supply Chain Operations Research (SCOR) model: Plan, Source, Make, Deliver, Return, and Enable.

- Supply chain management is the coordination of a network of independent organizations all involved in creating a desired product or service so that they function like one seamless organization. It is about the production of products and services and also how people, process, technology, equipment, infrastructure, money, and information all integrate efficiently and effectively to facilitate the flow of products and services from the raw material stage to finished products desired by consumers, to the benefit of everyone in the supply chain. The goals are to improve customer service while simultaneously reducing both inventory investment and operating expenses.

- Any organization that offers a product or a service has a supply chain: large or small, public or private, for-profit or nonprofit. We are all part of multiple supply chains as either suppliers, customers, or both.

- To understand a supply chain fully means to understand the flow of products and service, information, payments, and returns from end to end: Which entities form the links or nodes in the supply chain? Who are the suppliers, the manufacturers, the customers? How are the products being distributed?

- Supply chains exist in the service industry as well. Service firms offer intangible products, so customers are actually paying for the labor and intellectual property of the service provider. Supply chain models for service products operate differently from that of physical products as service products cannot be produced in advance or inventoried, and frequently the customer of a service product provides the tangible item that will receive the service.

- The basic concept of supply chain management goes back to the 1950s and has evolved significantly over time from initially being almost exclusively internally focused to now embracing collaboration and strategic partnerships with external trading partners. In the modern supply chain, companies focus on activities in their core competencies and enter into voluntary, trust-based relationships with trading partners for activities outside their core competencies.

- The underlying foundation of supply chain management consists of four functional areas: operations management, supply management, logistics management, and integration.

- There are two different strategic supply chain capability models: efficient and responsive. The type of product(s) a company is producing, functional or innovative, is one of the major considerations for determining which model is best suited for that supply chain.

- A push model is defined as a business response in anticipation of customer demand. The product is pushed through the supply chain toward the customer based on anticipated need. A pull model is defined as a response resulting from customer demand. The manufacturer waits for the customer to pull production of the product through operations with an order.

- A formal, stepwise, and robust process of defined tasks must be in place for the supply chain to be managed efficiently and effectively in order to deliver products when and where the customers wants them consistently.

- One of the key challenges in supply chain management is the need to manage or balance demand versus supply. There are many components or elements of demand and supply to consider. Safety stock inventory and supply flexibility can be employed as shock absorbers to help maintain the balance when unexpected occurrences alter the operations plan.

- Supply chain planning and execution can be viewed as two mirror image processes complementing one another: planning and procurement followed by execution and order fulfillment. Companies make a plan and then execute against that plan on a cyclical, ongoing basis. The process facilitates the flow of information, orders, products, and funds along the supply chain.

- Supply chain management provides value for both internal and external customers. Some of the major benefits are improving customer service, increasing revenues, lowering costs, providing a better utilization of assets, reducing uncertainty, and eliminating rush activities.

- Current trends in supply chain management include:

  - The impact of continued globalization on the complexity and competitiveness of the supply chain
  - Improving visibility and collaboration to combat increasing demand volatility and forecast inaccuracy
  - A focus on risk assessment and risk management
  - A focus on sustainability and greening the supply chain

REFERENCES

[1] *APICS Dictionary* (14th ed.). (2013). Chicago, IL: APICS. www.apics.org; Wisner, J., et al. (2014). *Principles of supply chain management: A balanced approach* (4th ed.). Boston, MA: Cengage Learning.

Chapter 2

Forecasting and Demand Planning

CHAPTER OUTLINE

Introduction

Key Terms

Forecasting

Fundamentals of Forecasting

Forecasting Techniques

Qualitative Forecasting

Quantitative Forecasting

Variation in Quantitative Forecasting

Time Series Models

Cause-and-Effect Models

Other Forecasting Models

Forecast Error

Mean Absolute Deviation

Mean Absolute Percent Error

Mean Squared Error

Forecast Bias

Running Sum of Forecast Errors

Tracking Signal

Bullwhip Effect

Collaborative Planning, Forecasting, and Replenishment

Summary

INTRODUCTION ....

Forecasting and demand planning are the key building blocks from which all downstream supply chain planning activities are derived.

The first step is forecasting, where the forecast is developed through data analysis and judgment. Organizations must have a formal forecasting process to develop an agreed upon set of numbers that becomes a driver for demand planning and its requisite components: financial planning, sales planning, marketing and promotional planning, production planning, procurement and inventory planning, logistics planning, and distribution planning.

The second step is demand planning, where management and other experts within the company review the forecast to ensure alignment with strategic requirements, business policy, and business knowledge, and make adjustments if necessary.

Forecasting and demand planning are crucial components of customer satisfaction.

KEY TERMS..

DEMAND is "the need for a particular product or component. The demand could come from any number of sources (e.g., a customer order or forecast, an interplant requirement, a branch warehouse request for a service part, the manufacturing of another product, etc.). At the finished goods level, demand data are usually different from sales data because demand does not necessarily result in sales (i.e., if there is no stock, there will be no sale). There are generally up to four components of demand: cyclical component, random component, seasonal component, and trend component."[1]

DEMAND PLANNING is "the process of combining statistical forecasting techniques and judgment to construct demand estimates for products or services across the supply chain from suppliers' raw materials to the individual consumer's needs. Items can be aggregated by product family, geographical location, product life cycle, etc. to determine an estimate of consumer demand for finished products and services. Numerous forecasting models are tested and combined with judgment from marketing, sales, distributors, warehousing, service parts, and other functions. Actual sales are compared with forecasts provided by various models and judgments to determine the best integration of techniques and judgment to minimize forecast error."[1]

DEPENDENT DEMAND is demand for an item that is directly related to other items or finished products (i.e., a component part or material used in making a finished product). Dependent demands are calculated and should <u>not</u> be forecasted. For example, the seat on a standard bicycle is a dependent demand item. If a company forecasts that it's going to sell 100 standard bicycles next month and creates a production plan to manufacture 100 standard bicycles, then the company knows that it will need 100 seats, because there is one seat on each standard bicycle. The company does not need to, and should not, forecast the demand for bicycle seats because the demand is directly related to the number of standard bicycles that it's going to manufacture. The number of seats is calculated based on the number of bicycles the company will manufacture rather than forecasted independently.

INDEPENDENT DEMAND is demand for an item that is unrelated to the demand for other items (i.e., a finished product or spare/service parts). The demand for finished products generally comes from the external customer and is independent from other items and may therefore need to be forecasted. Forecasting should be done for the independent demand items only. Dependent demand items can then be calculated from the forecast for the independent demand item using the bill-of-materials and material requirements planning, which will be detailed in Chapter 3. In other words, once the *independent* demand for the number of bicycles is forecasted, the *dependent* demand for seats, tires, handlebars, and so forth can be determined. It is important to note that an accessory for the bicycle would require a forecast because it is not inherently part of the production plan. In other words, a bike lock that is not packaged with the bike has its own independent demand because its demand is not necessarily related to the bike itself.

FORECAST is "an estimate of future demand. A forecast can be constructed using quantitative methods, qualitative methods, or a combination of methods, and it can be based on extrinsic (external) or intrinsic (internal) factors. Various forecasting techniques attempt to predict one or more of the four components of demand: cyclical, random, seasonal, and trend."[1]

FORECASTING is "the business function that attempts to estimate future demand for products so that they can be purchased or manufactured in appropriate quantities in advance."[1]

FORECASTING...

If managing the supply chain were a linear process, then the process would begin with the development of a forecast. Companies need to know what demand is or will be in order to begin to plan the use of their supply chain resources and execute against that plan effectively. Managing demand requires timely and accurate forecasts. The timelier the forecast, the more accurate the forecast is likely to be.

- SHORT-TERM forecasts cover a period up to six months and are generally reviewed on a weekly basis

- MEDIUM-TERM forecasts cover a period from six months to two years and are generally reviewed on a monthly basis

- LONG-TERM forecasts cover a period of two years or more and are generally reviewed on an annual or quarterly basis.

Forecasting is necessary, because it takes time to convert raw materials to a finished product delivered to the customer. Most customers do not want to wait for the time necessary to produce a product from start to finish. Most companies, therefore, cannot wait for demand to develop and then react to it. Companies must anticipate and plan for future demand so that they can react immediately to customer orders as they occur, which is why most manufacturers use a "make-to-stock" rather than "make-to-order" strategy. "Make-to-stock" manufacturers plan ahead and then deploy inventories of finished goods into distribution channels in anticipation of demand (i.e., use the push model).

© Nicotombo/Shutterstock.com

There are two important considerations about a forecast that must be stated:

- The first is that statistically speaking, the forecast will be inaccurate. Although it may be inaccurate, it is still useful. Forecasting is an imprecise science at best, but in the absence of any better information, the forecast is not something that companies can operate without. Because a forecast is an estimate of future demand, which may be inaccurate, the goal of the forecasting and demand planning process is to minimize forecast error in order to be as close to accurate as possible.

- The second important consideration is that the forecast is the basis for most "downstream" supply chain planning decisions. Good forecasting can benefit a company by facilitating more effective planning, which can lead to reduced inventories, reduced costs, reduced stockouts, and improved customer service. Bad forecasting can be the root cause for creating just the opposite. There is a familiar adage that applies to forecasting: "garbage in = garbage out." If a forecast is bad, everything else (i.e., the supply plan) based on that forecast will also be bad. As a result, some companies spend a lot of time and effort trying to figure out how they can best forecast because that will make everything else downstream flow more smoothly.

Companies must consider all factors that influence demand when forecasting, not only statistical data and information, but also knowledge about the marketplace, trends, marketing and sales efforts, competitor activity, and the like. Some considerations follow:

- Is the product seasonal?

- Is there a price increase coming?

- Is a new competitor entering the marketplace?

- Is the company's new product going to cannibalize one or more of its other products already on the market?

FUNDAMENTALS OF FORECASTING

There are some fundamental truths about forecasting in business about which supply chain managers should all be aware. These fundamentals can easily be forgotten at times, to the detriment of the quality and accuracy of forecasts. Supply chain managers should consider the following fundamentals when forecasting for their company:

Adapted from Jeff Robson, 8 Fundamentals of Forecasting in Business, Business Strategy Blog, June 26, 2012.

1. **Your forecast is most likely inaccurate.**

    - The question you should be asking is "How inaccurate is the forecast?"

    - Forecasts should include an estimate of error.

    - Forecasting is difficult mainly because people know it is likely to be inaccurate and nobody likes to be publicly and visibly inaccurate.

    - Nevertheless, a good forecast is essential in positioning the resources necessary to satisfy customer demands.

    - Forecasts require regular review as circumstances can change. You must be open to the first signs of change and be prepared to react quickly and decisively.

    - You must be willing to recognize and adapt to changing conditions. Don't fall in love with your forecast and ignore evidence that it may be inaccurate. Pride of authorship in this case can be deadly to the business.

2. **Simple forecast methodologies are better than complex methodologies.**

   - Simple forecast methods are easy to understand, analyze, and adjust as necessary.

   - Complicated forecast methods often hide key assumptions built into the model.

   - When key assumptions are obscured it can be hard to trace failures.

3. **A correct forecast does not prove that the forecast method is correct.**

   - Accurate forecasts could have been chance.

   - If you only question your methods when there is a large variance in the data, you'll miss all those times your forecast was just lucky – potentially hiding a multitude of sins.

4. **If you don't use the data regularly, trust it less when forecasting.**

   - The quality of your data is proportional to how often you use it.

   - When information is not regularly used, errors often remain undetected. Regular use of data helps identify mistakes and smooth out inconsistencies over time.

5. **All trends will eventually end.**

   - Many factors will affect the pattern you are trying to forecast.

   - It doesn't matter how accurately you predict the trend, in the future the variables will change and the forecast will be inaccurate.

   - Short-term forecasts are more accurate than long-term forecasts. The further out into the future you forecast, the more likely that changes over time will undermine your estimates.

6. **Most forecasts are biased, and it is hard to eliminate bias.**

   - When you have to make assumptions (i.e., which factors to include, how strongly to weight them, etc.), it is likely that you will be introducing some bias into the forecast.

   - A forecast process with bias will eventually get off track unless steps are taken to correct the course periodically. The best course of action is to measure for bias and then correct the bias routinely.

7. **Large numbers are easier to forecast than small numbers.**

   - Forecasts are more accurate for groups than for single items. Assuming that forecasts for each item in the group are as likely to be too high as too low, the low forecasts tend to balance out the high forecasts.

   - It's usually better to forecast the bigger number and work back the calculation to determine the associated numbers than to forecast the small, related products and then add them up to determine the bigger number.

8. **Technology is not the solution to better forecasting.**

   - Technology is not the answer; it is a tool to facilitate the process.

   - Robust forecasting comes from sound logic and methodology.

   - Create an appropriate strategy and then use technology to make it more successful.

FORECASTING TECHNIQUES

There are two main categories of forecasting techniques: **qualitative** and **quantitative** (figure 2.1). A forecast can be developed by using qualitative methods, quantitative methods, or a combination of methods, and it can be based on intrinsic (internal) or extrinsic (external) factors. Companies that forecast well generally use a combination of quantitative and qualitative techniques.

QUALITATIVE FORECASTING

QUALITATIVE FORECASTING TECHNIQUES are based on opinion, intuition, and judgment. This technique is generally used when data are not available, limited, or irrelevant for some reason. For example, when companies launch new products into the marketplace, they don't have any direct statistical or historical data they can rely on to create a forecast. Although they might be able to use a similar product launched in the past by themselves or even a competitor as a model, they don't actually have hard data on which to base the forecast, so they will need to incorporate some judgments or opinions. This is qualitative forecasting, and its success depends significantly on the skill and experience of the forecasters and what information is available to them. The more experiences that can be brought into the process, the better this type of forecast will be.

FIGURE 2.1

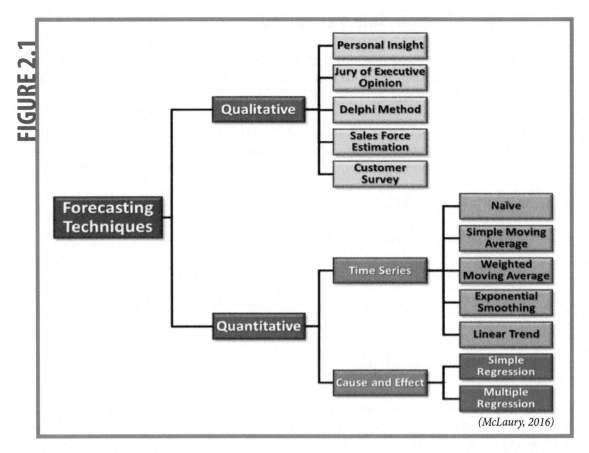

(McLaury, 2016)

Five major types of qualitative forecasting are outlined here: Personal Insight, Jury of Executive Opinion (or Management Estimate), Delphi Method, Sales Force Estimates, and Customer Survey.

1. **PERSONAL INSIGHT:** The forecast may be based on the insight of the most experienced, most knowledgeable, or most senior person available. Sometimes, this approach is the only option, but methods that include more people are generally more reliable.

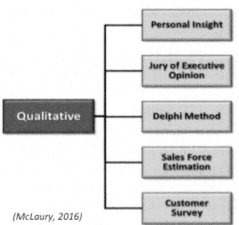

(McLaury, 2016)

2. **JURY OF EXECUTIVE OPINION or MANAGE-MENT ESTIMATE:** In an organization, those people who know the most about the marketplace and the product would likely form the jury or management panel determining the forecast. The

forecast relies upon a consensus of panel members. Generally, the panel conducts a series of forecasting meetings to discuss the forecast until the panel reaches a consensus.

Advantages:

- Decisions are enriched by the experience of competent experts.

- Companies don't have to spend time and resources collecting data by survey.

- It is very useful for new products.

Disadvantages:

- Experts may introduce some bias.

- Experts may become biased by other colleagues or a strongly opinionated leader.

3. DELPHI METHOD: This method is basically the same as the Jury of Executive Opinion except that the insights, opinions, and judgments of each of the participants is collected separately so that people are not influenced by one another. In the Delphi method, questionnaires are submitted to individual experts for their anonymous responses. Instead of meeting face-to-face, the experts submit their responses to a panel director. A summary of all the responses is given to the individual experts requesting that they modify their original response if they think it is necessary. This is done in several rounds until a consensus forecast is achieved. The use of summaries reduces the defensiveness group members experience when challenged in person. It also reduces the potential for "groupthink." The Delphi method can be time-consuming and is therefore best for long-term forecasts.

Advantages:

- Decisions are enriched by the experience of competent experts.

- Decisions are not likely a product of groupthink.

- It is very useful for new products.

Disadvantages:

- Experts may introduce some bias.

- If external experts are used there is a risk of loss of confidential information.

- Companies must spend time and resources collecting data by survey.

4. **SALES FORCE ESTIMATES:** This method is also basically the same as the Jury of Executive Opinion except that it is performed specifically with a group of salespeople. Individuals working in the sales function bring special expertise to forecasting because they maintain the closest contact with customers. The resulting forecast is a blend of the informed opinions of the group. This method can be improved by providing salespeople with incentives for accurate forecasts and by training the salespeople to interpret their interactions with customers better.

Advantages:

- No additional cost to collect data because internal salespeople are used.

- The forecast is more reliable because it is based on the opinions of salespeople in direct contact with customers.

Disadvantages:

- Salespeople may introduce some bias.

- Salespeople may not be aware of the economic environment.

- It is not ideal for long-term forecasting.

5. **CUSTOMER SURVEY:** This method is generally used for short-term forecasting where an organization conducts surveys with customers to determine the demand for their products and services and to anticipate future demand accordingly. Customers are directly approached and asked to give their opinions about the particular product. A customer questionnaire may be prepared for such times. Questionnaires should be simple and interesting so as to induce customers' responses. Customer surveys can be done in person (e.g., one-on-one, focus group), over the phone, by mail, email, or online.

When collecting information with questionnaires or surveys, the number of responses compared to the number of nonresponses or incomplete answers should be tracked to determine if the data are statistically valid. Response rates for some types of survey methods may be as low as 10%.

Rather than distribute a digital or tangible survey, some forecasters prefer a focus group, which is a small group of customers who are interviewed together to collect their input. An interviewer creates an environment that encourages different points of view without pressuring participants to vote or reach consensus. The company conducts several focus group sessions with different participants to identify trends and patterns. Careful analysis of the discussions provide clues and insights as to how a product or service is perceived by the group.

Advantages:

- It is a direct method of assessing information from the primary sources.

- It is simple to administer and comprehend.

- Consumer intercepts are usually held to gain a fast and quick overview.

- It does not introduce any bias or value judgment particularly in the census method if the questions are constructed carefully.

Disadvantages:

- Customers do not always answer the questionnaire.

- Poorly formed questions may lead to unreliable information.

- It is time-consuming and costly to survey a large population.

QUANTITATIVE FORECASTING ··

QUANTITATIVE FORECASTING TECHNIQUES use historical demand data to project future demand. Whereas qualitative techniques are more of an art form, quantitative techniques are more of

a science. In quantitative forecasting, historical demand data are used in conjunction with statistical models to create the forecast. Ideally, the historical data used should be actual demand data if available, rather than actual sales history. Actual sales history may reflect what the customer was forced to accept at the time due to limitations in available supply rather than what the actual customer demand was at the time.

The two main quantitative techniques are **time series models** and **cause-and-effect models**.

TIME SERIES MODELS are the most frequently used of any method and follow the premise that the future is an extension of the past. They

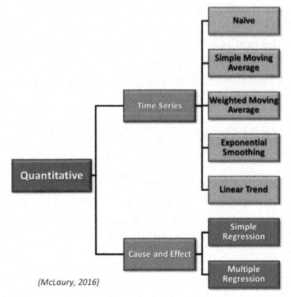

(McLaury, 2016)

are intrinsic forecasting techniques that incorporate data collected during specific time intervals such as days, weeks, and months.

For example, if a company's actual demand was 1,000 units per month for the last 24 months, a very basic time series model would project that the company is probably going to experience demand of 1,000 units per month going forward, all other things being equal. This simplistic example demonstrates the use of historical demand data to predict future demand.

Time series models tend to be best for short-term forecasting and should also include an estimate of the degree of potential error.

CAUSE-AND-EFFECT MODELS basically use the same historical demand data as time series models but make some assumptions and incorporate some independent variables in the effort to predict future demand more accurately. There is a "cause" (independent variable) and an "effect" (dependent variable). Cause-and-effect models are used where sufficient historical data are available, and the correlation between the dependent variable to be forecasted and the related independent variable(s) is well known.

Cause-and-effect forecasting models are extrinsic forecasting techniques because they evaluate the data based on some circumstance or event that will likely have an impact on the demand for a product or item. These approaches try to find a correlation, or a cause-and-effect relationship, between the indicator and overall market demand. Cause-and-effect models are more advantageous if they are based on recent independent variables (i.e., recent events). The more distant the event, the less useful it will be in achieving an accurate forecast. The key challenge is to choose an independent variable that has true correlation with the demand being forecasted.

The best practice for a company is to do some combination of intrinsic and extrinsic forecasting. Using internal information is powerful by itself, but external information can lend an additional layer of reliability by connecting external events to internal processes.

VARIATION IN QUANTITATIVE FORECASTING ....

Quantitative forecasting seeks to connect historical demand data with future demand probability. These predictions are seldom simple and must allow for variation in the demand. Variation can be problematic for forecast models if the nature of the variation is not understood, but understanding fluctuations in demand allows for a more complete forecast model.

TREND VARIATION: Trend variation is movement of a variable over time. Quantitative forecasts measure the rise or fall of demand for a product. Is the actual demand for an item increasing or decreasing over time; and is that pattern projected to continue into the future, and for how long?

A trend might be more easily observed by plotting actual demand on a graph over time to see whether there is an increase or decrease. Trends particularly occur at the beginning or the end of a product's lifecycle. When an item is new, the demand might be steadily increasing (trending up); when the product is mature, the demand might be steadily declining (trending down). The trend variation should be taken into consideration when creating a forecast for an item.

RANDOM VARIATION: Random variation is an instability in the data caused by random occurrences. These random changes are generally very short term, and can be caused by unexpected or unpredictable events such as weather emergencies, natural disasters, and the like. A sudden demand for wood may occur, for example, after a hurricane because many homes are damaged. As these variations are unexpected and unpredictable, they are normally excluded from the forecast data as abnormal demand. Manufacturers may provide a contingency for these potential variations through a mitigation strategy such as maintaining some additional stock (i.e., safety stock).

SEASONAL VARIATION: Seasonal variation is a repeating pattern of demand from year to year, or over some other time interval, with some periods of considerably higher demand than others. Demand may fluctuate depending on time of the year (e.g., seasonal weather, holidays). Seasonality is based on history repeating itself, and therefore can be predicted. Some industries and products have definitive seasons (e.g., snow shovels, swimsuits, Halloween candy, Christmas wrapping paper). These products predictably have large demand at certain times of the year and low demand the rest of the time. If seasonal variation is observed in the historical demand data, it is almost always built into the forecast unless there is some other overriding information to the contrary.

CYCLICAL VARIATION: Cyclical variation is a demand pattern that repeats like a seasonal variation but follows a wavelike pattern that can extend over multiple years and, therefore, cannot be easily predicted. These long-term cycles typically correlate with the general business or economic cycle. The stock market is an example of a cyclical variation. A "bull market" or a "bear market" can last for a long time, potentially even multiple years. Another example of a cyclical variation is a product going through its lifecycle, starting with a launch and rapid growth when it is new, leveling off when it reaches maturity, and then trailing off when it is in the decline stage.

TIME SERIES MODELS

The main purpose of a time series model is to collect and study the past data of a given time series in order to generate probable future values for the series. In other words, forecasts for future demand rely on understanding past demand. Accordingly, time series forecasting can be characterized as the act of predicting the future by understanding the past.

The following are a few basic forecasting techniques using time series data.

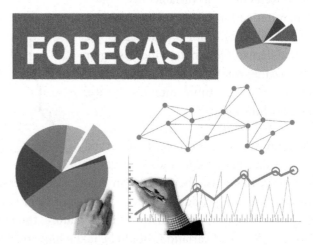

© one photo/Shutterstock.com

NAÏVE: Naïve forecasting sets the demand for the next time period to be exactly the same as the demand in the last (or current) time period. For example, if a company had an actual demand for 100 bicycles in June, using the naïve forecasting method for July, the forecast would be set at 100 bicycles and so on for subsequent months. This forecasting technique does not factor in any variations (i.e., trend, random, seasonal, or cyclical). It is most useful for products or items that have a very stable/flat trend such as mature products, or for use in comparison to other, more sophisticated forecasting techniques.

Advantages: This technique works for mature products and is very easy to determine.

Disadvantages: This technique works for mature products only. Any variations in demand will create inventory issues.

SIMPLE MOVING AVERAGE: Instead of using the most recent time period demand data to forecast demand for the next time period like naïve forecasting, a moving average uses a calculated average of demand during a specified number of the most recent time periods. A simple moving average is where all the data points are assigned equal weights.

For example, a four-month simple moving average takes the average monthly demand for the preceding four months to create the forecast for the next month.

Formula: (M1 + M2 + M3 + M4) / 4

Compute the simple moving average forecast for **July** using the following data:

	Month	Units Actual	Forecasted
		Actual	**Forecasted**
M6	January	90,000	
M5	February	110,000	
M4	March	80,000	
M3	April	90,000	
M2	May	100,000	
M1	June	120,000	
M	July		?

(120,000 + 100,000 + 90,000 + 80,000) / 4
= 390,000 / 4
= 97,500 units for the July forecast

As the actual demand data for each new time period are added, the oldest one is dropped and the average is recalculated (i.e., a "moving" average).

Advantages: This forecasting technique provides a very consistent demand over long periods of time and smooths out random variations. Including more time periods will smooth the amount of variation in the model.

Disadvantages: This forecasting technique generally fails to identify trends or seasonal effects. It will also create shortages when demand is increasing, because it lags behind actual demand. Adding more periods to the average actually increases the amount the forecast lags behind actual demand.

WEIGHTED MOVING AVERAGE: A weighted moving average is very similar to a simple moving average except that not all historical time periods are valued equally. In the previous example, all of the time periods were weighted equally, totaled up, and then divided by the number of periods to get the simple moving average. With a weighted moving average, different weight is applied to each time period according to its importance. The weight given to each time period is flexible so long as the weight for each time period is a positive number and all of the weights total 100%.

Formula: (W1 x M1) + (W2 x M2) + (W3 x M3) + (W4 x M4)

Perhaps the company feels that the most recent month or few months are more representative or relevant to the product's demand today than the demand data from the more distant past. In this case, the most recent past time period(s) would be given a greater percentage of the total weight and the more distant past time periods would be given a lesser percentage.

Compute the weighted moving average forecast for July using the following data:

	Month	Units Actual	Units Forecasted	Weight
M6	January	90,000		N/A
M5	February	110,000		N/A
M4	March	80,000		10%
M3	April	90,000		20%
M2	May	100,000		30%
M1	June	120,000		40%
M	July		?	
				100% TOTAL

(40% x 120,000) + (30% x 100,000) + (20% x 90,000) + (10% x 80,000)
= 48,000 + 30,000 + 18,000 + 8,000
= **104,000 units for the July forecast**

As the actual demand data for each new time period are added, the oldest one is dropped, the weighted percentages are reapplied, and the average is recalculated (i.e., a "moving" average).

Advantages: This forecasting technique is more accurate than a simple moving average if actual demand is increasing or decreasing—that is, if there is any trend variation. Properly weighted time periods provide accurate information for forecasts.

Disadvantages: Though better than a simple moving average, this technique will still lag behind actual demand to some degree. The challenging part of using a weighted moving average is deciding on the weight for each time period. There is no guideline to help decide which weights to use. Appropriate weighting relies on experience and knowledge about the product and the market.

EXPONENTIAL SMOOTHING: Exponential smoothing is a more sophisticated version of the weighted moving average. The equation requires three basic elements: last period's forecast, last period's actual demand, and a smoothing factor, which is a number greater than 0 and less than 1 (used as a weighting percentage).

The formula for calculating the forecast using exponential smoothing is the most recent period's demand multiplied by the smoothing factor, PLUS the most recent period's forecast multiplied by (one minus the smoothing factor).

> Forecast = (D x S) + (F x (1 – S))
> *Where:*
> D = last period's actual demand
> S = the smoothing factor represented in decimal form
> F = last period's forecast

Compute the exponential smoothing method forecast for July using the following data:

	Month	Units Actual	Units Forecasted	Smoothing Factor
M6	January	90,000	90,000	0.5
M5	February	110,000	92,500	0.5
M4	March	80,000	97,500	0.5
M3	April	90,000	90,000	0.5
M2	May	100,000	92,500	0.5
M1	June	120,000	95,000	0.5
M	July		?	

> (120,000 x 0.5) + (95,000 x (1 – 0.5))
> = 60,000 + (95,000 x 0.5)
> = 60,000 + 47,500
> **= 107,500 units for the July forecast**

The smoothing constant is not a given. It has to be determined based on the best judgment of a company's experts. The smoothing constant can be selected by experimenting with various constants in the historical data to see which one works best. Using the best possible smoothing constant is crucial to the accuracy of the forecast. In general, companies use a smoothing constant between 0.05 and 0.5. The higher the constant, the more weight that is given to the actual demand data from the preceding period. A constant of 0 would give no weight (0%) to the last period's demand, whereas a constant of 1.0 would give all of the weight (100%) to the last period's demand, which would then produce the same result as a naïve forecast.

Advantages: Exponential smoothing will create a forecast more responsive to trends than previous methods.

Disadvantages: Exponential smoothing will still lag behind trends, especially upward trends, because the smoothing factor would need to be greater than 1.0 to approach an accurate forecast. Picking an appropriate smoothing factor is essential for this method to work, but selection of a smoothing factor requires much experience and experimentation in order to arrive at a reliable value for the smoothing factor.

LINEAR TREND: Linear trend forecasting is used to impose a line best fit across the demand data of an entire time series.[2] A linear pattern is a steady increase or decrease in numbers over time. In other words, linear regression will always create a straight line that can be defined by a simple formula. There are no bends (i.e., variations) in a best fit line. If a best fit line is found, it can be used as the basis for forecasting future values by extending the line past the existing data and out into the future while maintaining the slope of the line.

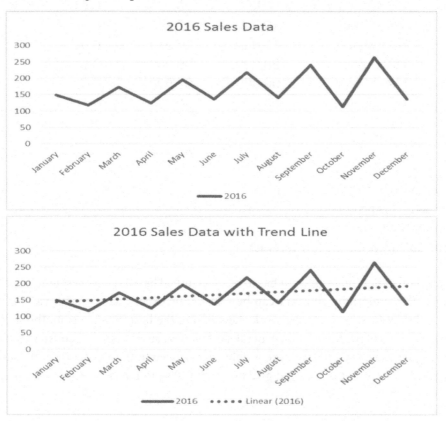

FUNDAMENTALS OF SUPPLY CHAIN MANAGEMENT

Advantages: When a best fit line is available, this method can provide an accurate forecast several time periods into the future. The use of linear regression allows these models to remain useful even amid random variation.

Disadvantages: While the overall trend is identified with linear regression, seasonal and cyclical variations are softened as the historical data becomes more expansive, making forecasts more useful for annual forecasts than monthly forecasts. In other words, linear regression will show the overall growth from year 1 to year 9 and be able to project year 12. It will not, however, generally show that demand increases in the summer and decreases in the winter (or some other variation), because the simple line is creating an average of sorts.

CAUSE-AND-EFFECT MODELS ....

© Technokrata/Shutterstock.com

There are two basic cause-and-effect models described here: simple linear regression and multiple linear regression. Regression uses the historical relationship between an independent and a dependent variable to predict the future values of the dependent variable (i.e., demand).

SIMPLE LINEAR REGRESSION attempts to model the relationship between a single independent variable and a dependent variable (the demand) by fitting a linear equation to the observed data. The equation describes the relationship between the independent variable and dependent variable as a straight line. For example, the demand might be dependent on how much money is spent on advertising and promotion: the more money spent, the higher the demand. The line that represents this relationship can be used to forecast demand with consideration of future values of the independent variable. In other words, if a company plans on investing more in advertising, it might be necessary to increase the forecast, or vice versa.

MULTIPLE LINEAR REGRESSION attempts to model the relationship between two or more independent variables and a dependent variable (i.e., demand) by fitting a linear equation to observed data. For example, the forecasted demand might be dependent on how much money is spent on advertising and promotion **and** on the selling price charged for the product. As with the previous example, forecasts can be adjusted with knowledge of the independent variables. If advertising is increased, and the price is lowered, it is likely appropriate to increase forecast demand.

Depending on the data and the number of independent variables, the mathematics involved can be complex. For example, if advertising is increased and the price is also increased, the impact on demand is not as obvious. The mathematics of multiple regression can help predict the impact on demand. Forecasting and statistical software packages can be useful to facilitate the computations required for this type of forecasting technique.

OTHER FORECASTING METHODS

There are numerous other forecasting models available and in use beyond what is covered in this text. The following are a few that may be worth further research.

- Drift Method

- Holt's Linear Trend Method

- Holt-Winters Seasonal Method

- Autoregressive Integrated Moving Average (ARIMA)

- Box-Jenkins

- X-11

- Econometric Model

- Input-Output Model

FORECAST ERROR

Because forecasts are almost always inaccurate, companies need to track the forecast against actual demand and measure the size and type of the forecast error. The size of the forecast error can be measured in units or percentages. In addition, calculating a value for the error may be useful to help justify the time and resources necessary to improve the forecasting process.

Forecast Error is the difference between the actual demand and the forecast demand. The error can be quantified as a unit value or as a percentage.

> Forecast error value = A – F
> Forecast error percentage = ((A – F) / A) x 100
> *Where:*
> A = actual demand
> F = forecast demand

Error measurement plays a critical role in tracking forecast accuracy, monitoring for exceptions, and benchmarking the forecasting process. Interpretation of these statistics can be tricky, particularly when working with low-volume data or when trying to assess accuracy across multiple items.

MEAN ABSOLUTE DEVIATION ....

MEAN ABSOLUTE DEVIATION (MAD) measures the size of the forecast error in units. It is calculated as the average of the unsigned (i.e., absolute) errors over a specified period of time. Absolute errors for a series of time periods are added and then divided by the number of time periods. The resulting value is the MAD measure of forecast inaccuracy. Whether the forecast is over or under the actual demand is irrelevant; only the magnitude of the deviation matters in the MAD calculation.

> $MAD = \Sigma(|A – F|) / n$
> *Where:*
> A = actual demand
> F = forecast demand
> n = number of time periods

MEAN ABSOLUTE PERCENT ERROR ....

MEAN ABSOLUTE PERCENT ERROR (MAPE) measures the size of the error in percentage terms. It is calculated as the average of the unsigned percentage error. Many companies use the MAPE as it is easier for most people to understand forecast error and forecast accuracy in percentage terms rather than in actual units. MAPE is a useful variant of the MAD calculation, because it shows the ratio, or percentage, of the absolute errors to the actual demand for a given number of periods.

MAPE = Σ ((|A – F|) / A) / n (expressed as a percentage)
Where:
A = actual demand
F = forecast demand
n = number of time periods

MAPE allows the magnitude of the forecast error to be clearly understood without needing detailed knowledge of the product.

MEAN SQUARED ERROR

MEAN SQUARED ERROR (MSE) magnifies the errors by squaring each one before adding them, and then dividing by the number of forecast periods. Squaring errors effectively makes them absolute, because multiplying two negative numbers results in a positive number.

MSE = Σ (A – F)^2 / n
Where:
A = actual demand
F = forecast demand
n = number of time periods

FORECAST BIAS

Forecast error can be the result of <u>bias</u>, which is a consistent deviation from the mean in one direction, either high or low. In other words, bias exists when the demand is consistently over- or under-forecast. A good forecast is <u>not</u> biased.

Σ Forecast error = Σ Actual demand – Σ Forecast demand

In this formula, if the sum of the forecast error is not zero, there is bias in the forecast. The size of the number reflects the relative amount of bias that is present. A negative result shows that actual demand was consistently less than the forecast, whereas a positive result shows that actual demand was greater than forecast demand.

Once bias has been identified, correcting the forecast error can be realized by adjusting the forecast by the appropriate amount in the appropriate direction (i.e., increase the forecast in the case of under-forecast [positive bias], and decrease it in the case of over-forecast [negative bias]).

A forecast process with bias will eventually create significant problems in the supply chain if left unchecked. Good supply chain planners are aware of these biases. A best practice is to measure for forecast bias routinely and then make corrections accordingly.

RUNNING SUM OF FORECAST ERRORS

RUNNING SUM OF FORECAST ERRORS (RSFE) provides a measure of forecast bias. RSFE indicates the tendency of a forecast to be consistently higher or lower than actual demand. A positive RSFE indicates that the forecasts were generally too low, underestimating the demand. In this situation, stockouts are likely to occur as companies are unable to meet customers' actual demand. A negative RSFE indicates that the forecasts were generally too high, overestimating demand. In this situation, excess inventory and higher carrying costs are likely to occur.

$$RSFE = \sum e_t$$
Where:
e_t = forecast error for period t

TRACKING SIGNAL

The tracking signal is a simple indicator that forecast bias is present in the forecast model. It determines if the forecast is within acceptable control limits and provides a warning when there are significant unexpected departures from the forecast. If the tracking signal falls outside the preset control limits, there is a bias problem with the forecasting method; and an evaluation of the way the forecast is generated is warranted. Tracking signals are most often used when the validity of the forecasting model is in doubt.

A smoke detector is a good analogy for a tracking signal. It is preset to allow for a certain range of smoke, but beyond that range the alarm (tracking signal) goes off and warns individuals that circumstances are outside the safe control limits. Individuals can then take action to correct the problem (or contact those individuals who can take the appropriate action).

The tracking signal is the ratio of the running sum of forecast errors to mean absolute deviation.

Tracking signal = RSFE / MAD

The RSFE is a cumulative sum that does not use absolute value for the errors. Therefore, the tracking signal could be either positive or negative to show the direction of the bias. Companies use a tracking signal by setting a target value for each period. If the tracking signal exceeds this target value, it would trigger a forecast review. It is important to remember that forecasts are seldom perfect, and any error in the forecast shows a bias. Tracking signals allow a system to acknowledge that the forecast will not be perfect but should be reasonably close.

BULLWHIP EFFECT

The bullwhip effect refers to the phenomenon that even minimal variability in customer demand can be distorted and amplified with increasing volatility upstream in the supply chain. That is, variability in customer demand is magnified as the supply chain participants become more remote from the end customer. This results in large variations on orders being placed upstream and inefficiencies all throughout the supply chain as suppliers react to their customers who are reacting to their customers. The reason for the effect can be attributed to individual supply chain participants second-guessing what is happening with ordering patterns in the absence of any other information or visibility. The serial nature of communicating orders up the chain with the inherent transportation delays of moving product down the chain induces more and more overcorrection with each successive link in the supply chain.

The bullwhip effect results from a host of issues:

- Customer demand is rarely perfectly stable, and businesses must forecast demand to position inventory and other resources properly. Forecasts, however, are based on statistics, and statistics are rarely 100% accurate.

- Companies often carry an inventory buffer called safety stock due to the knowledge that forecast errors are a given. Moving back across the supply chain from the end consumer(s) to raw material supplier(s), each supply chain participant has a greater observed variation in demand and thus greater need for safety stock.

- In periods of rising demand, downstream participants increase orders. In periods of falling demand, orders decrease or stop, and inventory accumulates. Variations are amplified as one moves upstream in the supply chain (i.e., further back from the end customer/consumer).

When the retailer feels a small demand ripple in the marketplace at the end of the supply chain, the retailer will then start adjusting its orders to the wholesalers, and the wholesaler in turn will adjust its orders to the distributor, the distributor to the factory, and so on back up the supply chain. When the new demand reaches the material or components supplier at the other end of the supply chain, the magnitude of fluctuation becomes unrecognizable. An overreaction due to uncertainty occurs throughout the entire supply chain.

HOW CAN THE BULLWHIP EFFECT BE ALLEVIATED? There is no single remedy that will completely mitigate the bullwhip effect, but there are some actions that supply chain participants can take collectively:

- Collaboration: The sharing of information through the use of electronic data interchange (EDI), point of sale (POS) data, and web-based information systems can facilitate needed collaboration.

- Synchronizing the supply chain: Supply chain participants can coordinate production planning and inventory management to minimize the need for reactionary corrections.

- Reducing inventory: Reducing overall supply chain inventory levels through the use of just in time (JIT), vendor managed inventory (VMI), and quick response (QR), all of which will be discussed later in this text, reduces overreactions to stockouts and decreases the chances of overages.

If the various participants work together to get closer to customers through collaborative planning, forecasting, and replenishment (CPFR), then the bullwhip effect can be greatly reduced and the accumulation of inventory and the inefficient use of resources throughout the supply chain can be minimized.

COLLABORATIVE PLANNING, FORECASTING, AND REPLENISHMENT

Collaborative planning, forecasting, and replenishment (CPFR) is "a process philosophy for facilitating collaborative communications"[1] whereby supply chain trading partners can jointly plan key supply chain activities from production and delivery of raw materials to production and delivery of final products to end customers. Collaboration encompasses business planning, sales forecasting, and all operations required to replenish raw materials and finished goods.

CPFR combines the intelligence of multiple trading partners who share their plans, forecasts, and delivery schedules with one another in an effort to ensure a smooth flow of goods and services across a supply chain. CPFR can significantly reduce the bullwhip effect and provide a plethora of benefits:

- Better customer service

- Lower inventory costs

- Improved quality

- Reduced cycle time

- Better production methods

CPFR requires a fundamental change in the way that buyers and sellers work together. The real value of CPFR comes from the sharing of forecasts among firms rather than firms relying on sophisticated algorithms and forecasting models to estimate demand.

Companies could forecast what they think their customers plan to buy from them, or customers could share their purchase plans with companies, so both sides could benefit.

SUMMARY

- Forecasting and demand planning are the key building blocks from which all downstream supply chain planning activities are derived.

- Demand is the need for a particular product or component. Demand planning is the process of combining statistical forecasting techniques and judgment to construct demand estimates for products or services across the supply chain from the suppliers' raw materials to the consumers' needs.

- A forecast is an estimate of future demand. Forecasting is the business function that attempts to estimate future demand for products so that they can be purchased or manufactured in appropriate quantities in advance. Forecasts, by their nature, are likely to be inaccurate but can still be useful. Forecasting is necessary, because it takes time to convert raw materials to a finished product that will be delivered to the customer.

- Dependent demand is demand directly related to other items or finished products (i.e., a component part or material used in making a finished product). Independent demand is demand for an item that is unrelated to the demand for other items (i.e., a finished product or spare/service parts).

- There are two main categories of forecasting techniques: qualitative and quantitative. Qualitative forecasting techniques are based on opinion, intuition, and judgment. These techniques are used when there is no/little historical data for the product. Quantitative forecasting techniques use historical demand data to project future demand. Quantitative forecasting is the more common method and involves two main qualitative techniques: time series models and cause-and-effect models.

- Time series models predict the future by understanding the past. Cause-and-effect models use the historical relationship between an independent and a dependent variable to predict the future values of the dependent variable (demand).

- Because forecasts are almost always inaccurate, companies need to track the forecast against actual demand and measure the size and type of the forecast error. Error measurement plays a critical role in tracking forecast accuracy.

- Mean absolute deviation (MAD), mean absolute percent error (MAPE), and mean squared error (MSE) are methods used to measure the size of the error.

- Running sum of forecast errors (RSFE) and tracking signals provide a measure and a warning of forecast bias.

- The bullwhip effect refers to the phenomenon that even minimal variability in customer demand can be distorted and amplified with increasing volatility as the participants become more remote from the end customer.

- Collaborative planning, forecasting, and replenishment (CPFR) is a collaboration process whereby supply chain trading partners can jointly plan key supply chain activities: from production and delivery of raw materials to production and delivery of final products to end customers. CPFR can significantly reduce the bullwhip effect.

REFERENCES ....

[1] *APICS Dictionary* (14th ed.). (2013). Chicago, IL: APICS. www.apics.org

[2] Harvey, A. C. (1989). *Forecasting, structural time series models and the Kalman filter*. Cambridge, UK: Cambridge University Press; McGuigan, J. R., et al. (2011). *Managerial economics* (12th ed.). Mason, OH: South-Western Cengage Learning; Robson, J. (2012, June). 8 fundamentals of forecasting in business. Business Strategy Blog, http://www.businessstrategyblog.com.au/2492/8-fundamentals-of-forecasting-in-business/

Chapter 3
Supply Chain Planning

CHAPTER OUTLINE

Introduction

Supply Chain Planning

Planning Goals and Objectives

Planning Responsibilities and Tasks

Supply Chain Planning Diagram

Business Planning

Sales and Operations Planning

Production Planning (Aggregate Production
  Planning)

Master Production Scheduling

Time Fencing

Basic Production Strategies

Bill of Materials

Material Requirements Planning

Capacity Planning

Distribution Requirements Planning

Enterprise Resource Planning Systems

INTRODUCTION ....

Supply chain planning is the element of supply chain management responsible for determining how best to satisfy the requirements created by the demand plan. Its objective is to balance supply and demand in a way that realizes the financial and service objectives of the company. It is a combination of all the planning processes across the supply chain, including aggregate production planning, master production scheduling, materials requirement planning, and distribution requirements planning. (Refer to Figure 3.2 later in the chapter.)

SUPPLY CHAIN PLANNING ....

Supply chain planning is hierarchical and can be divided into three broad categories:

- LONG RANGE (typically 1–3 years; can be as long as 10 years)
  Involves planning for major actions such as capital expenditures including the construction of facilities and major equipment purchase, and new product introduction plans (sales and operations planning and/or aggregate production planning). Example: Fictional Motor Company needs to increase manufacturing capacity to respond to an annual 5% increase in the demand for XL-150 pickup trucks over the next one to three years.

- INTERMEDIATE RANGE (typically 3–18 months)
  Involves planning the quantity and timing of end items—that is, specific make and model (master production scheduling). Includes sales planning; production planning; setting major resource levels such as manpower, inventory, contracting; and analyzing operating plans. Example: Fictional Motor Company plans to make 1,000 XL-150 pickup trucks per month for the next 3 to 18 months.

- SHORT RANGE
  Involves the detailed planning process for components and parts to support the master production schedule. Includes ordering and scheduling activities using information from the bill-of-materials, inventory system, purchasing system, and so forth (materials requirement planning). Example: Plan and order the components and materials needed for production of the XL-150 pickup trucks for delivery each week over the next 24 weeks (250 engines, 250 transmissions, seats, windows, etc.).

PLANNING GOALS AND OBJECTIVES......................................

The first step in supply chain planning is for the top management at the company to establish the desired high-level planning goals and objectives. **Example:** Meet demand within the limits of the available resources at the lowest overall cost, or obtain the resources necessary to meet demand at the lowest overall cost.

The next step is to determine what is necessary to achieve these goals and objectives. Identify the specific action steps. **Examples:** Build or acquire a new facility, hire more workers, buy more equipment.

This is followed by setting start and completion dates for each action item identified. **Example:** Begin hiring more workers in February and finish hiring by April.

Responsibility for each action item should be formally assigned to the appropriate individual or department within the company to execute. **Example:** The action item of hiring more workers would be assigned to the human resource manager or department within the company.

PLANNING RESPONSIBILITIES AND TASKS...........................

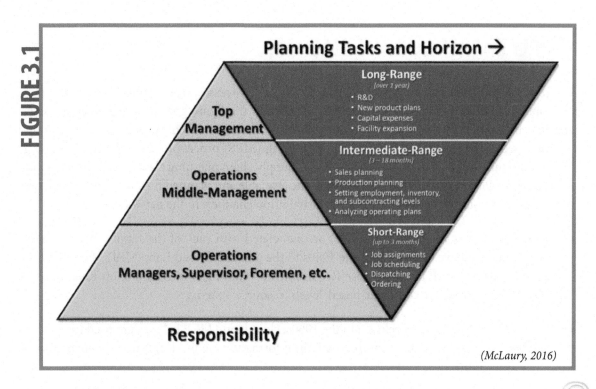

FIGURE 3.1

Planning Tasks and Horizon →

Long-Range
(over 1 year)
- R&D
- New product plans
- Capital expenses
- Facility expansion

Top Management

Intermediate-Range
(3 – 18 months)
- Sales planning
- Production planning
- Setting employment, inventory, and subcontracting levels
- Analyzing operating plans

Operations Middle-Management

Short-Range
(up to 3 months)
- Job assignments
- Job scheduling
- Dispatching
- Ordering

Operations Managers, Supervisor, Foremen, etc.

Responsibility

(McLaury, 2016)

Responsibility for the various levels of supply chain planning is generally held by different groups within a company. Figure 3.1 shows which group(s) are typically responsible for short-, intermediate-, and long-range planning.

As <u>long-range</u> planning encompasses making strategic decisions and controlling the level of major resources, it is usually the responsibility of top management in an organization. This level of planning sets the direction the company will follow into the future

<u>Intermediate-range</u> planning translates the long-range plan into an executable plan and schedule in the near time frame. It details the specific products to be produced against a specific time schedule, and allocates the resources needed to achieve the long-range plan. This level of planning is best managed by midlevel operations management people who have the knowledge and information about the operations necessary to develop the plan.

<u>Short-range</u> planning encompasses converting the intermediate level plan into a detailed sequence of steps and actions necessary to execute the plan in the immediate time frame. This is the planning level where the plan becomes a reality, materials are obtained, products are produced, and orders are filled. This level of planning is best managed by the individuals within an organization who are the most directly involved with these activities—the managers, supervisors, supply chain planners, and foreperson of the manufacturing operations.

SUPPLY CHAIN PLANNING DIAGRAM

Figure 3.2 shows the sequence of supply chain planning processes, from top to bottom, and their relationship to each other. The hierarchy of processes in the figure goes from the long-range aggregated Business Planning and Sales and Operations Planning (S&OP) processes down through the intermediate range Master Production Scheduling (MPS) process to the detailed short-range Material Requirements Planning (MRP) process. Supply chain planning also includes Distribution Requirements Planning (DRP), which allocates the available and planned finished product inventory out to the various warehouses serving the distribution channels in the network.

Figure 3.2 also shows which planning steps are associated with each of the supply chain management concepts that have evolved from the 1960s to the present; Closed Loop MRP, Manufacturing Resource Planning (MRP II), Enterprise Requirements Planning, and Distribution Requirements Planning (DRP). These are computer-based "push" resource systems.

- CLOSED LOOP MRP: Developed in the 1960s, closed loop MRP is "a system used for production planning and inventory control, with an information feedback feature that enables plans

FIGURE 3.2

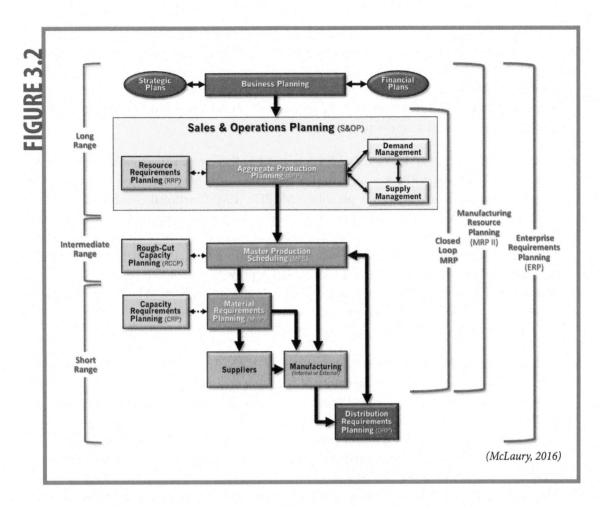

(McLaury, 2016)

to be checked and adjusted. Closed Loop MRP synchronizes the purchasing or materials procurement plans with the master production schedule. The system feeds back information about completed manufacture and materials on hand into the MRP system, so that these plans can be adjusted according to capacity and other requirements. The system is called a closed loop MRP because of its feedback feature."[2] It incorporates the aggregate production plan, the master production schedule, the material requirements plan, and the associated capacity planning tools needed to check the feasibility of the plan.

- MANUFACTURING RESOURCE PLANNING (MRP II): Evolving in the 1980s, manufacturing resource planning (MRP II) is "an integrated information system used by businesses. Manufacturing Resource Planning (MRP II) evolved from early Materials Requirement Planning (MRP) systems by including the integration of additional data, such as employee and financial needs. The system is designed to centralize, integrate and process information for effective decision making in scheduling, design engineering, inventory management and cost control in manufacturing. MRP II is a computer-based system that can create detail production schedules using realtime data to coordinate the arrival of component materials with machine and labor availability. MRP II is used widely by itself, but also as a module of more extensive enterprise resource planning (ERP) systems."[2] It incorporates the closed loop MRP system and adds the strategic, business, and financial plans.

- ENTERPRISE REQUIREMENTS PLANNING (ERP): Evolving in the 1990's, Enterprise Requirements Planning (ERP) is a process that interfaces with manufacturing to act as an extension of manufacturing resource planning (MRPII). ERP functionality includes all aspects of production planning and scheduling, material planning and inventory control, purchasing, manufacturing, capacity planning, distribution and logistics, as well as planning for the finance and human resource activities of the supply chain. ERP is typically implemented through a software platform of integrated functional modules providing computerized management of all aspects of the enterprise's supply chain. The ERP software application facilitates the sharing of information and the real-time communication and collaboration across multiple business functions necessary for the supply chain to operate efficiently and effectively.

- DISTRIBUTION REQUIREMENTS PLANNING (DRP): The DRP is "1) the function of determining the need to replenish inventory at branch warehouses. A time-phased order point approach is used where the planned orders at the branch warehouse level are 'exploded' via MRP logic to become gross requirements on the supplying source. In the case of multilevel distribution networks, this explosion process can continue down through the various levels of regional warehouses (master warehouse, factory warehouse, etc.) and become input to the master production schedule. Demand on the supplying sources is recognized as dependent, and standard MRP logic applies. 2) More generally, replenishment inventory calculations, which may be based on other planning approaches such as period order quantities or 'replace exactly what was used,' rather than being limited to the time-phased order point approach."[1]

BUSINESS PLANNING ....

The business plan, with its long-term focus, provides the company's direction and objectives for the next 2 to 10 years. Management gathers input from the various organizational functions such as finance, marketing, operations, and engineering, to develop the business plan. The plan states the company's objectives for profitability, growth rate, and return on investment. It is then typically updated and reevaluated annually. It is also typically used as the starting point for developing the organization's production plan or aggregate production plan.

SALES AND OPERATIONS PLANNING ....

Sales and operations planning (S&OP) is an iterative business management process that determines the optimum level of manufacturing output.

S&OP is a process that brings all the demand and supply plans for the business (sales, marketing, development, production, sourcing, and finance) together to provide management with the ability to strategically direct the business to achieve a competitive advantage.

- "It is the definitive statement of the company's plans for the intermediate to long term, covering a horizon sufficient to plan for resources, and to support the annual business planning process."[1]

- It links the strategic plans for the business with its execution, and provides a way for management to determine resource needs and to keep a handle on the business without having to review the plans at the detailed level.

- It is performed at least once a month and is reviewed by management at an aggregate (product family) level.

- Generally, issues are "bubbled-up" to senior management on an exception basis. Middle management and operational management are expected to try to resolve issues first whenever possible.

Monthly S&OP meetings are essential to decision making. Senior management meets to discuss the various trade-offs between customer service, inventory investments, production capabilities, supply availability, and distribution concerns. The process strives to determine how to best apply the company's resources to strike an optimum balance between maximizing profit and satisfying the company's most important operational goals.

The S&OP process follows some standard steps:

- Review the current plan.

- Review current demand and forecasts for changes and trends.

- Identify capacity and material/product shortages and propose solutions.

- Evaluate product portfolio changes for adding new products and phasing out older products.

- Ensure that the plan meets financial targets.

- Hold a formal S&OP meeting, typically monthly, to review the plan, major changes, and proposed scenarios, to determine and decide on the resource adjustments necessary to meet the company's objectives.

PRODUCTION PLANNING (Aggregate Production Planning).......

Production planning, or aggregate production planning (APP), is an integral part of the business planning process. It is "a process to develop tactical plans based on setting the overall level of manufacturing output (production plan) and other activities to best satisfy the current planned levels of sales (sales plan or forecasts), while meeting general business objectives of profitability, productivity, competitive customer lead times, and so on, as expressed in the overall business plan. The sales and production capabilities are compared, and a business strategy that includes a sales plan, a production plan, budgets, pro forma financial statements, and supporting plans for materials and workforce requirements, and so on, is developed. One of its primary purposes is to establish production rates that will achieve management's objective of satisfying customer demand by maintaining, raising, or lowering inventories or backlogs, while usually attempting to keep the workforce relatively stable. Because this plan affects many company functions, it is normally prepared with information from marketing and coordinated with the functions of manufacturing, sales, engineering, finance, materials, and so on."[1]

Aggregate production planning is the hierarchical planning process that translates annual business and marketing plans, and demand forecasts, into a production plan for a product family (products that share similar characteristics) in a plant or facility. The aggregate plan identifies the resources needed by operations management to support the business plan over the next 6 to 18 months. It details the aggregate production rate and size of the workforce, which enables planners to determine the amount of inventory to be held; the amount of overtime authorized; any subcontracting, hiring, or firing of employees; and backordering of customer orders.[2]

Developing the aggregate production plan includes:

1. Determining the demand for each period covered by the aggregate planning horizon

2. Determining the available capacity for each period covered by the aggregate planning horizon

3. Identifying any constraints which may influence the plan

4. Determining the direct labor and material costs and the indirect manufacturing costs for each product or product family covered by the aggregate production plan

5. Identifying or developing strategies and contingency plans to manage the potential upside or downside in the market

6. Agreeing on a plan that best meets the planning goals and objectives

It is also advisable to test or challenge the plan, if possible, to determine how robust the plan is, and whether or not additional strategies or contingency plans need to be developed.

Individual products are not represented in the plan as it would be cumbersome to include every product, so a company typically develops the APP by major product family.

Example: A cosmetic company may produce many different products, such as mascara or lipstick, and each with different colors, different styles, and package sizes. Including all of these in a plan would be cumbersome. The aggregate plan considers a product grouping such as "tubes of lipstick" or "bottles of mascara" as a product measure for aggregate planning purposes.

The aim is to develop the aggregate production plan to cover all of the operations resources (machines, labor, and inventory), to produce the amount of product needed over a certain period of time. The aggregate plan will then specify, for a particular period, how many units of product are produced, how much labor is needed, and how much inventory is on hand. Using product families reduces the level of detail but still provides the information needed for decision making. Some common terms of output used in the aggregate plans are *units, gallons, pounds, standard hours,* and *dollars.*

Aggregate production planning is an iterative and ongoing process. The plan should be updated once every three months, rolling the plan out three more months into the future each time, or whenever there is a major change—whichever comes first. The APP is an intermediate plan and does not need to be updated continuously. Updating the APP too frequently will add instability to the company's operations.

Aggregate Production Planning Goals

For the aggregate production planning process to be value added, it must strive to achieve some high-level goals, including:

- Meeting demand

- Using capacity efficiently

- Achieving the inventory targets

- Minimizing costs:

- Labor
- Inventory
- Plant and equipment
- Subcontract

Available capacity versus demand:

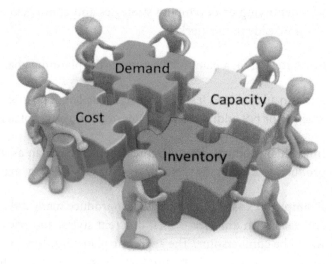

- If capacity and demand are **nearly equal** emphasis should be placed on meeting demand as efficiently as possible.

- If capacity is **greater than demand** the firm might choose promotion and advertising in order to increase demand.

- If capacity is **less than demand** the firm might consider subcontracting a portion of the workload to an outside third party.

Aggregate Production Planning Strategies

In order for the APP to achieve the desired goals, demand and supply must be kept in balance. If the APP projects a potential imbalance in demand and supply, there are some strategies typically employed by companies to remedy the projected imbalance before it actually occurs. The following are some strategic actions companies can take on both the demand and supply sides of the plan to avoid the imbalance.

DEMAND STRATEGIES:

- Influencing demand: Companies can try to influence projected demand so that it aligns better to available production capacity (e.g., airlines and hotels offering weekend discounts, telecommunication companies offering weekend rates, off-season purchase discounts, early bird specials, happy hour). These can be facilitated through advertising, promotional plans, and price discount strategies.

- Backordering: Accept that demand will be greater than supply capabilities during high demand periods and allow some demand to go unfulfilled. However, this action

may create a negative customer experience and impact the company in both the short and long term.

- Counter-seasonal product mix: Develop a product mix with opposing trends (e.g., opposite seasons) that level the cumulative required production capacity (e.g., manufacture lawn mowers for the summer and snow blowers for the winter).

SUPPLY STRATEGIES:

- Change inventory levels:

    - Increase inventories: Build stock in advance of demand in order to use available capacity.

    - Decrease inventories: Temporarily reduce inventory below normal safety stock levels during peak demand periods to meet customer requirements.

- Change capacity:

    - Vary production output through overtime or idle time.

    - Vary workforce size by hiring or layoff.

    - Use part-time workers.

    - Subcontract the work.

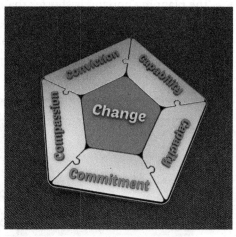

The output of the aggregate planning process is the aggregate production plan, which guides development of the master production schedule (refer to figure 3.2).

MASTER PRODUCTION SCHEDULING ....

"The Master Production Schedule (MPS) represents what the company plans to produce expressed in specific configurations, quantities, and dates. It becomes a set of planning numbers that drives material requirements planning. The master production schedule must take into account the forecast, the production plan, and other important considerations such as backlog, availability of material, availability of capacity, and management policies and goals."[1]

NOTE: For the service industry, the master production schedule may be the **appointment log or book**, where capacity (e.g., skilled labor or professional service) is balanced with demand.

Unlike the APP, which is expressed as product families, the MPS is expressed as specific finished goods. It is a detailed <u>disaggregation</u> of the aggregate production plan, listing the exact end items to be produced by a specific period, and includes how operations will use available resources. This allows the company to make informed commitments to customers.

 "MPS is the plan that drives the business and commits resources and materials (costs) to meet the plan. The plan is what the business can achieve not necessarily what the customer wants."[4] The MPS is a statement of production, not a statement of demand. As such, individual products can be finished ahead of time (i.e., before they are required to meet demand) and held in inventory rather than finished as needed. The master production scheduler is the person responsible for balancing customer service and capacity usage (see figure 3.3).

- The MPS is reviewed and updated as necessary—weekly or even daily.

- The planning horizon is shorter than APP, but longer than the lead time to produce the item. <u>Example</u>: If the lead time to produce an item is 2 months, then the planning horizon of MPS must be more than 2 months but generally not as far out into the future as the 18 months covered by the APP. Typically the planning horizon of MPS is 3 to 12 months.

FIGURE 3.3

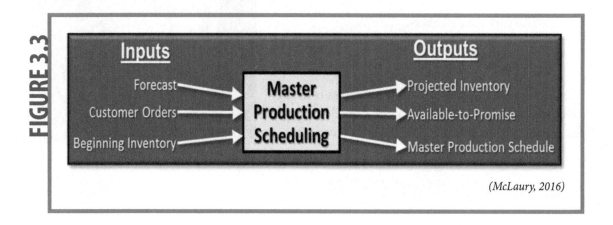

(McLaury, 2016)

Example: Aggregate Production Plan → Master Production Schedule

FIGURE 3.4

	Jan	Feb	Mar	Apr	May	Jun
Aggregate Production Plan						
Lawn Mowers	200	300	400	300	300	200
Master Schedule						
Push Mowers	100	100	100	100	100	100
Self-Propelled Mowers	75	150	200	125	100	75
Riding Mowers	25	50	100	75	100	25
Total Mowers	200	300	400	300	300	200
Master Production Schedule (MPS)						
Forecast (Self-Propelled Mowers)	75	150	200	125	100	75
Customer Orders	75	100	175	100		
Projected Available Balance [100]	175	225	200	250	150	75
Available-to-Promise (ATP)	75	50	100	75	75	75
Master Production Schedule (MPS)	150	150	150	150	0	0

(McLaury, 2016)

Planning Formula

Beginning Inventory (projected available balance from the end of the previous period), plus production (i.e., the MPS) quantity for the current period, minus the demand (i.e., customer orders or forecast) for the current period, equals the projected ending inventory (i.e., projected available balance) for the current period (see figure 3.4).

Available-to-promise (ATP) is a business function that provides a response to customer order enquiries, based on resource availability. It generates available quantities of the requested product, and delivery due dates.

It represents "the uncommitted portion of a company's inventory and planned production maintained in the master schedule to support customer order promising."[1] In simple terms, it is a calculation to determine how much inventory the company will have at the end of each period that has not already been promised/planned/allocated to future customer orders. This information will help the company respond to new customer orders or inquiries, determining whether the company will have enough available inventory to deliver against these new customer orders or not.

Three basic methods of calculating the ATP quantities:

1. Discrete Available-to-Promise [(on hand + supply – ordered) per period]

2. Cumulative Available-to-Promise *without look ahead*

3. Cumulative Available-to-Promise *with look ahead*

Discrete Available-to-Promise

1. Add the beginning inventory to the MPS [planned production] for period 1, subtracting the committed customer orders (CCOs) from period 1 up to but not including the period of the next scheduled MPS.

2. For all subsequent periods, there are two possibilities:

   – If no MPS has been scheduled for the period, the ATP is zero.

   – If an MPS has been scheduled for the period, the ATP is the MPS minus the sum of all the CCOs from that period up to the period of the next scheduled MPS.

3. If an ATP for any period is negative, the deficit must be subtracted from the most recent positive ATP, and the ATP quantities must then be revised to reflect these changes.

TIME FENCING ....

Because MPS is the plan that drives the business, even small changes in the MPS can cause major changes in the detailed production schedule and the material plan, creating nervousness and instability throughout the organization. To minimize the impact of the inevitable changes in MPS that will occur, many companies have adopted a time fencing policy separating the planning horizon into a firmed time period and a planned time period. This means that the business agrees that it will not change the MPS within a given window of time (e.g., the first six weeks of the plan).

- FIRMED TIME PERIOD: From the current date out several weeks into the future

  – A firm time fence is established at the outer limit of this period to signify when changes can no longer be made automatically or without prior approval.

  – The planning system or master production scheduler is not allowed to automatically make changes in the firmed time period, only recommend changes.

- Recommended changes must be reviewed and approved by an authorized person(s) who will then initiate the appropriate action.

- **PLANNED TIME PERIOD:** From the end of the firmed time period to the end of the planning horizon

  - The planning system or the master production scheduler can create or make changes to planned orders in this time period based on the data and planning logic determined by the company, without prior approval.

  - Figure 3.5 illustrates an example.

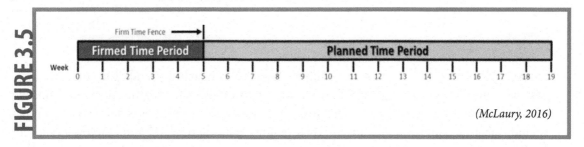

(McLaury, 2016)

While this time fencing policy may help to minimize the nervousness and instability in the MPS created by changes, it can be extremely difficult to stick to as there is a tradeoff between maintaining the stability and effectiveness of the plan, and supporting a customers' urgent requirements.

BASIC PRODUCTION STRATEGIES ....

The three basic production strategies that companies use to complete the production plan are the level production strategy, the chase production strategy, and the mixed production strategy.

1. **LEVEL PRODUCTION STRATEGY:** Relies on a constant output rate while varying inventory and backlog according to fluctuating demand. This strategy may be adopted in cases where the changeover is long, or it's inefficient to stop/start. The company relies on variable finished goods inventory and backlogs to meet demand. This strategy works well for make-to-stock firms. Examples include plywood, steel, light bulbs, razors. **Example:** The established stable workforce has a capacity to produce 50 units per demand time period. If customer demand decreases, the workforce is kept stable and excess inventory is produced. If the demand increases, the workforce is kept stable and the incremental demand is satisfied through any available excess inventory or by accepting a backlog (i.e., unfulfilled customer demand) until such time as there is sufficient excess inventory to supply the shortfall (see figure 3.6).

FIGURE 3.6

Customer Demand	Workforce	Finished Output of Goods or Services	Backlog or Inventory
10	Constant Number of Workers	50	40 Inventory
20	Constant Number of Workers	50	30 Inventory
80	Constant Number of Workers	50	30 Backlog get shortfall from inventory

(McLaury, 2016)

2. **CHASE PRODUCTION STRATEGY:** Adjusts capacity to match demand. The company hires and lays off workers to match the finished product output to fluctuating demand. Finished goods inventory remains constant. This strategy works well for make-to-order firms. Examples include airplane companies, because of their lengthy training time. Union employees are sent back to the union hall, waiting to be recalled and collect unemployment in the interim. Another example is workers who harvest crops. **Example**: The established stable workforce has a capacity to produce 20 units per demand time period. If the demand drops to 10 units, the company would fire/lay off up to half the workforce. If the demand increases to 30 units, the company would hire up to an additional 50% to meet demand (see figure 3.7).

FIGURE 3.7

Customer Demand	Workforce	Finished Output of Goods or Services
10	Fire	10
20	Stable Workforce	20
30	Hire	30

(McLaury, 2016)

MIXED OR HYBRID PRODUCTION STRATEGY: Maintains stable core workforce while using other short-term means such as overtime, subcontracting, and part-time helpers, to manage short-term demand. Examples include construction companies and retail stores at holiday season (see figure 3.8).

FIGURE 3.8

Customer Demand	Workforce	Finished Output of Goods or Services
10	Stable Workforce	10
20	Work Overtime	20
50	Work Overtime & Outsource some Output	50
80	Overtime, Part Time Help and Outsource	80

(McLaury, 2016)

BILL OF MATERIALS..

The **bill of materials (BOM)** is a document that shows an inclusive listing of all component parts and assemblies, and the quantity of each, needed to produce or assemble a single unit of a parent item. "It is used in conjunction with the master production schedule to determine the items for which purchase requisitions and production orders must be released. A variety of display formats exist for bills of material, including the single-level Bill of Materials, indented Bill of Materials, modular (planning) Bill of Materials, transient Bill of Materials, matrix Bill of Materials, and costed Bill of Materials. . . The Bill of Materials may also be called the formula, recipe, or ingredients list in certain process industries."[1]

The following are different types of bills of material used in supply chain planning:

- SINGLE LEVEL BILL OF MATERIALS: Display of components that are directly used in a parent item, together with the quantity required of each component (i.e., the planning factor). Shows only the relationships one level down.[1]

- **MULTILEVEL BILL OF MATERIALS:** Display of all the components directly or indirectly used in a parent, together with the quantity required of each component (i.e., the planning factor). If a component is a subassembly, blend, intermediate, for example, all its components and all their components also will be exhibited, down to purchased parts and raw materials.[1] This is often presented as an indented bill of materials.

- **PLANNING BILL OF MATERIALS:** "An artificial grouping of items or events in bill-of-material format used to facilitate master scheduling and material planning. It may include the historical average of demand expressed as a percentage of total demand for all options within a feature or for a specific end item within a product family and is used as the quantity per in the planning Bill of Materials."[1]

EXAMPLE OF HOW THE BOM IS USED: The recipe for baking a cake includes a list of ingredients and the instructions on how to actually combine those ingredients to make a cake. The list of ingredients is the bill of materials, which in this example might include 4 cups of flour, 1 cup of water, 4 eggs, 1 cup of sugar, etc. The bill of materials tells you which ingredients and how much of each ingredient you need to produce each individual "cake."

In this example the cake is an independent demand item, and the ingredients are dependent demand items, defined as follows:

INDEPENDENT DEMAND: Demand for an item that is unrelated to the demand for other items (e.g., a finished product or spare/service parts). The demand for finished products generally comes from the external customer, is independent from other items, and may therefore need to be forecasted. It can be affected by trends, seasonal patterns, and general market conditions.

For example, if we have been selling 10 cakes per week for the past few months, we can use this information to create a forecast of how many cakes we expect to sell for the next few weeks/months. This estimate/forecast for the independent demand item (i.e., cake) becomes the basis for determining how many cakes we will produce in our production plan to satisfy the projected demand.

DEPENDENT DEMAND: Demand that is directly related to, or derived from, the bill of materials structure for other items or finished products (a raw material, component part, packaging material, subassembly, etc.) used in making a finished product or parent item. Dependent demands are calculated and should not be forecasted.

For example, if we are going to bake a cake, and the BOM states that we need 4 cups of flour for one cake, the total amount of flour that we need is entirely dependent on how many cakes we are going to make. Flour is one of the dependent demand items of the cake, which is the independent demand item in this example. If we plan to make 10 cakes per week, and per the BOM we need 4 cups of flour for each cake, we will need 40 cups of flour in total each week to make the planned 10 cakes per week. No forecast or estimation is needed for the flour because we can calculate exactly how much we need based on the planned number of cakes.

Example: Single Level Bill of Materials

FIGURE 3.9

Independent Demand - The external demand for an item that is unrelated to the demand for other items (e.g., finished product). The demand for these items is forecasted and can be affected by trends, seasonal patterns, and market conditions.

Dependent Demand - the internal demand for items that are assembled or combined to make up the final product (e.g., component parts). Demand for these items is calculated based on the demand of the final product in which the parts are used, by using the planning factor.

Table	Quantity Per *
Leg	4
End	2
Side	2
Top	1
Hardware Kit	1

* Planning Factor

(McLaury, 2016)

Figure 3.9 is a single level BOM showing that for every table that is produced, 4 legs, 2 ends, 2 sides, 1 top, and 1 hardware kit are required. The finished product (i.e., the table) is an independent demand item forecasted based on anticipated external demand. The component parts (leg, end, side, top, and hardware kit) are dependent demand items in which the demand is calculated based on the number of tables that are planned for production.

Example: Multilevel Bill of Materials

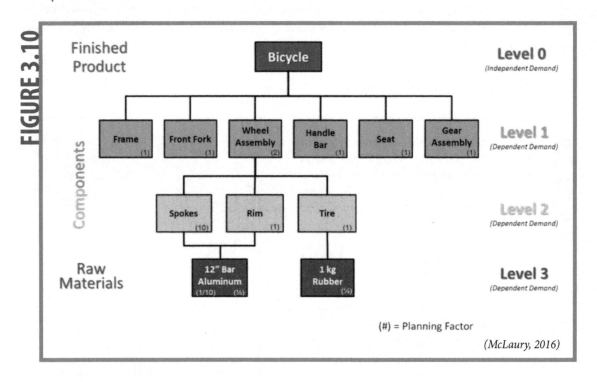

FIGURE 3.10

(McLaury, 2016)

Figure 3.10 is a multilevel BOM showing the parent and component relationships and the specific units of each component (i.e., the planning factor) needed to produce one unit of the parent item. In this example, the parent item (i.e., finished product) is the bicycle and all of the other items are component parts of the bicycle. Some of the component parts such as the wheel assembly also have their own component parts such as the spokes, rim, and tire. The bicycle is Level 0; the wheel assembly is Level 1; the spokes, rim, and tire are Level 2; and so forth.

MATERIAL REQUIREMENTS PLANNING ••••••••••••••••••••••••••••••••••••••

"Material Requirements Planning (MRP) is a set of techniques that uses Bill of Materials data, inventory data, and the master production schedule to calculate requirements for materials. It makes recommendations to release replenishment orders for material. Further, because it is time-phased, it makes recommendations to reschedule open orders when due dates and need dates are not aligned. Time-phased MRP begins with the items listed on the MPS and determines (1) the quantity of all components and materials required to fabricate those items and (2) the date that the components and material are required. Time-phased MRP is accomplished by exploding the Bill of Materials (see Key Terms Used In MRP), adjusting for inventory quantities on hand or on order, and offsetting the net requirements by the appropriate lead times."[1]

The authorized MPS is a critical input to MRP, which is the next planning level below the MPS. The MRP uses the MPS, bill of materials data, and inventory records to calculate specific requirements for materials in specific time frames. The MPS tells the MRP what the company plans to build and when. The MRP logic then uses this information along with the BOM and the inventory data to calculate the materials needed to build the products in the schedule and plan the procurement or production of those materials in quantity and in time to meet the schedule. Notice that as we move from the business plan down through the aggregate production plan, MPS, and then MRP, we progressively become more specific and detailed, as well as more immediate in terms of the planning horizon.

Key Terms Used in MRP

- GROSS REQUIREMENT: A time-phased requirement prior to netting out on-hand inventory and lead-time

- NET REQUIREMENT: The unsatisfied item requirement for a specific time period: gross requirement for period minus current on-hand inventory

- PROJECTED ON-HAND INVENTORY: Projected closing inventory at the end of a period: beginning inventory minus gross requirements, plus scheduled receipts plus planned receipts from planned order releases

- PLANNED ORDER RELEASE: A specific order for a specific item and quantity to be released to the shop or the supplier

- FIRMED PLANNED ORDER: A planned order that can be frozen in quantity and time so that the MRP computer logic cannot automatically change when conditions change; established by the planner or supply chain manager to prevent system nervousness (This can aid planners working with MRP systems to respond to material and capacity problems by firming up selected planned orders.)

- SCHEDULED RECEIPT: A committed order awaiting delivery for a specific period

- TIME BUCKET: Unit of time or time period used in MRP (e.g., days, weeks, months)

- PARENT: Item generating demand for lower-level components

- **COMPONENTS:** Parts demanded by a parent

- **PLANNING FACTOR:** The number/quantity of each component or material needed to produce a single unit of the parent item

- **EXPLOSION:** The process of converting a parent item's planned order releases into component gross requirements

- **PEGGING:** Relates the gross requirements for a component part to the planned order releases of the parent item, so as to identify the source(s) of the item's gross requirements (Pegging can be thought of as active where-used information.)

- **LOT SIZE:** Order size for MRP logic

- **SAFETY STOCK:** "A quantity of stock planned to be in inventory to protect against fluctuations in demand or supply. Over planning supply versus demand can be used to create safety stock."[1]

MRP Input

In order for the MRP logic to work, the following data are required:

1. The independent demand information (i.e., finished product forecast from the MPS)

2. Parent-component relationships from the BOM

3. Inventory status of the final product and each of the components and materials

4. Released, firmed, or planned order releases for the final product and each of the components and materials

MRP Output

MRP systems have capabilities of providing management with a wide range of outputs. These typically include:

1. **PLANNED ORDERS:** a schedule indicating the amount and timing of future orders

2. **ORDER RELEASES:** authorizing the execution of planned orders

3. **CHANGES TO PLANNED ORDERS:** revisions of due dates or order quantities, including the cancellation of orders if necessary

4. **PERFORMANCE-CONTROL REPORTS:** measure deviations from plans such as deliveries and stockouts, as well as providing info that can be used to assess cost performance

5. **PLANNING REPORTS:** predict future inventories, procurement contracts, and data for future assessment of material requirements

6. **EXCEPTION REPORTS:** recognizes inconsistencies within the report such as errors in overdue or late orders, etc.

Advantage: MRP provides detailed planning information for all products and materials.

Disadvantages: MRP results in loss of visibility, which is especially acute for products with a deep BOM, and it ignores capacity and shop floor conditions.

Example: Material Requirements Planning

Figure 3.11 highlights part of the BOM for a bicycle, which will be used to demonstrate how the MRP is determined. To illustrate, each bicycle (finished product) requires 2 wheel assemblies. Each wheel assembly requires 10 spokes. Each spoke requires 1/10 of a 12-inch bar of aluminum.

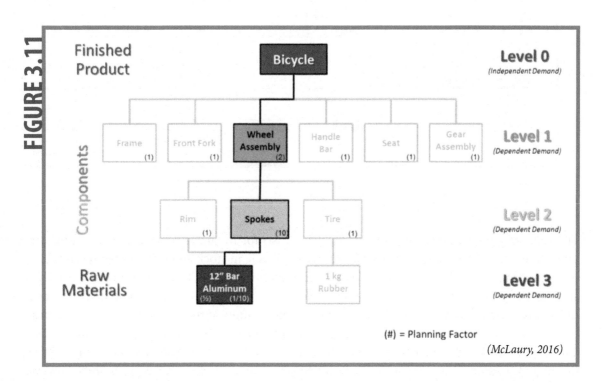

(McLaury, 2016)

In figure 3.12, the bicycle and each of these component parts are entered into a simple MRP template along with their relevant planning information, including independent demand forecast, scheduled receipts, beginning inventories, lot sizes, lead times, safety stock requirements, and the like, to be planned for the next eight weeks.

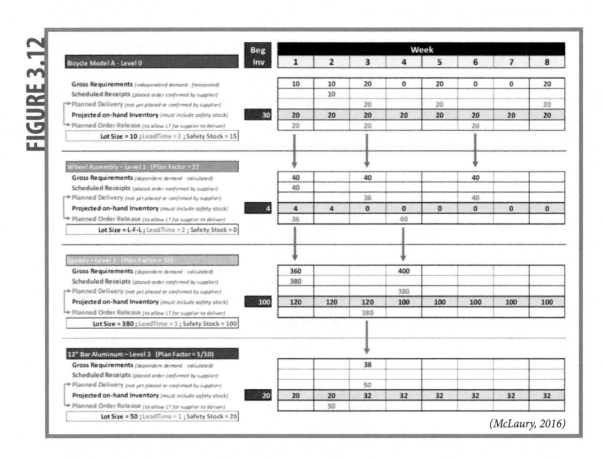

(McLaury, 2016)

BICYCLE MODEL A (LEVEL 0):

The gross requirements (i.e., finished product forecast) for the bicycle has been entered for each week. There is a beginning inventory of 30 bicycles already in stock and a scheduled receipt for 10 units confirmed for delivery in Week 2. For Week 1, start with 30 units of beginning inventory, and subtract the gross requirements of 10 units in Week 1, leaving a projected on-hand inventory of 20 units at the end of Week 1. For Week 2, start with the 20 units at the end of Week 1, and subtract the 10 units of gross requirements for Week 2, and add the scheduled receipts of 10 units in Week 2 to end the week with 20 units. For Week 3, start with 20 units at the end of Week 2, and subtract the 20 units of gross requirements in Week 3. This would end Week 3 with zero (0) units; however, this item has a safety stock policy of 15 units, so an order must be planned to bring the projected week-ending inventory up to a least 15 units. As this item also has a lot size of 10 units, orders must be placed in increments of 10 units. Consequently, a delivery of 20 units must be planned (i.e., planned delivery) for Week 3 bringing the projected on-hand Inventory at week end to 20 units. The lead time for this item is 2 weeks, so the planned delivery of 20 units must be released to the supplier in Week 1 (i.e., planned order release) for delivery in Week 3. Each of the succeeding weeks 4 through 8 follows the same logic.

WHEEL ASSEMBLY (LEVEL 1):

The gross requirements for the wheel assembly (dependent demand item) are calculated directly from the planned order releases of the bicycle (i.e., the parent item) as the wheel assemblies must be available to produce the bicycles when the planned orders for the bicycles are released (see red arrows in figure 3.11). As there are 2 wheel assemblies required for every bicycle produced (i.e., the planning factor), the gross requirements for the wheel assemblies in Week 1, Week 3, and Week 6 are 40 units each. There is a beginning inventory of 4 wheel assembly units already in stock, and a scheduled receipt for 40 units confirmed for delivery in Week 1. For Week 1, start with 4 units of beginning inventory, and subtract the gross requirements in Week 1 of 40 units, and add the scheduled receipts in Week 1 of 40 units, to end the week with 4 units of projected on-hand inventory. For Week 2, there are no gross requirements, scheduled receipts, or planned deliveries in Week 2, so the projected on-hand inventory of 4 units is carried forward. For Week 3, start with 4 units at the end of Week 2, and subtract the 40 units of gross requirements in Week 3. Because demand exceeds available supply resulting in a shortage of 36 units, a delivery must be planned for Week 3. The lot size is lot-for-lot (LFL), meaning that any quantity can be ordered. In addition, there is no safety stock requirement for this item, so the planned delivery in Week 3 can be established at 36 units to resolve the projected shortfall. The lead time for this item is 2 weeks, so the planned delivery of 36 units must be released to the supplier in Week 1 (planned order release) for delivery in Week 3. Each of the succeeding weeks 4 through 8 follows the same logic.

SPOKES (LEVEL 2):

The gross requirements for the spokes (dependent demand item) are calculated directly from the planned order releases of the wheel assembly (i.e., the parent item), as the spokes must be available to produce the wheel assemblies when the planned orders for them are released (see red arrows in figure 3.11). As there are 10 spokes required for every wheel assembly produced (i.e., the planning factor), the gross requirements for the spokes in Week 1 are 360 units, and in Week 4 are 400 units. There is a beginning inventory of 100 spoke units already in stock, and a scheduled receipt for 380 units confirmed for delivery in Week 1. For Week 1, start with 100 units of beginning inventory, and subtract the gross requirements in Week 1 of 360 units, and add the scheduled receipts in Week 1 of 380 units, to end the week with 120 units of projected on-hand inventory. For Week 2 and Week 3, there are no gross requirements, scheduled receipts, or planned deliveries, so the projected on-hand inventory of 120 units is carried forward. For Week 4, start with 120 units at the end of Week 3, and subtract the 400 units of gross requirements in Week 4. Because demand exceeds available supply resulting in a shortage of 280 units, a delivery must be planned for Week 4. The lot size is 380 units, and there is a safety stock requirement of 100 units for this item, so the planned celivery in Week 3 can be established at the 380 unit lot size to resolve the projected shortfall, and end the week with the 100 units of safety stock required. The lead time for this item is one week, so the planned delivery of 380 units must be released to the supplier in Week 3 (planned order release) for delivery in Week 4. Each of the succeeding weeks 5 through 8 follows the same logic.

12-INCH ALUMINUM BAR (LEVEL 3):

The MRP calculations for the 12-inch aluminum bar follows the same logic as for the spokes.

MRP Process

The MRP process can be done manually, but it is usually computer based, because it is an iterative process and can be quite extensive depending on the number of items to be planned during each cycle. Most companies have a software package that will handle this calculation, whether it is a Microsoft Excel type spreadsheet application, or an ERP system such as SAP. Companies run MRP at least once per month and most run MRP much more frequently, up to and including daily. The planning horizon also varies among companies. It can be as short as three months and as long as multiple years.

CAPACITY PLANNING..

Capacity is defined as the capability of a system to perform its expected function. Capacity planning is "the process of determining the amount of capacity required to produce in the future. This process may be performed at an aggregate or product-line level (resource requirements planning), at the master-scheduling level (rough-cut capacity planning), and at the material requirements planning level (capacity requirements planning)."[1] Organizations must balance the production plan with capacity.

Capacity planning is essential to determining optimum utilization of resource and it plays an important role in the decision-making process (e.g., decisions to extend existing operations, modification to product lines, starting new products). This directly impacts how effectively the organization deploys its resources in producing products. Effective capacity planning is dependent upon such factors as production facility layout, design and location, product line or mix, production technology, human resources, operational structure, and external supply structure.

Standard Steps in the Capacity Planning Process:

1. Estimate future capacity requirements.

2. Evaluate existing capacity and facilities and identify gaps.

3. Identify alternatives for meeting requirements.

4. Conduct financial analyses of each alternative.

5. Assess key qualitative issues for each alternative.

6. Select the alternative to pursue that will be best in the long term.

7. Implement the selected alternative.

8. Monitor results.

The following are the major capacity planning tools:

Resource Requirement Planning (RRP): "Capacity planning conducted at the business plan level. The process of establishing, measuring, and adjusting limits or levels of long-range capacity. Resource planning is normally based on the production plan but may be driven by higher level plans beyond the time horizon for the production plan (e.g., the business plan). It addresses those resources that take long periods of time to acquire. Resource planning decisions always require top management approval."[1]

Rough-Cut Capacity Planning (RCCP): "The process of converting the master production schedule into requirements for key resources, often including labor; machinery; warehouse space; suppliers' capabilities; and, in some cases, money. Comparison to available or demonstrated capacity is usually done for each key resource. This comparison assists the master scheduler in establishing a feasible master production schedule. Three approaches to performing RCCP are the bill of labor (resources, capacity) approach, the capacity planning using overall factors approach, and the resource profile approach."[1] RCCP is a gross capacity planning technique that does not consider scheduled receipts or on-hand inventory quantities when calculating capacity requirements. It is a statement of the capacity required to meet gross production requirements.

RCCP verifies that sufficient capacity is available to meet the master schedule. It is used to both balance required and available capacity and negotiate changes to the master schedule and/or available capacity. The master schedule can be adjusted by changing master schedule dates and increasing or decreasing master schedule quantities. Capacity can be adjusted by adding or removing shifts, using overtime or temporary labor, and adding or removing equipment.

CAPACITY REQUIREMENT PLANNING (CRP): "The function of establishing, measuring, and adjusting limits or levels of capacity. The term capacity requirements planning in this context refers to the process of determining in detail the amount of labor and machine resources required to accomplish the tasks of production. Open shop orders and planned orders in the MRP system are input to CRP, which through the use of parts routings and time standards translates these orders into hours of work by work center by time period. Even though rough-cut capacity planning may indicate that sufficient capacity exists to execute the MPS, CRP may show that capacity is insufficient during specific time periods."[1] There is an old adage, "the devil is in the details," and CRP is where the detailed production plan is vetted against available and planned capacity to ensure that the plan can really be executed.

CRP uses the information from the RCCP, plus MRP outputs on existing inventories and lot sizing. The result is a load report or load profile for each work center to help plan production requirements. This will indicate where capacity is inadequate or idle, allowing for imbalances to be corrected by adjustments in labor or equipment or the use of overtime or additional shifts.

DISTRIBUTION REQUIREMENTS PLANNING ....

"The function of determining the need to replenish inventory at branch warehouses. A time-phased order point approach is used where the planned orders at the branch warehouse level are 'exploded' via MRP logic to become gross requirements on the supplying source. In the case of multilevel distribution networks, this explosion process can continue down through the various levels of regional warehouses (master warehouse, factory warehouse, etc.) and become input to the master production schedule. Demand on the supplying sources is recognized as dependent, and standard MRP logic applies."[1]

Distribution requirements planning (DRP) is designed to optimize the movement of inventory in a multi-warehouse environment so that demands can be met effectively and efficiently without relying on excessive inventory. Companies that use DRP include those in wholesale or manufacturing that have regional demand supplied by one or more warehouses or manufacturing plants. DRP enables supply transfers from one warehouse to another, rather than having to issue a purchase order to an external supplier, or initiate a production order in a manufacturing plant. Suggestions are based on the closest warehouse in a chain of supplying warehouses, resulting in stock being supplied from oversupplied warehouses to undersupplied warehouses with a demand.

Key elements of DRP include:

- Forecast demands

- Current inventory levels

- Target safety stock

- Recommended replenishment quantities

- Replenishment lead times

DRP works by either a push or a pull method. The push method sends goods down through the network based on a forecast. This method generally has lower costs because shipments are planned and stored centrally; however, service levels can suffer if central planning is too far removed from the actual demand. The pull method uses the fulfillment of actual customer orders to move the inventory down through the network. This provides more availability for customers because local management controls the availability of the goods; however, managing distribution inventory can be difficult because small changes in customer demand can generate large swings in demand higher up the network, due to the bullwhip effect.

ENTERPRISE RESOURCE PLANNING SYSTEMS ....

An enterprise resource planning (ERP) system is a "framework for organizing, defining, and standardizing the business processes necessary to effectively plan and control an organization so the organization can use its internal knowledge to seek external advantage."[1]

An ERP system automates and integrates core business processes such as taking customer orders, scheduling operations, and keeping inventory records and financial data. ERP systems can drive huge improvements in the effectiveness of any organization by:

- Assisting in defining business processes and ensuring there is compliance throughout the supply chain

- Protecting critical business data through well-defined roles and security access

- Enabling a company to plan the workload based on existing orders and forecasts

- Providing the tools to give a high level of service to customers

- Translating data into decision-making information

To realize the full benefits of an ERP system it should be fully integrated into all aspects of the business from the customer facing front end, through planning and scheduling, to the production and distribution of products to the end customer.

FIGURE 3.13

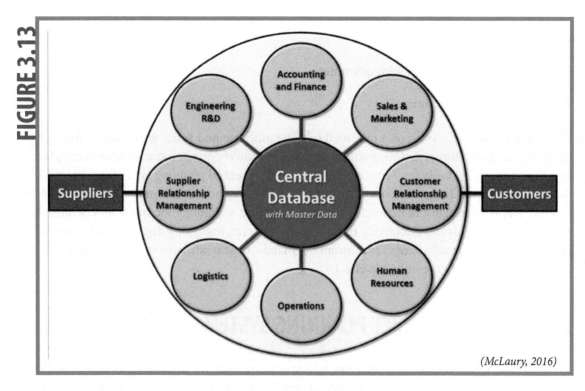

(McLaury, 2016)

The basic goal of using an enterprise resource planning system is to provide one central repository for all information that is shared by all the various supply chain functions to improve the flow of data across the organization (see figure 3.13).

ERP software typically consists of multiple enterprise software modules, which can be purchased as part of a system or individually, based on what best meets the specific needs and technical capabilities of the organization. Each ERP module is focused on one area of business process.

Major ERP applications include:

- Accounting and Finance

- Customer Relationship Management

- Human Resource Management

- Manufacturing

- Supplier Relationship Management

- Supply Chain Management

Advantages:

- The added visibility offered by the ERP system leads to more efficient and effective use of the firm's resources and reduced supply chain inventories.

- It helps to standardize manufacturing processes.

- It measures performance and communicates via a standardized method.

Disadvantages:

- It takes substantial time and capital investment to implement.

- The ERP system is complex.

- Firms tend to adapt existing processes to meet the functionality or capabilities of the ERP system, which may not be the most optimal for the firms' business.

ERP System Developers

- **LARGE ENTERPRISE ERP:** SAP, Oracle, Microsoft

- **MID-MARKET ERP:** Infor, QAD, Lawson, Epicor, Sage, IFS

- **SMALL BUSINESS ERP:** Exact Globe, Syspro, NetSuite, Visibility, Consona, CDC Software, Activant Solutions

ERP Implementation

There are two basic types of ERP implementation:

1. **BEST-OF-BREED:** Companies pick the best application for each individual function for their particular business needs regardless of the supplier/software developer, and then integrate the various systems together.

- **Advantage:** Companies can obtain the best system for each function to meet the specific needs of the company.

- **Disadvantages:** Software may not integrate well; may not be able to take advantage of upgrades and enhancements as each will require a reintegration.

2. SINGLE INTEGRATOR SOLUTION: Companies evaluate and pick a single vendor for all the desired applications.

   - **Advantages:** Functions are already integrated, tested, and debugged. No compatibility issues or data translation issues. Can take advantage of system upgrades and enhancements more easily than the best-of-breed solution.

   - **Disadvantages:** Single integrator software solutions are generally costly, and require a significant number of resources, people, and time to implement. Companies may be paying for functionality that they do not need. It may not be the best solution for individual functions.

Major causes of ERP implementation problems include:

- Lack of top management commitment

- Lack of adequate resources

- Lack of proper training (both initial and ongoing)

- Lack of communication

- Incompatible system environment

REFERENCES

[1] *APICS Dictionary* (14th ed.). (2013). Chicago, IL: APICS. www.apics.org

[2] Sanders, N. (2013, December). *The definitive guide to manufacturing and service operations.* Upper Saddle River, NJ: Council of Supply Chain Management Professionals, Pearson Education, Inc.

[3] Investopedia.com. (2016). Retrieved from http://www.investopedia.com/

[4] Master production scheduling. (2016). Supplychain-mechanic.com. Retrieved from http://supply-chain-mechanic.com/?p=69

Chapter 4

Inventory Management

CHAPTER OUTLINE

Introduction

Inventory

Categories of Inventory

Inventory in the Service Industry

Functions of Inventory

Inventory Management

Inventory Stocking Levels

Inventory Costs

Inventory Investment

Independent and Dependent Demand

Inventory Policy

Economic Order Quantity Model

Other Types of Inventory Systems

Stock Levels and Replenishment

Inventory Optimization

Inventory Control Tools

Measuring Inventory Performance

Summary

INTRODUCTION

A key decision in any product-based supply chain is how much inventory to keep on hand. Maintaining adequate finished product inventory allows a company to fill customer orders immediately, and maintaining adequate materials inventory allows a company to support manufacturing operations and the production plan while avoiding delays. Failing to manage inventory adequately can lead to significant issues and inefficiencies throughout the supply chain, including dissatisfied customers, lost sales and revenue, and higher costs, just to name a few. Inventory is usually one of the company's largest assets, so careful management of that asset is an essential business requirement.

INVENTORY

Inventory represents the quantities of goods and materials that are held in stock. APICS defines inventory as "those stocks or items used to support production (raw materials and work-in-process items), supporting activities (maintenance, repair, and operating supplies), and customer service (finished goods and spare parts)."[1]

© iQoncept/Shutterstock.com

Inventory includes finished product(s), all the materials used for production, and all of the other materials and supplies needed to run a business (office and break room supplies, spare parts for equipment, cleaning and maintenance supplies, etc.). Most companies segregate their production inventory from their nonproduction inventory. They may even have separate procurement groups that individually handle the buying activities for production versus nonproduction items.

Inventory Is an Asset and Potentially a Liability

While inventory can be one of a company's largest assets, it can also be a significant liability if it is not managed well. Some inventory may be necessary to maintain operations and ensure that products are available when customers demand them, but too much inventory ties up capital that could otherwise be used for purposes such as research and development, marketing and sales, stockholder dividends, salary increases, and so forth. Too much inventory can be a liability if it becomes unusable due to expiration, obsolescence, damage, or spoilage. In addition, the more inventory a company holds, the more space that must be used, and space costs money whether a company owns and maintains its own warehouse or rents space from an outside public or contract warehouse. In addition to storage costs, a company may also have to pay for utilities, security, insurance, taxes, and the like, to hold inventory. Simply put, the more inventory a company holds, the more costs are generated.

CATEGORIES OF INVENTORY

There are four main categories of inventory:

- Raw Materials

- Work in Process (WIP)

- Finished Goods

- Maintenance, Repair, and Operating (MRO) supplies

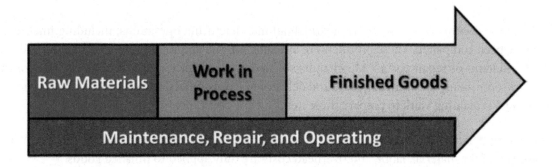

RAW MATERIALS are "purchased items or extracted materials that are converted via the manufacturing process into components and products."[1]

Any company that produces a product generally starts with some type of raw material, component part, or starting material. There are entire strategies around the question of how much raw material a company should hold in inventory. Do they want to buy it from their supplier and have it delivered to their operation just in time for when it is needed? Or do they want to buy and hold a larger quantity for strategic reasons? Companies might be willing to increase costs by storing excess inventory if they fear there may be a potential shortage of the material or suspect that there is an upcoming price increase and want to buy at the current lower price. The ultimate decision for how much raw material to buy and when could lie at either end of the spectrum or anywhere in between.

WORK IN PROCESS (WIP) is "a good or goods in various stages of completion throughout the plant, including all materials from raw material that has been released for initial processing up to completely processed material awaiting final inspection and acceptance as finished goods."[1] Work-in-process inventory is sometimes also referred to as "work-in-progress" inventory.

Due to the range of potential stages of completion that WIP encompasses, and the fact that materials in WIP may be in a state of continuous transformation, many companies view WIP as the "black hole" of inventory as they may not have very good or very timely visibility into this part of their inventory.

Best practice generally suggests minimizing the amount of work-in-process inventory in the manufacturing area, because too much WIP may clutter up the physical space and impede the process flow. In a LEAN manufacturing environment, which will be discussed in Chapter 8, the WIP inventory should be so minimal that it is almost immaterial.

Because it can be time consuming to calculate the amount of WIP inventory, determine the percentage of completion, and assign a cost to WIP, it is also a standard practice in many companies to minimize the amount of WIP inventory on hand just prior to the end of a reporting period.

FINISHED GOODS are "those items on which all manufacturing operations, including final testing, have been completed. These products are available for sale and/or shipment to the customer as either end items or repair parts."[1] Merchandise owned by a retailer that is sitting on the shelf or in the stockroom, ready for immediate sale and delivery to its customers, is considered finished goods. There is no remaining work to prepare these items for the consumer.

From a cost perspective, finished goods are usually worth much more than raw materials or WIP, because all of the material, labor, and overhead costs are fully applied to finished goods.

The amount of finished goods inventory that a company decides to maintain is a strategic decision:

- Companies can decide to operate a **make-to-order** supply chain where the finished goods are not produced until a customer order is received, and the raw materials may not even be ordered from the supplier(s) in advance. Once the customer order is received, the materials are ordered/delivered, the finished goods are produced, and the product shipped to the customer immediately upon production. Little to no finished goods inventory is maintained by the manufacturer in a make-to-order supply chain strategy.

- Companies can alternatively decide to operate a **make-to-stock** supply chain where product is produced prior to receipt of a customer order. A forecast and demand plan are created for the finished goods based on anticipated demand. The raw materials are ordered in advance and the finished goods are produced against the production plan, which is based on the anticipated demand, and then held in inventory until a customer order is received. Significant amounts of finished goods inventory can sometimes be maintained by the manufacturer in a make-to-stock supply chain strategy when large demand is forecast.

Each of these strategies, and variations of these strategies, involves making trade-offs among inventory investment, operating costs, and customer service.

MAINTENANCE, REPAIR AND OPERATING (MRO) SUPPLIES are "items used in support of general operations and maintenance such as maintenance supplies, spare parts, and consumables used in the manufacturing process and supporting operations."[1] These are materials that you need to run the manufacturing operation and the business but do not end up as part of the finished product. Some MRO items are consumed during the process of converting raw materials into finished goods (e.g., oil for the manufacturing equipment). Other MRO items are used to facilitate the manufacturing operation (cleaning supplies, spare parts, etc.), and still other MRO items may be used to facilitate the company's administrative activities (office supplies, coffee for the break room, etc.).

MRO inventory is separate from production inventory, but it is just as important. It needs to be stored and accounted for similarly to production items. As companies need MRO items to run their operations, a shortage of one or more of these items may cause a supply disruption. Frequently these items are expensed at the time they are purchased, and there may be a separate function, group, or individual who plans and orders these MRO items from those who plan and order production items.

INVENTORY IN THE SERVICE INDUSTRY ....

Companies in the service industry do not maintain inventory of services, because services are basically produced and consumed immediately upon demand. Companies in the service industry can, however, maintain inventory of "facilitating products," which are those items that are used to help facilitate the service being provided. For example, a car rental service provides the vehicles necessary to offer the rental service. The rental vehicles are facilitating products that can be inventoried in advance of providing the rental service. Restaurants offer dining services that involve preparing and serving the food, providing the seating area, ambiance, cleanup, parking and valet, among other amenities. Restaurants cannot inventory the actual dining service; they can only begin the service when the customers arrive. Restaurants can, however, inventory the food, tableware, and other elements of the dining operation as these are facilitating products necessary to provide the dining service. Restaurants can even prepare some of their meal options in advance such as salads or deserts (i.e., inventory these facilitating products so they are ready to go when the customers arrive for the dining service). Supply chains in the service industry will be covered in more detail in Chapter 12.

FUNCTIONS OF INVENTORY

There are four basic function of inventory, or reasons why companies hold inventory:

1. To meet customer demand (cycle stock)

2. To buffer against uncertainty in demand and/or supply (safety stock)

3. To decouple supply from demand (strategic stock)

4. To decouple dependencies in the supply chain

© Mr. High Sky/Shutterstock.com

1. To Meet Customer Demand:

- Meeting customer demand is the purpose of "cycle stock."

- Maintaining finished goods inventory allows a company to immediately fill customer orders. A customer places an order which can then be shipped/delivered to him or her from the available inventory.

- Maintaining raw materials inventory helps a company ensure that the necessary materials will be available to begin or continue the production plan/schedule uninterrupted.

- To facilitate meeting customer demand, companies may develop inventory deployment strategies to ensure that the product is available when and where the customers want it. Inventory deployment strategies range from having all of the available inventory centrally located to having the inventory geographically dispersed to multiple locations (e.g., distribution centers or retail outlets). The more dispersed the inventory is, the more likely it will be that a higher level of inventory will be needed to ensure adequate availability at all locations for all customer demand.

2. To Buffer against Uncertainty in Demand and/or Supply:

- A company may decide to maintain some inventory of finished goods and/or raw materials due to uncertainty in demand. In the absence of actual customer orders, the company may create a sales forecast (i.e., estimate demand based on the information that it has about what customers may want). The demand plan is not likely to be 100% accurate. If the estimates are on the low side (i.e., under-forecasted for any reason), and there is more demand than expected, the company will not be able to satisfy all of the demand unless it has proactively created a buffer or "safety stock" of finished goods inventory from which to satisfy this unanticipated demand. Similarly, the company may decide to create a safety stock of raw materials in addition to, or in place of, finished goods safety stock to buffer for any unanticipated demand.

- A company may also decide to maintain some inventory of finished goods and/or raw materials due to uncertainty in supply. Unexpected disruptions in supply can create a shortage, which leads to unfulfilled demand and/or interrupted production plans and schedules. Suppliers, whether internal or external, may be late with delivery for any number of reasons or deliver a quantity less than what was ordered, leading to a shortage. Even raw materials or finished goods delivered on time and in full may be effected by quality problems and be unusable or unsalable. Because of the uncertainty of supply, some companies may proactively decide to create a buffer or safety stock of raw materials and/or finished goods inventory from which to satisfy demand in the event of a disruption and shortage.

- This is the purpose of "safety stock": an incremental quantity of stock kept in inventory to protect against fluctuations in either demand or supply or a combination of both. Safety stock will be detailed later in this chapter.

3. **To Decouple Supply from Demand:**

- There are a number of reasons why a company may want to buy an amount of raw materials or produce an amount of finished goods that differs from what is specifically required by the demand plan. This can result in inventory being held.

- One reason to hold inventory may be to achieve economies of scale in purchasing, manufacturing, and/or transportation. A company may receive a price break or discount from a supplier for buying a larger quantity than is specifically required, or receive a lower per unit transportation cost for transporting a larger quantity in a truckload volume than in a less-than-truckload volume. If the price break, discount, or lower per unit transportation cost is sufficient to offset the extra holding cost incurred as a result of the additional inventory, then the decision to buy the larger quantity is justified. Inventory can also be used as a hedge against price increases.

- Another reason to hold inventory may be the decision to manufacture a finished product in full production lots rather than smaller quantities, because it may be more economical, more efficient, offer more consistent and better quality control, or be more appropriate for equipment operating requirements.

- In each of these examples the additional quantity purchased or manufactured results in inventory that may be held for some period of time before it is used or sold.

4. TO DECOUPLE DEPENDENCIES IN THE SUPPLY CHAIN:

- Inventory can be held between dependent operations in manufacturing to decouple the dependency of the operations. Sequential operations in manufacturing are dependent upon previous operations (i.e., production steps), to continue the manufacturing process. If there is a disruption of an upstream (previous) operation due to a material shortage, labor issue, equipment problem, etc., then all downstream (subsequent) operations will also be disrupted. If some inventory of materials or work in process is maintained between operations, then operations downstream from the disruption may be able to continue the manufacturing process for some period of time, perhaps even until the disruption is resolved. This inventory helps to decouple some of the dependencies in the supply chain.

- Inventory can also be used to smooth or level demand requirements when demand is irregular, seasonal, and so forth. For example, if a company manufactures and sells seasonal products such as snow blowers or lawn mowers, the demand for those products is likely to peak during the season and fall off significantly in the off-season. It may be very inefficient for the company to adjust manufacturing capacity to match the demand in each season. The company may decide to adopt a level production strategy where they establish a steady manufacturing output rate based on the anticipated annual volume. The company can build up inventory when demand is low, keeping workers busy during slack times, so that when demand picks up, the increased inventory can be slowly depleted through normal in-season sales and the company does not have to react by increasing production. The company can avoid excessive overtime and the hiring, training, and other associated labor costs associated with hiring more workers to meet the increased demand. It can also avoid layoff costs and the potential loss of skilled workers in the off-season associated with production cutbacks. This strategy might even prevent the idling or shutting down of facilities.

This type of level production strategy is designed to smooth the peaks and valleys in demand, allowing the company to maintain a constant level of output and a stable workforce.

The steady manufacturing output rate means that the company will overproduce against demand in the off-season in order to create inventory to meet the higher demand in-season when it will be underproducing against demand. By shifting demand requirements to earlier time periods and leveling the demand, inventory levels throughout the year vary significantly. If inventory levels could not fluctuate in this way, the manufacturing output—and associated labor, materials, and costs—would need to fluctuate.

This tactic is commonly used by retailers who routinely build up inventory months before the demand for their product peaks (e.g., at Halloween, at Christmas, the back-to-school season).

INVENTORY MANAGEMENT

INVENTORY MANAGEMENT is defined as "the branch of business management concerned with planning and controlling inventories."[1] Inventory management can help a company be more profitable by lowering the cost of goods sold and/or by increasing sales.

Small cost reductions from the application of sound inventory management principles can result in a significant increase in net income. Efficient inventory processes during the production phase of a product's life simultaneously reduce costly work stoppages and inventory storage costs. Reducing the amount of finished inventory that is held in stock reduces storage costs for the item. So long as the production and distribution channels for a given product are efficient, these inventory savings translate into more profit while selling the product for the same price. The stated advantages of maintaining smaller inventories are predicated on the notion of having sufficient supply as inventory management must balance two competing considerations: (1) reduce the amount of inventory held in stock, and (2) ensure there is enough inventory to satisfy customer demand.

Effective inventory management balances these two considerations to achieve the stated goals of lowering costs and increasing sales. Although sales are still tied to demand, customers cannot satisfy their demand if an item is out of stock. Not having product available for customers when they place orders is one of the self-defeating mistakes a company can make. There are some products customers do not expect to receive immediately, but any stockout adds delays in delivering a finished product to the customer or adds cost to the manufacturer. If manufacturing supplies are out of stock, the company may have to expedite delivery of materials, expedite new production, spend extra money working overtime, and use premium modes of transportation, to satisfy the customer demand. Any of these remedies effectively negate any cost savings generated from maintaining lower inventory levels, and not investing in one of these costly solutions will likely lead to upset customers, effectively decreasing future sales.

Balance in inventory management is crucial. Effective inventory management can yield decreased costs and/or increased sales, but sometimes companies may opt to concentrate on one end or the other and accept the potential trade-offs of their inventory decision:

- If a company's supply chain strategy is to operate an **efficient capabilities model**, the company can choose to maintain a somewhat more reduced level of inventory held at a centralized location, which may potentially be more remote from the customer(s). This strategy decreases the overall inventory costs, but increases the risk of a customer service issue.

- If a company's supply chain strategy is to operate a **responsive capabilities model**, the company can choose to maintain a somewhat higher level of inventory held at multiple decentralized locations which may potentially be closer to the customer(s). This strategy increases the overall inventory costs, but reduces the risk of a customer service issue occurring.

So, what is the right amount of inventory? The answer to that question is, "It depends." There are many factors that go into determining the right amount of inventory for a particular company/product. It depends on the supply chain strategy and setup, the type of product(s), customers' expectations, customer service objectives, product shelf life, among other factors.

INVENTORY STOCKING LEVELS

As introduced earlier in this chapter, there are various levels of stock held by companies to meet customer demand, to buffer against uncertainty in demand and/or supply, to decouple supply from demand, and to decouple dependencies in the supply chain (see figure 4.1).

The three main inventory stocking levels are:

- Cycle stock

- Safety stock

- Strategic stock

In addition, pipeline inventory, which is external to the company, may have an impact on decisions that companies make about how to manage and control their inventory resources.

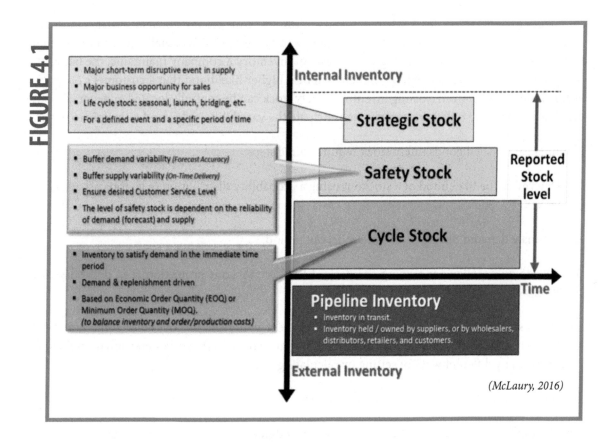

FIGURE 4.1

- Major short-term disruptive event in supply
- Major business opportunity for sales
- Life cycle stock: seasonal, launch, bridging, etc.
- For a defined event and a specific period of time

- Buffer demand variability *(Forecast Accuracy)*
- Buffer supply variability *(On-Time Delivery)*
- Ensure desired Customer Service Level
- The level of safety stock is dependent on the reliability of demand (forecast) and supply

- Inventory to satisfy demand in the immediate time period
- Demand & replenishment driven
- Based on Economic Order Quantity (EOQ) or Minimum Order Quantity (MOQ).
  (to balance inventory and order/production costs)

Internal Inventory

Strategic Stock

Safety Stock

Cycle Stock

Reported Stock level

Time

Pipeline Inventory
- Inventory in transit.
- Inventory held / owned by suppliers, or by wholesalers, distributors, retailers, and customers.

External Inventory

(McLaury, 2016)

Cycle Stock

Cycle stock is the most active component of inventory. It is the inventory that a company builds to satisfy its immediate demand. Cycle stock "depletes gradually as customer orders are received and is replenished cyclically when supply orders are received."[1] The amount of cycle stock that a company holds is dependent on various factors, including anticipated and actual demand in the immediate time period, supply replenishment lead time, and supply replenishment order quantities. Unless a company is operating in a pure make-to-order type environment, companies carry some amount of cycle stock.

Safety Stock

Safety stock is "a quantity of stock planned to be in inventory to protect against fluctuations in demand or supply. Over planning supply versus demand can be used to create safety stock."[1]

Among the functions of inventory are protection against higher than anticipated demand, late delivery of replenishment supplies, and poor quality of a supplier's products. It is very common for companies to carry safety stock when demand and/or lead time are not constant. Safety stock, also known as "buffer stock," is inventory that is above and beyond what is actually needed to meet anticipated demand. Generally, the higher the level of inventory a company maintains, the better the company's customer service will be as there will be a higher likelihood that a customer's order can be filled immediately from existing inventory. Safety stock can be centrally located or geographically dispersed depending on where companies anticipate the variability in demand or supply to occur.

Planning for finished goods safety stock requires three steps:

1. Determine the likelihood of a stockout using a probability distribution (e.g., forecast accuracy/error).

2. Estimate demand during a potential stockout period.

3. Decide on a policy concerning the desired level of stockout protection (i.e., desired service level).

Companies operating in a make-to-stock environment will generally maintain some amount of safety stock whether based on a management decision or on a safety stock determination formula. There are many different ways of setting or calculating safety stock.

SETTING SAFETY STOCK LEVELS BY MANAGEMENT DECISION/POLICY

Each of the following may be based on experience, judgment, intuition, or historical data:

1. Specifying some dynamic forward demand coverage (2 weeks, 4 weeks, etc.)

2. Establishing and maintaining a fixed quantity of safety stock inventory

3. Setting safety stock based on an ABC analysis of products in the company's portfolio (explained later in the chapter in "Other Types of Inventory Systems")

CALCULATING SAFETY STOCK VIA FORMULA

1. (Maximum daily usage − Average daily usage) × Total replenishment lead time

2. $k \times \sqrt{LT} \times (1.25 \times MAD)$

   Where:

k	Desired customer service level (safety factor). Derived from a normal distribution curve. Sample values for k are 2.33 for 99%, 2.03 for 98%, 1.64 for 95%, etc.
$\sqrt{LT}$	The square root of the lead time necessary to fully replenish inventory.
1.25 x MAD	MAD = mean absolute deviation of the difference between the actual demand and the forecast demand. The absolute forecast error expressed as a unit quantity.
	The value *1.25 x MAD* represents an adjusted increase in the MAD by 25%. The increase helps to define the safety stock that is needed in case of unexpected demand. Any demand increase above 25% would not be covered. The value of the constant can vary from company to company and even item to item.

Strategic Stock

Strategic stock, also known as "anticipation stock," is additional inventory above and beyond cycle stock and safety stock. Cycle stock and safety stock are both maintained continuously to support demand and the ongoing uncertainty in both demand and supply. Strategic stock is generally used for a very specific purpose or future event and for a defined period of time (i.e., neither continuous nor ongoing).

There are many potential reasons that a company may decide to carry some strategic stock: hedging a currency exchange, taking advantage of a price discount, protecting against a major short-term disruptive event in supply, taking advantage of a major business opportunity, and/or providing for lifecycle changes (seasonal demand, new product launch, transition protection or bridging, etc.). Companies do not routinely carry strategic stock, and many companies never carry strategic stock, which is why it is depicted as a smaller box in figure 4.1.

Strategic stock can also be the result of smoothing or leveling the demand requirements when demand is irregular, seasonal, and the like. Shifting supply plans forward from peak demand periods to off-peak demand periods to maintain a level production strategy produces a strategic stock (i.e., a temporary increase in inventory levels). This is also sometimes called "build stock," "seasonal inventory," or "seasonal stock."

Pipeline Inventory

The first three types of stock in the upper half of figure 4.1 (cycle stock, safety stock, and strategic stock) are inventory, which is internal to the company. In the lower half of figure 4.1 you will see pipeline inventory, which is external to the company.

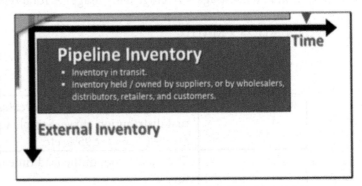

Pipeline inventory is "inventory in the transportation network and the distribution system, including the flow through intermediate stocking points."[1] Pipeline inventory is in-transit, either out to the distribution channels or already out in the market being held by wholesalers, distributors, retailers, and even consumers. The ownership of this inventory has been transferred to the company's downstream trading partners/customers, but pipeline inventory may still influence decisions the company makes regarding how it manages and controls its internal inventory.

Companies make inventory decisions regularly to remain competitive and to maintain their inventory strategy. In addition to factors such as the type of distribution network and the type and nature of the finished products in the supply chain, a company should consider all of the inventory in the supply chain holistically (i.e., internally and externally) when determining how much safety stock and/or strategic stock to hold.

- If pipeline inventory is high, it might be less critical for the company to maintain higher levels of safety and strategic stocks. A short-term supply disruption causing a temporary backorder (i.e., an unfilled customer order or commitment) to intermediary customers such as wholesalers and distributors might not necessarily turn into a major market stockout, because there is a lot of inventory moving downstream.

- Conversely, if pipeline inventory is low, any issue that happens in the marketplace will likely have a larger and more immediate impact on the overall supply situation and, therefore, more safety and/or strategic stock may be warranted.

Obsolete Inventory

A company may also experience some level of obsolete inventory. These are "inventory items that have met the obsolescence criteria established by the organization. For example, inventory that has been superseded by a new model or otherwise made obsolescent. Obsolete inventory will never be used or sold at full value. Disposing of the obsolete inventory may reduce a company's profit."[1] Simply put, obsolete inventory is stock that is expired, damaged, or no longer needed. Writing this obsolete inventory off of the books and disposing of it may be a difficult decision to make as all or part of the obsolete product's value may be lost. Unusable inventory does, however, take up space and cost money to maintain, so it may be better to absorb the loss as soon as an item has met the obsolescence criteria than delay and continue to lose money on storage and related fees. However, there may be a cost associated with the actual disposal of the obsolete inventory, depending on the type and method of disposal. Some companies may find ways to donate this inventory to a nonprofit organization if it has any remaining value, which not only helps the nonprofit but also avoids disposal costs and may result in a tax benefit for the company.

INVENTORY COSTS

The categories of costs associated with inventory are described as follows:

DIRECT COSTS are expenditures that are directly traceable to the volume of units produced. Examples are labor, materials, and expenses specifically related to the production of a product.

INDIRECT COSTS are expenditures that cannot be traced directly to the volume of units produced. Examples are depreciation, administrative expenses, overhead, MRO items, buildings, equipment, and utilities. Indirect costs may be either fixed or variable and are typically allocated to a cost object as defined by individual company policy.

FIXED COSTS are expenditures that do not vary with the volume of units produced. Examples are rent, property tax, and salaries of certain personnel, all of which are independent from the output. Fixed costs are frequently time related (i.e., paid on a weekly, monthly, or annual basis). They are generally referred to as overhead costs. Fixed costs are, however, not permanently fixed; they are fixed only for the relevant period of time.

Whether a company manufactures 1 unit, 100 units, or 1,000 units, a manufacturing facility is needed. The cost is fixed in the immediate time period regardless of how many units are produced. Even if no units are produced, there is still a cost for the building, depreciation, insurance, security, maintenance, and so forth. The building represents a fixed cost no matter whether the building is owned or leased by the company. However, in the long run, the fixed cost may change as the building depreciates, the lease expires and is renewed, etc. At that point it will become a new or revised fixed cost.

VARIABLE COSTS are expenditures that vary directly with a change of even one unit in the volume produced. Examples are direct labor and materials consumed, sales commissions, and allocated overhead. Variable costs rise as production increases and fall as production decreases. Generally, the cost of goods sold (COGS) are variable costs.

ORDER COSTS are the direct labor cost incurred when a purchaser places an order. Order costs are "used in calculating order quantities, [they are] the costs that increase as the number of orders placed increases. It includes costs related to the clerical work of preparing, releasing, monitoring, and receiving orders, the physical handling of goods, inspections, and setup costs, as applicable."[1] Every time an order is placed, regardless of the quantity of the order, there is a cost associated with processing the order.

CARRYING COSTS are "the cost of holding inventory, usually defined as a percentage of the dollar value of inventory per unit of time (generally one year). Carrying cost depends mainly on the cost of capital invested as well as the costs of maintaining the inventory, taxes and insurance, obsolescence, spoilage, and space occupied. Such costs vary from 10 percent to 35 percent annually, depending on type of industry. Carrying cost is ultimately a policy variable reflecting the opportunity cost of alternative uses for the funds that have been invested in inventory."[1] Carrying costs are also called "holding costs."

Hidden Costs of Inventory

Having too much or too little inventory on hand can create hidden costs that will negatively impact a company. Companies need to be aware of these hidden costs.

Financial resources tied up in too much inventory are not available for other purposes (e.g., research and development, marketing and sales, shareholder dividends and salary increases). Excess inventory makes meeting customer demand easier, but it might also be masking underlying problems with the supply chain. Moreover, excess inventory sitting on shelves means quality control issues may take longer to uncover, eventually leading to future inventory and manufacturing costs.

Too little inventory, on the contrary, leads to production disruptions due to unavailability of materials, which can cause loss of sales and revenue from dissatisfied customers, cancelation of orders, idle workers and equipment, extra machinery setups, loss of quantity discounts on purchases, and more. Longer replenishment lead times and reduced responsiveness to customers ultimately yield lower sales.

INVENTORY INVESTMENT ....

As discussed earlier in this chapter, inventory is typically a significant asset for a company, but it can be a liability as well. Companies should measure inventory investment routinely to ensure that their inventory practices do not adversely affect their competitiveness. Two common measures companies use are **absolute inventory value** and **inventory turnover**.

ABSOLUTE INVENTORY VALUE is defined as "the value of the inventory at either its cost or its market value. Because inventory value can change with time, some recognition is taken of the age distribution of inventory. Therefore, the cost value of inventory is usually computed on (1) a FIFO, i.e., first in first out basis, meaning that the oldest inventory is used/sold first, (2) a LIFO, i.e., last in first out basis, meaning the newest inventory is used/sold first, or (3) a standard cost basis, to establish the cost of goods sold."[1] Absolute inventory value is the cost of all finished goods and materials a company has on hand. This value may be required for reporting on financial statements such as a company's balance sheet.

© Iconi Bestiary/Shutterstock.com

INVENTORY TURNOVER is "the number of times that an inventory cycles, or 'turns over,' during the year. A frequently used method to compute inventory turnover is to divide the average inventory level into the annual cost of sales. For example, an average inventory of $3 million divided into an annual cost of sales of $21 million means that inventory turned over seven times."[1] (See figure 4.2.) Generally, the more turns, the better. The more times inventory is replenished, the less opportunity there is for it to expire, become obsolete, spoil, or become damaged. Inventory turnover measures the speed with which inventory passes through an organization or supply chain. It is a measure of managerial prowess. If a company can turn inventory over very quickly, it likely means that it is converting raw material expenditures into sales revenue very quickly, utilizing the inventory asset to generate income very efficiently.

FIGURE 4.2

$$\text{Inventory Turnover Ratio} = \frac{\text{Cost of Goods Sold (COGS)}}{\text{Average Inventory @ Cost}}$$

aka, Cost of Sales or Cost of Revenue

(McLaury, 2016)

INDEPENDENT AND DEPENDENT DEMAND

INDEPENDENT DEMAND is "the demand for an item that is unrelated to the demand for other items. Demand for finished goods, parts required for destructive testing, and service parts requirements are examples of independent demand."[1] Independent demand is usually based on actual customer orders or some type of forecast, which by its nature creates some uncertainty and variability. The potential for variability is even greater when there is a lack of collaboration with customers. The uncertainty is a key driver in determining what inventory management model to use. Independent demand items are typically managed using a "replenishment philosophy" (i.e., reordered when the currently inventory diminishes to a predefined level). These inventory ordering models are stochastic or deterministic and include fixed-order quantity and fixed-time period order quantity, which are discussed later in this chapter.

DEPENDENT DEMAND is "demand that is directly related to or derived from the bill of material structure for other items or end products. Such demands are therefore calculated and need not and should not be forecast. A given inventory item may have both dependent and independent demand at any given time. For example, a part may simultaneously be the component of an assembly and sold as a service part."[1] Inventory management and determination for dependent demand items is considerably different from independent demand items, because there is significantly less uncertainty and variability. The variability for a dependent demand item is directly related to how much variability there is for the end item, from which its demand is derived. Dependent demand items are typically managed using a "requirements philosophy" (i.e., only ordered as needed based on higher level components or products). These inventory ordering models include material requirements planning, kanban, and drum-buffer-rope.

INVENTORY POLICY

An inventory policy is "a statement of a company's goals and approach to the management of inventories."[1] Inventory policies establish target inventory levels for all products and materials and the methods and systems used to achieve and maintain target goals.

Inventory policies address the fundamental inventory concerns:

1. When to review inventory?

2. When to order replenishment inventory?

3. How much inventory to order?

WHEN TO REVIEW INVENTORY

There are two basic approaches of inventory reviews that determine when replenishment orders must be placed, and each involves some trade-offs:

- **CONTINUOUS REVIEW:** In this method, inventory levels are continuously reviewed. As soon as the inventory/stock falls below a predetermined level (i.e., reorder point), a replenishment order is triggered. A continuous review system is more costly to conduct than a periodic review system, but it potentially requires less safety stock because inventory is constantly monitored and replenishment actions are taken more quickly.

  Advantages: Continuous inventory review systems allow for real-time updates of inventory, which can make it easier to know when to replenish. This method also facilitates accurate accounting, because the inventory system can generate real-time costs of goods sold.

  Disadvantages: The continuous inventory review system is costly to implement. The hardware and software necessary to run the system can be expensive to purchase, install, and maintain.

- **PERIODIC REVIEW:** In this method, inventory levels are reviewed at a set frequency (weekly, monthly, etc.). At the time of review, if the stock levels are below the predetermined level (i.e., reorder point), then an order for replenishment is placed, otherwise no action is taken until the next cycle. This method segments the inventory items into review "buckets" (i.e., time periods), making it easier to manage when using a manual process, when the number of items involved is extremely large, or when constraints exist. A periodic review system is less expensive to implement and operate than a continuous review system. However, since inventory items are only reviewed periodically, there is a greater risk of inventory dropping well below the reorder point trigger between review points and there is a corresponding greater potential need for safety stock.

  Advantages: Periodic inventory review systems reduce the time spent analyzing inventory, which allows more time for other aspects of running the business. These systems are less expensive than continuous counterparts.

Disadvantages: It may not provide accurate inventory counts for businesses with high sales volume. You must make assumptions between inventory review periods regarding inventory counts, which can make it difficult to determine when reordering items is necessary. It also can make inventory accounting less accurate.

WHEN TO ORDER REPLENISHMENT INVENTORY

Most, if not all, inventory replenishment systems use some type of predetermined reorder point to trigger a replenish order. A reorder point is "a set inventory level where, if the total stock on hand plus [the stock] on order falls to or below that point, action is taken to replenish the stock. The order point is normally calculated as forecasted usage during the replenishment lead time plus safety stock."[1] The reorder point is the lowest inventory level at which a new order must be placed to avoid a stockout. This means that the reorder point is set at the level of remaining inventory that is sufficient to cover all of the demand that is projected to occur during the lead time necessary to receive the replenishment supply.

REORDER POINT WITHOUT SAFETY STOCK: If the replenishment lead time is 10 days, and the projected demand is 5 units per day, the reorder point should be set at 50 units of remaining inventory. When inventory drops down to 50 units, a replenishment order is triggered for delivery in 10 days: 5 units of demand per day x 10 days of lead time needed for replenishment = reorder point of

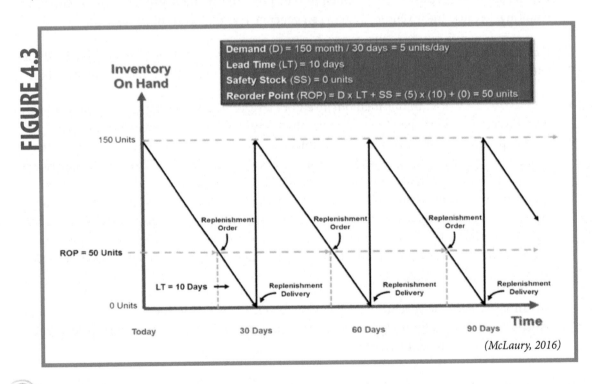

(McLaury, 2016)

50 units of remaining inventory. (See figure 4.3.) In this example the replenishment order will be delivered to the company just as the inventory drops to zero but not after, avoiding a stockout. If the replenishment order is placed <u>after</u> the remaining inventory drops below 50 units, then the company will likely run out of stock before the replenishment order is received 10 days later.

Reorder Point with Safety Stock: If the replenishment lead time is 10 days, and the projected demand is 5 units per day, **and the company has a desired safety stock of 25 units**, the reorder point should be set at 75 units of remaining inventory. When inventory drops down to 75 units, a replenishment order is triggered for delivery in 10 days: 5 units of demand per day x 10 days of lead time needed for replenishment + safety stock of 25 units = reorder point of 75 units of remaining inventory. (See figure 4.4.) In this example the replenishment order will be delivered to the company 10 days after the order is placed when there are still 25 units remaining in inventory. This safety stock of 25 units will help to ensure that a stockout is avoided by protecting for an upside in demand (i.e., > 5 units/day) during the time it takes to replenish the inventory, a late delivery of the replenishment order from the supplier (i.e., > 10 days to deliver), or potentially both. If the replenishment order is placed <u>after</u> the remaining inventory drops below 75 units but <u>before</u> inventory drops below 50 units, the safety stock will help to mitigate the risk of a stockout before the replenishment order is received 10 days later. If the inventory drops below 50 units before the replenishment order is placed, the safety stock will have been consumed and the company will likely run out of stock before the replenishment order is received 10 days later.

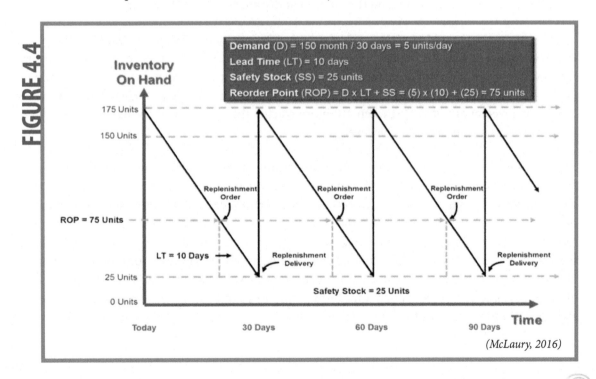

FIGURE 4.4

Inventory On Hand

Demand (D) = 150 month / 30 days = 5 units/day
Lead Time (LT) = 10 days
Safety Stock (SS) = 25 units
Reorder Point (ROP) = D x LT + SS = (5) x (10) + (25) = 75 units

175 Units
150 Units
ROP = 75 Units
LT = 10 Days
25 Units
0 Units

Replenishment Order
Replenishment Delivery
Safety Stock = 25 Units

Today   30 Days   60 Days   90 Days   Time

(McLaury, 2016)

How much inventory to order

The two most common inventory ordering system categories are:

- Fixed-Order Quantity

- Fixed-Time Period

FIXED-ORDER QUANTITY is "an inventory system, such as Economic Order Quantity, in which the same order quantity is used from order to order. The time between orders (i.e., order period) then varies from order to order."[1] In this fixed-order quantity model, inventory is monitored on a continuous basis. When the inventory position drops to a predetermined reorder point, the same predetermined fixed-order quantity is placed.

This approach would be similar to an individual driving a car and paying attention to the fuel gauge. When the fuel gauge shows that fuel is depleted down to a predetermined level (e.g., ¼ of a tank remaining), the person pulls into the nearest fuel station to refill the tank (i.e., replenish the fuel inventory) back to the full level again. The reorder point for fuel is ¼ of a tank and the fixed-order quantity is ¾ of a tank, the amount needed to restore the fuel inventory to the full level. The time interval between refills may vary depending on how much driving is done and, therefore, how much fuel is burned. The reorder point and the order quantity are both fixed, however.

FIXED-TIME PERIOD QUANTITY is "a method of inventory planning that measures actual inventory levels at regular intervals of time; either an order is placed every time, or a check of inventory levels is made and an order placed if needed. Often the quantity ordered varies from period to period as inventory is restored to a predetermined level."[1] This model may also be referred to as the "min-max inventory model" (i.e., when inventory reaches the minimum allowable level, the item is reordered to its maximum allowable level).

In this model, inventory levels are checked in fixed-time intervals rather than continuously like in the fixed-order quantity model, and the quantity ordered varies based upon the inventory position when checked versus a target level. The review interval and the target inventory level are set based on factors and criteria determined by the company. Inventory is then checked at the prescribed intervals (e.g., every week), and the remaining inventory at that point in time is measured against the target inventory level. If the actual inventory is below the target inventory level, an order is placed with a quantity necessary to restore the inventory level back to the target level. The amount of inventory ordered will potentially vary from period to period based on the remaining inventory at each time interval checked.

The formula for this model is:

Q = R – IP
Where:
Q = order quantity
R = target inventory level
IP = inventory position

This method would be similar to a person who drives a car and only checks the fuel gauge every fifth day. If the fuel gauge shows that fuel is anywhere below a full tank remaining, the person pulls into the nearest fuel station to refill the tank (i.e., replenish the fuel inventory to the full level again). The target fuel inventory level is a full tank, and the reorder quantity will vary with each fifth-day check depending on how much driving is done and, therefore, how much fuel was burned between the fixed-time period intervals. This approach might be adopted when an individual knows that normal driving will never take his or her car to a dangerously low fuel level in the given time period. This person would likely not pick a time interval of 10 days if that time period might lead to an empty tank (i.e., a stockout).

The biggest difference between the fixed-order quantity method and the fixed-time period quantity method is in the timing and quantities of the orders placed.

With the <u>fixed-order quantity</u> method, inventory is checked on a continual basis and the system is set up to place orders as needed, regardless of time since last reorder. This system has an advantage of providing greater system responsiveness, but it also requires administrative processes to be in place to operate on a continual basis.

With the <u>fixed-time period order quantity</u> method, an unexpected surge in demand could lead to a stockout, because the inventory level is not checked on a continuous basis. This system, therefore, potentially requires carrying more safety stock inventory than the fixed-order quantity system.

ECONOMIC ORDER QUANTITY MODEL..

ECONOMIC ORDER QUANTITY (EOQ) is "a type of fixed order quantity model that determines the amount of an item to be purchased or manufactured at one time. The intent is to minimize the combined costs of acquiring and carrying inventory."[1]

EOQ is a quantitative decision model based on the trade-off between the inventory carrying costs and the order costs. The objective of this model is to find the point of intersection of these two costs in order to find the order quantity that bears the lowest total cost to meet projected demand. The optimal order quantity will become the quantity for every order placed until the next EOQ is calculated. It is important to note that the EOQ is a real calculation, but its worth is limited because the variables do not hold true over time. The calculation is still good as a baseline for ordering, but a supply chain manager will need to make adjustments.

The basic EOQ formula is:

$$EOQ = \sqrt{\frac{2 \times \text{Order Cost} \times \text{Annual Demand Volume}}{\text{Annual Carrying Cost \%} \times \text{Unit Cost}}}$$

EOQ = The square root of 2 *times* the Order cost *times* the Annual demand volume *divided* by the Annual carrying cost percentage *times* the Unit cost.

ORDER COSTS (which were defined earlier in this chapter) are costs that are incurred each time an order is placed. These costs include order preparation costs, order transportation costs, and order receipt processing costs. Order costs are not impacted by the volume of inventory being ordered, only by the number of orders being placed per year.

ANNUAL DEMAND VOLUME is the projected cumulative quantity of the item to be consumed/sold over the course of a year.

CARRYING COSTS (which were defined earlier in this chapter) are "the cost of holding inventory, usually defined as a percentage of the dollar value of inventory per unit of time (generally one year)." These costs include the cost of capital (i.e., the interest paid on borrowed money, or the lost opportunity cost of the money used to buy the inventory), taxes on the inventory held in storage, insurance, obsolescence, and physical storage. Carrying costs vary depending on how much inventory is bought and held. The annual carrying cost percentage is the carrying cost computed for a year and then expressed as a percentage of the cost of the inventory item. Companies typically adopt a standard such as 20% to use for this calculation.

UNIT COST is the total expenditure incurred by a company to produce, store, and sell one unit of a particular product or service. Unit costs include all fixed costs, or overhead costs, and all variable costs, or direct material costs and direct labor costs, involved in production.

Demand volume and the carrying cost must both be expressed in annual quantity terms for the formula to produce the desired results.

EOQ Example:

Order Cost	$25 per order
Annual Demand Volume	5,000 units
Annual Inventory Carrying Cost (%)	20% per year
Unit Value @ Cost	$5 per unit

$$EOQ = \sqrt{\frac{2 \times 25 \times 5,000}{0.20 \times 5.00}} = \sqrt{\frac{250,000}{1}} = \sqrt{250,000} = 500$$

Proof:

Annual Order Cost is (5,000/500 x $25.00) = 10 x $25 = $250

Annual Carrying Cost is [500/2 x (5 x 0.20)] = 250 x 1 = $250

FIGURE 4.5

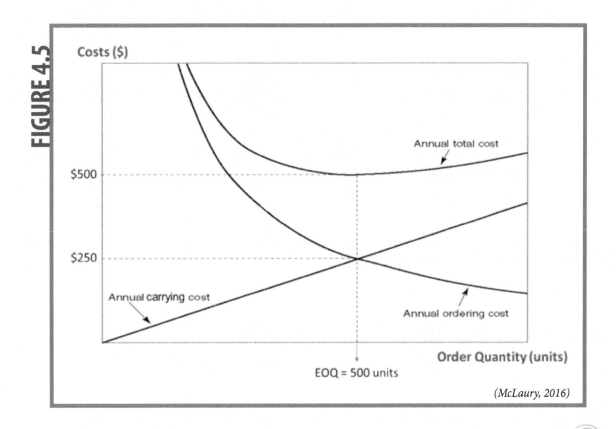

(McLaury, 2016)

Explaining the EOQ Graph

The EOQ graph (figure 4.5) displays the relationship between ordering cost and carrying cost. The Total Cost line is, in fact, the sum of these two costs (i.e., the sum of the other lines). The Carrying Cost line shows the costs for holding inventory based on the number of items held. As more items are held (moving right on the x-axis), the carrying costs also rise. The *Ordering Cost* line shows how much it costs <u>per item</u> for orders of different quantities. As the size of each order increases (again, moving right on the x-axis), the cost per item decreases. Unlike carrying costs, ordering costs cannot be represented with a simple straight line.

The Order Cost line does not typically begin with a zero value (touching the y-axis) as there are no order costs until an order is placed. If the order is for a single unit, the line would begin at 1 on the x-axis. If there are minimum order requirements, the line would start at this minimum quantity. As this line moves toward the right, it will consistently get lower as the ordering costs are shared by more and more items in the order, but the line will never reach zero ($0). There is a point of diminishing return, however, and this is why the Total Cost line eventually turns back up: The savings generated by placing a larger order no longer offset the carrying costs of the additional items.

The EOQ is specifically targeted at finding the point of greatest return, where the savings generated by larger orders combined with the carrying costs for those items is the lowest. As described earlier, this point is the intersection of the Carrying Cost and Order Cost lines. To the left of this point, carrying costs are lower, but the price per item is significantly higher. To the right of this intersection, the carrying costs for the items are higher, but the order costs have decreased slightly, failing to offset the increased carrying costs. It is important to note that the EOQ generates an idealized value that may not be possible in the real world (i.e., fractions of items or quantities not allowed by manufacturers). Moving just a little to the left or right of the intersection will still allow a company to realize much of the savings from identifying an EOQ.

Assumptions of the EOQ Model

The EOQ model involves some assumptions that must hold true for the model to deliver the desired results:

- The model must be calculated for one product at a time.

- The demand must be known and constant throughout the year.

- The delivery replenishment lead time is known and does not fluctuate.

- Replenishment is instantaneous. There is no delay in the replenishment of the stock, and the order is delivered in the quantity that was demanded (i.e., in one whole delivery).

- The purchase price (i.e., unit cost) is constant and no discounts or price breaks are factored into the model.

- Carrying cost is known and constant.

- Order cost is known and constant.

- Stockouts are not allowed

PRACTICAL CONSIDERATIONS OF EOQ

As mentioned earlier, the assumptions outlined above rarely hold true over time in the real world. Supply chain managers typically need to consider aspects that might alter the way they use the EOQ model. Some of the more practical considerations which supply chain managers must consider include the following:

- **Volume Economies of Scale:**

  - Individual Item Purchase Price Discounts. These discounts provide a lower perunit cost when larger quantities are ordered. If the volume discount is sufficient to offset the added cost from carrying additional inventory, then ordering a larger volume may be a desirable option, assuming obsolescence will not be an issue. To facilitate this decision, enterprise resource planning (ERP) systems must be programmed with quantity discount logic to work with the EOQ formula to determine optimum order quantities.

  - Multiple-Item Purchase Price Discounts. EOQ is calculated for one product at a time and does not consider any discounts for multiple item purchases, which would lower the unit cost of an item. If you purchase a combination of items from a supplier you may be able to take advantage of a volume discount based on the total volume across all the items purchased rather than just an individual item's volume.

  - Transportation Freight-Rate Discounts. Carriers generally offer a rate discount for larger volume shipments. A general rule of thumb for transportation is that the larger the shipment, the lower the cost per unit. Ordering a larger quantity may mean that you can take advantage of full truckload shipment rates, which will lower the per unit transportation costs. These adjustments will vary the order cost at different order quantities, which is not accounted for in the standard EOQ model.

- **Constraints:**

  - <u>Limited Capital</u>. The EOQ model may generate an order quantity that the company does not have sufficient available funds to purchase at one time. Capital limitations, which the model does not consider, may require that supply chain managers reduce the order quantity.

  - <u>Storage Capacity</u>. Similar to limited capital, the EOQ model may generate an order quantity that the company does not have sufficient storage capacity to handle at one time. Storage capacity limitations, which the model does not consider, may also require that supply chain managers reduce the order quantity.

  - <u>Transportation</u>. The nature of the item being transported may dictate the need for specialized or dedicated transportation, which may in turn impact the quantity per order. Certain commodities may be susceptible to time, temperature, contamination, or other types of issues necessitating the use of dedicated transport conveyances to prevent commingling of products in a conveyance. Other products may be very high value and susceptible to theft requiring dedicated transport conveyances to ensure a direct (i.e., nonstop) secure delivery. In these cases, supply chain managers may want to increase order quantities to fill up the conveyance and to also make fewer shipments per year.

  - <u>Obsolescence</u>. The EOQ model may generate an order quantity that would create spoilage or obsolescence based on the item nearing or reaching the end of its lifecycle before consumption, because too much was ordered at one time. To resolve this issue, ERP systems may also include additional programming to determine the maximum order quantity for an item reaching the end of the product lifecycle.

  - <u>Production Lot Size</u>. The supplier may require the company to order an item in full production lot sizes, particularly if the supplier does not have any other customers for that item. Similarly, the company may want to order an item in full production lot sizes, for various reasons (to ensure a consistent quality, due to the lot size of a key raw material, etc.).

  - <u>Unitization</u> (i.e., buying in full pack, case, pallet configurations). Similar to production lot size, the supplier may require the company to order an item in full pack, case, or pallet configurations, particularly if the supplier does not have any other customers for that item. Similarly, the company may want to order an item in full pack, case, or pallet configurations for various reasons of its own.

As a result of these and other considerations, companies may calculate EOQ for use as a baseline and make management decisions on how the output is used in practice. Management overrides may be necessary in response to some of the considerations outlined above.

OTHER TYPES OF INVENTORY SYSTEMS ....

The following are other types of inventory systems that are essentially variations on the continuous and periodic review methods:

- **ABC system** is a type of inventory system that utilizes some measure of importance to classify inventory items and allocate control efforts accordingly. This system takes advantage of what is commonly called the 80/20 rule, which holds that 20% of the items usually account for 80% of the value. The ABC classification is typically in decreasing order of annual dollar volume (price multiplied by projected volume) or other similar criteria. The ABC principle states that effort and cost can be saved by applying less stringent controls on low volume/value items than that which is applied to high volume/value items. This principle is applicable to inventory, purchasing, sales, and the like. Not all items/products are equal, just like not all customers and not all suppliers are equal. Some are more important than others. An ABC classification helps to identify which inventory items are more important and which ones should receive the majority of efforts in optimizing inventory.

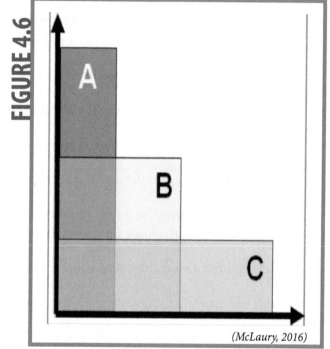

FIGURE 4.6

(McLaury, 2016)

The typical breakdown of an ABC classification is as follows (figure 4.6):

- Category A contains the most important items and typically represents 10% to 20% of the items and 50% to 70% of the value.

- Category B contains moderately important items, and typically represents 20% of the items and 20% of the value.

- Category C contains the least important items, and typically represents 60% to 70% of the items and 10% to 30% of the value.

- **Bin systems** is a type of inventory system that uses either one or two bins to hold a quantity of the item being inventoried (figure 4.7). It is mainly used for small or low value items. When the inventory in the first bin has been depleted, an order is placed to refill or replace the inventory.

The second bin is set up to hold enough inventory to cover demand during the replenishment lead time so as to last until the replacement order arrives.

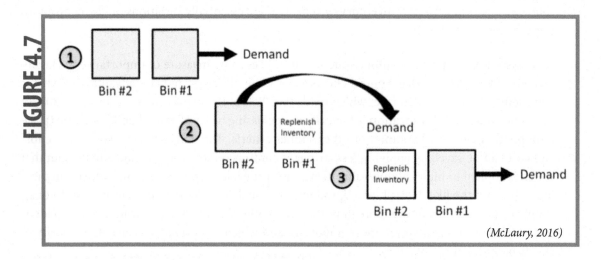

FIGURE 4.7

(McLaury, 2016)

- **Target stock level** (TSL) is a type of periodic inventory review system. TSL is the level of inventory that is needed to satisfy all demand for a product or item over a specific time period.

    - TSL = [Demand × (Lead time + Review time)] + Safety stock

    - In a min-max inventory system, the TSL is the equivalent of the maximum.

    - It is equal to the order point plus a variable order quantity.

    - It is also known as an order-up-to-inventory level.

- **Base stock level systems** are a type of inventory system that triggers a replenishment order whenever a withdrawal is made from inventory.

    - Replenishment order quantity is equal to the quantity withdrawn from inventory.

    - This will maintain the inventory at a base stock level.

    - It is used primarily for very expensive items (e.g., airplane engines).

- **"Single-period" inventory model** is a type of inventory system in which inventory is only ordered for a one-time stocking. The objective is to maximize profit.

- Often referred to as the newsboy or newsvendor problem, because newspapers are usually printed only once per day in a certain quantity and immediately become obsolete when the next issue is printed the following day. Magazines suffer similar short product lifespans.

- This model is used by vendors preparing for a very small sales window (e.g., fireworks for the Fourth of July, Christmas trees, Halloween costumes, Easter decorations).

STOCK LEVELS AND REPLENISHMENT ....

Figure 4.8 looks rather complicated and can be intimidating, but it illustrates how the various types of stock relate to the process of supply and demand under a dynamically increasing demand pattern. For illustrative purposes, figure 4.8 represents finished goods only.

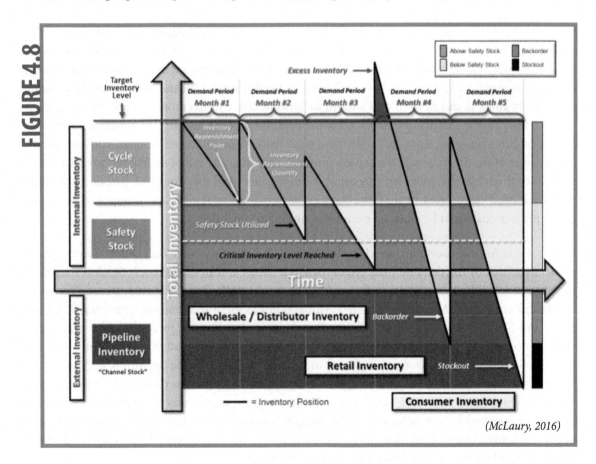

(McLaury, 2016)

The top half of the figure shows the internal inventory, which consists of cycle stock and safety stock, while the bottom half of the figure shows the external pipeline inventory (or channel stock) divided into Wholesale, Retail, and Consumer inventories for illustrative purposes. These stock levels comprise the total inventory as indicated by the vertical axis. The horizontal axis represents time moving forward from left to right.

MONTH #1: Starting near the top left of the diagram, the current inventory is exactly at the Target Inventory Level to begin the Demand Period for Month #1. As time moves forward through Month #1, inventory is depleted at a constant rate (as indicated by the black diagonal line) exactly as anticipated by the demand plan, and Month #1 ends by depleting the entire Cycle Stock as planned. Replenishment lead time is one month, and an inventory replenishment order was placed earlier according to the demand plan. The inventory replenishment order quantity is equal to the projected demand for the following month and is the Target Inventory Level. This projected demand is represented by the peak at the beginning of Month #2. The replenishment order arrives on time and returns the inventory back up to the target inventory level to begin the demand period for Month #2.

MONTH #2: As time moves forward through Month #2, inventory is depleted at a rate greater than anticipated by the demand plan and <u>all</u> of the Cycle Stock and <u>some</u> of the Safety Stock is used to meet customer demand. **As this is the very purpose of maintaining safety stock inventory, this is perfectly acceptable. In fact, if safety stock is never used to adjust for the uncertainty in demand, then safety stock is not needed and should be eliminated**. An inventory replenishment quantity equal to the projected demand was placed at the beginning of the month. The replenishment order arrives on time; however, since actual demand was greater than projected demand and necessitated use of some of the Safety Stock, the replenishment order quantity is not sufficient to return the inventory to the target inventory level to begin the demand period for Month #3. The demand might not be adjusted yet in order to see if the increase in demand was temporary or might be persistent, or the projections might be adjusted even without longitudinal data.

MONTH #3: As time moves forward through Month #3, inventory is again depleted at a rate greater than anticipated by the demand plan. <u>All</u> of the Cycle Stock and <u>all</u> of the Safety Stock is used to fill the unexpected volume of customer demand. Again, as this is the purpose of safety stock inventory, this is still acceptable. Month #3 ends at a critical point as all of the internal inventory (i.e., Cycle Stock and Safety Stock) has been depleted. Recognizing that the company might be under-forecasting projected demand, in the absence of any additional or collaborative information about why demand is increasing, an inventory replenishment order is placed at the beginning of Month #3 to arrive at month-end, but for a quantity significantly larger than previous orders. The replenishment order arrives on time; however, since a significantly larger quantity was ordered than in previous months, the replenishment order quantity returns the inventory to a level in excess of the target to begin the demand period for Month #4. The black line at the end of Month #3 is above the target inventory level indicating that inventory is above, or in excess of, target.

Month #4: As time moves forward through Month #4, inventory is now being depleted at a rate even more significant than the previous two months. The company is now forced to use <u>all</u> of the Cycle Stock and <u>all</u> of the Safety Stock, and there are now Wholesaler/Distributor orders that cannot be filled as inventory is insufficient to satisfy the demand. The black line at the end of Month #4 is dipping into the Wholesale/Distributor inventory, indicating unfulfilled demand. These unfulfilled customer orders are known as "backorders."

Wholesalers/Distributors can/will continue to sell their pipeline inventory to their downstream supply chain partners (i.e., Retailers and Consumers) until their stocks are depleted as well. At this critical point, customer service has been negatively impacted as the company's immediate customers (i.e., Wholesalers/Distributors) have unsatisfied demand.

Again, recognizing that they may be under-forecasting demand, the company placed an inventory replenishment order at the beginning of Month #4 to arrive at month-end for a quantity similar to what was ordered at the beginning of Month #3. The replenishment order arrives on time; however, since actual demand was once again significantly greater than projected demand and all Excess, Cycle, and Safety Stock were depleted, leaving the product on backorder with the Wholesalers/Distributors, the replenishment order quantity is not sufficient to return the inventory to the target inventory level to begin the demand period for Month #5. The black line at the end of Month #4 stops below the target inventory level.

Month #5: As time moves forward through Month #5, inventory is again being depleted at the accelerated rate experienced in Month #4 and all internal and external inventory, including Wholesaler/Distributor <u>and</u> Retailer inventory, is fully depleted, creating a stockout in the marketplace. A <u>stockout</u> is the most serious inventory situation as it means that there is no inventory available anywhere internally or externally to support any further demand. At this point, customer service is significantly and critically impacted at all levels. Damage to the brand and the company reputation may occur, and business may be lost to competitors. Lost business may be temporary until replenishment inventory is available, or this lost business might be permanently lost to competitors.

COLLABORATIVE PLANNING, FORECASTING AND REPLENISHMENT (CPFR): Figure 4.8 illustrates the scenario for inventory chasing demand, reacting to an increasing demand pattern without any additional information or collaboration with your trading partners to know what is really happening. CPFR is "a collaboration process whereby supply chain trading partners can jointly plan key supply chain activities from production and delivery of raw materials to production and delivery of final products to end customers. Collaboration encompasses business planning, sales forecasting, and all operations required to replenish raw materials and finished goods. A process philosophy for facilitating collaborative communications."[1] It is a process designed to avoid or mitigate the type of situation depicted in figure 4.8. CPFR helps an organization to be proactive and get out in front of the situation before it spirals out of control.

INVENTORY OPTIMIZATION

All of the methods and approaches mentioned in this chapter look to optimize the inventory held by a company. The optimization point is the intersection of inventory costs and customer service goals, and this point will be varied for different companies based on their capacities and philosophy. Identifying the appropriate inventory buffers is essential in realizing a company's mission, but these buffers can be set for individual sites or for an entire system. In single-echelon inventory optimization, a distribution site is treated essentially as an island that holds needed inventory to meet the needs of its customers, separate from upstream components. In multi-echelon inventory optimization (MEIO), inventory needs are established across various sites and levels of the supply chain, upstream and downstream, to meet the needs of the entire system's customers. MEIO initiatives typically reduce inventory by 10% to 30% while improving service levels, resulting in dramatically improved profitability and more satisfied customers. MEIO involves identifying many variables and constants, but the result is significant information for improving inventory operations.

INPUTS:

- **Desired Service Level** is normally a user provided input. The desired service level depends on the item in question: its sales attributes, demand, profitability, and associative relationship to the other items. Users normally define groups of items that have similar attributes and desired service levels.

- **Demand** is the historical and projected demand for the item.

- **Supply** is the historical and projected supply of the item.

- **Supply Lead Time** is the historical lead time of the supplies. The lead time may vary for every order that is fulfilled even when using the same item/vendor/distribution center combinations. This time-series data allows for the variability of such lead time and helps the inventory optimization engine determine the probability that a specific projected supply will be realized on the needed date.

OUTPUTS:

- Recommended safety stock levels

- Recommended safety stock locations

- Recommended reorder levels

- Recommended order quantities

- Inventory can typically be reduced by 10% to 30% by rightsizing inventory held at all stages (i.e., echelons) of the supply chain.

- MEIO programs normally reduce overall inventory while meeting or improving service levels.

- Decreasing the amount of on-hand inventory frees up capital that would otherwise be tied up in inventory.

- The total logistics burden includes costs for warehousing, insurance, labor, expedited shipping, and so forth. Eliminating inventory removes its associated logistics cost, which can amount to 10% of inventory value.

- Obsolete inventory is a write-off that represents lost revenue. Most companies can expect to save a portion of the COGS of optimizable obsolete inventory. Savings can range from a few percentage points to substantially higher for companies with many new product introductions or high rates of product churn.

- Shortages and stockouts can be reduced. These inventory issues lead to both fulfillment delays and permanently lost revenue due to cancelled orders. Lowering the lost order rate results in higher revenue generation. MEIO can reduce the percentage of permanently lost orders within the optimizable inventory by a significant amount.

INVENTORY CONTROL TOOLS

Many inventory control tools exist in today's market. Those that incorporate barcode tracking or radio frequency identification (RFID) tagging generally offer the most flexibility and ease of use.

Barcode Systems

Barcode systems help businesses and organizations track products, prices, and stock levels for centralized management in a computer software system allowing for incredible increases in productivity and efficiency. The lines and patterns on a barcode are actually representations of numbers and data, and their use allows basic information about a product to be read by an optical scanning device, a barcode scanner, easily and automatically. The scanner is connected to a computer system that supplies information to the scanner (e.g., the price of the item in a grocery store), and receives information from the scanner (i.e., the product sold) and, therefore, removes it from inventory. The computer control of the barcode system vastly reduces the time it takes to record necessary information and eliminates the potential for human data entry error.

Barcodes started out with simple one-dimensional (linear) designs, consisting of basic black lines that could only be read by specially designed barcode scanners. However, today barcodes come in many shapes and sizes and a wide range of designs; many can even be read by mobile phones and other devices. The barcodes can be classified in one of two categories: linear (1D) and two dimensional (2D).

LINEAR (1D) BARCODES are "a series of alternating bars and spaces printed or stamped on parts, containers, labels, or other media, representing encoded information that can be read by electronic readers. A bar code is used to facilitate timely and accurate input of data to a computer system."[1]

© Horvats/Shutterstock.com

Barcoding is "a method of encoding data using bar code for fast and accurate readability."[1]

Barcoding inventory is a quick and efficient way of monitoring stock levels. Data error rates for barcoding are significantly less than those for manual methods, and efficiency rates are higher as less time is required not only to set up initial data, but also to gather and generate reports.

Linear barcodes do have some limitations: they are one dimensional, can only be read horizontally, and can only hold a maximum of 85 characters. The 1D barcode is nearing the end of its lifespan. As 2D scanners become more affordable and newer technology becomes more accessible, the linear barcode will become obsolete.

2D BARCODES are graphical images that store information both horizontally <u>and</u>

© LABELMAN/Shutterstock.com

vertically. As a result of that construction, 2D barcodes can store over 7,000 characters, allowing transmission of almost two paragraphs of information.

By moving to 2D barcodes, businesses are able to convey much more complex information, like expiration dates and serial numbers, without the need for any additional scanning. 2D barcodes allow users to customize the data captured and the way it is stored. This flexibility increases the ability of organizations to achieve their specific goals and create a database catered to their needs.

2D barcode scanners are much more versatile than linear barcode scanners in that they can scan from any angle. They can also scan multiple barcodes in one scan.

© Shutterstock.com

A barcode reader (or barcode scanner) is an electronic device that can read barcodes and transmit the data to a computer. These might be handheld cordless devices, corded devices that attach directly to a PC's USB port, or computers with integrated laser scanners.

A basic inventory tracking system consists of software and a barcode scanner. Inventory items (e.g., finished products or raw materials) have barcode labels affixed so that when an item is removed from stock, the barcode can be scanned in order to reduce the available count in the inventory tracking software, instead of having to enter the information manually. Real-time access to location, quantity, destination, and so forth, allows inventory managers the flexibility to make the decisions outline earlier in this chapter.

Radio Frequency Identification

Radio frequency identification (RFID) is the successor to the barcode. RFID is "a system using electronic tags to store data about items. Accessing these data is accomplished through a specific radio frequency and does not require close proximity or line-of-sight access for data retrieval."[1] The RFID tags can be either active or passive. An active RFID tag broadcasts information and contains its own power source. A passive RFID tag does not send out data and is not self-powered. Electromagnetic energy is transmitted from the reader in order to obtain the information from passive tags. As the tags pass through/near the reader, the reader pulls information from the tag (e.g., a security tag on a product that sends a signal when it passes through a reader at the front of a store).

The biggest advantages that RFID has over barcodes is that RFID does not require direct line of sight to read a tag, it can provide much more information, and the information on the tag is updatable.

RFID works like a barcode, but unlike the barcodes you see in retail stores that have

1) **Chip:** holds information about the physical object to which the tag is attached

2) **Antenna:** transmits information to a reader (e.g., handheld, warehouse portal, store shelf) using radio waves

3) **Packaging:** encases the chip and antenna so that tag can be attached to physical object

to pass in front of scanners to be identified, an RFID tag is triggered by a radio frequency from an antenna and transmits informaiton back via radio frequency through the antenna to a reader that converts it into digitial informaton for use by a software package (see figure 4.9). Significantly more information can be programmed onto an RFID tag than can be relayed with a linear barcode. A linear barcode usually provides a product code or serial number, whereas an RFID tag can include more and different kinds of information such as lot number, expiration date, and even manufacturing instructions.

RFID tags have excellent potential for warehousing and asset tracking, because they can relay information over a longer distance (up to 100 meters in some cases), making it possible to know exactly how much of something you have in real time, and reducing the risk of miscounted inventory.

Some of the ways RFID can be utilized in the supply chain include:

- MATERIALS MANAGEMENT: Goods can be counted and logged automatically as they enter the supply warehouse. Items, cases, and/or pallets traditionally used barcodes, which workers

FIGURE 4.9

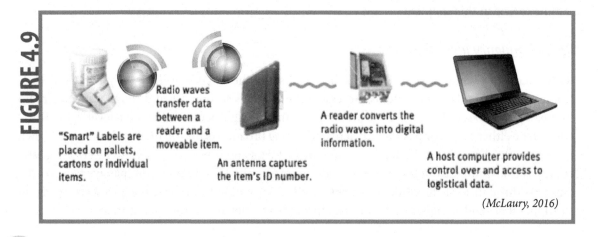

"Smart" Labels are placed on pallets, cartons or individual items.

Radio waves transfer data between a reader and a moveable item.

An antenna captures the item's ID number.

A reader converts the radio waves into digital information.

A host computer provides control over and access to logistical data.

(McLaury, 2016)

had to scan indiviudally when receiving them in the warehouse. With RFID, those items can be read all at once by a portal reader placed at the dock door as they are unloaded from the truck. Unloading an inbound container which may take a least a couple of hours to individually scan, sort, and count, may take less than 30 minutes with RFID-tagged cartons.

- MANUFACTURING: Assembly instructions encoded on RFID tags can provide information to computer-controlled assembly devices even while the product is moving down the line in production.

- DISTRIBUTION: Shipments leaving the distribution center can automatically update the enterprise resource planning (ERP) system to trigger an invoice to the customer, notify the customer of delivery tracking information, and initiate a replenishment order with the supplier.

- RETAIL STORE: Use of these tags can eliminate checkout lines. If a grocery store tagged every item with an RFID tag, shoppers could place items in their carts and then simply roll the cart past the reader to complete their purchase. If that shopper has a store card with an RFID tag, the reader could even automatically charge the customers card. Just like with barcodes, RFID systems could update inventory as soon as a purchase is complete; however, the RFID tags could also help employees idenitfy products customers took off the shelf and then placed onto a different shelf after changing their minds. These misplaced products are still technically in the store inventory because they have not left the store, but they have been effectively removed since customers will not find them until they are placed back where they belong. RFID tags could alert a reader to an incorrect position and even inform an employee about where it belongs, information a barcode cannot supply.

Unfortunately, RFID hasn't yet gained much traction due mainly to the high cost of the tags, which cost as much as $0.20 each, compared to barcodes, which costs a fraction of a penny each. The other major hurdle facing mass adoption of RFID technology is that in order to reap the real rewards of RFID, the entire end-to-end supply chain must implement RFID technology. At its current price, this is an extremely expensive endeavor that requires purchasing new equipment at every level of the supply chain.

Software

The backbone of inventory management in any organization is the inventory control software that maintains the systemic record of product location, quantity, inventory transactions, and resupply orders. While some organizations are small enough to use a spreadsheet as their primary inventory management tool, most are using databases with a menu-driven user interface. Some organizations use off-the-shelf software, while others have internal development teams. Business model differences call for different solutions.

Hardware

The software requires input to manage the inventory. Servers, desktops, dumb terminals, RF devices, asset tags, RFID tags, scannable barcode label printers, and point of sale devices can all play a role as an inventory management tool. Selecting the right tools to balance labor versus infrastructure is part of the art of inventory management.

MEASURING INVENTORY PERFORMANCE ....

Companies use several measurements specifically for analyzing inventory:

- UNITS: the number of units available

- DOLLARS: the amount of dollars tied up in inventory

- DAYS/WEEKS/MONTHS OF SUPPLY: (Avg. on-hand inventory) / (Avg. usage)

- INVENTORY TURNS: (Cost of goods sold) / (Average inventory at cost)

Inventory turnover is a measure of operational efficiency. Specifically, it tells you how many times inventory is being sold and purchased over a given time period. A low turnover rate may indicate overstocking, obsolescence, or deficiencies in the product line or marketing effort.

It is important to note that every dollar saved in inventory drops right to the bottom line as pure savings. It's a dollar-for-dollar savings for the company. Any dollar not spent on inventory is a dollar that can be invested in research and development, marketing and sales, dividends for shareholders, to take as profit, and so forth. This immediate effect on the bottom line is one reason why companies measure their inventory continuously and try to reduce their inventory investment as much as possible. Effective inventory management can potentially generate a significant amount of savings.

Other related measures that can indicate how well an inventory management system is working include the following:

- SERVICE LEVEL is "a measure (usually expressed as a percentage) of satisfying demand through inventory or by the current production schedule in time to satisfy the customers' requested delivery dates and quantities. In a make-to-stock environment, level of service is sometimes calculated as the percentage of orders picked complete from stock upon receipt of the customer order, the percentage of line items picked complete, or the percentage of total dollar demand picked complete. In make-to-order and design-to-order environments, level of service is the percentage of times the customer requested or acknowledged date was met by shipping complete product quantities."[1]

- ORDER FILL RATE is "a measure of delivery performance of finished goods, usually expressed as a percentage. In a make-to-stock company, this percentage usually represents the number of items or dollars (on one or more customer orders) that were shipped on schedule for a specific time period, compared with the total that were supposed to be shipped in that time period. In a make-to-order company, it is usually some comparison of the number of jobs or dollars shipped in a given time period (e.g., a week) compared with the number of jobs or dollars that were supposed to be shipped in that time period."[1]

- LINE ITEM FILL RATE is the total number of line items filled divided by the total number of line items ordered. This metric applies to products or orders that contain multiple products.

SUMMARY

- Inventory serves a useful purpose in the supply chain; however, companies can help minimize the need for inventory by carefully managing those factors that drive inventory levels up. Every dollar saved in inventory drops right to the bottom line as pure savings.

- There are four main categories of inventory: raw materials; work in process (WIP); finished goods; and maintenance, repair, and operating (MRO) supplies.

- There are four basic function of inventory: to meet customer demand (cycle stock), to buffer against uncertainty in demand and/or supply (safety stock), to decouple supply from demand (strategic stock), and to decouple dependencies in the supply chain.

- There are three main inventory stocking levels: cycle stock, safety stock, and strategic stock.

- Pipeline inventory may have an impact on decisions that companies make about how to manage and control their inventory resources

- There are six categories of costs associated with inventory: direct costs, indirect costs, fixed costs, variable costs, order costs, and carrying costs.

- Inventory items can be divided into two main types: independent demand and dependent demand items. The systems for managing these two types of inventory differ significantly:

- The two classic systems for managing independent demand inventory are continuous review and periodic review systems.
- The systems for managing dependent demand inventory are material requirements planning, kanban, and drum-buffer-rope.

- The reorder point is the lowest inventory level at which a new order must be placed to avoid a stockout. The reorder point is set at a level of remaining inventory that is enough to cover all of the demand that is projected to occur during the lead time necessary to receive the replenishment supply.

- The economic order quantity (EOQ) minimizes total annual order costs and carrying costs. Even if all the assumptions don't hold true in the long term, the EOQ gives a good indication of whether or not current order quantities are reasonable.

- Inventory optimization is finding optimal inventory strategies and policies related to customer service and return on investment over several echelons of a supply chain.

- Inventory control tools help to facilitate the management of inventory, improving efficiency and reducing errors.

- Measuring inventory performance is essential as companies cannot improve what they do not measure. Companies measure their inventory in an effort to reduce their inventory investment and generate savings.

REFERENCE ....

[1] *APICS Dictionary* (14th ed.). (2013). Chicago, IL: APICS. www.apics.org

SOURCE

Chapter 5
Purchasing Management

CHAPTER OUTLINE

Introduction
Defining Procurement and Purchasing
The Basic Purchasing Process
Financial Significance of Purchasing
Make versus Buy Decision
Supplier Selection
Organization of Purchasing
International Purchasing
Government and Nonprofit Purchasing
World-Class Procurement

INTRODUCTION ....

"Purchasing is a managerial activity that goes beyond the simple act of buying. It includes research and development for the proper selection of materials and sources, follow-up to ensure timely delivery; inspection to ensure both quantity and quality; to control traffic, receiving, storekeeping and accounting operations related to purchases."[1]

Purchasing has become a critical function within most organizations, responsible for spending as much as half of the revenues that the company receives from sales, in order to obtain the materials and services necessary for the company to succeed. More money is often spent on the purchase of materials and services than for any other expense.

In business today, the purchasing function has evolved into a core competency within most companies, performing the vital role of finding and developing suppliers, and bringing in external expertise that can be highly valued by the company.

DEFINING PROCUREMENT AND PURCHASING ....

PROCUREMENT: The process of selecting and vetting suppliers, negotiating contracts, establishing payment terms, and the actual purchasing of goods and services.

- Procurement is concerned with acquiring all of the goods, services, and work that is vital to an organization.

- Procurement is the overarching or umbrella term within which the functions of purchasing management, strategic sourcing, and supplier relationship management can be found (see figure 5.1).

The objectives of a world-class procurement organization are:

1. To support the organization's goals and objectives

2. To support operational requirements

3. To manage the procurement process and the supply base efficiently and effectively

4. To develop strong relationships with key suppliers

5. To develop strong relationships with other functional groups within the organization

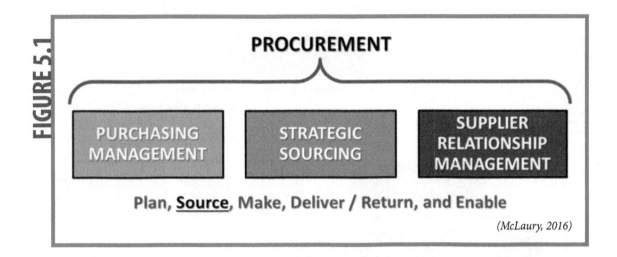

FIGURE 5.1

PROCUREMENT

| PURCHASING MANAGEMENT | STRATEGIC SOURCING | SUPPLIER RELATIONSHIP MANAGEMENT |

Plan, <u>Source</u>, Make, Deliver / Return, and Enable

(McLaury, 2016)

PURCHASING: The <u>action</u> of obtaining merchandise, capital equipment; raw materials, services, or maintenance, repair, and operating (MRO) supplies in exchange for money, or its equivalent.

- Purchasing is the process of how goods and services are ordered.

- Purchasing is typically described as the transactional function of procurement for goods or services.

PURCHASING is also a term commonly used in industry to represent the <u>function</u> of, and the responsibility for, procuring materials, supplies, and services for an organization.

- It can be a separate department or organization within a company, or it can be part of the supply chain management department or organization within a company.

- Many companies have a Chief Procurement Officer or Chief Purchasing Officer as part of their executive leadership team. See figure 5.2.

Purchasing Terms

The following are some key purchasing terms and definitions used in this text:

- E-PROCUREMENT: The business-to-business purchase and sale of supplies and services over the Internet.

- MERCHANTS: Wholesalers and retailers who purchase for resale.

FIGURE 5.2

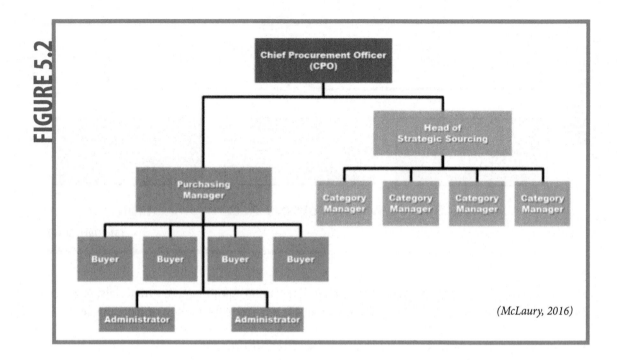

(McLaury, 2016)

- **INDUSTRIAL BUYERS:** Individuals within an organization who purchase raw materials for conversion into products, and/or purchase services, capital equipment, and MRO supplies.

- **CONTRACTING:** A term often used for the **acquisition of services**

- **SUPPLY MANAGEMENT:** A newer term that encompasses all acquisition activities beyond the simple purchase transaction.

  - The "Identification, acquisition, access, positioning, and management of resources an organization needs or potentially needs in the attainment of its strategic objectives." *Institute of Supply Management (ISM)*

- **REQUEST FOR INFORMATION (RFI):** "An inquiry to a potential supplier about that supplier's product or service for potential use in the business. The inquiry can provide certain business requirements or be of a more general exploratory nature."[1]

- **REQUEST FOR PROPOSAL (RFP):** A detailed low-level capabilities evaluation document that is used to precisely determine a supplier's capability and interest in the production of a customized product or service.

- REQUEST FOR QUOTE (RFQ): A document generally used to solicit bids from interested and qualified suppliers for goods or services that the organization needs to obtain.

- BID: A tender, proposal, or quotation submitted in response to a solicitation from a contracting authority.

- COMPETITIVE BIDDING: Offers submitted by multiple individuals or firms competing for a contract, privilege, or right to supply specified services or merchandise.

- PURCHASE REQUISITION: Document that defines the need for goods and/or services. An internal document. Does not constitute a contractual relationship with any external party.

- PURCHASE ORDER (PO): The buyer's offer to the supplier to acquire goods or services. Becomes a legally binding contract only when accepted by the supplier.

The Role of Purchasing in an Organization

The primary goals of purchasing are to:

1. Ensure an uninterrupted flow of materials and services for the company.

2. Obtain materials and services at the best value, meaning the best quality at the best prices, with the best service, in the most economic order quantities.

3. Secure reliable alternative sources of supply as necessary to manage risk.

4. Optimize customer satisfaction by using the knowledge and expertise of the supply base to provide high quality at the lowest total cost.

   - Actively seek better materials and reliable suppliers

   - Work with the expertise of strategic suppliers to improve quality and materials and finished goods

   - Involve suppliers and purchasing personnel in new product design and development efforts

5. Maintain good relationships with suppliers.

THE BASIC PURCHASING PROCESS..

The industrial purchasing process can vary from one organization to another, but there are some key common elements, and a number of inputs, interfaces, communications, and outputs involved in the process.

The process usually starts with a demand for a material, component, or a service and progresses through the following steps:

1. A need is identified, and a **purchase requisition** is created/issued.

   - Request for goods or services submitted to the procurement/purchasing organization for action.

   - Typically initiated by a user within an organization.

2. Obtain authorization as necessary.

   - A purchase requisition may be routed to an authorized approver(s) depending on the type of material or service being requested and/or the dollar value of the request.

   - Multiple authorizations, in a prescribed sequence, to various management levels of the organization, may be necessary if the value exceeds a specific predetermined threshold.

3. Identify and evaluate potential suppliers.

   - May be determined from a list of company-approved suppliers.

   - Alternatively, may use a **request for information** (RFI) to collect information from potential suppliers on their capabilities and interest in supplying the material or service.

4. Make supplier selection.

   - If the buyers already knows which supplier they will buy the item from, move to the next step.

   - If not, a **competitive bidding** process may be initiated. A request for proposal (RFP) or a request for quotation (RFQ) may be issued to qualified suppliers, to identify proposed alternatives for supplying the desired material or service, and to obtain price and availability information.

     a. Buyer issues a **RFP** for items that have not been previously purchased, or not purchased from a specific supplier being evaluated. Supplier(s) provides the proposal to supply the item(s) including price and delivery.

b. Buyer issues a **RFQ** for routine or repeat purchased items. Supplier(s) provides a price and delivery quote on the specific item(s) requested.

- A supplier is selected from the RFP or RFQ **bids** received based on criteria determined by the buyer, including price, availability, quality, delivery costs.

5. A **purchase order** (PO) is created and delivered to the supplier.

   - A PO is generated and forwarded to the supplier to inform the supplier of the intent to purchase.

   - The purchase order will identify the item(s) to be procured, the quantity required, the requested delivery date(s), and the price to be paid. It will also identify the delivery location and any terms and conditions that relate to the order.

   - The PO is the buyer's formal offer to the supplier to obtain the item(s).

   - The PO becomes a binding contract only when accepted by supplier.

6. Supplier confirmation of the PO

   - The supplier formally agrees to supply the item(s) per the specifications, terms, and conditions described on the PO.

   - The PO then becomes a legally binding contract between the buyer and the supplier for the item(s) specified.

7. Fulfillment

   - The supplier ships/delivers the item(s) to the buying organization as per the PO.

8. Receipt of goods

   - Once the item(s) arrives at the designated location, the buyer will typically conduct some form of receipt process where the item(s) are checked to ensure that they conform to the details of the PO, including quality and quantity.

   - A confirmation of receipt may also be sent to the supplier.

9. Invoice

   - Supplier prepares an invoice for the item(s) ordered and transmits to the buyer. The invoice either accompanies the item(s) or is sent separately.

10. Reconciliation

   – The invoice may need to be reconciled to the purchase order and goods receipt before payment is made. This step is sometimes referred to as a "three-way match."

11. Payment

   – Invoice payment processed using an appropriate payment method assuming the item(s) is received and meets all of the criteria established on the PO.

12. Reclamation of taxes

   – In some situations, the supplier will be obligated to charge a tax, but the buyer may be eligible to retain some or all of the tax based on corporate status.

13. Close out the PO

   – If the PO has been received complete, and all terms and conditions have been met, then it should be closed out in the purchasing system (whether manual or automated).

14. Analysis

   – Measurements of the efficiency and accuracy of the procurement process.

   – Specific PO data and information captured and used during periodic supplier performance meetings.

In leading procurement organizations, every step will be completed, although some will be completed automatically by the e-procurement system using defined rules, particularly for low-dollar value or nonstrategic purchases

e-Procurement

The "electronic" requisitioning, receiving, and reconciliation of the received goods, e-procurement involves the automation of the nonstrategic and transactional activities that would otherwise consume the majority of a buyer's time. It provides increased enterprise level visibility of all purchases.

© Tashatuvango/Shutterstock.com

The term describes the automation through web-enabled tools of many elements of the purchasing process including:

- The issue, collection, and analysis of bids

- Execution and analysis

- Award of business via reverse auction

e-Procurement tools typically automate all or part of the following processes:

- Solicitation development tools (i.e., RFI, RFP, RFQ)

- Reverse auctions

e-Procurement may not work well for every type of purchase. Examples include the procurement of critical items that are only available through a few suppliers; where procuring an item involves complex negotiations; or where the potential to lower costs through an e-procurement process is minimal.

Advantages of an e-Procurement System

- TIME SAVINGS: A reduction in the time between recognizing the need for an item and the release and receipt of an order for that item

- COST SAVINGS: Lower overhead costs in the purchasing area

- ACCURACY: A reduction in errors; a virtual elimination of manual paperwork and paperwork handling

- REAL TIME: Improved communication both within the company and with suppliers

- MOBILITY: Access to purchase requisition and purchase order information through the use of mobile devices and the internet, allowing actions to be taken regardless of where a person is located at any given time

- TRACKABILITY: The ability to track the status of purchase requisitions, orders, and information

- MANAGEMENT: Allows purchasing personnel to spend less time on processing of purchase orders and invoices, and more time on strategic value-added purchasing activities

- **BENEFITS TO THE SUPPLIERS:** Customer orders can be received and confirmed faster by the supplier, and receipts and invoices can be processed faster by the buyer, facilitating the supplier's receipt of revenue.

Small Value Purchases

Purchases of small value, noncritical items may take as much time to process as purchases of higher value, critical items. In an effort to minimize the amount of valuable purchasing resource time spent on small value purchases, there are some tools and techniques that companies can use to reduce this processing time and cost. These tools and techniques will allow the purchasing group to transfer some of the routine transactional purchasing activities for small value purchase to users or others within the company, thereby freeing up time for these valuable purchasing resources to work on more critical or strategic purchasing activities.

- **CREDIT CARD/CORPORATE PURCHASING CARD (P-CARD):** A form of company charge card that allows goods and services to be procured without using a traditional purchasing process

- **BLANKET OR OPEN-END PURCHASE ORDERS:** A purchase order that the buyer negotiates with its supplier, which can incorporate multiple delivery dates over a period of time (often a year). It is typically used for frequently needed expendable goods. Once negotiated, authorized users within the buyer's company can arrange for the necessary items, quantities, and delivery dates directly with the supplier.

- **BLANK CHECK POs:** A term used to describe a situation in which an usually high level of trust is afforded to the supplier by the buyer. The supplier can supply items to the buyer as needed without confirming pricing in advance. This may be used when the buyer is not exactly sure what item(s) will be needed and cannot, therefore, create a blanket PO.

- **PETTY CASH:** An accessible amount of money kept by an organization for expenditure on small items. A typical example of when this might be used is a company sending someone out with petty cash to buy coffee and donuts for a business meeting.

- **STOCKLESS BUYING OR SYSTEM CONTRACTING:** An arrangement in which a supplier holds the items ordered by the buyer in its own warehouse, and releases them when required by the buyer.

- **STANDARDIZATION AND SIMPLIFICATION OF MATERIALS AND COMPONENTS:** The concept of limiting the alternatives or options of some small value purchases in order to maximize the volume and potentially obtain better pricing. Example: creating a catalog or listing of a set number and type of office supplies to be order from a supplier.

- ACCUMULATING SMALL ORDERS TO CREATE A LARGE ORDER: The concept of volume consolidation for small value purchases. Example: having an administrator collect all of the individual departments' office supply needs throughout the month and placing one monthly order for delivery rather than allowing multiple deliveries.

- USING A FIXED ORDER INTERVAL: Establishing a set schedule with a supplier to deliver a predetermined amount of inventory of an item. Example: water supplier delivers a fixed number of water bottles for the water cooler in a department on a fixed time schedule (e.g., delivers two 10-gallon water bottles to the XYZ Department every Monday morning).

FINANCIAL SIGNIFICANCE OF PURCHASING ....

Purchasing activities can have a significant and profound impact on the financials of an organization. The following are a few examples of the financial significance of purchasing.

Profit-Leverage Effect

The profit-leverage effect states that a decrease in purchasing expenditures directly increases profits before taxes (assuming no decrease in quality or purchasing total cost). The bottom line impact is a dollar saved is a dollar of profit to be used for such things as shareholder dividends, employee pay increases, investments, company reinvestments in R&D, or marketing and sales, among others.

- As shown in figure 5.3, a 10% cost reduction generates significantly more profit before taxes than does a 10% sales increase.

FIGURE 5.3

PROFIT LEVERAGE EFFECT		Baseline Simplified P&L	Increase Sales 10%	Decrease COGS 10%
Sales		$1,000,000	$1,100,000	$1,000,000
Cost of Goods Sold (COGS)	50%	($500,000)	($550,000)	($450,000)
Administrative Costs	45%	($450,000)	($495,000)	($450,000)
Profit Before Tax		$50,000	$55,000	$100,000
% Change			10%	100%

(McLaury, 2016)

- This is one of the main reasons that procurement managers are under significant pressure from senior management to reduce purchase costs.

Return on Assets Effect

RETURN ON ASSETS (ROA) EFFECT states that with the exact same number/value of assets, a decrease in purchasing expenditures significantly increases the return on those assets compared to a comparable increase in sales. A high ROA indicates managerial prowess in generating profits with lower spending.

FIGURE 5.4

RETURN ON ASSETS EFFECT		Baseline Simplified P&L	Increase Sales 10%	Decrease COGS 10%
Sales		$1,000,000	$1,100,000	$1,000,000
Cost of Goods Sold (COGS)	50%	($500,000)	($550,000)	($450,000)
Administrative Costs	45%	($450,000)	($495,000)	($450,000)
Profit Before Tax		$50,000	$55,000	$100,000
Assets		$500,000	$500,000	$500,000
Return on Assets		10%	11%	20%

(McLaury, 2016)

- As shown in figure 5.4, a 10% cost reduction generates a significantly higher ROA than does a 10% sales increase, given the same number/value of assets.

Inventory Turnover Effect

Inventory is an asset but it also represents financial capital tied up and not available for use in other parts of the business. The purchasing function in an organization is frequently responsible for supply management and therefore plays a large part in the amount of inventory the company holds.

- Inventory turnover represents the number of times the company sold through inventory in a given time period.

- It is the costs of goods sold (COGS) divided by the average inventory.

- A high turnover ratio is beneficial because it means the company is generating sales efficiently to sell inventory.

- A low turnover ratio is unfavorable as it means the company is not selling through products efficiently. The company is likely making/buying too much inventory for demand and/or the company is throwing out expired or unsalable products.

Total Cost of Ownership

TOTAL COST OF OWNERSHIP (TCO) is the sum of all the costs associated with every activity of the supply stream.[1] The four elements of cost are quality, service, delivery, and price (QSDP).

TCO is the sum of the cost elements in QSDP (i.e., Quality + Service + Delivery + Price).

- Each element of QSDP has an impact on the TCO.

- The main insight that TCO offers is that the acquisition cost is often a very small portion of the total cost of ownership.

Procurement professionals recognize that although the purchase price of an item remains very important, it is only one part of the total cost of ownership. Other factors beyond purchase price must also be considered when making the decision to buy an item. This makes sense when you consider that acquisition costs account for only 25% to 40% of the total cost for most products and services. The balance of the total cost includes operating, training, maintenance, warehousing, environmental, quality, and transportation costs as well as the cost to recover the product's value later on.

Factors to consider:

- **Quantity discounts** may be offered as an inducement to encourage buyers to purchase larger quantities.

- **Cash discounts** may be offered for prompt payment of invoices.

- **Value-added services** may also be offered. Services may include special delivery, special packaging, preparation of promotional displays, and subassembly operations in a supplier's plant.

- **Administrative expenses** are associated with the procurement activity itself such as screening potential suppliers, negotiation, order preparation, and order transmission.

- **Poor supplier quality** costs related to defective finished goods, scrap, rework, recycling, or recovery of materials must also be considered, as well as related warranty administration and repair costs.

The elements comprising the TCO can be viewed in three categories: pre-transaction costs, transaction costs, and post-transaction costs (see figure 5.5).

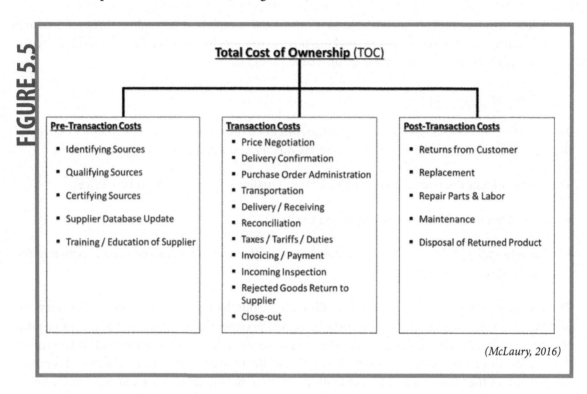

FIGURE 5.5

Total Cost of Ownership (TOC)

Pre-Transaction Costs	Transaction Costs	Post-Transaction Costs
▪ Identifying Sources	▪ Price Negotiation	▪ Returns from Customer
▪ Qualifying Sources	▪ Delivery Confirmation	▪ Replacement
▪ Certifying Sources	▪ Purchase Order Administration	▪ Repair Parts & Labor
▪ Supplier Database Update	▪ Transportation	▪ Maintenance
▪ Training / Education of Supplier	▪ Delivery / Receiving	▪ Disposal of Returned Product
	▪ Reconciliation	
	▪ Taxes / Tariffs / Duties	
	▪ Invoicing / Payment	
	▪ Incoming Inspection	
	▪ Rejected Goods Return to Supplier	
	▪ Close-out	

(McLaury, 2016)

PRE-TRANSACTION COSTS involve all of the activities carried out prior to executing the actual buy and sell transaction; and all of the costs associated with identifying a need, finding and qualifying sources, site visits, inspections/audits, administratively establishing new sources of supply, and any approvals necessary.

TRANSACTION COSTS involve all of the activities carried out as part of the actual buy and sell transaction. These costs include the purchase price, placing and managing the order, transportation, tariffs and duties, incoming inspections, rejected product handling, late deliveries, missing documentation, expediting, and invoice processing/payment.

POST-TRANSACTION COSTS involve all of the activities carried out following the actual buy and sell transaction. All of the costs associated with defective/rejected finished products, field failures, repair, replacement or warrantee costs, loss of customer goodwill, and so forth.

MAKE VERSUS BUY DECISION

The make versus buy decision is the act of deciding whether to produce an item internally or buy it from an external supplier. Make versus buy is a <u>strategic decision</u> and every company must decide what and how much they want to make versus buy. Some companies want to produce as much as they can internally, while others are content to buy most, if not all, of their materials

© SNEHIT/Shutterstock.com

externally. Factors to consider in the decision include costs, available capacity, proprietary and/or specialized knowledge, quality considerations, skill requirements, volume, and timing.

- MAKE: Producing (i.e., manufacturing) materials or products internally (i.e., in operations owned by the company).

- BUY/OUTSOURCE: Buying materials and/or components from suppliers instead of making them in-house (i.e., buying from a third-party external source).

In determining the make-or-buy decision, it is important to analyze all of the expenses associated with developing the capability to make a product, in addition to all of the expenses associated with buying the product. The assessment should include qualitative and quantitative factors. It should also consider only relevant expenses.

- QUANTITATIVE factors primarily involve the incremental costs of making or purchasing the component, such as the availability of manufacturing facilities, needed resources, and manufacturing capacity. Fixed and variable costs can be determined with certainty or by estimation.

- QUALITATIVE factors are more subjective and include such things as control over quality, the reliability and reputation of the potential suppliers, and the impact of the decision on customers and suppliers.

Reasons for Making

Following are some of the more common reasons companies cite for the decision to make an item rather than buy it.

- To protect proprietary technology

- No competent supplier exists

- Better control over continuity of supply

- To achieve an overall lower cost

- Better quality control

- To use existing idle capacity and/or labor

- Better control of lead time

- More control of transportation and warehousing cost

- Quantity not sufficient to interest a supplier

- Political, regulatory, environmental, or social

Reasons for Buying (or Outsourcing)

Following are some of the more common reasons companies cite for the decision to buy an item rather than make it.

- If it is a nonstrategic item

- If it provides a cost advantage, especially for components that are nonvital to the organization's operations. Suppliers may provide the benefit of economies of scale

- If insufficient capacity is an issue, where a firm may be at or near capacity and subcontracting from a supplier may make better sense

- When temporary capacity constraints are a factor; the concept of "extended workbench," which involves short-term supplementing internal capacity with external capacity during time of constraint or overloaded work centers

- Lack of expertise, such as when a firm may not have the necessary technology and expertise

- Quality concerns, meaning suppliers may have better technology, process, skilled labor

- To achieve multisourcing strategy, using an external supplier in addition to an internal source

- Inventory considerations, such as when a company opts to have the supplier hold inventory of the item or the materials required to produce the item

- Brand strategy, where the company can take advantage of a supplier's brand image, reputation, and popularity

Outsourcing Risks and Benefits

There are some risks associated with outsourcing to consider:

- Potential loss of control over production decisions, intellectual property, etc.

- Increased reliance on suppliers, moving strategic direction away from manufacturing and toward external supply

- Increased need for supplier management: more suppliers means more supplier management activities

There are also some benefits of outsourcing to consider. These include allowing companies to:

- Concentrate on their core competencies by outsourcing noncore competencies.

- Reduce staffing levels, for the staff no longer needed due to shifting work volume to external supply.

- Reduce internal management problems, from the reduced staffing levels.

- Accelerate reengineering efforts by tapping into the knowledge and expertise of external suppliers to add to the company's knowledge and expertise.

- Improve manufacturing flexibility, from the potential use of the capacity from the work now shifted to an external source of supply.

Additional Make versus Buy Concepts

- **In-sourcing** (also known as back sourcing): This involves reverting back to in-house production when external quality, delivery, and services do not meet expectations.

- **Co-sourcing**:

  1. The sharing of a process or function between internal staff and an external provider
  2. Using dedicated staff at an external provider that work exclusively under your control and direction

Other Types of Make versus Buy Decisions

The following are two types of strategic make versus buy decisions beyond just individual products or materials, involving larger aspects of the company. Refer to figure 5.6.

- BACKWARD VERTICAL INTEGRATION: Refers to a company acquiring one or more of its suppliers. **Example:** a manufacturer buying the key supplier of a critical material to take ownership of this aspect of its supply chain.

- FORWARD VERTICAL INTEGRATION: Refers to a company acquiring one or more of its customers. **Example:** a manufacturer buying a wholesaler/distributor to take ownership of this aspect of its supply chain.

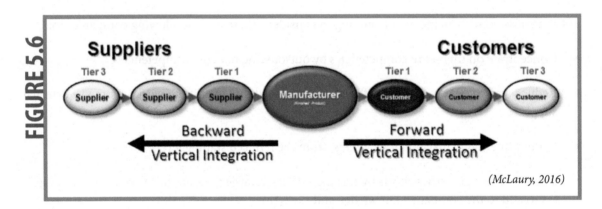

FIGURE 5.6

(McLaury, 2016)

SUPPLIER SELECTION ....

Supplier selection is typically conducted by a cross-functional team led by the purchasing function. It may involve members of the company's financial group, quality group, risk management group, manufacturing department, engineering group, among others.

The process of selecting suppliers is complex and should be based on multiple standard criteria using evaluation forms or scorecards. The following are some commonly used supplier selection criteria:

- Product and process technologies

- Reliability

- Quality

- Order system and cycle time

- Cost

- Willingness to share information

- Capacity

- Service

- Communication capability

- Location

ORGANIZATION OF PURCHASING

The way in which a purchasing department is structured is directly dependent on the way in which the company operates. There is no ideal organization for purchasing, but most companies will organize the purchasing function so as to maximize its impact, and to generate more value for the company and the end customers.

The three general organization structures presented in this text are centralized purchasing, decentralized purchasing, and a hybrid purchasing structure.

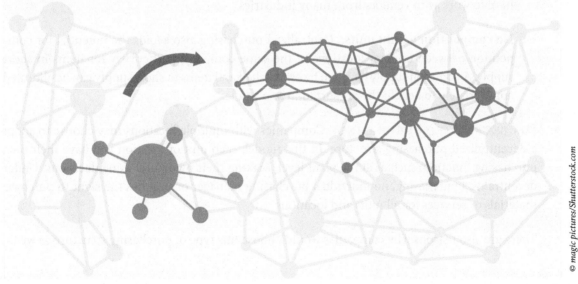

© magic pictures/Shutterstock.com

- CENTRALIZED PURCHASING: Larger companies often establish a centralized purchasing structure with all of the purchasing staff reporting to a purchasing executive such as a chief purchasing officer or chief procurement officer (CPO). The centralized purchasing organization will typically be located at the company's corporate office and make all the purchasing decisions for the whole company including for any plants or satellite offices.

  There are a number of reasons why companies would choose this type of purchasing structure.

  - **Leverage from concentrated volumes**: By having a centralized purchasing organization, the company is able to leverage the total spend when negotiating with suppliers. This should allow the purchasing organization to obtain the best price and terms from suppliers by offering them a commitment to buy in larger quantities.

  - **Control**: Centralized purchasing gives a company a higher degree of control over the purchasing process. Decentralized purchasing disperses activities across the organization, involving a greater number of people and less control of the purchasing process.

  - **Avoiding duplication**: Centralized purchasing avoids the possible duplication of roles and efforts across multiple locations. Decentralized purchasing means that purchasing personnel at multiple locations will essentially be performing the same role and potentially be purchasing the same items.

  - **Specialization**: Centralized purchasing organizations allow purchasing professionals to specialize in one area. For example, a purchasing clerk could work with vendors who provide steel products, whereas if they were in a smaller purchasing department they would have to work with vendors from many industries.

  - **No competition within units**: Centralized purchasing also avoids the potential for competition between units or locations of the same company, particularly for items in short supply. A common supply base can be established and items in short supply can be allocated appropriately to benefit the organization as a whole.

- DECENTRALIZED PURCHASING: Companies with multiple locations may choose to adopt a decentralized purchasing structure. In this model, each unit or location will have their own purchasing function, such as at the plant level, making their own purchasing decisions. Under decentralized purchasing, no individual purchasing manager or unit has the right to purchase materials or services for all units and locations.

  There are also reasons why companies would choose this type of purchasing structure as well.

- **Diverse business needs**: Decentralized purchasing may be more appropriate for companies with diverse business units having very different needs from one another, or for companies that have acquired another company and not assimilated them into their core business model.

- **Local sourcing**: Local purchasing functions will likely have better knowledge of local requirements, will frequently have closer ties to local suppliers, and may be able to obtain better pricing, better quality, and lower transportation costs.

- **Speed:** Where locations require the delivery of items at a moment's notice, the centralized purchasing model may not be appropriate. If a stockout is imminent, and/or manufacturing will be stopped, a local supplier may be able to deliver the same day, whereas centralized purchasing will likely deal with a national supplier who might not be able to offer the same response.

- **Less bureaucracy:** No heavy investment is required initially. Purchase orders can be placed quickly. The replacement of defective materials takes less time.

• HYBRID PURCHASING ORGANIZATION: Many companies have tried to adopt a mix of centralized and decentralized purchasing, where business units or locations have the purchasing responsibility for certain items, and the central purchasing organization has responsibility for other items. The two main types of hybrid purchasing organization are:

- **Centralized – Decentralized:** Typically for a large organization with centralized control. Large national contracts will be centralized at the corporate level and smaller specific items will be decentralized at the business unit or location level.

- **Decentralized – Centralized**: Typical for a large multiunit organization. There will be decentralized purchasing at the corporate level and centralized purchasing at the business unit or location level. Business units will buy all of their own materials and services and the corporate level will buy only those items needed for the corporate operations.

INTERNATIONAL PURCHASING..

International purchasing involves the worldwide search for suppliers who can meet the right quality at the right price, quantity, and delivery. It is identifying, developing, and accessing the optimal sources of supply for the business regardless of the location. Opening up the purchasing function to the global market affords a company more choices and more access to innovation, information, and technology.

There are many good reasons for a company to consider global sourcing, including:

- The opportunity to improve quality, cost, and delivery performance

- To exploit global efficiencies, such as access to low cost labor and materials; tax breaks and low trade tariffs

- To respond to insufficient domestic capacity

- To achieve access to better process and product technology

- Due to a change in the domestic business environment

- To take advantage of reciprocal trade and countertrade arrangements

Companies interested in pursuing international purchasing arrangements must develop or acquire specialized skills and knowledge to deal with international suppliers, logistics, communication, political environment, and other issues.

Some of these specialized aspects involve:

- IMPORT BROKERS: Agents licensed by the governmental regulatory authority to conduct business on behalf of importers, for a service fee. They take the burden of filling out import paperwork, and clearing products through customs barriers for importers

- IMPORT MERCHANTS: A person or company engaged in the purchase and sale of imported commodities for profit. They buy and take title to the goods being imported and then sell the goods domestically.

- TRADING COMPANIES: Buy products in one country and sell them in different countries where they have their own distribution network. Trading companies mostly work with high production volume products such as raw materials, chemicals, generic pharmaceuticals, etc. They may carry a wide variety of goods (such as from a catalog).

- TARIFFS: Duties, taxes, or customs imposed by the host country for imported or exported goods.

- NONTARIFF BARRIERS: Quotas, licensing agreements, embargoes, laws and regulations imposed on imports and exports.

- COUNTERTRADE: International trade by exchange of goods rather than by currency.

There are some potential challenges to international purchasing that companies should consider and plan for prior to adopting this strategy, including:

- The potential lack of knowledge and skills concerning international trade policies and procedures

- Awareness and cost of required tariffs and duties

- The difficulty in communicating with suppliers due to language barriers, varying time zones, working weeks, holidays

- Locating, evaluating, sourcing, and expediting in global markets

- Payments and currency management

- Longer time span for negotiations

- The potential for cultural, political, and labor problems

- Protection against product liability and quality management issues

- Potentially longer transportation lead times necessitating additional inventory

- Specific and varying documentation requirements

- Handling legal matters and the process for settling disputes

GOVERNMENT AND NONPROFIT PURCHASING ....

Government purchases are expenditures made in the private sector by all levels of government. Nonprofit purchases are expenditures made in the private sector by all types of nonprofit organizations. Public purchasing for the government and the nonprofit sector is somewhat different from private industrial purchasing and is characterized by:

COMPETITIVE BIDDING: A transparent procurement method in which bids from competing suppliers are invited by openly advertising the scope, specifications, and terms and conditions of the proposed contract as well as the criteria by which the bids will be evaluated. Competitive bidding aims at obtaining goods and services at the lowest prices by stimulating competition, and by preventing favoritism.

A **sealed bid** is a document enclosed in a sealed envelope and is submitted in response to invitation to bid.

- OPEN COMPETITIVE BIDDING: The sealed bids are opened in the presence of anyone who may wish to be present, and evaluated for award of a contract.

- CLOSED COMPETITIVE BIDDING: The sealed bids are opened in the presence of authorized personnel only.

- The contract is usually awarded to lowest priced responsive and responsible bidder.

Bidders are generally required to furnish **bonds** as incentive to ensure that the successful bidder will fulfill the contract awarded.

- **Bid bond** is a debt secured by a bidder for the purpose of providing a guarantee that the successful bidder will accept the contract once awarded. If not, the bond would be forfeited.

- **Performance bond** is a debt secured by a bidder for the purpose of providing a guarantee that the work will be on time and meet specifications.

- **Payment bonds** is a debt secured by a bidder for the purpose of providing protection against third-party liens not fulfilled by a bidder.

Some key regulations that rule government and nonprofit procurement include:

- **Federal Acquisition Streamlining Act** (1994), which removed restrictions on bids less than $100,000. Purchases less than $2,500 can be made without bidding.

- **Buy American Act** (1933) basically states that purchases (whether by the government or by third parties) using federal funds must be bought from a U.S. source if the cost of the goods from the U.S. source is not more than a specific differential above the foreign source for the goods.

- **Green purchases** involve a variety of federal, state, and local initiatives to include environmental and human health considerations when making purchases.

WORLD-CLASS PROCUREMENT

"World-class procurement organizations outperform their peers by striving to provide unique value beyond cost reduction, including becoming a trusted advisor to the business, driving supplier innovation, and focusing on risk management, according to new research from The Hackett Group, Inc."[2]

The Hackett Group's research identified five key areas where world-class organizations are adopting procurement strategies to differentiate themselves:

1. BEING A TRUSTED ADVISOR TO THE BUSINESS: Having a high level of involvement in the company's budgeting and planning cycle. They are considered valued business partners by the organization, not gatekeepers or administrators.[2]

2. DRIVING SUPPLIERS TO INNOVATE: Effective at harnessing the intellectual capital of their suppliers to bring new and innovative solutions to bear, helping to influence—not just support—the business strategy.[2]

3. PROVIDING ANALYTICS-BACKED INSIGHTS: Working closely with the business during operations planning and budgeting periods to provide predictive insights on supply markets, to the point that analytics, market intelligence, and benchmarking are offered on demand as a service to key stakeholders.[2]

4. PROTECTING THE BUSINESS FROM RISK: Have formal risk management programs that includes completing supplier risk assessments and working with finance and other stakeholders to determine the best mitigation strategy when risk exposure is identified.[2]

5. TAKING AN AGILE APPROACH TO STAFFING: Talent management sets procurement leaders apart from the pack, they provide more training and invest more in retention planning, and they pay higher salaries. They require substantially fewer FTEs than peer groups and are more productive overall.[2]

REFERENCES

[1] *APICS Dictionary* (14th ed.). (2013). Chicago, IL: APICS. www.apics.org; Westing, J. H., Fine, I. V., & Zenz, G. J. (1976). *Purchasing management: Materials in motion.* New York, NY: John Wiley & Sons Publishing.

[2] Hackett Group, Inc. (2014). How world-class procurement organizations outperform; Focus on becoming trusted advisors, driving supplier innovation. Retrieved from http://www.thehackettgroup.com/about/research-alerts-press-releases/2014/08142014-how-world-class-procurement-organizations-outperform.jsp

Chapter 6
Strategic Sourcing

CHAPTER OUTLINE

Introduction
Sourcing Strategies
Supplier Selection
Strategic Alliances
Supplier Certification Programs
Additional Sourcing Concepts
Ethics and Sustainability

INTRODUCTION ....

What Is Strategic Sourcing?

Sourcing is the process of identifying a company that provides a needed good or service. **Strategic sourcing** is a comprehensive approach for locating and sourcing <u>key suppliers</u>, which often includes the business process of analyzing the total spend by material category (see figure 6.1).

- The focus of strategic sources is on development of long-term relationships with trading partners who can help the buyer meet profitability and customer satisfaction goals.

Strategic sourcing can be further defined as an institutional procurement process; "an approach to supply chain management that formalizes the way information is gathered and used so that an organization can leverage its consolidated purchasing power to find the best possible values in the marketplace." (Rouse, 2016) "Strategic sourcing requires analysis of what an organization buys, from whom, at what price and at what volume." (Rouse, 2016) ". . . it differs from conventional purchasing because it places emphasis on the entire life-cycle of a product, not just its initial purchase price."[1]

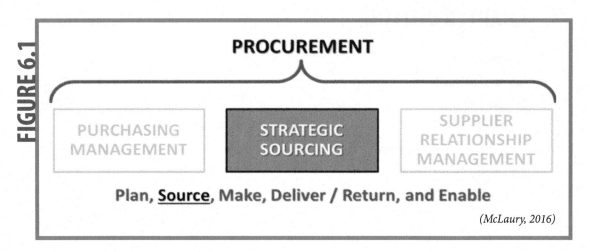

FIGURE 6.1

PROCUREMENT

PURCHASING MANAGEMENT

STRATEGIC SOURCING

SUPPLIER RELATIONSHIP MANAGEMENT

Plan, <u>Source</u>, Make, Deliver / Return, and Enable

(McLaury, 2016)

To become a world-class procurement organization companies must consider strategic sourcing to be integral to their overall strategy. There are four competencies that enable strategic sourcing and create value throughout the supply chain:

1. To meet current demand by ensuring that the goods get where they are needed, when they need to be there

2. To anticipate and meet future demand

3. To do so in a customer-driven environment

4. To manage the flow of information throughout the extended supply chain

Drivers of Strategic Sourcing

Strategic sourcing is intended to manage an organization's external resources in support of the mission, vision, and long-term goals. There are seven main drivers of strategic sourcing to consider when developing sourcing strategies:

1. Improve long-term financial performance

2. Increase customer focus

3. Improve product quality

4. Reduce the cost of materials

5. Reduce delivery cycle times (i.e., lead times)

6. Optimize the number of global suppliers (Note: for most companies, this means a reduction in the number of suppliers.)

7. Deliver more innovative products, in less time, and less expensively than competitors

Objectives of Strategic Sourcing

Following the drivers of strategic sourcing, the specific objectives of strategic sourcing surround the reduction of cost while simultaneously maintaining or improving quality:

- Improve the value-to-price relationship (i.e., achieve cost reductions while maintaining or improving quality/service)

- Understand category buying and management process, to identify improvement opportunities

- Examine supplier relationships across the entire organization

- Develop and implement multiyear contracts with standardized terms and conditions across the organization

- Leverage the entire organization's spend

- Share best practices across the organization

SOURCING STRATEGIES ....

Strategic sourcing involves managing purchasing transactions in a strategic way providing the analysis and ability to make adjustments based on price, the evaluation of supplier performance, and the overall needs of the organization.

A regular review of an organization's sourcing strategy is a must in order to achieve significant agreed upon results. The high-level sourcing strategies utilized in today's business environment include:

- INSOURCING: Producing goods or services using a company's own internal resources.

- OUTSOURCING: The traditional definition involves purchasing an item or service externally, which had been produced using a company's own internal resources previously. The term has more recently become synonymous with the concept of buying an item from an external source of supply regardless of whether the item had been produced using a company's own internal resources previously.

- SINGLE SOURCING: A sourcing strategy where there are multiple potential suppliers available for a product or service; however, the company decides to purchase from only one supplier. This is in contrast to a situation where there is only one supplier for an item (i.e., sole sourced). Sole source is not truly a strategy as there really isn't a choice, and there is very little opportunity for a company to negotiate price or service.

- MULTIPLE SOURCING: Purchasing a good or service from more than one supplier. Companies may use multiple sourcing to create competition between suppliers in order to achieve higher quality and lower price.

Strategies for Functional versus Innovative Products

When developing successful sourcing strategies companies will likely adopt different strategies for functional products versus innovative products, the differences being:

- FUNCTIONAL PRODUCTS: MRO items and other commonly low profit margin items with relatively stable demands and high levels of competition (office supplies, food staples, etc.)

  - Potential Strategy: Multiple sourcing with several reliable, low cost suppliers

- INNOVATIVE PRODUCTS: Items characterized by short product lifecycles, volatile demand, high profit margins, and relatively less competition (e.g., technology products such as the iPhone)

- Potential Strategy: Single sourcing with an innovative, high-tech, cutting edge, market leading supplier; develop a long-term partnership

A framework for sourcing strategy development can utilize the following steps (additional and more in-depth steps will be discussed later in this chapter):

1. Classify the company's products and suppliers as belonging to either the functional or innovative category.

2. Develop strategic sourcing goals and strategies for each category.

3. Create the sourcing team (typically a cross-functional team led by procurement team).

4. Develop a team strategy and communication plan.

5. Identify the targeted spend area(s) and conduct a spend analysis.

6. Gather information on supplier capabilities; use RFI.

7. Develop a supplier portfolio (i.e., a profile of each supplier in each category).

8. Develop a future state (i.e., vision of what the company wants the future to look like).

9. Conduct supplier selection and negotiation.

10. Implement supplier relationship management (SRM; see Chapter 7).

Spend Analysis

A spend analysis is the process of collecting, cleansing, classifying, and analyzing expenditure data with the purpose of decreasing procurement costs, improving efficiency, and monitoring compliance.

The basic steps for conducting a spend analysis include:

- Defining the scope

- Identifying all data sources

- Gathering and consolidating all data into one database

- Cleansing the data (finding and correcting errors) and standardizing it for easy review

- Categorizing the data

  A typical spend analysis consists of:
  - The total historic expenditure and volumes

  - Expenditures categorized by commodity and subcommodity

  - Expenditures categorized by division, department, and/or user

  - Expenditures categorized by supplier

  - Future demand projections or budgets

- Analyzing the data

  - For the best deals per supplier

  - To ensure that all purchases are from preferred suppliers

  - To reduce the number of suppliers per category

- Repeating the process on a regular schedule

General Portfolio Spend Categories

Companies can generally apportion their total spend into the following four main categories:

1. NONCRITICAL: Items that involve a low percentage of the company's total spend and involve very little supply risk

2. BOTTLENECK: Items that present unique procurement problems (where supply risk is high, availability is low, and there are only a small number of alternative suppliers)

3. LEVERAGE: Commodity items where many alternatives of supply exist and supply risk is low (Spend for these items is generally high, and there are potential procurement savings.)

4. STRATEGIC: Strategic items and services that involve a high level of expenditure and are vital to the company's success

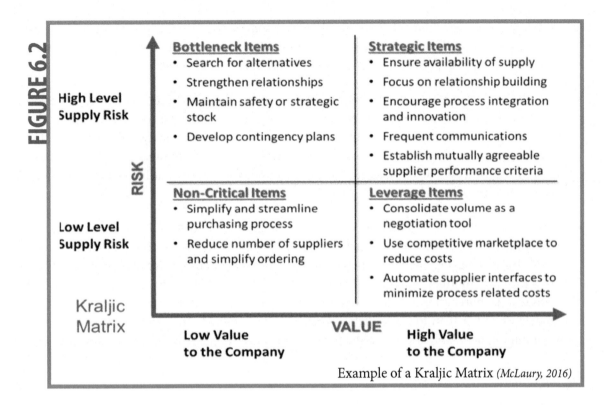

FIGURE 6.2

Bottleneck Items
- Search for alternatives
- Strengthen relationships
- Maintain safety or strategic stock
- Develop contingency plans

Strategic Items
- Ensure availability of supply
- Focus on relationship building
- Encourage process integration and innovation
- Frequent communications
- Establish mutually agreeable supplier performance criteria

Non-Critical Items
- Simplify and streamline purchasing process
- Reduce number of suppliers and simplify ordering

Leverage Items
- Consolidate volume as a negotiation tool
- Use competitive marketplace to reduce costs
- Automate supplier interfaces to minimize process related costs

High Level Supply Risk

Low Level Supply Risk

RISK

VALUE

Low Value to the Company

High Value to the Company

Kraljic Matrix

Example of a Kraljic Matrix *(McLaury, 2016)*

Sourcing Strategies by Category

Figure 6.2 is an example of a Kraljic matrix, which shows the plotting of each of the sourcing strategies, where the vertical axis is Risk, and the horizontal axis is Value, Bottleneck items and Strategic items are high risk, and Strategic items and Leverage items are high value. There are different sourcing strategies that can and should be used for each category.

- BOTTLENECK ITEMS: Two major strategies are searching for alternative sources of supply that might be able to alleviate the unique sourcing problems, and strengthening the relationship with each supplier to maximize the opportunity for success. Efforts to integrate the supplier with the company's operations may also help to resolve the supply problems. Items in this category are candidates for maintaining safety or strategic stock and also for the development of contingency plans in the event of a supply disruption.

- STRATEGIC ITEMS: Strategies to ensure the availability of supply, and encourage process integration and innovation, should help to reduce the risk of a supply disruption. Companies should develop a formal supplier relationship management program with these suppliers to build the relationship. Using value management techniques such as value engineering, reducing complexity, and early supplier involvement in product design are some of the ways that procurement can work with suppliers toward that goal. Frequent communications coupled with mutually established and agreed upon supplier performance criteria and measurement are critical.

- LEVERAGE ITEMS: The main strategy for items in this category is to consolidate all of the volumes and use the competitive marketplace to generate the lowest total cost of ownership. This is the category where procurement professionals can really use their analytical and negotiation skills to generate savings. Another aspect of the strategy may be to automate supplier interfaces to minimize process-related costs, and build longer term agreements utilizing automated payment methods to simplify the buying activity.

- NONCRITICAL ITEMS: Because items in this category are both low risk and low value, the strategy here is for procurement to reduce their level of effort and focus. The transactional costs associated with buying these items may actually exceed the purchase price of these items. These are most likely routinely purchased items which may be suitable candidates for delegating the transactional purchasing activities to users within the company based on some predetermined guidelines, rather than to use valuable procurement personnel's time to process. Simplifying, streamlining, standardizing, and reducing the number of suppliers will facilitate this strategy.

Supplier Base

A supply base is defined as "the group of suppliers from which a firm acquires goods and services."[1]

Over time as a company matures and grows, its supplier base tends to grow as well. All too frequently, companies have more suppliers than they truly need or than they can manage effectively. Managing suppliers takes time and resources, and every supplier-related activity costs money, including monitoring and reporting supplier performance, conducting supplier audits, performing site visits, maintaining up-to-date supplier information in the company database, and of course all of the transactional aspects of RFPs, RFQs, POs, invoice payments, and the like. This is one reason why a company might want to conduct a supply base rationalization program.

Supply base rationalization, or supply base optimization, involves selectively and systematically determining the right number of suppliers, with the right capabilities, to achieve the company's overall business objectives. Rationalizing or optimizing the supply base could mean either reducing or increasing the number of suppliers a company works with, as well as potentially increasing or enhancing the opportunity presented to new or existing suppliers.

The current trend is companies emphasizing long-term strategic supplier alliances consolidating volume into one or fewer suppliers, resulting in a smaller supply base. Buyer-supplier partnerships are easier to manage with a rationalized supply base and can result in:

- Reduced purchase prices

- Fewer supplier management problems

- Closer and more frequent interactions between buyer and supplier

- Greater levels of quality and delivery reliability

SUPPLIER SELECTION

Supplier selection is the process a company uses to choose a supplier. The process involves selecting the best and/or the most appropriate supplier based on an assessment of the supplier's capabilities. Selecting suppliers is a complex process and should be based on multiple criteria using formal evaluation forms or scorecards. Typical criteria used to assess suppliers includes:

- Management, organization, and strategic fit

- Reputation and references

- Amount of past business

- Reliability

- Quality systems

- Order system and cycle time (i.e., lead time)

- Cost

- Supplier's willingness to share information

- Capacity

- Service performance

- Supplier's product and process technologies

- Communication capability, both in terms of the method in which they communicate and whether they are proactive in communicating, particularly if there are issues

- Location/proximity to the company's operations

- Warranties and claim policies

The supplier selection process is usually conducted by a cross-functional team led by the procurement organization and typically includes representatives responsible for quality, finance, engineering, etc. The process can be time consuming and costly. It can involve travel to potential supplier sites, and interviews with suppliers and with the suppliers' other customers. Accordingly, evaluation and selection can take weeks or months.

How Many Suppliers Are Needed?

Determining the optimal number of suppliers to use for each good or service being purchased is not an easy task. There is no standard rule. Generally, companies should use the fewest number of suppliers that they can without increasing risk significantly.

SINGLE-SOURCE SUPPLIER STRATEGY: The following are some reasons a company may opt for a single-source supplier strategy:

- To establish a good relationship with the supplier

- To reduce quality variability

- To achieve the lowest cost, as 100% of volume will be with the single source

- To achieve transportation economies

- If the single-source supplier has a proprietary product or process

- If the volume is too small to split between multiple suppliers

With a single-source supplier strategy, a buyer is likely to experience significant bargaining power, better transparency, easier relationship management, and better supplier responsiveness. While these are valid reasons and advantages to a single-source supplier strategy, there is potentially also an increased risk of supply problems or shortages. If the single-source supplier has a problem, it could quickly result in a supply disruption for the company. Therefore, it may be preferable to keep the number of single-sourced suppliers at a minimum if possible.

MULTIPLE SOURCING SUPPLIER STRATEGY: The following are some reasons a company may opt for a multiple sourcing supplier strategy:

- If the company needs more capacity than can be accommodated by a single source

- To spread the risk of a supply disruption among multiple trading partners

- To create competition on price, delivery, and other services

- To take advantage of more sources of information

- To meet a requirement involving some special kinds of business

If a company adopts a multiple sourcing supplier strategy, the risk of a major supply disruption may be reduced. Most businesses depend on a continuity in the flow of products or services and should not underestimate the importance of reduced dependency on a single source of supply. When a disruption occurs in the supply of products or services due to quality issues, production or processing problems, capacity constraints, financial difficulties, etc., the purchasing company can be significantly impacted and potentially irreparably damaged.

When choosing between a single and a multiple sourcing supply strategy, it is not about one strategy being better than the other strategy. It is about what strategy better meets the needs of business.

Preferred Suppliers

A preferred supplier is a supplier of choice; generally one that has achieved a specific and exceptional level of performance over time as measured by a set of criteria agreed upon by both buyer and supplier. Preferred suppliers are typically trusted partners who know the buyers organization, processes, procedures, and requirements. They usually provide a higher value than their competitors and are characterized as reliable, responsive, flexible, and cost effective.

Preferred suppliers are commonly used to provide:

- Product and process technology, and expertise

- Product development and value analysis

- Information on latest trends in materials, processes, or designs

- Capacity for meeting unexpected demand

- Cost efficiency due to economies of scale

STRATEGIC ALLIANCES ....

In general terms, a strategic alliance, in the context of strategic sourcing, is an agreement between a buyer and a supplier to pursue a set of agreed upon objectives, while remaining independent organizations. These companies have decided to share information and resources to achieve a mutual benefit.

Preferred suppliers are potentially ideal candidates for a strategic alliance.

The benefits of these types of arrangements can vary, but the most basic benefits are the potential to increase revenue and profits for both parties, the potential to create a competitive advantage or block a competitor from gaining market share, to mitigate risks and ensure a continuity of supply, and to position the partners for future strategic opportunities.

A strategic alliance is a natural extension of a supplier development program in which "technical and financial assistance is given to existing and potential suppliers to improve quality and/or due date/performance."[1] Strategic alliances can be very advantageous for both the buyer and the supplier. They can result in better market penetration, access to new technologies and knowledge, and a higher return on investment. Eventually the arrangement could extend to a company's second-tier suppliers as key first-tier suppliers begin to form their own alliances.

Tapping into Strategic Supplier's Knowledge

As noted, strategic alliances can create access to previously untapped knowledge. Strategic sourcing partners offer buyers the opportunity to extend their own intellectual capabilities by involving their external partner base in their product development process. The two most common ways to accomplish this are through:

- EARLY SUPPLIER INVOLVEMENT (ESI): "The process of involving suppliers early in the product design activity and drawing on their expertise, insights, and knowledge to generate better designs in less time, and designs that are easier to manufacture with high quality."[1] These strategic supply partners become more involved in the internal operations of the buyer's company, particularly with respect to new product and process design, working with buyers to do concurrent engineering, and designing products specifically for manufacturability.

- VALUE ENGINEERING: Activities help the buyer's company to reduce costs, improve quality, and reduce new product development time. The goal is to satisfy the product's performance requirements at the lowest possible cost. This typically involves considering the availability of materials, production methods, transportation issues, limitations or restrictions, planning and organization. Benefits can include a reduction in lifecycle costs, improvement in quality, and a reduction in environmental impact, to name just a few.

Value engineering involves buyers and suppliers working together:

- Identifying the materials and other key aspects of a product

- Analyzing those materials and key aspects

- Developing alternative solutions for delivering those functions with the aim of achieving reduced costs, improved quality, and reduced development time

- Assessing the alternative solutions

- Determining the costs of the alternative solutions

- Selecting the alternatives with the highest likelihood of success for further development

Negotiating Win-Win Strategic Alliance Agreements

When negotiating an agreement, there are two basic negotiating strategies from which the parties can choose:

1. DISTRIBUTIVE NEGOTIATIONS: A process that leads to a self-interested, one-sided outcome

2. INTEGRATIVE OR COLLABORATIVE NEGOTIATIONS: A process where both sides work together to maximize the outcome or create value. A win-win result. This negotiating strategy requires open discussions and a free flow of information between the parties.

© Iconic Bestiary/Shutterstock.com

Successful integrative or collaborative negotiations start with a clearly expressed understanding of how each company wants to benefit from the collaboration. Desired benefits may or may not be readily apparent. Confirming the alignment between both parties regarding motivation, contribution, financial benefit, and the management of the alliance are essential to a successful conclusion to the agreement and to continuing success into the future. Consequently, negotiations are not about each company obtaining the most value, but more about establishing a relationship that works well for both parties.

Rewarding Supplier Performance

Another important aspect of a strong supplier alliance is implementing a supplier rewards and recognition program. Recognition of a supplier is the identification of exceptional performance, contributions, and/or capabilities.

Rewarding suppliers for outstanding performance motivates and encourages them to continue to strive for excellence in their products, services, and operations. Recognizing and rewarding suppliers strengthens and fosters strong and productive supplier relationships.

Reward incentives can include the promise of future business, some form of public recognition such as a plaque, an awards dinner, an honors ceremony, a press release, or formal communication to the supplier's senior leadership team. Recognition programs encourage performance improvements by rewarding suppliers with additional benefits, cash back for achieving performance-based objectives, and strategic or preferred supplier status.

Rewarding suppliers provides an incentive to surpass performance goals.

Pain and Gain Share Provisions

A supplier rewards and recognition program could also be reflected as part of the formal supply agreement in the form of pain and gain share provisions. Agreements could be constructed and negotiated to spell out in detail the gains (rewards) and pains (penalty) that the supplier will realize for either exceptional or poor performance. This is sometimes referred to as a "Pain and Gain Share Agreement." Both parties would mutually agree on the provisions and the positive and negative outcomes. Generally this will only be acceptable to both parties if both pain and gain provisions are included.

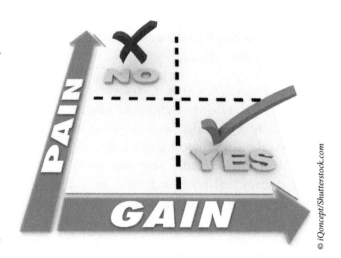

© iQoncept/Shutterstock.com

- **PAIN:** Using a penalty or punishment is a negative outcome for poor performance, cost overruns, quality problems:

    - Buyer could impose a financial penalty (i.e., fine) on the supplier for poor performance.

    - Buyer could reduce future business with the supplier for poor performance.

- Buyer could implement a bill-back amount equal to, or a percent of, the incremental costs resulting from poor performance.

- GAIN: Using a reward as a positive outcome from exceptional performance:

  - Buyer could award a financial bonus to the supplier for exceptional performance.

  - Buyer could award more business and/or longer contracts to the supplier.

  - Buyer could share a portion of any cost reductions developed by the supplier which benefit the buyer.

  - Buyer could provide access to in-house training seminars, conferences, tools and information, or other resources to the supplier.

  - Buyer could publicly recognize the supplier and/or confer a special status on the supplier such as "Preferred Supplier," "Partner," or "Supplier of the Year."

SUPPLIER CERTIFICATION PROGRAMS

One of the elements for building a strong strategic supplier partnership is having a well-defined and established supplier certification program.

Supplier certification is defined as "certification procedures verifying that a supplier operates, maintains, improves, and documents effective procedures that relate to the customer's requirements. Such requirements can include cost, quality, delivery, flexibility, maintenance, safety, and ISO quality and environmental standards."[1]

© Victor Correia/Shutterstock.com

- Supplier certification programs are used to differentiate strategic supplier alliance candidates from others.

- Companies may choose to develop <u>internal</u> certification programs, and may also require <u>external</u> certifications such as ISO 9000 / ISO 14000, as part of their overall certification process.

The following is a list of certification components that a company might consider when evaluating its suppliers for a certification program:

- "The supplier measures its quality performance

- The supplier uses parts-per-million (ppm) as its quality unit of measure, not percent defective

- The supplier has quality performance goals

- The supplier has a documented record of continuous quality improvement over several years

- The supplier's quality efforts are focused on preventing defective items from being produced rather than detecting defective items that have already been produced

- The supplier has formalized quality documentation, training programs, and the like to ensure that quality is sustainable through personnel changes

- The supplier knows its standard deviation

- The supplier can demonstrate how it uses tools to determine whether or not its processes are in control

- The supplier has a quality-related certification like ISO9001

- The supplier has implemented a leading quality improvement program like Lean, Six Sigma, or Lean Six Sigma

- The supplier has implemented a quality improvement program with its own suppliers

- The supplier has won a prestigious quality award such as the Malcolm Baldrige National Quality Award"[1]

One of the benefits of a supplier certification program is being able to reduce the amount of time and resources necessary for the buyer to conduct incoming inspections of products and materials from certified suppliers. These suppliers can be trained on the buyer's procedures and methods for testing the products or materials they supply to the buyer so that they can test these items before they are transferred to the buyer, and provide the buyer with a certificate of analysis with each shipment or lot. Buyers may then opt to only test items periodically on incoming inspection rather than with each delivery or lot, providing that the periodic testing confirms the supplier's results.

External Certifications

External certification can be very beneficial for a company, because having an independent third party verify that the products or services supplied by the company meet specific and internationally recognized requirements will add credibility. It is also worth noting that certification is actually a legal or contractual requirement in some industries.

Suppliers that are externally certified, such as "ISO 9001:2008 certified," are preferred by procurement departments because of the following:

- They have to conform to an externally defined set of standards for quality, delivery of service, etc.

- They are easier for procurement to initially qualify and periodically audit.

- Certification is done by an external register agency alleviating some of the procurement workload.

- They are open to sharing supply chain information.

- They want to build relationships with their customers.

- They have formal processes in place for continuous improvement.

- They have to be recertified every three years.

ADDITIONAL SOURCING CONCEPTS ....

The following are some additional sourcing concepts of note.

Reverse Auctions

Reverse auctions are a sourcing technique where prequalified suppliers access a website at prearranged time and date, and try to underbid competitors to win the buyer's business. The buyer makes potential sellers aware of the intent to buy a specified good or service. During the course of the actual reverse auction event, the sellers bid against one another to secure the buyer's business, driving the price to be paid for the item down.

Vendor Management Inventory

Vendor management inventory (VMI) is an inventory replenishment arrangement where the supplier directly monitors the buyer's inventory and refills the stock automatically when necessary, without the customer initiating a purchase order. VMI arrangements transfer the responsibility for managing the inventory located at a customer's facility back to the vendor (i.e., supplier, manufacturer) of that inventory based on a predetermined set of parameters. This arrangement reduces the buyer's workload and benefits both buyer and supplier.

- From the <u>buyer's</u> perspective:

  - The supplier tracks the inventories.

  - The supplier determines the delivery schedule and order quantities.

  - The buyer can take ownership at the stocking location.

  - The buyer may be able to avoid taking ownership until the material is actually being used, thereby reducing inventory carrying costs and improving cash flow.

- From the <u>supplier's</u> perspective:

  - The supplier avoids ill-advised orders from the buyer.

  - The supplier decides inventory setup and shipments.

  - The supplier has access to more information from the buy to aid in planning.

  - The supplier may have an opportunity to educate the buyer about other products or services offered by the supplier.

VMI arrangements can help to stabilize the supply chain. It reduces the risk of major disruptions that can affect all the companies that are linked directly and indirectly through the supply chain. It reduces the potential for the bullwhip effect.

Co-Managed Inventory

Co-managed inventory (CMI) is an arrangement where a specific quantity of an item is stored at the buyer's location. Once it is used, the item is replaced by the supplier, with the knowledge and approval of the buyer. In CMI, the buyer provides systems access to the supplier, and the supplier takes responsibility for managing the replenishment process in the buyer's system accordingly. The supplier reviews all of the available information and generates orders in the buyer's system. The primary difference between CMI and VMI is that in CMI the supplier is just recommending an order, which is not confirmed until and unless the buyer approves it. In VMI, the order created by the supplier is a confirmed order and the supplier is responsible to deliver the product and bill the buyer for the materials delivered.

JIT 2

The concept of JIT 2 is very similar to VMI and CMI, except that with JIT 2 a representative of the supplier is actually embedded in the buyer's organization. The employee is on the payroll of the supplier but works for the buyer and is empowered to forecast demand, monitor inventory, and place orders. The arrangement involves the buyer granting the supplier access to potentially proprietary or sensitive data. JIT 2 benefits both buyers and suppliers, from day-to-day operational improvement, to strategic advances in the structure of the supply chain organization.

ETHICS AND SUSTAINABILITY ....

As the discipline of supply chain management has been increasingly recognized for the value that it brings to an organization, supply chain professionals have been tasked with a larger role, and an evolving set of responsibilities over the years. That role has expanded to include responsibility for ensuring that not only does the company act in an ethical manner, but that it holds its supply partners to a high ethical standard as well. Companies should seek to replace suppliers who do not exhibit strong corporate morals and behave ethically. Supply partners are an extension of the company and can have a significant negative impact on the company and its reputation. There are several significant cases in the recent past where this has occurred.

Business Ethics and Ethical Sourcing

Most companies today have some type of corporate social responsibility program. Frequently these programs also require suppliers to agree to abide by a supplier code of conduct in order to be considered an approved supplier. Some key terms and concepts related to ethics include:

- CORPORATE SOCIAL RESPONSIBILITY (CSR) is the practice of business ethics.

- BUSINESS ETHICS is the application of ethical principles to business. The two main ethical approaches are:

  - UTILITARIANISM: An ethical act that creates the greatest good for the greatest number of people, and should be the guiding principle of conduct.

- RIGHTS AND DUTIES: Some actions are just right in and of themselves, regardless of the consequences. Think; Do the right thing!

- ETHICAL SOURCING is that which attempts to take into account the public consequences of organizational buying, or to bring about positive social change through organizational buying behavior. This involves the procurement organizations ensuring that the products being sourced are acquired in a responsible and sustainable way. The people involved in producing these products should be treated fairly and work in a safe environment. The environmental and societal impacts must also be considered as part of the sourcing process.

Ethical Policies

Companies that seek to create ethical policies to ensure compliance in this areas should:

- Create a supplier code of conduct and require all suppliers to formally agree to abide by the code as a condition of being an approved supplier.

- Inform suppliers of ethical sourcing expectations and create specific provisions within supplier agreements accordingly.

- Determine where all purchased goods originate and the manner in which they are made.

- Have knowledge of their suppliers' workplace principles.

- Seek independent verification of supplier compliance with ethical standards.

- Include ethics as part of their supplier performance rating system.

- Routinely report supplier compliance to key stakeholders.

Sustainable Sourcing

Sustainability is an integral part of ethical business practices. Sustainability in the supply chain is defined as the ability to meet the current needs of the supply chain without hindering the ability to meet future needs in terms of economic, environmental, and social challenges. In simple terms, do not mortgage the future for the present.

For organizations to establish and achieve a sustainable sourcing strategy they will have to set and meet strong, realistic, measurable, and achievable targets. Companies must understand their supplier's sustainability impact and initiatives, considering things like worker safety, wages, working conditions, human rights, and so forth.

Establishing a sustainable procurement process takes work and the company involved must understand the value of incorporating sustainable standards into its sourcing goals.

Sustainable Sourcing Strategies

Sustainable sourcing strategies should include elements such as:

- Growing the company through the launch of new sustainable products

- Increasing resource efficiencies which will also help to reduce costs

- Ensuring that the products or materials used meet environmental objectives for things like waste reduction, reuse, and recycling

- Linking company brands to the social consciousness of consumers

- Building intangible assets such as social and environmental responsibility; increasing consumer awareness of sustainable sourcing and sustainability (e.g., go green).

REFERENCES

[1] *APICS Dictionary* (14th ed.). (2013). Chicago, IL: APICS. www.apics.org; Rouse, M. (2016). *Strategic sourcing*. Whatsit.com. Retrieved from http://searchfinancialapplications.techtarget.com/definition/strategic-sourcing; Dominick, C. (2016). A 12-point supplier quality checklist; and Do you practice supplier quality management? Next Level Purchasing, Inc. Retrieved from http://www.nextlevelpurchasing.com/articles/supplier-quality-management.php

Chapter 7
Supplier Relationship Management

CHAPTER OUTLINE

Introduction
Successful Partnerships
Keys to Successful Partnerships
Supplier Performance Evaluation
Supplier Certification
Supplier Development
Supplier Recognition
Supplier Relationship Management Systems
Trends in Supplier Relationship Management
Summary

INTRODUCTION ....

Supplier relationship management (SRM) is the discipline of strategically planning for, and managing, all interactions with the third-party organizations that supply goods and/or services to an organization in order to maximize the value of those interactions. Most supply professionals view SRM as an organized approach to defining what they need and want from a supplier and establishing and managing the company-to-company link to obtain those needs. The focus of SRM is to develop two-way, mutually beneficial relationships with strategic supply partners delivering greater levels of innovation and competitive advantage than would be achieved by operating independently.

In many ways, SRM is similar to customer relationship management. Just as companies interact with customers, so do they interact with suppliers—negotiating contracts, purchasing, managing logistics and delivery, collaborating on product design, and more. SRM is a recognition that various interactions with suppliers are not unique and/or insular; in reality they are comprising a relationship, one that can and should be managed in a coordinated and systematic way across functional business units (the entire organizations supply chain), and continue throughout the SRM lifecycle.

Supplier relationship management starts with identification of suppliers and is followed by measuring their qualifications, understanding their performance ability, and determining their stability in the marketplace.

Supplier relationship management helps an organization work with suppliers for better performance and returns on their investment. It helps an organization to reduce their procurement expenses. It also coordinates between business processes and suppliers relationship, as seen in figure 7.1.

FIGURE 7.1

SRM seeks to improve profits and to reduce costs using tools such as:

- SOURCING ANALYTICS: Drives deep category and supplier insights by using market leading tools to process vast amounts of data

- SOURCING EXECUTION: The tactical operation of strategic sourcing performed by a procurement organization

- PROCUREMENT EXECUTION: The tactical operation of purchasing/procurement performed by a procurement organization

- PAYMENT AND SETTLEMENT

- SUPPLIER SCORECARDING: A way to track performance metrics; ccan be associated with various categories, depending on the supplier's role within your enterprise

- PERFORMANCE MONITORING: Tool that enables end users, administrators, and organizations to gauge and evaluate the performance of a given system

SRM is often a part of the rollout of strategic sourcing and is typically applied with suppliers:

- Providing high volumes of a product/service

- Providing lesser quantities of a crucial product/service

- Serving many business units of a company or organization

- Where intensive engineering, manufacturing, and/or logistics interaction is essential

SUCCESSFUL PARTNERSHIPS ....

Strong and successful supplier partnerships involve a mutual commitment between the buyer and the supplier over an extended time, to work together to the mutual benefit of both parties, sharing relevant information and the risks and rewards of the relationship. Successful partnerships rely on achieving a win-win for the buyer and supplier. This requires adopting a strategic perspective as opposed to a tactical position. A strategic perspective involves long-term thinking—that is, looking at relationships not for what's happening today, but for what you want to get out of the relationship over the long run. That makes a big difference in the approach to creating a partnership. One of the most important aspects is creating a win-win situation. If you focus on the tactical or hold a very short-term view, you will look at what's best for you regardless of whether it is best for the supplier or not. If you think strategically, you will look at not only what you need to win but also what your supplier needs to win as well. It does a company no good in the long run to just beat up on their suppliers. The company may feel that they have won in the short term, but in the long term they may lose their suppliers and do themselves more harm than good. If you want to be successful in the long run, you will need your suppliers to be successful as well. There has to be mutual benefits; both sides have to feel that there's a benefit in the relationship. If you have different strategies, different perspectives, and different goals and objectives, it's not going to work. You have to share the risks and rewards.

KEYS TO SUCCESSFUL PARTNERSHIPS ·······································

If you value your suppliers, developing partnerships with some or most of those suppliers may be very important for the future of your business. There are some keys to developing successful partnerships with your suppliers.

Building Trust

© Lictmeister/Shutterstock.com

With trust, partners are more willing to work together, find compromise solutions to problems, work toward achieving long-term benefits for both parties, and go the extra mile. SRM requires a consistent approach and defined set of behaviors to foster trust over time. It also requires new ways of collaborating with key suppliers, and actively changing existing policies and practices that can hurt collaboration and limit the potential value to be derived from supplier relationships.

No partnership is going to work if you don't trust one another. Building trust can be as easy as just laying your cards out on the table: "Here's what I need to get out of this relationship; I'm neither trying to game the system nor deceive you in any way, what I need is . . ." or "I'm willing to pay you a fair amount of money for your services, I value you as a partner, I will treat you as an extension of my organization." If you can start to work together from there, you will start to build trust. The big problem with trust is that it is lost a lot faster than it is built. You can make one misstep and then your partners won't trust you and it is extremely difficult to regain trust once it is broken. You may know that from personal experience. If you had a trusting relationship with someone and they did something that caused you to feel like they are not on your side anymore, it is very difficult to trust that person again. It is the same with organizations.

Building trust may mean that you have to make some compromises. Compromising shows partners that you are willing to work with them and that you recognize that they have needs from the partnership as well. Usually, a good relationship involves compromise on both sides. Both parties give a little bit to get a lot more out of the longer-term relationship.

Shared Vision and Shared Objectives

Strong, successful partnerships involve all parties having a shared vision and shared objectives. If a company wants to establish a strategic partnership with a supplier, then they both need to be on the same page. If the company, for example, wants to grow and expand its business, but the supplier does not share that goal or objective because the supplier wants to maintain its size and market position, the partnership is not likely to succeed.

Example:

Company N has a long-term relationship with Trucking Company K, which handles all of Company N's internal shipments between its local manufacturing facilities and internal warehouses. Trucking Company K also handles shipments going to and from the local airport and ocean port. Company N approaches Company K saying, "You are a great partner, and we would like to have you start to do some of our long-haul trucking, taking our product out to the ultimate customers in addition to handling our local short haul transportation. It is a very expensive product, but we trust you." Trucking Company K responds, "Well, thank you very much for your confidence and trust in our company, but we don't have the capability to handle your long-haul trucking requirements, and that is not the business we want to be in. We don't want to develop into a long-haul trucker, we want to remain in the short-haul business." Clearly, the two companies did not share the same vision or the same objectives. Trucking Company K may be a great partner, but didn't want to expand and evolve its business. If you don't have the same vision, and you don't have the same objectives, then you're not going to be able to build or expand on an existing partnership.

Personal Relationships

Most good long-term business relationships start out with personal relationships between individuals. Companies come together through people and it is these people that need to build the relationship between the companies. Developing a relationship on a personal level between company counterparts will potentially facilitate the process of developing a long-term successful partnership between the companies. If you are going to share information and negotiate, it helps if you get to know your counterpart and begin to build some trust with them. It is the people who communicate and make things happen in any strategic partnership.

© Texelart/Shutterstock.com

Mutual Benefits and Needs

Clearly, if both parties in a potential relationship don't see a way to have their needs met or if they don't both see the benefits of the relationship, one or both will not value the relationship and it is not likely to succeed, or maybe even to begin. Partnership should result in a win-win situation, which can only be achieved if both companies have compatible needs. An alliance is much like a marriage, and if only one party is happy, then the marriage (i.e., alliance) is not likely to last.

Commitment and Top Management Support

Partnerships are more likely to be successful when top management of both companies is actively supporting the partnership. That support must flow down through the ranks of managers and staff to ensure everyone understands the potential benefits to be derived. Having the support of senior management will facilitate the process of securing resources, funding, and decision making related to the partnership, making it easier to operate and move the partnership forward. In addition, as issues arise which need the attention of senior management on either side of the partnership, having their buy-in and support

© iDraw/Shutterstock.com

from the start will also help to facilitate and ease the process of obtaining their decisions or approval to resolve issues.

Change Management

Organizations are facing faster, more complex, more interdependent, and more cross-functional change than ever before. Changes in business and business relationships occur frequently and sometimes in unanticipated ways. Any relationship or partnership will inevitably face the need to make changes. If the change is not managed well, it has the potential to derail the partnership. Therefore, having a formal and robust change management process, which both parties have agreed upon in advance, is critical to the long-term health of the relationship. Applying change management enables organizations in a partnership to deliver results on each change more effectively and build competencies that grow the partnership's capacity to handle more changes.

Information Sharing and Lines of Communication

Communication is a big part of a supplier relationship—any relationship for that matter. A strong communications plan that considers how best to share and distribute information among, within, and between partners is a necessary part of good partnership management. The frequent sharing of information and having open lines of communication fosters an ongoing dialogue, which is so important because it helps to reduce the risk of assumptions and encourages partners to stay focused on their shared vision.

© 6kor3does/Shutterstock.com

Within a supplier partnership, two main communications strategies should be considered. The first is a plan to share information about the partnership internally, within your own organization and with your supply partners. With a good internal communications strategy in place, you can then reach out externally to begin to build and share your message in hopes of successfully implementing your partnership's goals and objectives. Partners should collaborate in planning their communications strategies at the beginning of the partnership, considering each other's policies, procedures, needs, and objectives.

Most companies will set up both formal and informal communication. Formal communication, for example, would be to have a regular interval review meeting with the supplier. The partners meet and discuss items on a set agenda, talking about what's happening in their businesses, what new products are planned for launch, new services and new markets, reviewing performance, and discussing issues and potential resolutions. Informal communication, for example, would be if something happens in the day-to-day operation and someone at the organization where the activity is happening needs to notify someone at the other organization quickly. What develops is an informal communication chain primarily between individuals at the operations level of both organizations who then determine if something needs to be more formally communicated. Informal communications may go a long way toward building the relationship. If both parties know that the other is going to notify them promptly and honestly if something happens, then trust will be maintained, and these types of ad hoc communications generally take place informally.

Capabilities

For a supplier relationship to be effective and successful, suppliers must have the right technology and capabilities to meet the buyers cost, quality, and delivery requirements in a timely manner.

In the example introduced earlier under "Shared Vision and Shared Objectives," Trucking Company K, who was handling all the internal transportation for Company N, didn't have the capability to become a long-haul trucker for Company N, and didn't want to develop that capability. Without this capability, the relationship will not evolve beyond the present. Company N will want to develop a supplier relationship with a supplier who has the desired capability and this may even alter the current relationship with Company K.

If a company chooses to partner with a supplier based on its needs and the supplier's current capabilities, and does not consider whether the supplier's capabilities are in line with the company's long-term strategy, it may find that the supplier is not capable of supporting its needs in the long term. If a company, for example, is planning to expand its business into a new market that is projected to increase volume requirements from a supplier, and the supplier does not have the capability to meet the new volume requirements, the company is not likely to achieve its expansion goal through this partnership.

A supplier's capability is an essential aspect of the health and success of any buyer-supplier relationship.

Continuous Improvement

"The act of making incremental, regular improvements and upgrades to a process or product in the search for excellence."[1]

Continuous improvement is an ongoing effort to improve products, services, or processes. These efforts can seek incremental improvement over time or breakthrough improvement all at once. Making a series of small improvements over time results in the elimination of waste in a system, making the system more efficient and cost effective.

FUNDAMENTALS OF SUPPLY CHAIN MANAGEMENT

Continuous improvement should be an integral part of the SRM process and evolution. Buyers and suppliers must be willing to continuously improve their processes and capabilities in meeting customer requirements.

The process commonly utilized in continuous improvement is: plan, do, check, act.

- PLAN: Identify an opportunity and plan for change.

- DO: Implement the change on a small scale.

- CHECK: Use data to analyze the results of the change and determine whether it made a difference.

- ACT: If the change was successful, implement it on a wider scale and continuously assess your results. If the change did not work, begin the cycle again.

© My Porfolio/Shutterstock.com

Other methods of continuous improvement often considered are Six Sigma, LEAN, and total quality management, which emphasize employee involvement and teamwork, measuring and systematizing processes, and reducing defects and cycle times.

Performance Metrics

Performance metrics are quantifiable indicators used to assess how well an organization or business is achieving its desired objectives. These measures are typically tied to an organization's strategy. Measures related to quality, cost, delivery, and flexibility are generally used to evaluate suppliers. Metrics should be (1) understandable, (2) easy to measure, and (3) focused on real value-added results. The best performance measures are S.M.A.R.T (specific, measurable, achievable, relevant, and time oriented).

When evaluating suppliers, a multicriteria approach is best, as it gives the company a better overall picture of the supplier's performance. For simplicity purposes, it is also preferable to build these measurement targets around the end goals that are being sought (price, cost, quality, specific logistics details, order cycle times, lead time, etc.) rather than on the means or subcomponent activities that add up to accomplishing the end goal. For example, an order cycle time target has within it an order receipt time, an order processing time, and order filling time, and a transportation transit time, which are all means or subcomponent measures. Avoid over-requiring means or subcomponent measurements of suppliers, and focus instead on measuring the supplier against the end goal, which is what's really important.

An important performance metric related to SRM is the <u>total cost of ownership (TCO)</u>. In supply chain management, the total cost of ownership of the supply delivery system is the sum of all the costs associated with every activity of the supply stream. The main insight that TCO offers to the supply chain manager is the understanding that the acquisition cost is often a very small portion of the total cost of ownership. TCO is made up of <u>all</u> costs associated with the acquisition, use, and maintenance of a good or service, which not only must be considered today, but over the life of the product. For this reason, TCO is sometimes called "lifecycle cost analysis."

It is important to actively monitor a supplier's performance and provide visibility and feedback on supplier performance at each stage of the evaluation process.

Relevant metrics include:

- Supplier price and cost performance

- Product receipt quality

- Delivery performance

- Contractual and standard compliance

- Financial stability

- Participation in product development

- Cooperativeness in third-party production management

- Support of both ethics and sustainable practices

SUPPLIER PERFORMANCE EVALUATION

Successful companies embrace their suppliers, viewing them as partners in helping to grow the business. Making sure that this is a mutually beneficial partnership will impact the price you are negotiating today and the quality of service you get in the future. Supplier performance evaluation against a set of mutually agreeable criteria can help to ensure that both parties in the relationship know exactly what is expected, and if expectations are being met. If done well, this will eliminate ambiguity and confusion.

At the start of the supplier relationship, determine what characteristics a supplier needs to have, demonstrate, or maintain to continue doing business with your company. Create specific performance criteria for tracking and evaluating your suppliers on a regular basis (monthly, quarterly, and/or annually).

Along with developing SRM performance metrics, it is best to ensure value measurement is established and put in place as well. A suggested tool for monitoring performance and identifying areas for improvement is the joint, two-way performance scorecard. A scorecard should include a combination of quantitative and qualitative measures, including how key participants perceive the quality of the relationship. These key performance indicators (KPIs) are shared between customer and supplier and reviewed jointly, reflecting the fact that the relationship is two way and collaborative, and that strong performance on both sides is required for it to be successful.

One method of evaluating the performance of key suppliers is the weighted-criteria evaluation system, which should consist of the following components:

1. Select the key dimensions of performance mutually acceptable to both customer and supplier and follow the agreed method of evaluation.

2. Assign a weight to each dimension.

3. Monitor and collect supplier performance data.

4. Evaluate the actual performance of the supplier for each dimension on a scale from 0 to 100.

5. Multiply the dimension rating by the weight for that rating, for each dimension, and then sum the overall score.

6. Classify suppliers based on their overall score:

   – Certified, Preferred, Acceptable, Conditional, Developmental, Unacceptable—according to a criteria scale that the company finds appropriate

7. Audit and perform ongoing certification review.

Figure 7.2 is an example of a high-level outline of the criteria categories in a weighted-criteria evaluation system.

Follow-up actions to take with suppliers based on their performance category:

1. PREFERRED: Work with these suppliers in maintaining a competitive position and on new product development.

2. ACCEPTABLE: Require a plan from these suppliers outlining how they will achieve Preferred status.

3. DEVELOPMENTAL: Require corrective actions from these suppliers on how they will achieve Acceptable status. Look for alternative suppliers if these do not achieve acceptability within a fixed period of time (e.g., three months).

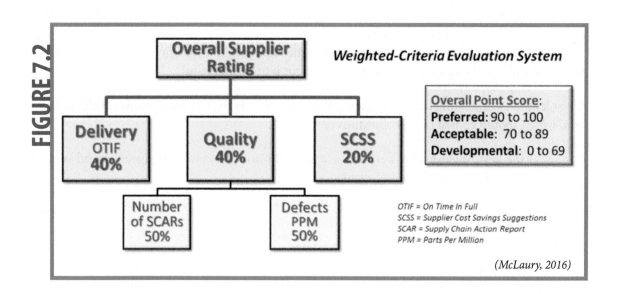

FIGURE 7.2

Overall Supplier Rating

Weighted-Criteria Evaluation System

Overall Point Score:
Preferred: 90 to 100
Acceptable: 70 to 89
Developmental: 0 to 69

Delivery
OTIF
40%

Quality
40%

SCSS
20%

Number of SCARs
50%

Defects
PPM
50%

OTIF = On Time In Full
SCSS = Supplier Cost Savings Suggestions
SCAR = Supply Chain Action Report
PPM = Parts Per Million

(McLaury, 2016)

FIGURE 7.3

Performance Measure	Rating	x	Weight	=	Final Value
Quality Defects (PPM)	90		0.25		22.50
Delivery OTIF	85		0.20		17.00
Cost	80		0.15		12.00
Responsiveness	95		0.10		9.50
Innovation	85		0.10		8.50
Corporate Social Responsibility	90		0.10		9.00
Customer Complaints	90		0.10		9.00
Total Score			1.00		87.50

(McLaury, 2016)

Based on the criteria established earlier in this example, the supplier in figure 7.3 would be in the Acceptable category, and the company should work with this supplier on areas in need of improvement to become a Preferred supplier.

SUPPLIER CERTIFICATION ....

SUPPLIER CERTIFICATION: "Certification procedures verifying that a supplier operates, maintains, improves, and documents effective procedures that relate to the customer's requirements. Such requirements can include cost, quality, delivery, flexibility, maintenance, safety, and ISO quality and environmental standards."[1]

One of the key reasons that a company might certify a supplier is to eliminate or minimize incoming inspections, saving the company time and money. By certifying a supplier to provide the quality testing on the product(s) it supplies, the company is transferring that responsibility to the supplier, which requires trust and a strong partnership.

Training and developing supply partners to consistently meet supplier certification criteria is important to achieve and maintain a supplier certification.

Benefits of Supplier Certification

The typical benefits of a supplier certification program include:

- Building long-term relationships

- Reducing time spent on incoming inspections

- Decreasing the supplier base, because if a company develops a strong relationship with a supplier(s) and certifies the supplier, the risk to the continuity of supply becomes lower, and the company will not likely need as many suppliers as a result

- Recognizing excellence

Criteria Used in Internal Certification Programs

The typical criteria in a supplier certification program includes (but is not limited to):

- No incoming product lot rejections (e.g., less than 0.5% defective) for a specified time period

- No incoming nonproduct rejections (e.g., late delivery) for a specified time period

- No significant supplier production-related negative incidents for a specified time period

- ISO 9000 / Q 9000 certified or successfully passing a recent, onsite quality system evaluation

- Mutually agreed-upon set of clearly specified quality performance measures

- Fully documented process and quality system with cost controls and continuous improvement capabilities

- Supplier's processes stable and in control

External Certification: International Organization for Standards

The International Organization for Standardization (ISO) is the world's largest developer of voluntary international standards. It was founded in 1947, and has since then published more than 21,000 international standards covering almost all aspects of technology and business. Today, the ISO has members from 163 countries and about 150 people working full time for the Central Secretariat in Geneva, Switzerland.

Organizations that become ISO certified and request and receive written permission from the ISO can display the ISO logo. ISO certification is highly sought after in the business world as it represents achieving and maintaining a stand of excellence verified by an independent third-party organization.

Two ISO standards commonly used in supplier certification programs are:

ISO 9000

- A series of management and quality standards in design, development, production, installation, and service.

- Companies wanting to sell in the global market will want to seek ISO 9000 certification.

The following are eight quality management principles on which the ISO 9000 series quality management system standards are based:

1. Customer focus—understand current and future customer needs

2. Leadership—establish unity of purpose and direction of the organization

3. Involvement of people—people are the essence of an organization

4. Process approach—a desired result is achieved through a managed process

5. Systems approach to management—managing interrelated processes

6. Continual improvement—performance improvement is a permanent objective

7. Factual approach to decision making—decisions are based on facts and data

8. Mutually beneficial supplier relationship—interdependent benefits create value for both an organization and its suppliers.

ISO 14000

- A family of standards for environmental management

- The benefits include reduced energy consumption, environmental liability, waste and pollution, and improved community goodwill.

SUPPLIER DEVELOPMENT

Supplier development is the technical and financial assistance given to existing and potential suppliers to improve quality and/or due date performance. In simpler terms, it can be described as a buyer's activities to improve a supplier's capabilities. A supplier's knowledge of, and technology used to produce, the commodity they supply can be leveraged through supplier development initiated by the manufacturer to reduce costs and lower project risks.

Supplier development programs should be designed to achieve:

- Lower supply chain total cost

- Increased profitability for all supply chain participants

- Increased product quality

- Near-perfect on-time delivery at each point in the supply chain

A supplier development program must be aimed at improving suppliers performance, not bullying them into charging less or simply auditing and rewarding them. Supplier development is all about providing suppliers with what they need to be successful in the supply chain.

Two of the most important functions of a supplier development program are:

- Providing information about products, expected sales growth, etc. Poor communication and a lack of information translates into additional costs (usually in the form of just-in-case inventory). Suppliers need to become extensions of their customers.

- Training suppliers in the application of LEAN and Six Sigma / quality tools. Asking suppliers to lower their price without giving them the knowledge on how to lower their costs (through LEAN implementation, for example) is not sustainable in the long term. This tactic will drive suppliers out of business, which goes against the purpose of supplier development.

The typical approach to supplier development is based on the following process steps:

1. Identify <u>critical</u> products and services.

2. Identify <u>critical</u> suppliers.

3. Form a cross-functional team internally to work with the supplier(s).

4. Meet with the top management at the supplier(s) to obtain their support and involvement.

5. Identify key development needs and projects.

6. Define details of the agreement and the action plan.

7. Monitor the status of the projects / action plan and modify strategies as necessary.

With a robust supplier development program, companies can establish trust through a heightened commitment to their supply partners.

SUPPLIER RECOGNITION

A supplier recognition program is just what it sounds like—a program to recognize suppliers who achieve the high performance standards necessary to meet customer expectations.

The success of the business can depend on the quality and performance of the company's suppliers. Therefore, it is always a good practice for a company to have innovative supplier recognition programs in order to recognize their achievements and reward them for their exceptional performance and services. There are several key benefits of such programs that make them valuable for a business organization.

- MOTIVATE SUPPLIERS TO PERFORM BETTER: Effective programs that recognize and reward suppliers for their performance can motivate them to continue to excel in terms of their quality, pricing, and delivery commitments. In a highly competitive business environment, strong and motivated suppliers can be a crucial competitive advantage for a business. Therefore, the company must take care to develop and nurture its supplier network with innovative recognition and reward schemes.

- HELP TO IMPROVE SUPPLIER LOYALTY AND COMMITMENT: In today's competitive environment, supplier loyalty cannot be taken for granted. Reputed suppliers are always in demand from a number of competitors, and their supply capacity is limited. Therefore, the business organization needs to ensure that it continues to receive privileged support from its key suppliers. Supplier support is important to ensure that customer delivery commitments are maintained. When there is a peak demand for the company's product, it may fail to exploit the market opportunity fully if it does not have adequate supplier support to meet that demand in the peak season.

- ENCOURAGE SUPPLIERS TO ADAPT TO THE COMPANY'S CULTURE: If the company treats its suppliers as a part of the family and engages in supplier recognition programs periodically, it can help to bring the suppliers closer to the corporate values, ethics, and principles of the company. They tend to identify themselves with the values and policies of the organization, and adapt to its culture more easily. This helps to consolidate the relationships with suppliers for the long run. It also fosters a better understanding of each other's needs and creates a win-win situation for both parties.

- HELPS TO CREATE ENTRY BARRIERS FOR COMPETITORS: Strong and mutually rewarding relationships with suppliers can lead to the creation of stiffer entry barriers for new competitors. If the suppliers trust the company, they may like to sign deals of exclusivity with the company for certain crucial components. The company can give them a buyback assurance for their entire production capacity. In such a situation, it becomes difficult for too many competitors to enter the business if they do not have access to critical supply sources.

- ENCOURAGES SUPPLIER PARTICIPATION IN PRODUCT INNOVATION: Recognition to suppliers also brings about their enthusiasm to work closely with the company on new product development. A number of products require a close interaction and cooperation between the company and the suppliers during the development stages. Involvement of suppliers from an early stage helps to achieve the lowest costing and minimizes quality issues in the long run. Therefore, recognition of the value that a supplier can bring to an organization is important to achieve the overall organizational objectives.

Companies should recognize and celebrate the achievements of their best suppliers.

- A simple thank you goes a long way to show appreciation. Providing a recognition letter of appreciation (often supported by a wall plaque) is a good way to start a recognition program.

- Companies can establish supplier awards. Award winners exemplify true partnerships, continuous improvement, organizational commitment, and excellence.

- Award-winning suppliers serve as role models for other suppliers and motive them to strive to achieve the award.

A properly developed and active supplier recognition program can and will make major contributions to the organization, its suppliers, and its customers and stakeholders. If a company is going to keep and utilize suppliers, there should be a motivation plan that reaches them. Future success depends on the supply chain; therefore, the supplier recognition program should support building a better and more competitive supply chain.

SUPPLIER RELATIONSHIP MANAGEMENT SYSTEMS ....

When considering development of a supplier relationship program there are several technologies available to support development. The key is to ensure that the system(s) being considered can in fact gather and track a supplier's performance data across all business units and/or locations.

The reason for, and a benefit of, a system is to provide a more comprehensive and objective view of supplier performance, which in turn can be used when making sourcing decisions. Such a system will also help in identifying and addressing supplier performance issues. It is important to recognize that an SRM system can only be implemented in line with other necessary business process changes. The SRM system is part of the process, not the whole process by itself.

The following are five key points to consider in the development and implementation of an SRM system:

1. Automation is meant to handle routine transactions.

2. Integration spans multiple departments, processes, and software applications.

3. Visibility of information and clear and concise process flows are vital.

4. Collaboration occurs through information sharing.

5. Optimization of processes and decision making are necessary.

Based on the technology and methods now available to assist in the evaluation and certification process, an organization will find it easier to make better, faster, and more informed decisions about potential suppliers. Systems can enhance the process; however, training and understanding of the system are critically important. Implementing simple systems is still a better value and provides a greater success rate than implementing complicated (often expensive) systems. The key to any system is to ensure that the staff has agreed to the system and its abilities, and that the information that it will yield will in fact be useful to all parties involved both at the supplier and organizational levels.

TRENDS IN SUPPLIER RELATIONSHIP MANAGEMENT ....

1. CLOSE ALIGNMENT OF SOURCING AND NEGOTIATION WITH SUPPLIER RELATIONSHIP MANAGEMENT

   Many companies are determining their supplier negotiation strategies by tying them to their category management strategy, and to what type of relationship and goals they have with the supplier.

2. FOCUS ON CROSS-FUNCTIONAL ENGAGEMENT

   SRM success depends on internal relationship management as much as external relationship management.

   Strategic SRM requires coordination and alignment with suppliers, and with internal functions. Mixed messages cause supplier confusion, compromised trust, missed opportunities, inefficiencies, increased risk, and lost leverage.

   A best practice cross-functional governance structure for strategic supplier relationships involves SRM teams at both the company and supplier levels, each led by a relationship manager, who along with executive sponsors from both organizations, form a steering committee to lead the process.

3. FOCUS ON INNOVATION

Customers and suppliers work with each other regularly or often on innovation projects. Companies that engage in more innovation with suppliers report higher ROI from their efforts. Companies estimating ROI from innovation from/with their suppliers report much higher results than from internal innovation efforts.

4. INVESTMENT IN PEOPLE AND "SOFT SKILLS"

Treat suppliers with the courtesy and respect due all people in all interactions. Be candid, and able to disagree (even forcefully), without being disagreeable. Hold <u>both</u> sides to the same standards. Actively search out opportunities for mutual benefit. Actively seek to cultivate mutual trust.

5. MORE ROBUST MEASUREMENT

Benefits of strategic partnerships with suppliers are numerous.

For customers:

- Preferred access to the supplier's best people

- Increased operating efficiencies

- Lower costs

- Improved quality

- Enhanced service

- Influence over supplier investments and technology roadmaps

- Preferred access to supplier ideas

- Increased innovation from and with suppliers, leading to lower costs and incremental revenue

- Sustainable competitive advantage

For suppliers:

- Greater visibility into customer purchasing plans

- Increased operating efficiencies

- Longer term customer commitments; greater predictability of future business

- Increased scope of business and revenue

- Lower costs of sales; increased margins

- Opportunities to develop, pilot, and showcase innovative solutions

- Deeper insights into customer strategy and plans

- Ability to align investments leading to increased ROIC

- Sustainable competitive advantage

SUMMARY

- Supplier relationship management (SRM) is the discipline of strategically planning for, and managing, all interactions with the third-party organizations that supply goods and/or services to an organization in order to maximize the value of those interactions. Supplier relationship management helps an organization work with suppliers for better performance and returns on their investment.

- Strong and successful supplier partnerships involve a mutual commitment between the buyer and the supplier over an extended time, to work together to the mutual benefit of both parties, sharing relevant information and the risks and rewards of the relationship. This requires adopting a strategic perspective as opposed to a tactical position.

- The keys to developing successful partnerships with your suppliers are:

  - Building trust

  - Having a shared vision and shared objectives

  - Building personal relationships

- Identifying mutual benefits and needs

- Securing commitment and top management support

- Managing change

- Sharing information and maintaining open lines of communication

- Understanding suppliers capabilities

- Implementing a continuous improvement program

- Establishing performance metrics

- Successful companies embrace their suppliers, viewing them as partners in helping to grow the business. Making sure that this is a mutually beneficial partnership will impact the price you are negotiating today and the quality of service you get in the future. Supplier performance evaluation against a set of mutually agreeable criteria can help to ensure that both parties in the relationship know exactly what is expected, and if expectations are being met.

  - One method of evaluating the performance of key suppliers is the weighted-criteria evaluation system.

- The main reason for supplier certification is for the company to eliminate or minimize incoming inspections, saving the company time and money. Companies can implement internal or external certifications or a combination of both. One external certification partner commonly used in industry is the International Organization for Standards (ISO).

  - ISO 9000 is a series of management and quality standards in design, development, production, installation, and service.

  - ISO 14000 is a family of standards for environmental management.

- Supplier development is the technical and financial assistance given to existing and potential suppliers to improve quality and/or due date performance. In simpler terms, it can be described as a buyer's activities to improve a supplier's capabilities.

- A supplier recognition program is established to recognize suppliers who achieve the high performance standards necessary to meet customer expectations. It is always a good practice for a company to have innovative supplier recognition programs in order to recognize their achievements and reward them for their exceptional performance and services.

- The reason for, and a benefit of, an SRM system is to provide a more comprehensive and objective view of supplier performance, which in turn can be used when making a sourcing decisions. Such a system will also help in identifying and addressing supplier performance issues.

- The current trends in supplier relationship management are:

  - Close alignment of sourcing and negotiation with supplier relationship management

  - Focus on cross-functional engagement

  - Focus on innovation

  - Investment in people and "soft skills"

  - More robust measurement

REFERENCES

1 *APICS Dictionary* (14th ed.). (2013). Chicago, IL: APICS. www.apics.org; Influx Connect. (n.d.). A robust supplier incentive program. Retrieved from http://influxconnect.com/?q=node/1146

MAKE

Chapter 8

Operations Management with LEAN and Six Sigma

CHAPTER OUTLINE

Introduction

Manufacturing Strategies

Total Cost of Manufacturing

LEAN and Six Sigma

Introduction to LEAN

Key Elements of LEAN Manufacturing

Introduction to Six Sigma

Six Sigma Methodology

Six Sigma Training and Certification Levels

Total Quality Management

Quality Gurus

Voice of the Customer

Cost of Quality

Quality Tools

Statistical Process Control

Acceptance Sampling

Implementing LEAN and Six Sigma

INTRODUCTION ....

Operations Management

Operations management refers to the design, execution, and control of the operations that convert resources into desired goods and services, aligned with the company's business strategy. In simple terms, it is the business function responsible for managing the process to create goods and services. Major activities in operations management beyond product creation often include, product development, managing purchases, inventory control, production operations, quality control, storage, and logistics. The focus is on the efficiency and effectiveness of processes including the measurement and analysis of those processes. The goal of operations management is not only to convert materials and labor into goods and services as efficiently as possible, but also control costs to maximize the profit of the company. The nature of how operations management is carried out varies by company and depends on the nature of the products or services in the portfolio.

In this text we will specifically focus on the operations management areas of manufacturing strategies, LEAN manufacturing, and Six Sigma.

MANUFACTURING STRATEGIES ....

Companies must develop a manufacturing strategy that suits the type(s) of products that they produce, their customers' expectations, and their strengths. Manufacturing strategies can vary significantly depending on the product and/or the customer requirements. Developing a manufacturing strategy that suits a company's strengths is essential for establishing and maintaining an effective supply chain.

In this section we will review four key manufacturing strategies; make-to-stock (MTS), make-to-order (MTO), assemble-to-order (ATO), and engineer-to-order (ETO). We will also review the implications to customer delivery lead time with each of these manufacturing strategies.

- MAKE-TO-STOCK (MTS): "A production environment where products can be, and usually are, finished before receipt of a customer order. Customer orders are typically filled from existing stocks, and production orders are used to replenish those stocks."[1]

  - Make-to-stock means to manufacture products for stock based on demand forecasts. The more accurate the forecast is, the less likely excess inventory will be created, and the less likely a stockout will occur. Therefore, the critical issue is how to forecast demands accurately.

- Most daily necessities such as foods, sundries, and textiles are MTS-type products.

- One issue of MTS is the potential to have excess inventory. Companies that operate a MTS model struggle to make the correct product at the correct time in the correct quantities.

- MTS features economies of scale, large volumes, long production runs, low variety, and multiple distribution channels.

- MAKE-TO-ORDER (MTO): "A production environment where a good or service can be made after receipt of a customer's order. The final product is usually a combination of standard items and items custom-designed to meet the special needs of the customer."[1]

  - The MTO strategy only manufactures the end product once the customer places the order, creating additional wait time for the consumer to receive the product but allowing for more flexible customization.

  - The MTO strategy relieves the problems of excessive inventory that is common with the traditional MTS strategy.

  - MTO is not appropriate for all types of products. It is appropriate for highly configured products such as computer servers, aircraft, ocean vessels, bridges, automobiles, or products that are very expensive to keep in inventory.

  - MTO relies on relatively small quantities, but more complexity.

- ASSEMBLE-TO-ORDER (ATO): "A production environment where a good or service can be assembled after receipt of a customer's order. The key components (bulk, semi-finished, intermediate, subassembly, fabricated, purchased, packing, and so on) used in the assembly or finishing process are planned and usually stocked in anticipation of a customer order. Receipt of an order initiates assembly of the customized product. This strategy is useful where a large number of end products (based on the selection of options and accessories) can be assembled from common components."[1]

  - ATO is a hybrid strategy between a MTS strategy where products are fully produced in advance, and the MTO strategy where products are manufactured once the order has been received. The ATO strategy attempts to combine the benefits of both strategies—that is, getting products into customers' hands quickly while allowing for the product to be customizable.

  - The ATO strategy requires that the basic parts for the product are already manufactured but not yet assembled. Once an order is received, the parts are assembled quickly and sent to the customer.

- ATO is when base components are made, stocked to a forecast, but products are not assembled until the customer order is received

- ENGINEER-TO-ORDER (ETO): "Products whose customer specifications require unique engineering design, significant customization, or new purchased materials. Each customer order results in a unique set of part numbers, bills of material, and routings."[1]

  - The essence of ETO is building a unique product every time. There may be components that are common from one product to another, but not in the same quantity as in repetitive manufacturing.

  - It is a more dramatic evolution of a MTO supply chain.

  - The cost of poor quality can be very high with an ETO strategy. The warranty costs and the cost of rework to replace an item in a complex assembly can have a serious negative effect on profit margins. Quality must be part of the entire process, and not just part of purchasing and manufacturing—the typical focus of a repetitive manufacturer.

  - ETO is used when products are unique and extensively customized for the specific needs of individual customers

The choice of strategy is the major determining factor in the **total cycle time** or **lead time** the customer experiences.

As shown in figure 8.1, each manufacturing strategy involves completion of different aspects of the supply chain prior to receiving a customer order, and accordingly, the customer will experience different lead times depending on which manufacturing strategy has been established.

- MTS: The product is already produced and available in the warehouse when the customer order is received, so the customer will only experience the customer delivery lead time.

- ATO: The product design is complete and the components/materials have already been procured when the customer order is received, so the customer will experience the manufacturing (e.g., assembly) and customer delivery lead times.

- MTO: The product design is the only element complete when the customer order is received, so the customer will experience the procurement, manufacturing, and customer delivery lead times.

- ETO: Since no supply chain elements have been completed when the customer order is received, the customer will experience the full cumulative supply chain lead time.

216

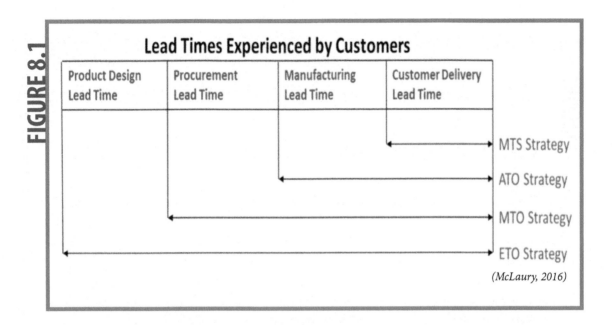

(McLaury, 2016)

Manufacturing Strategies for Manufacturing Processes

There are four basic manufacturing processes from which companies can choose to produce their product(s) depending on various factors, including the level of customization required by the customer, the type of product being produced, complexity, volume, and cost. Each of these manufacturing processes aligns more closely with one or two specific manufacturing strategies. Figure 8.2 summarizes these four manufacturing processes.

- JOB SHOP: "A type of manufacturing process used to produce items to each customer's specifications. Production operations are designed to handle a wide range of product designs and are performed at fixed plant locations using general-purpose equipment."[1] Job shops produce small lots of a variety of products, which require a unique setup and sequence of process steps to create a custom product for each customer.

  - Characteristics: A job shop manufacturing process is characterized as being highly flexible, with a large variety of products, very long lead times, low volumes, low labor requirements, low fixed costs, but high variable costs.

  - Examples: Metal fabrication shops, print shops, custom cabinet making

  - Manufacturing Strategies: ETO or MTO are the manufacturing strategies that are most closely aligned with the job shop process.

FIGURE 8.2

Manufacturing Process	Flexibility	Product Variety	Volume	Fixed Costs	Variable Costs	Lead Time	Manufacturing Strategy
Job Shop	Highly Flexible	Very High	Very Low	Low	High	Very long	ETO / MTO
Batch	Somewhat Flexible	High	Low	Moderate	Moderate	Long	MTO / ATO
Line Flow	Somewhat Inflexible	Limited	High	Moderate	Moderate	Short	ATO / MTS
Continuous Flow	Highly Inflexible	Very Limited	Very High	High	Low	Very short	MTS

(McLaury, 2016)

- **BATCH:** "A type of manufacturing process used to produce items with similar designs and that may cover a wide range of order volumes. Typically, items ordered are of a repeat nature, and production may be for a specific customer order or for stock replenishment."[1]

  - Characteristics: A batch manufacturing process, in comparison to a job shop process, is characterized as being less flexible, with a more narrow variety of products, long lead times, slightly higher volumes, moderate labor requirements, and moderate fixed and variable costs. In batch processing, some of the components for the final product may be produced in advance.

  - Examples: Manufacturing component parts for a production line, manufacturing clothing, or furniture

  - Manufacturing Strategies: MTO or ATO are the manufacturing strategies that are most closely aligned with the batch process.

- **LINE FLOW:** "A form of manufacturing organization in which machines and operators handle a standard, usually uninterrupted, material flow. The operators generally perform the same operations for each production run. A flow shop is often referred to as a mass production shop or is said to have a continuous manufacturing layout. The plant layout (arrangement of machines, benches, assembly lines, etc.) is designed to facilitate a product 'flow.' Some process industries (chemicals, oil, paint, etc.) are extreme examples of flow shops. Each product, though variable in material specifications, uses the same flow pattern through the shop. Production is set at a given rate, and the products are generally manufactured in bulk."[1]

- – Characteristics: A line flow manufacturing process is characterized as being somewhat inflexible, with a limited variety of products, short lead times, and high volumes. Products are standardized allowing a better organization of resources than with job shop or batch processing. The sequence of operations in line flow is generally fixed, and production orders are not linked to customer orders as is typical in job shop and batch processing.

  - – Examples: Automobiles, computers, appliances, household goods

  - – Manufacturing Strategies: ATO or MTO are the manufacturing strategies that are most closely aligned with the line flow process.

- • CONTINUOUS FLOW: "A production system in which the productive equipment is organized and sequenced according to the steps involved to produce the product. This term denotes that material flow is continuous during the production process. The routing of the jobs is fixed and setups are seldom changed."[1]

  - – Characteristics: A continuous flow manufacturing process is characterized as being inflexible, with a very limited variety of products, very short lead times, very high volumes, high fixed costs, and low variable costs. This type of manufacturing process involves standardized production with rigid line flows and tightly linked process segments. The process is often operated 24/7 to maximize utilization and to avoid expensive stops and starts.

  - – Examples: Gasoline, laundry detergent, chemicals

  - – Manufacturing Strategies: MTS is the manufacturing strategy that is most closely aligned with the continuous flow process.

TOTAL COST OF MANUFACTURING..

Total cost of manufacturing (TCM) consists of all the costs associated with production, procurement, inventory, warehousing, and transportation. All of these costs are impacted by the manufacturing strategy. Since TCM results from the functional integration of manufacturing, procurement, and logistics, it is important for companies to design a supply chain strategy (and adopt a manufacturing strategy) that achieves the lowest TCM across the entire process.

Key points:

- • TCM is the complete cost of producing and delivering products to your customers.

- TCM incorporates both fixed and variable costs.

- TCM is generally expressed as a cost per unit for each product.

Relationship of TCM Elements to Volume and Manufacturing Strategy

- Per unit procurement and production costs go <u>down</u> as volume goes up. Generally, a step function applies as more capital (i.e., fixed cost) will be required to produce more as volume grows beyond the existing output capabilities.

- Per unit inventory and warehousing costs go <u>up</u> as volume goes up. The company will produce and manage more inventory and therefore will likely need more warehouse storage space, insurance, and potentially pay more inventory taxes, among other things.

- Per unit transportation costs go <u>down</u> as volume goes up, but level off at high volumes (economies of scale in transportation until the container/conveyance is filled up).

LEAN AND SIX SIGMA

LEAN: "A philosophy of production that emphasizes the minimization of the amount of all the resources (including time) used in the various activities of the enterprise. It involves identifying and eliminating non-value-adding activities in design, production, supply chain management, and dealing with customers. Lean producers employ teams of multiskilled workers at all levels of the organization and use highly flexible, increasingly automated machines to produce volumes of products in potentially enormous variety. It contains a set of principles and practices to reduce cost through the relentless removal of waste and through the simplification of all manufacturing and support processes."[1] LEAN is an operating philosophy of waste reduction and value enhancement. Elements of what is today known as LEAN were originally created as part of the Toyota Production System (TPS) by key Toyota executives.

SIX SIGMA: "The six sigma approach is a set of concepts and practices that key on reducing variability in processes and reducing deficiencies in the product. Important elements are (1) Producing only 3.4 defects for every one million opportunities or operations; (2) Process improvement initiatives striving for six sigma-level performance. Six sigma is a business process that permits organizations to improve bottom-line performance, creating and monitoring business activities to reduce waste and resource requirements while increasing customer satisfaction."[1] It is an enterprise and supply chain–wide philosophy that emphasizes a commitment toward excellence, encompassing suppliers, employees, and customers.

LEAN and **Six Sigma** <u>complement</u> one another:

- LEAN focuses on eliminating wastes and improving efficiency.

- Six Sigma focuses on reducing defects and variations.

The combination of LEAN and Six Sigma creates a faster and better supply chain.

INTRODUCTION TO LEAN ....

- Starting in the 1910s, Henry Ford's mass production line created a first breakthrough by using continuous assembly and line flow systems.

- In the 1940s, Toyota executives, Taichii Ohno and Shigeo Shingo, created the Toyota Production System (TPS), which incorporated Ford's production system and other techniques to form the basis of what is now known as LEAN.

- The term LEAN was first coined by John Krafcik in 1988, and the definition was expanded in the book, *The Machine that Changed the World* (Womack, Jones, & Roos, 1990).

- In the 1990s, supply chain management combined and incorporated the concepts of:

  - <u>Quick Response,</u> which is the rapid replenishment of a customer's stock by a supplier with direct access to data from the customer's point of sale; emphasizes speed and flexibility.

  - <u>Efficient Consumer Response (ECR),</u> which is a strategy to increase the level of services to consumers through close cooperation among retailers, wholesalers, and manufacturers

  - <u>Just in Time (JIT),</u> which is an inventory strategy to decrease waste by receiving materials only when and as needed in the production process, thereby reducing inventory costs; requires and accurate demand forecast to be effective

  - <u>Keiretsu Relationships,</u> which involve companies both upstream and downstream of a manufacturing process, remaining independent, but working closely together for mutual benefit

- The combination of these approaches and concepts have emerged as the philosophies and practices known as LEAN manufacturing.

Lean is a culture, it is _not_ a toolbox of methods or ideas. LEAN provides _value_ for customers through the most efficient use of resources possible. It has become standard in many industries.

Implementing LEAN often results in:

- Large cost reductions

- Improved quality

- Increased customer service

To know how LEAN provides value for customers, we need to understand what is meant by the term "value."

- Value is the **inherent worth** of a product as judged by the customer, and reflected in its selling price and market demand.

- Value is further defined as anything for which the customer is willing to pay

In most processes, there are value added process steps and nonvalue added process steps.

- **Value Added** process steps actually transform or shape a product or service that is eventually sold to a customer. Example: a process step that actually assembles component items into a finished product, adds value to the product.

- **Nonvalue Added** process steps take time, resources, and/or space, but do not actually add value to the product or service. Example: the process step of moving the component parts to the assembly equipment does not actually add value to the product. The overall process would be better and more efficient if this step could be minimized or eliminated.

LEAN is composed of three elements working in unison:

- LEAN manufacturing

- Total quality management

- Respect for people

LEAN manufacturing is a natural fit within the discipline of supply chain management as all of the LEAN goals and objectives help to facilitate an efficient and effective supply chain. Supply chain management strives to incorporate LEAN elements by:

- Satisfying internal as well as external customer demand

- Communicating demand forecasts and production schedules up and down the supply chain, to reduce/eliminate the bullwhip effect

- Quickly moving products into and through the production process

- Optimizing inventory levels across the supply chain (internally and externally)

- Increasing the value, capabilities, and flexibility of the workforce through cross-training

- Extending collaboration and alliances beyond just first-tier suppliers and customers to include second- and third-tier suppliers and customers as well

KEY ELEMENTS OF LEAN MANUFACTURING

There are many different aspects of LEAN manufacturing and each company may value various aspects differently. The following are some of the more common elements of LEAN manufacturing:

© Mathias Rosenthal/Shutterstock.com

1. Waste reduction

2. Lean layouts

3. Inventory, setup time, and changeover time reduction

4. Small batch scheduling and uniform plant loading

5. Lean supply chain relationships

6. Workforce empowerment and respect for people

7. Continuous improvement

Waste Reduction

Waste reduction is the number one objective of LEAN. Waste in the context of LEAN and supply chain management is the expenditure of one or more resources for no purpose or value. Companies can reduce costs and add value by eliminating waste from the production system. Waste can occur in many forms. Refer to figure 8.3 for the eight categories of waste, and use the mnemonic "DOWN TIME" to remember them.

FIGURE 8.3

Waste	Description
Defects	Anything that does not meet the acceptance criteria
Overproduction	Production before it is needed, or in excess of customer requirements. Providing a service that is not needed.
Waiting	Elapsed time between processes when no work is being done
Non-Utilized Talent	Underutilizing people's talents, skills or knowledge. De-motivating the workforce by not asking for input or recognizing success
Transportation	Unnecessary movement of materials or products
Inventory	Excess products or materials not being processed
Motion	Unnecessary movement of people. Multiple hand-offs
Extra-Processing	Unnecessary steps in a process. Redundancies between processes. More work or higher quality than required by the customer

(McLaury, 2016) Adapted from GoLeanSixSigma.com

Any or all of these wastes may exist in a company or with a particular process.

Before waste is removed, processes are less efficient, generally take longer to complete, and are often scattered, which can negatively affect customers.

After waste is removed, processes are more efficient, streamlined, and take less time to complete, resulting in more satisfied customers (see figure 8.4).

The elimination of waste can deliver many benefits. Reducing waste results in:

- Reduced cycle times

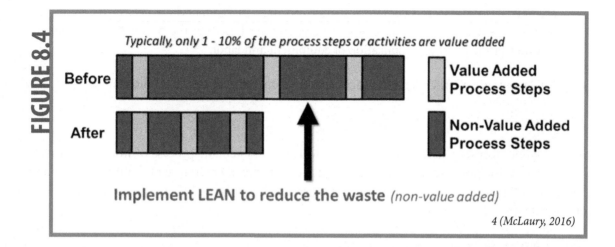

FIGURE 8.4

Typically, only 1 - 10% of the process steps or activities are value added

Before

After

☐ **Value Added Process Steps**

■ **Non-Value Added Process Steps**

Implement LEAN to reduce the waste *(non-value added)*

4 (McLaury, 2016)

- Greater throughput

- Better productivity

- Improved quality

- Reduced costs

All of these can improve customer satisfaction and provide the company with a competitive advantage!!

Lean Layouts

The second element is lean layouts, which involve moving people and materials when and where needed, and as soon as possible.

- Lean layouts are very visual, meaning that the lines of visibility are unobstructed, with operators at one processing station or workcenter able to monitor the progress of work at another workcenter.

  – Communication between workstations can be facilitated through the use of a kanban, which is "[a] method of just-in-time production that uses standard containers or lot sizes with a single card attached to each. It is a pull system in which work centers signal with a card that they wish to withdraw parts from feeding operations or suppliers. The Japanese word kanban, loosely translated, means card, billboard, or sign but other signaling devices such as colored golf balls have also been used. The term is often used synonymously for the specific scheduling system developed and used by the Toyota Corporation in Japan."[1] A kanban contains information that is passed between stations, and authorizes production or the movement of materials to the next workstation.

- Lean layouts can also incorporate a manufacturing cell model where sets of machines are grouped together or in close proximity to one another based on the products or component parts they produce, saving duplication of equipment and labor.

- Lean layouts are often U shaped to facilitate easier operator and material movements.

THE CONCEPT OF 5-S

A lean layout incorporates the concept of 5-S, which is a systematic process of workplace organization. It is a discipline designed to help build a quality work environment, both physically and mentally. 5-S is also considered part of the broader idea known as visual control, visual workplace, or visual factory.

The 5-S process steps are:

1. SORT: Keep only necessary items in the workplace, eliminate the rest.

2. STRAIGHTEN: Organize and arrange items to promote an efficient workflow.

3. SHINE: Clean the work area so it is neat and tidy.

4. STANDARDIZE: Schedule regular cleaning and maintenance.

5. SUSTAIN: Stick to the rules. Maintain and review the standards.

There is a place for everything, and everything should be in its place.

Inventory, Setup Time, and Changeover Time Reduction

The third element of LEAN involves inventory, setup time, and changeover time reduction.

- Excess <u>inventory</u> is a waste.

  - Some inventory may be necessary, but excess inventory takes up space; costs money to hold and maintain; costs money to protect, secure, and insure; and it ties up financial capital which could be used for other aspects of the business (e.g., R&D, marketing and sales, improvements, dividends, pay increases).

  - Reducing inventory levels can free up capital and reduce holding costs. In addition, there is less likelihood of waste being created by obsolescence, expiry, spoilage, or damage with lower inventory levels.

What do you see? . . . a river flowing smoothly

© ehrlif/Shutterstock.com

Now that the water level is lower what do you see?

© Frantisek Czanner/Shutterstock.com

- Traditionally, supply chains work as a push system, where inventory is carried to cover up problems. Reducing inventory levels can also uncover production problems. Refer to the following analogy.

  - The water represents inventory. When the water level is high, you don't see the rocks beneath the water, and don't know they are there.

  - The rocks represent hidden obstacles, problems, and issues. These dangers are hiding just beneath the surface.

  - Inventory can hide the underlying problems, but they are still there and can potentially create major issues in the supply chain.

- Lowering inventory will help to expose the hidden problems. Once the problems are detected, they can be solved. The end result will be a smoother running supply chain with less inventory investment.

- <u>Setup Time</u> and <u>Changeover Time</u> are both considered waste as they are intervals when the equipment is not performing its intended function—that is, producing product.

  - Setup time is the time taken to prepare and format the manufacturing equipment and systems for production.

  - Changeover time is the time taken to adapt and modify the manufacturing equipment and systems to produce a different product or a new batch of the same product.

  - While setting up the equipment is a necessary function, if the setup time can be minimized, the difference will be more time available to produce. Both setup and changeover are non-value added operations and should be minimized as much as possible.

Small Batch Scheduling and Uniform Plant Loading

The fourth element of LEAN is small batch scheduling and uniform plant loading.

In a LEAN manufacturing environment, the ideal schedule is to produce every product as quickly as possible and at the same rate as customer demand. In the real world, material availability, labor availability, and setup or changeover time influences the scheduling of large batches.

SMALL BATCH SCHEDULING

Large batches can exacerbate the bullwhip effect as production in large batches creates an uneven workload as production is not synchronized with customer demand, and an uneven demand for

FUNDAMENTALS OF SUPPLY CHAIN MANAGEMENT

upstream processes, making a pull system impossible. Throughput times in manufacturing go up and work-in-process inventory goes up, creating more waste in the system.

Think of a snake trying to swallow a large meal.

LEAN manufacturing attempts to reverse this though small batch scheduling or small lot production. If demand can be leveled and setup/changeover times can be reduced, smaller batches will facilitate producing at the same rate as customer demand. Production in small batches creates a smooth workload as production can be synchronized with customer demand, and a smooth demand for upstream processes, facilitating a pull system. It increases flexibility allowing the company to respond to changes in customer demands more quickly. Throughput times in manufacturing go down, and work-in-process inventory goes down, thus eliminating or minimizing waste in the system. The company can also get the product to the customer more quickly. Small batch scheduling can reduce costs by reducing inventory, while also increasing flexibility to meet customer demand.

Uniform Plant Loading

In a manufacturing environment, unless demand is perfectly flat, or capacity is highly variable, it is likely that demand will exceed capacity, not reach capacity, or both, at various points in the planning horizon. Matching the production plan to follow demand exactly can contribute to inefficiency and waste.

The technique of uniform plant loading involves shifting planned production forward and planning production up to the available capacity in earlier time periods, in order to meet demand in later time periods, where the production necessary to meet demand would have otherwise exceeded the available capacity. In figure 8.5, the Original Plan shows that production would be under capacity in the first seven months of the year and overcapacity in the final five months of the year. Both in-

FIGURE 8.5

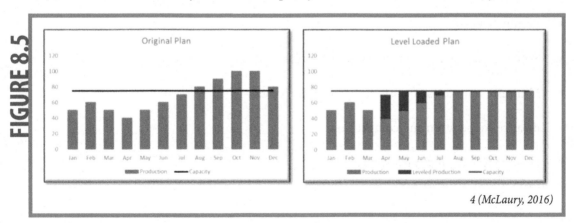

4 (McLaury, 2016)

stances would result in an inefficient use of resources and a potential customer service failure in the second half of the year. The Level Loaded Plan shows the shifting of some of the production from the final five months of the year, forward into the first half of the year where capacity is available. And while this "front-loading" or "leveling" of the plan creates some temporary excess inventory, it is a better utilization of the company's resources and avoids a customer service failure in the second half of the year. This more "uniform" plan helps suppliers better plan production as well.

Lean Supply Chain Relationships

The fifth element is lean supply chain relationships.

LEAN represents a new way of thinking about supply chain partners; its principles require cooperative supplier and customer relationships that balance cooperation with competition. Cooperation involves a variety of collaborative relationships including supplier and customer partnerships, and strategic alliances, which are a key feature of LEAN supply chain management. Companies develop lean supply chain relationships with key supplier and with key customers. Supply chain partners must work together to remove waste, reduce cost, and improve quality and customer service. Mutual dependency and benefits occur among these partners.

Lean supply chain relationship principles are:

- Focus on the value stream

- Eliminate waste

- Synchronize the flow of products and information

- Minimize transactional costs and production costs

- Balance cooperation and competition

- Ensure visibility and transparency

- Develop quick response capabilities

- Manage uncertainty and risk

- Align core competencies and complementary capabilities

- Foster innovation and knowledge-sharing

Workforce Commitment and Respect for People

The sixth element is workforce commitment and respect for people.

WORKFORCE COMMITMENT

For LEAN manufacturing to work, managers must support its principles by providing subordinates with the skills, tools, time, and other resources necessary to identify problems and implement solutions.

Management has the responsibility for motivating and engaging large numbers of people to work together toward a common goal such as LEAN manufacturing. Defining and explaining what that goal is, sharing a path to achieving it, motivating people to take the journey, and assisting them by removing obstacles are management's reason for being.

© lp studio/Shutterstock.com

One of the fundamental elements of LEAN manufacturing is that management must be totally committed to the "customer-first" philosophy. Typically, organizations think of the customer only in terms of the person or organization that purchases the final product. LEAN manufacturing promotes the view that each succeeding process, workstation, or department is the customer. It is management's responsibility to ensure that all team members and all departments realize their dual role: they are both the customers of the previous operation and the suppliers to the next operation downstream.

RESPECT FOR PEOPLE

People are the most valuable resource in any company. Without good people the business will not succeed. When people do not feel respected themselves, they tend to lose respect for the company.

This can become a major problem at any time but particularly when you are trying to implement LEAN. Most people want to perform well in their jobs. They want to feel like they have contributed to the company goals. A company that respects people will appreciate their workers' efforts and keep them in high regard. Some of the more basic ways a company can ensure that their people know they are respected include frequent communication, actively listening to their ideas, praising good performance, and providing help and support when necessary.

In a LEAN manufacturing environment:

- A flatter hierarchy than traditional organizations is embraced.

- Ordinary workers are given greater responsibility.

- Supply chain members work together in cross-functional teams.

- The goal regarding the workforce is <u>NOT</u> to reduce the number of people in an organization, but to use the people resources more wisely and more efficiently.

The role of workers, management, and suppliers in a LEAN manufacturing environment:

- ROLE OF WORKERS: Workers are given greater responsibility and their expanded duties include improving the production process, monitoring quality, and correcting quality problems. Workers often work in teams and form quality circles to facilitate these expanded responsibilities.

- ROLE OF MANAGEMENT: Management must create the cultural change needed for LEAN to succeed. They provide an atmosphere of cooperation, empower workers to take action based on their ideas, and develop incentive systems to encourage and reward lean behaviors.

- ROLE OF SUPPLIERS: A key element of LEAN is to build lean supply chain relationships with suppliers over the long term. Suppliers are expected to help improve process quality and share information. The goal is to have fewer but more strategic supply partners.

Continuous Improvement

The seventh element is continuous improvement.

In the context of LEAN manufacturing, continuous improvement is a method for identifying opportunities for streamlining work and reducing waste. Continuous improvement can be viewed as a formal practice or an informal set of guidelines. Continuous improvement helps to streamline workflows; and efficient workflows save time and money, allowing the company to reduce wasted time and effort.

© alexmillos/Shutterstock.com

- The continuous improvement approach helps to reduce process, delivery, and quality problems such as machine breakdown problems, setup problems, and internal quality problems

INTRODUCTION TO SIX SIGMA

What Is Six Sigma?

Six Sigma is a quality management process that seeks to improve the quality of process outputs by identifying and removing the causes of defects (errors) and minimizing the variability in manufacturing and business processes. The goal of Six Sigma is to attain less than 3.4 defects per million opportunities (DPMO). Six Sigma is a structured and data-driven approach to drive a near-perfect quality goal (i.e., "Zero Defects").

© nasirkhan/Shutterstock.com

Six Sigma History

- The modern-day concept of Six Sigma was originated by Motorola in 1980. Bill Smith, a Motorola engineer, is credited with coining the term "Six Sigma."

- In the early to mid-1980s, Motorola developed the new standard, created the methodology, and copyrighted it as well.

  - Motorola has documented more than $16 billion in savings as a result of Six Sigma.

- Thousands of companies around the world have adopted Six Sigma as a way of doing business. This is a direct result of many of America's leaders openly praising the benefits of Six Sigma (e.g., Jack Welch of General Electric Company). Six Sigma became famous when Welch made it central to his successful business strategy at General Electric in 1995.

  - GE reported $200 million in savings in the first year of implementation (1996).

SIX SIGMA METHODOLOGY

There are three main foundational aspects of Six Sigma:

1. QUALITY IS DEFINED BY THE CUSTOMER: Customers expect performance, reliability, competitive prices, on-time delivery, good service, clear and correct transaction processing, and more. It is vital to provide what the customers need to achieve customer satisfaction.

2. USE OF TECHNICAL TOOLS: Six Sigma provides a statistical approach for solving any problem and thereby improves the quality level of the product as well as the company. All employees should be trained to use technical tools (e.g., statistical quality control and the seven tools of quality). Six Sigma is concerned with the permanent fix to quality problems and seeks to identify and correct the root cause of the problem.

3. PEOPLE INVOLVEMENT: Six Sigma follows a structured methodology, and has defined roles for the participants. A company must involve all its employees in the Six Sigma program, and provide opportunities and incentives for them to focus their talents and ability to satisfy customers. All employees are responsible to identify quality problems. It is important that all Six Sigma team members have a well-defined role with measurable objectives. Under Six Sigma, the members of an organization are assigned specific "roles" as follows:

   - Senior Leader: Defines the goals and objectives in the Six Sigma initiative.

   - Implementation Leader: Supervises the Six Sigma initiative.

   - Coach: Six Sigma expert or consultant who sets a schedule, defines result of a project, and who mediates conflict, or deals with resistance to the program.

- <u>Sponsor</u>: High-level individual within the company that acts as a problem solver for the Six Sigma initiative.

- <u>Team Leader</u>: Oversees the work of the Six Sigma team and acts as a liaison between the sponsor and the team members.

- <u>Team Member</u>: Executes specific Six Sigma assignments.

- <u>Process Owner</u>: Takes responsibility for a process after the Six Sigma team has completed its work.

Six Sigma has two key methodologies:

- **DMADV** methodology:

  Define --> **M**easure --> **A**nalyze --> **D**esign -->**V**erify: a data-driven quality strategy for designing products and processes. This methodology is used when the company wants to create a new product design or process that is more predictable and defect free.

- **DMAIC** methodology:

  Define --> **M**easure --> **A**nalyze --> **I**mprove -->**C**ontrol: a data-driven quality strategy for improving processes. This methodology is used when the company wants to improve an existing business process. DMAIC is the most widely adopted and recognized Six Sigma methodology in use. It defines the steps a Six Sigma practitioner typically follows during a project.

This text will focus on the DMAIC methodology, which consists of the following five steps.

- <u>Define the problem</u>: The focus should be on the customers' expectation of the process.

- <u>Measure the problem and process</u>: Map out the current process. Determine the frequency of defects.

- <u>Analyze the data and the process</u>: Identify the root cause(s) of the problems and defects. Determine why, when, and where defects occur.

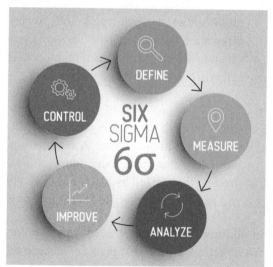

© Petr Vaclavek/Shutterstock.com

- Improve the process: Find solutions to fix or reduce the root cause(s) of the problems, and prevent problems from occurring. Implement and verify the solution(s).

- Control and sustain the improvement solutions: This ensures that the process stays fixed. "Bake" the solutions into the process permanently.

SIX SIGMA TRAINING AND CERTIFICATION LEVELS ....

There are multiple Six Sigma certification levels based on training, knowledge, and experience. These people conduct Six Sigma projects and implement improvements.

- YELLOW BELT: Has a basic understanding of Six Sigma methodology and the tools in the DMAIC problem-solving process. A team member that reviews processes and process improvements in support of a Six Sigma process improvement project. A person who has passed the Green Belt certification exam but has not yet completed a Six Sigma project.

- GREEN BELT: A Six Sigma trained individual that can work as a team member on complex project and lead small, carefully defined Six Sigma projects. On complex Six Sigma projects, Green Belts work closely with the Black Belt team leader to assist with data collection and analysis, and to keep the team functioning through all phases of the project.

- BROWN BELT: A Six Sigma Green Belt who has passed the Black Belt certification examination but has not yet completed a second Six Sigma project.

- BLACK BELT: A full-time quality professional who has a thorough knowledge of Six Sigma philosophies and principles, and possesses technical and managerial process improvement/innovation skills. Leads the Six Sigma project team and problem-solving efforts. Identifies projects and selects project team members. Trains and coaches project teams. A Black Belt is typically mentored by a Master Black Belt.

- MASTER BLACK BELT: Is a career path. A Master Black Belt has successfully led 10 or more teams through complex Six Sigma projects. A proven change agent, leader, facilitator, and technical expert in Six Sigma. A seasoned individual with a proven mastery of process variability reduction, and waste reduction. Acts as an advisor to executives, and a coach and mentor on projects that are led by Black and Green belts. Functions as the keeper of the Six Sigma process, and can effectively provide Six Sigma training at all levels.

In addition, every project needs organizational support. Six Sigma champions and executives set the direction, ensure that projects succeed and add value, and that selected projects fit within the organizational plan.

TOTAL QUALITY MANAGEMENT

Total quality management (TQM) is a management philosophy based on the principle that every employee must be committed to maintaining high standards of work in every aspect of a company's operations, focused on meeting customer needs and organizational objectives. TQM is a combination of quality and management tools designed to increase business and reduce losses resulting from wasteful practices.

When implemented, Six Sigma is an integral part of TQM. Its key principles are as follows:

© nasirkhan/Shutterstock.com

- Management Commitment

- Employee Empowerment

- Fact-Based Decision Making

- Continuous Improvement

- Customer Focus

There is no single academic formalization of total quality, but noted quality gurus W. Edwards Deming, Philip Crosby, Joseph Juran, and Kaoru Ishikawa, among others, contributed to the basic framework:

- This discipline and philosophy of management institutionalizes planned and continuous improvement.

- Quality is the outcome of all activities that take place within an organization.

- All functions and all employees must participate in the improvement process.

- Organizations need both quality systems and a quality culture.

QUALITY GURUS

Each of these quality gurus (i.e., experts) significantly contributed to our current understanding and practice of quality management today.

- **W. Edwards Deming** is widely considered the father of TQM. He is the creator of the Plan-Do-Check-Act model. He stressed management's responsibility for quality, and he developed 14 points to guide companies in quality improvement. He has been credited with the quote, "In God we trust, all others bring data."

  Deming's 14 points:

  1. Create constancy of purpose to improve product and service
  2. Adopt the new philosophy
  3. Cease dependence on inspection to improve quality
  4. End the practice of awarding business on the basis of price
  5. Constantly improve the production and service system
  6. Institute training on the job
  7. Institute leadership
  8. Drive out fear
  9. Break down barriers between departments
  10. Eliminate slogans and exhortations
  11. Eliminate quotas
  12. Remove barriers to pride of workmanship
  13. Institute program of self-improvement
  14. Put everyone to work to accomplish the transformation

- **Philip Crosby** coined the phrase "quality is free" (which is also the title of his book) as defects are costly. He introduced the concepts of zero defects, and focus on prevention and not inspection. Philip Crosby demonstrated what a powerful tool the cost of quality could be to raise awareness of the importance of quality. He referred to the measure as the "price of nonconformance" and argued that organizations choose to pay for poor quality. He has been credited with the quote, "Quality is the result of a carefully constructed cultural environment. It has to be the fabric of the organization, not part of the fabric."

  He introduced the four absolutes of quality:

  1. The definition of quality is conformance to requirements.
  2. The system of quality is prevention.
  3. Performance standard is zero defects.
  4. The measure of quality is the price of nonconformance.

- **Joseph Juran** defined quality as "fitness for use." He developed the concept of the cost of quality. He has been credited with the quote, "Without a standard, there is no logical basis for making a decision or taking action." He was a proponent of concepts of quality planning, quality control, and quality improvement.

- <u>Quality Planning:</u> Identify internal/external customers and needs:

  - Develop products satisfying those needs.

  - Mangers must set goals, priorities, and compare results.

- <u>Quality Control:</u> Determine what to control:

  - Establish standards of performance.

  - Measure performance, interpret the differences, and take action.

- <u>Quality Improvement:</u> Show the need for improvement:

  - Identify projects for improvement.

  - Implement remedies.

  - Provide control to maintain improvement.

- **Kaoru Ishikawa** developed one the first tools in the quality management process, the cause-and-effect diagram, or the Ishikawa (fishbone) diagram. With this tool, the user can see all possible causes of a problem to help find the root cause. He emphasized use of all seven of the basic quality tools. He is also known as the father of quality circles and helped bring this concept into the mainstream. Further, Ishikawa was a proponent of continuous customer service, meaning that a customer should continue receiving service even after receiving the product.

VOICE OF THE CUSTOMER

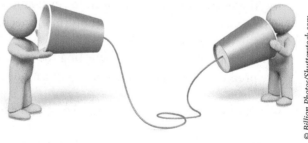

© Billion Photos/Shutterstock.com

Voice of the customer (VOC) is a term used in business to describe the in-depth process of capturing internal and external customers' stated and un-stated expectations, preferences, likes, and dislikes. Total quality management is all about meeting or exceeding customer expectations, so capturing the VOC is essential for TQM to be successful.

The VOC can be captured in a variety of ways: direct discussion or customer interviews, market surveys, focus groups, customer specifications, observation, warranty data, field reports, complaint logs, among others. The data are used to identify the quality attributes needed for a process or product.

COST OF QUALITY ....

Cost of quality is an approach that supports a company's efforts to determine the level of resources necessary to prevent poor quality, and to evaluate the quality of the company's products and services. Any cost that would not have occurred if quality was perfect, contributes to the cost of quality. This information will help a company to determine the benefits and savings generated by potential process improvements.

Cost of quality can be divided into "the cost of good quality" involving prevention and appraisal costs, and "the cost of poor quality" involving internal and external failure costs.

Cost of Good Quality

- **Prevention Costs** are incurred to prevent or avoid quality problems. These costs are associated with the design, implementation, and maintenance of the quality management system. They are planned and experienced before actual products or materials are acquired or produced. They include:

  - Establishment of specifications for incoming materials, processes, products, and services

  - Creation of quality plans

  - Quality training (development, preparation, and maintenance of programs)

  - Creation and maintenance of the quality system

- **Appraisal Costs** are associated with the measuring and monitoring of activities related to quality. These costs are associated with the evaluation of purchased materials, processes, products, and services to ensure that they conform to specifications. They include:

  - Testing, evaluating, and inspecting the quality of incoming materials, process setups, and products, against agreed upon specifications

  - Quality assessment and approval of suppliers

  - Performing audits to confirm that the quality system is operating properly

Cost of Poor Quality

- **Internal Failure Costs** are incurred to fix defects discovered before the product or service is delivered to the customer. These costs occur when the product or service does not meet the designed quality standards, and are identified before the product or service is delivered to the customer. They include:

- Defective product or material that cannot be used, sold, or repaired

- Correction of defective material or errors (e.g., rework and repairs)

- Unnecessary work or inventory resulting from errors, poor organization, or poor communication

- Analysis activities required to establish the root causes of internal product or service failures

- **External Failure Costs** are incurred to fix defects discovered by customers. These costs occur when the product or service that does not meet the designed quality standards are not detected until after the product or service is delivered to the customer. They include:

  - All work and costs associated with handling and responding to customer complaints

  - All work and costs associated with failed products that must be replaced or services that are repeated under a warranty

  - All work and costs associated with the repair and servicing of returned products and products still in the field

  - All work and costs associated with the handling and investigation of rejected or recalled products, including return transportation costs

QUALITY TOOLS ···

Seven quality tools are commonly used in making quality management decisions based on facts. Any one or any combination of the tools may be helpful depending on the circumstances, and none of the tools are mandatory in Six Sigma. There are a number of software programs available to support these tools.

The seven tools most commonly used for quality control and improvement are:

1. CAUSE-AND-EFFECT DIAGRAM (Ishikawa or fishbone diagram): Tool used to aid in brainstorming and isolating the cause(s) of a problem. The function is to identify the factor(s) that are causing a defect(s) so that improvement actions can be taken. Typically, the potential factors are identified by those familiar with the process involved. Major factors could be grouped using the four Ms: materials, machinery, methods, and manpower. It is commonly used in combination with the Five Whys and Five Hows technique to help identify the root cause. See figure 8.6 for an example.

FIGURE 8.6

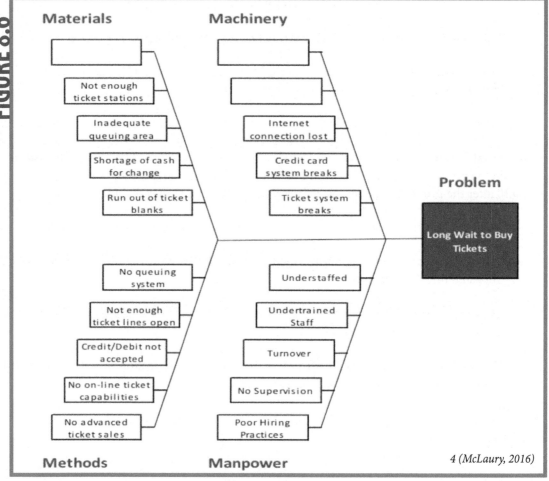

4 *(McLaury, 2016)*

2. CHECK SHEET: A simple way of gathering data so that decisions can be based on facts. Check sheets are commonly used to determine the frequencies for specific problems. They could also be used to correlate the number of defects to other variables such as the day of the week or month of the year, to see if there is any significant variation or pattern. The data gathered in a check sheet can also be used as input to a Pareto chart for analysis. See figure 8.7 for an example.

3. CONTROL CHART: Plots representative samples of the selected values from a process, in sequence over time. Control charts are used to study how a process changes over time. A control chart always has a median line for the average, an upper line for the upper control limit, and a lower line for the lower control limit. These lines are determined from historical data. By comparing current data to these lines, conclusions can be drawn regarding whether the process variation is in control or out of control. (Refer to "Statistical Process Control" later in this chapter.) A sample measurement outside the control limits therefore indicates that the process is no longer stable, and is usually a reason for corrective action. See figure 8.8 for an example.

FIGURE 8.7

Check Sheet
Frequency of Customer Problems at Movie Theater

Problem	Dates							TOTAL
	Sunday	Monday	Tuesday	Wednesday	Thursday	Friday	Saturday	
No Parking				5	12	15	17	49
Long Wait for Tickets	14	16	15	18	16	19	20	118
Tickets Sold Out	11	16	13	15	11	16	12	94
Long Wait for Concessions	11	15	12	11	12	15	13	89
Concessions Sold Out	5			12	13	15	15	60
Poor Seats			11	12	11	11	13	58
Poor Picture/Sound Quality			1	2	4	3	2	12
Temperature in Theater	1	2	2	3	1	2	1	12
Traffic Congestion on Exit				11	11	13	12	47
Other	2					3	5	10
TOTAL	44	49	54	89	91	112	110	549

4 (McLaury, 2016)

FIGURE 8.8

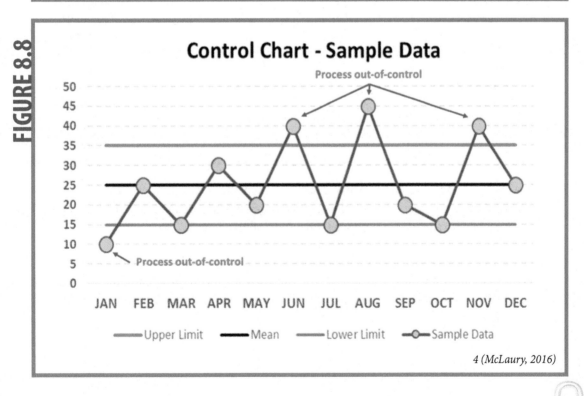

Control Chart - Sample Data

4 (McLaury, 2016)

4. FLOWCHART: A picture of process steps in sequential order. It is comprised of annotated boxes representing process steps to show the flow of products or customers. It helps users understand how a process progresses toward completion, and to identify where process improvements can be made. See figure 8.9 for an example.

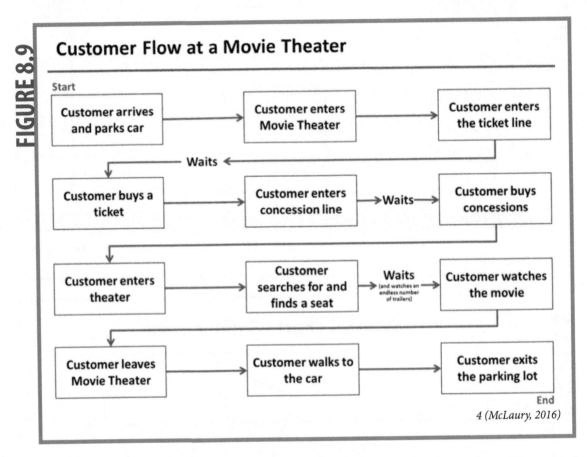

FIGURE 8.9

Customer Flow at a Movie Theater

4 (McLaury, 2016)

5. HISTOGRAM: Another form of bar chart in which the measurements represent a range of values of some parameter. Besides the central tendency and spread of the data, the shape of the histogram can also be of interest. See figure 8.10 for an example.

6. PARETO CHART: A bar graph. The lengths of the bars generally represent the frequency that specific defects occur, and are arranged with the longest bars on the left and the shortest bars on the right. A Pareto chart will visually depict which defects are more significant. See figure 8.11 for an example.

FIGURE 8.10

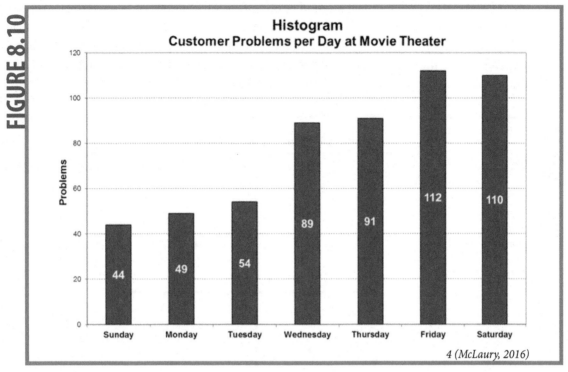

Histogram
Customer Problems per Day at Movie Theater

4 (McLaury, 2016)

FIGURE 8.11

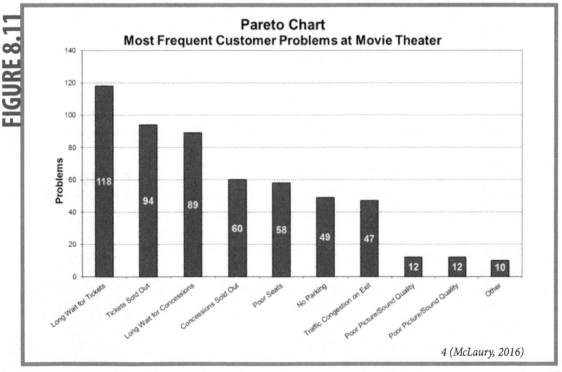

Pareto Chart
Most Frequent Customer Problems at Movie Theater

4 (McLaury, 2016)

7. **SCATTER DIAGRAM:** Graphical method of observing whether or not two parameters are related to each other. Data are plotted with one variable on each axis. If the variables are correlated, the data points will fall along a line or curve. The tighter the points hug the line, the better the correlation of the relationship, and one can be used to predict the other. See figure 8.12 for an example.

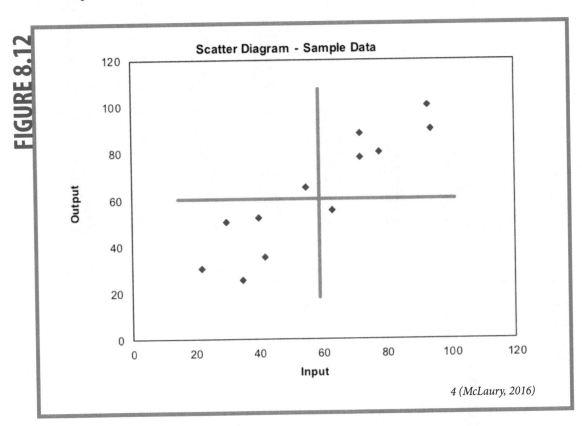

FIGURE 8.12

Scatter Diagram - Sample Data

4 (McLaury, 2016)

The Five Whys and the Five Hows Technique

The Five Whys and Five Hows technique is a questioning process designed to drill down into the details of a problem or a solution to find the root cause and the best corrective measure. Originally developed by Sakichi Toyoda, who stated "that by repeating why five times, the nature of the problem as well as its solution becomes clear." The Five Whys are used to reach the root cause of a problem and the Five Hows are used to develop the details of a root solution to a problem. Both are designed to bring clarity and refinement to a problem statement or a potential solution. This technique is typically used in conjunction with the cause-and-effect diagram.

STATISTICAL PROCESS CONTROL ....

Statistical process control (SPC) is a method for monitoring, controlling, and improving a process through statistical analysis. All processes exhibit intrinsic variation and SPC is the application of statistical methods and procedures, such as control charts, to analyze that inherent variability to achieve and maintain a state of statistical control. Variations can be natural (i.e., expected and random which cannot be controlled), or assignable (i.e., having a specific cause which can potentially be controlled).

© antkevyv/Shutterstock.com

Sometimes processes exhibit excessive variation that produces undesirable or unpredictable results, and SPC is used to reduce that variation to improve process capability.

- Companies:

    - Gather process performance data.

    - Create control charts to monitor process variability.

    - Then collect sample measurements of the process over time and plot on charts.

- SCP allows firms to:

    - Visually monitor process performance.

    - Compare the performance to desired levels or standards.

    - Take corrective action.

ACCEPTANCE SAMPLING ....

Acceptance sampling is the selection of a set of items from a product lot to test as a representative sample of the entire lot. Sampling lets you draw conclusions or make inferences about the population from which the sample is drawn. Acceptance sampling is useful when the cost of testing is high compared to the cost of passing a defective item, or when testing is impractical or destructive. It is a compromise between doing 100% inspection and doing no inspection at all. Sampling is also less time consuming than testing every item.

However, acceptance sampling can result in errors:

- Manufacturer's risk: A buyer rejects a shipment of good quality units because the sample quality level did not meet standards (type I error).

- Consumer's risk: A buyer accepts a shipment of poor quality units because the sample falsely provides a positive answer (type II error).

IMPLEMENTING LEAN AND SIX SIGMA ....

LEAN and Six Sigma are complementary principles providing the customer with the best possible quality, cost, and delivery. There is significant overlap, and the two initiatives approach their common purpose from somewhat different angles:

- LEAN focuses on waste reduction, whereas Six Sigma emphasizes variation reduction and the elimination of defects.

- LEAN achieves its goals by using less technical tools such as lean layouts, continuous improvement, and respect for people, whereas Six Sigma uses technical tools such as root cause analysis, statistical process control, and DMAIC.

The most common and successful implementations begin with LEAN, reducing waste, and using value stream mapping to make the workplace as efficient and effective as possible. Typically this is followed by implementing the more technical Six Sigma statistical tools to resolve process problems. Both LEAN and Six Sigma require strong management support to incorporate these principles into the standard way of doing business. One way companies have found success is by forming a Lean Six Sigma team with subject matter experts to lead the company-wide implementation effort.

REFERENCE ....

[1] *APICS Dictionary* (14th ed.). (2013). Chicago, IL: APICS. www.apics.org; GoLeanSixSigma.com. (2016). What is waste? Retrieved from https://goleansixsigma.com/8-wastes/

DELIVER AND RETURN

Chapter 9

Logistics: Warehousing, Transportation, and Reverse Logistics

CHAPTER OUTLINE

Introduction

Logistics

Warehousing

Functions of a Warehouse

Types of Warehouses

Which Warehouse Type to Choose

Warehouse Networks

LEAN and Green Warehousing

Third-Party Logistics

Transportation

Transportation Company Classifications

Major Modes of Transportation

Transportation Pricing and Considerations

Transportation Regulation

Transportation Deregulation

Other Transportation Intermediaries

Technology and Trends in Transportation

Logistics Management Software Applications

Reverse Logistics

Summary

INTRODUCTION ....

Up to this chapter, discussion has centered on the supply chain elements of Plan, Source, and Make. In this chapter we begin with the Deliver and Return aspects of the SCOR model. Logistics will be discussed in general, followed by a more detailed discussion of warehousing, transportation, and reverse logistics. The next few chapters will cover the other aspects of Deliver and Return, including global logistics and international trade, customer relationship management, and supply chain in the service industry.

LOGISTICS ....

As noted earlier in this text, many people confuse supply chain management with logistics, and consider them interchangeable terms. Logistics is part of supply chain management, specifically the part involving warehousing, transportation, and reverse logistics activities.

Logistics is "that part of supply chain management that plans, implements and controls the efficient, effective flow and storage of goods, services and related information from the point of origin to the point of consumption in order to meet customer requirements," as per the Council of Supply Chain Management Professionals (CSCMP) official definition.

Logistics is necessary to accomplish three things:

1. To move goods and materials from suppliers to buyers

2. To move goods and materials between sites, either internally or between internal and external sites

3. To move finished goods out to customers

Referring back to figure 1.2 (excerpt shown here), you see that logistics covers the flow on the left side from supplier to buyer, the flow in the middle moving goods and materials between sites (internal and external), and the flow on the right side going out to customers, whether the customer is a wholesaler, distributor, or retailer, or even the final consumer of a product. Logistics covers all of these movement activities.

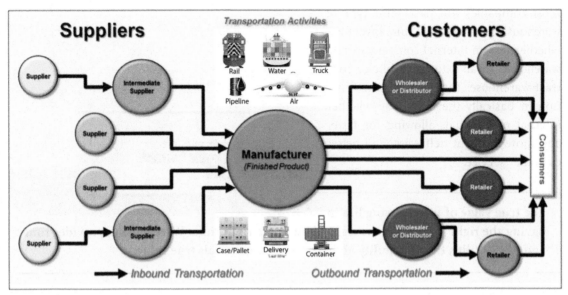

(McLaury, 2016)

Products have little value to the customer until they are moved to the customer's point of consumption. In other words, the customer cares very little about transportation and logistics activities on the front end of the supply chain. They are more interested and more directly impacted by the transportation and logistics activities on the back end when the product is actually in proximity to where they are going to use it, whether that is a wholesaler, a distributor, a retailer, or the actual end consumer. **The real value delivered by the logistics function is ensuring that the product is delivered at the right time and to the right location**—everything else up to that point is a necessary but nonvalue added activity. Although logistics on the front end of the supply chain is necessary to move materials from suppliers to manufacturers and out to wholesalers, the real value only occurs when the product is in the possession of the actual customer.

WAREHOUSING..

A <u>warehouse</u> is a facility used to store inventory.

<u>Warehousing</u> is all "the activities related to receiving, storing, and shipping materials to and from production or distribution locations."[1] Warehousing is the function that allows a company to store all of the types of inventory (i.e., raw materials, work in process, and finished goods) the company may have or need. Decisions driving warehouse management include site selection, the number of warehouse facilities in the network, the layout of the warehouse(s), and the methods of receiving, storing, and retrieving products and materials.

Most companies will have some type of warehousing operation to store inventory, whether it is an internal company owned warehouse, or an external public or contract warehouse. These warehouses function in basically the same way whether internal or external, allowing for faster and more frequent deliveries, and better customer service.

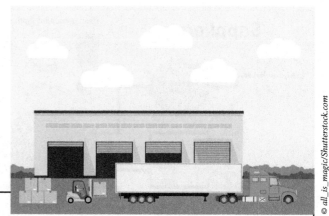

The true value of warehousing lies in having the right product in the right place at the right time. Warehousing provides time and place utility, the availability necessary to give materials true value.

FUNCTIONS OF A WAREHOUSE ....

Following are the basic functions of a warehouse:

- **RECEIVING:** Function encompassing the physical receipt of material, identification, inspection for conformance with the purchase order (quantity and damage), put-away (delivery to a warehouse storage location), and preparation of receiving reports.

- **STORAGE:** The safe and secure retention of parts or products for future use or shipment. Includes placing goods into storage and retrieval of goods from storage.

- **PICKING:** Withdrawing components from stock to make assemblies or finished goods, or withdrawing finished goods from stock to ship to a customer.

- **PACKING:** Placing one or more items of an order into an appropriate container for safe shipping, and marking and labeling the container with customer shipping destination data and other information that may be required.

- **SHIPPING:** Function for the outgoing shipment of parts, components, and products. Includes packaging, marking, weighing, and loading for shipment.

Warehouse operations may also perform other activities including functioning as:

- **CONSOLIDATION POINT:** Warehouse operation that receives products from suppliers, sorts them, and then combines them with similar shipments from other suppliers for further distribution.

- **BREAK BULK:** Warehouse operation that divides full truckloads of items from a single source or manufacturer into smaller, more appropriate quantities for use or further distribution.

- **QUALITY INSPECTIONS:** Incoming and outgoing.

- **REPACKAGING:** For specific customer orders.

- **ASSEMBLY OPERATION:** Warehouse operation that puts products together with other items/ components before shipping them out to the final customer. Examples include:

  - Literature
  - Spare parts
  - Advertising materials

Each of these will be described further in this chapter.

TYPES OF WAREHOUSES..

There are different types of warehouses that companies must consider. This text will review:

- Public
- Contract
- Private

- Consolidation
- Break bulk
- Cross docking

Public Warehousing

A public warehouse is a business that provides storage and related warehouse functions to companies on a short- or long-term basis, generally from month to month. They typically own their own equipment and hire their own staff to manage the operations of the facility. A public warehouse is often divided into zones for a variety of goods, and can include temperature-controlled storage, dry storage, and general storage.

Fees are generally a combination of a monthly storage fee plus a pallet-in fee and a pallet-out fee. The storage and handling fees in a public warehouse will also vary based on exactly what is being stored and handled. So, Customer A may be charged more than Customer B per pallet within the same public warehouse. The reasons could include the size and weight of the palletized loads, how high the pallets can be stacked, how fragile they are, the risk of theft, the value of goods, any hazards associated with the goods, and so forth. Public warehouses may also have some nominal transaction or document fees, and account management fees. The fee structure can be based on each pallet moved/stored or based on each square foot used by a client.

Public warehouses also offer a variety of al la carte services including order picking and order packing, order consolidation, cross docking, packaging services, kitting, returns processing, inspection services, inventory management, physical inventory counts, assembly operations, and shipping. They charge their clients a fee for each of the services the client uses in addition to the fees for storage and handling.

Although most companies see public warehousing as a short-term solution, it can often turn into a long-term relationship as companies become accustomed to the convenience of the public warehouse services. Companies that own and operate public warehouses will invest significantly in their facilities to remain competitive. They offer clients increasing levels of flexibility in order to retain existing clients and to attract additional clients. Public warehouses offer companies a range of labor solutions up to and including a dedicated workforce. In a longer term arrangement, they may also allow clients to bring in their own ERP or warehouse software so that the public warehouse in essence becomes a satellite location of the client providing real-time data.

PUBLIC WAREHOUSING OFFERS A VARIETY OF ADVANTAGES BECAUSE OF ITS FLEXIBILITY:

a. NO CAPITAL INVESTMENT: A major advantage is there is no capital investment from the user/client for warehousing. Public warehousing immediately takes away the need for a company to own and operate storage infrastructure, including the staff and security that go along with it. In this way, public warehousing is a variable cost component.

b. TAX AVOIDANCE: Because the user company doesn't own the property, the user is not subject to property taxes, which can be substantial.

c. FLEXIBILITY: Because a company can establish a short-term public warehouse commitment, if business conditions change, the company is not tied into a long-term commitment, and they can reduce or expand their storage needs accordingly.

d. ACCOMMODATES SEASONALITY: Seasonal businesses have the option of expanding and contracting their public space on a monthly basis. You only pay for space in the month you are using it, allowing storage costs to vary directly with seasonal volume.

e. CAPABILITY TO EXPAND: Public warehousing provides an economical and practical means to grow into new markets and geographies for companies that are expanding, particularly in the short term.

f. LOWER COSTS AND REDUCED RISK: Compared to other types of warehousing, public warehousing is usually less costly. Because there is no long-term commitment, users can switch to another public warehouse facility in a short period of time, often within 30 days, if there is another location that may have lower rent or fees.

g. ACCESS TO LOWER FREIGHT RATES: Because public warehouses handle the requirements of a number of companies, their volume allows them to negotiate consolidated freight rates rather than much higher less-than-truckload freight rates that result from shipping small quantities at a premium.

h. ACCESS TO SPECIAL FEATURES AND SERVICES: Most public warehouses can offer specialized services (e.g., broken-case handling, packaging services for manufacturer products for shipping, breakbulk services, and freight consolidation services) because they can consolidation volume with noncompetitor clients who use the same public warehouse. Most public warehouses have some special features that makes them unique. Examples of special features are:

   – Temperature-controlled storage (cool, cold, and frozen)

   – Crane capabilities

   – Ultraclean segregated areas

   – Guard service 24/7/365

   – Dedicated docking areas for special customers

   – Special staff functions like customer service, inventory ordering, etc.

   – Office space to rent for customer's sales, accounting, etc.

i. KNOWLEDGE OF EXACT STORAGE AND HANDLING COSTS: When a company uses a public warehouse, it knows exactly how much is being spent on storage and handling costs, because the monthly bill displays all necessary information. This allows the user to forecast costs for each different level of activity. Companies that operate their own private facilities often find it difficult to determine the exact fixed and variable costs.

PUBLIC WAREHOUSING ALSO HAS SOME <u>DISADVANTAGES</u>:

a. SYSTEMS COMPATIBILITY: There is the potential of incompatible computer systems. Public warehouses may not have a system to suit the needs of a specific customer and they are unlikely to invest in a new system for just one client.

b. LACK OF SPECIALIZED SERVICES: Most public warehouse facilities provide local services which may not be what the company requires. The specialized services that a company needs may not always be available in a desired location.

c. SPACE AVAILABILITY: Public warehousing space may not be available when and where a company wants it. Shortages can occur from time to time, particularly during a peak season, which may adversely affect the client company.

CRITERIA FOR CHOOSING A PUBLIC WAREHOUSE

Because of the increasing competition between the public warehouse operators, companies should review the capabilities of each potential public warehouse to identify which would be the best fit. Each company will have a number of factors that need to be considered when selecting a public warehouse. Companies have a variety of reasons why they require an outside warehouse in addition to their short-term and long-term needs, and the price they are willing to pay for the service. Companies are likely to weigh criteria such as geographical location, the type of technology needed versus what is available, whether the public warehouse has the capability to expand if more space is needed, and how flexible the public warehouse is to respond to changes in volume or other needs.

Contract Warehousing

A contract warehouse is a variation of public warehousing that handles the shipping, receiving, and storage of goods for a specific client on a contract basis. The contract can be for either an entire building or a defined portion of square-foot or cubic-foot space within a building. This type of warehouse usually requires a client to commit to services for a particular period of time. The length of time varies, often stated in years rather than months. The fee structure also varies based on transactions; it may be a fixed cost, cost-plus, or a combination of both. The company providing the space handles the employees, equipment, and maintenance expenses. They are also responsible for most incidental expenses, which further reduces costs.

Many of the advantages of pubic warehousing also apply to contract warehousing.

ADDITIONAL ADVANTAGES OF CONTRACT WAREHOUSING:

- **LOGISTICS EXPERTISE:** Contract warehousing companies provide a great deal of expertise for logistics demands. Contractors will be experienced in warehouse operations and supply chains. They often have knowledge that business owners don't. Because there is a long-term associated setup, it is in their interest to see that the client company's needs are met.

- **SERVICES:** The longer term nature of contract warehousing generally results in the client company obtaining specialized services that are tailor-made to suit their needs.

- **COST:** Facilities and specialized services that are provided under contract warehousing are similar to those provided by a private warehouse; however, these facilities come at a cheaper price, because significant capital costs are involved in the construction and maintenance of a private warehouse, whereas a contract warehouse is owned and operated by a third party that bears the burden of the capital costs.

- **FEES:** In the case of public warehousing, the client company is charged storage fees, and inbound and outbound transactions fees, and the user is expected to pay for any additional services that are desired. Contract warehousing also requires the client company to pay a fee for the services rendered; however, due to the longer commitment, the services provided in the contract can be bundled and negotiated, usually at a lower cost.

- **CONTROL:** A public warehouse results in the client company having to relinquish control, whereas contract warehousing offers a compromise by allowing the client company a certain degree of control at a reasonable price. In contrast, a private warehouse allows absolute control but at a higher capital cost than a contract warehouse.

DISADVANTAGES OF CONTRACT WAREHOUSING:

- **DURATION:** The client company is expected to enter into a contract for a specific period of time (generally three years). A public warehouse allows the client to store goods for both short and long periods of time, allowing flexibility when it comes to duration, which a contract warehouse limits.

Private Warehousing

A private warehouse is a storage facility that is owned by the company that owns the goods being stored in the facility. It is also known as proprietary warehousing. Private warehouses are generally established by companies that have a large volume or large value of goods being stored, or the need for some type of specialized storage or handling. They can be operated as a separate division within a company if desired, and they can be co-located onsite with manufacturing, or at an offsite location.

Advantages of private warehousing:

- **Control:** Private warehousing offers users significant control over their storage needs and they can be constructed to meet user specifications. Companies can also control product placement within a facility providing access to products when an organization needs them. It allows the company to integrate the warehousing function more easily into its total logistics system. The company has clear visibility of inventory control, internal material flow, handling, supervision, and associated cost control.

- **Flexibility:** Offers the company greater flexibility in designing and operating the warehouse to suit the needs of its customers and the characteristics of the products. The company can install specialized handling for its products if necessary and modify the facility through expansion or renovation to facilitate product changes, which is not possible in a public warehouse.

- **Cost:** Operating cost can be 15% to 25% lower if the company achieves at least 75% utilization.

- **Labor:** There is the prevailing belief that greater care goes into handling and storage when the company's own workforce operates the warehouse. This means that the company can utilize the expertise of its technical specialists. A company may also be able to better utilize its overall workforce. During a down period in manufacturing, the company could shift manufacturing workers over to the warehouse temporarily to help. Or, vice versa, during a down period in the warehouse, or a peak in manufacturing, the company might be able to shift warehouse workers over to manufacturing temporarily.

- **Tax Benefits:** Depreciation allowances on buildings and equipment help to reduce taxes.

- **Intangible Benefits:** When a company distributes its products through a private warehouse, it gives its customers a sense of permanence and continuity of business operations. The customer perceives the company as a stable, dependable, and long-term supplier of products.

Disadvantages of private warehousing:

- **Flexibility:** In the short term, it is very difficult for a private warehouse facility to respond to changes in the external environment, and expand or contract to meet increases or decreases in demand. Flexibility in strategic location is also an issue as private warehouses can't respond quickly to changes in market location and preferences, and this may mean that excellent business opportunities may be lost. If you own the warehouse, it is not easy to just pick up and move to another location if the market changes, which is an advantage in a public warehouse setting.

- **Fixed Size and Costs:** When demand is low, the company still assumes the fixed costs as well as the lower productivity linked to unused warehouse space. However, the disadvantages can be minimized if the company is willing and able to rent out part of its space.

- **High Opportunity Cost Risk:** The ROI on other investments may be greater if funds are channeled into other profit-generating opportunities rather than investing in a warehouse. Because the ROI is about the same as the company's other investments, most companies find it advantageous to use a combination of public and private warehousing. It is best to use private warehousing to handle the basic inventory levels required for the least cost logistics in markets where the volume justifies ownership. Any extra volume can be stored in the public warehouse during peak periods if the private warehouse is full. There is also the potential of not being able to sell the warehouse in the future if it is no longer needed.

- **High Startup Cost:** Companies have to generate enough capital to build or buy a warehouse. A warehouse is often a long, risky investment. In addition, there is the cost of hiring and training employees, and the purchase of material handling equipment. The high cost necessitates high and steady demand volumes for the investment to make sense. In addition, a high fixed cost alternative becomes less attractive in times of high interest rates, because it is more costly to secure the necessary financing.

Consolidation Warehousing

A consolidation warehouse receives products from suppliers, sorts them, and then combines them with similar shipments from other suppliers into larger, more economical, shipping loads for further distribution. In other words, small flexible shipments in, and large economical shipments out. The goal is maximizing transportation utilization while minimizing costs.

The concept is similar to carpooling where several individuals in the same area come together and meet at one place, and then take one car to work instead of taking several different cars. The cost to each person is significantly less than it would have been if they went separately. Consolidation of freight shipments works in basically the same way.

Consolidation warehouses are typically established at a strategic location between suppliers and customers. Ideally, in order to minimize the total transportation costs, the consolidation warehouse should be located closer to the supply base so that the smaller LTL shipments travel the shorter distance and can be consolidated more quickly into the larger FTL shipments traveling the longer distance to the customer. Usually a third-party logistics (3PL) provider manages and maintains the warehouse and the information system needed to run it, and these operations can either be client-dedicated or multiple-user facilities.

Figure 9.1 provides an example of the flow of products through a consolidation warehouse. Products are shipped from three separate plants or suppliers into the consolidation warehouse, usually in less-than-truckload (LTL) shipments. At the warehouse, the products are received and combined together to be shipped out to a customer in a larger full truckload (FTL) shipment.

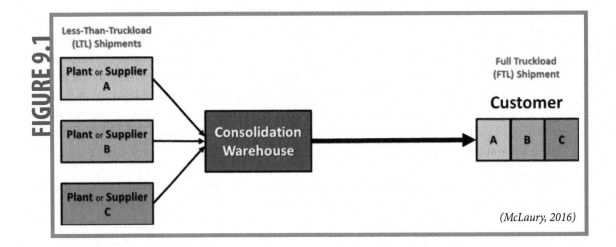

FIGURE 9.1

Less-Than-Truckload (LTL) Shipments

Plant or Supplier A

Plant or Supplier B

Plant or Supplier C

Consolidation Warehouse

Full Truckload (FTL) Shipment

Customer

A B C

(McLaury, 2016)

Break Bulk Warehousing

A break bulk warehouse is similar to a consolidation warehouse except that the incoming shipments are generally truckloads of homogeneous items from a single plant or supplier. The break bulk warehouse sorts or splits the items into individual orders or shipments and arranges for local delivery.

Similar to consolidation warehouses, break bulk warehouses are also typically established at a strategic location between suppliers and customers. In contrast to the consolidation warehouse location, in order to minimize total transportation costs, the break bulk warehouse should be located closer to the customer base so that the smaller LTL shipments travel the shorter distance to the customers, while the larger FTL shipments from the single supply source travel the longer distance before arriving at the break bulk warehouse.

Figure 9.2 provides an example of the flow of products through a break bulk warehouse. Products are shipped from a single plant or supplier into the break bulk warehouse, usually in FTL shipments. At the warehouse, the products are received and sorted or split into individual orders to be shipped out to customers in LTL shipments.

In both consolidation warehousing and break bulk warehousing, a 3PL provider frequently manages the warehouse and the information system(s) needed to run it. These operations can either be client-dedicated or multiple-user facilities.

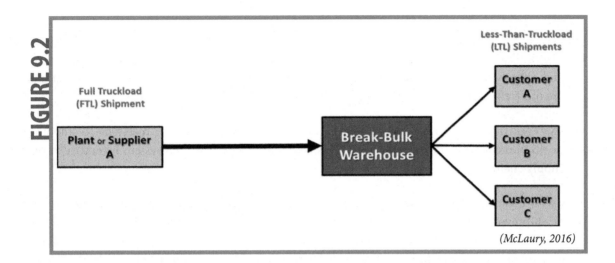

FIGURE 9.2

Less-Than-Truckload
(LTL) Shipments

Full Truckload
(FTL) Shipment

Plant or Supplier
A

Break-Bulk
Warehouse

Customer
A

Customer
B

Customer
C

(McLaury, 2016)

Cross-Docking Warehouse

Cross docking is the logistics practice of unloading materials from an incoming truck or railcar and loading these materials directly onto outbound trucks or railcars, with little or no storage in between. This is a type of consolidation and/or break bulk warehouse. The advantages of cross docking are to speed throughput times, reduce inventory investment, and reduce storage space requirements.

Cross docking takes place in a distribution terminal usually consisting of dock doors on two sides (inbound and outbound) with minimal storage space on site. The name *cross docking* refers to receiving products through an inbound dock and then transferring them across to the outbound dock. Once the inbound shipment has been received, the products can be moved either directly or indirectly to the outbound destinations. Products can be unloaded, sorted and screened to identify their end destinations, and then moved to the other end of the cross-dock terminal via materials handling equipment such as a forklift, conveyor belt, or pallet truck. When the outbound transportation has been loaded, the products can then be shipped out to customers.

The main reasons that cross docking is implemented are as follows:

- To provide a central site for products to be sorted and similar products combined to be delivered to multiple destinations in the most productive and fastest method possible

- To combine numerous smaller product loads into one method of transport to save on transportation costs (i.e., consolidation)

- To break down large product loads into smaller loads for transportation to create an easier delivery process to the customer (i.e., deconsolidation or break bulk)

CROSS-DOCKING PROVIDES CERTAIN ADVANTAGES:

- **OPERATIONAL EFFICIENCY:** As the material does not have to be stored at the warehouse, and directly moves from the receiving docks to the shipping docks, the warehouse operations are more efficient.

- **INVENTORY EFFICIENCY:** As the inventory moves directly from the receiving to shipping docks, there is no storage at the warehouses, and that reduces the total system inventory in the supply chain.

Figure 9.3 illustrates a cross-docking warehouse operation. On the left side of the diagram are inbound shipments of products from four suppliers. Once these products are received and unloaded, they can be sorted, reconfigured, and moved across the dock to ship outbound to the four customers, as shown on the right side of the diagram. Notice that each customer is being shipped a different configuration of the four products.

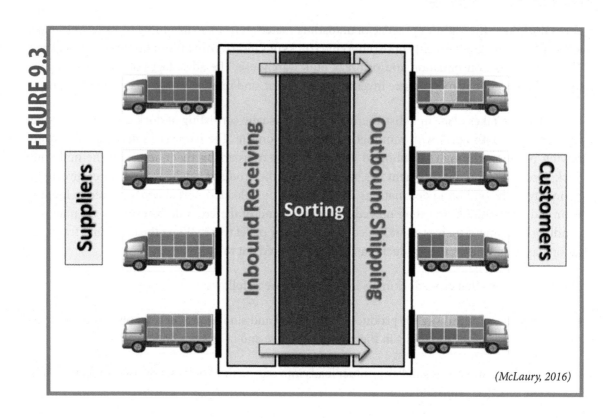

FIGURE 9.3

Suppliers — Inbound Receiving — Sorting — Outbound Shipping — Customers

(McLaury, 2016)

Figure 9.4 illustrates the difference with and without a cross-docking warehouse operation in this scenario. Without cross docking, each of the four suppliers must make LTL shipments to each of the four customers for a total of 16 LTL shipments. This will very likely cost significantly more than the eight FTL shipments (i.e., four inbound and four outbound), which will be completed as shown using the cross-docking operation.

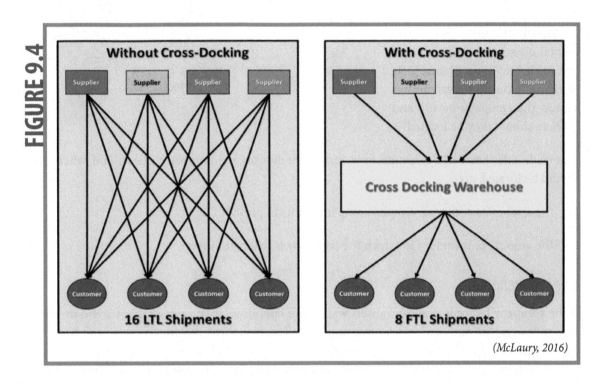

(McLaury, 2016)

With cross docking, larger and fewer shipments translate to lower overall transportation costs. Additionally, both suppliers and customers will experience a much more efficient use of their resources because each will only make or receive one shipment rather than four.

WHICH WAREHOUSE TYPE TO CHOOSE

To choose the most appropriate warehousing facility, the company should consider all of the services desired, the level of control that is required, and the length of time the storage facility would be required. Cost would also play a very important role when choosing between a privately owned and operated warehouse, and a warehouse owned and managed by a third party.

WAREHOUSE NETWORKS ....

A warehouse network is simply the number of, and the relationship between, the warehouses that a company has in its organizational structure. The fundamental questions to be answered in establishing a warehouse network are "How many warehouses should the company have?" and "Where should they be located?"

Map © Shutterstock.com

The trade-offs that will determine how many warehouses the company needs, and where they should be located, are:

1. The level of customer service the company wants to provide

2. The amount of inventory in which the company is willing to invest

Single Warehouse

If the company has only one centralized warehouse operation, then operating costs and inventory will be lower. Having fewer warehouses requires a less complicated infrastructure, and less or no duplications of equipment, warehouse staff, and managers. With fewer warehouses, the network becomes more centralized and the company will have its best people, equipment, and inventory systems concentrated in fewer places. This can be beneficial to customer service in that the warehouse can more actively focus on the needs of its customers. However, the centralized network may take longer to deliver product to some customers who are remote from the central location.

Multiple Warehouses

If the company establishes multiple warehouses that are geographically dispersed throughout the market they will likely be able to distribute product to their customers much faster than if they only have a centralized warehouse, assuming that they maintain adequate inventory in each warehouse. Every part of the market could potentially be better served through a multiple warehouse network. As responsiveness and delivery service increase, however, warehouse operating costs and inventory costs also increase as each warehouse costs money to staff and operate. Trade-offs between costs and customer service must be considered. A basic fact is that as the number of warehouses increase, the network becomes more decentralized, which may or may not be beneficial.

Hybrid Approach (Hub-and-Spoke Network)

Companies may choose to do some type of a hybrid approach to balance costs and inventory against customer service. One such network configuration is a "hub-and-spoke," where there is a centralized warehouse (i.e., the "hub"), which holds most of the inventory, linked to a series of smaller decentralized and geographically dispersed warehouses (i.e., the "spokes"), which hold only a small amount of inventory to support the local area in the immediate time frame. The hub warehouse feeds the spoke warehouses with inventory as necessary on a regular basis. Operating costs are lower because the spoke warehouses are smaller than in a purely decentralized model. Inventory is also lower than in a purely decentralized model as all of the safety stock is held centrally, which generally means that less total safety stock is required because all of the risk and uncertainty that the safety stock is protecting against is managed centrally. On the other side, customer service is generally better than in a purely centralized model, because some of the inventory is maintained in the spoke warehouses closer to the customers. For this model to work well, the demand in the local areas must be well understood and monitored closely.

Warehouse Network Strategies

Whether a company determines that it needs one or multiple warehouses, it will also have to determine which location strategy makes the most sense for its business. This strategy decision will be different from one business to another depending on the nature of the business and how many customers and suppliers interact with the company. The three main warehouse network location strategies are:

- MARKET POSITIONED STRATEGY: Warehouses are set up close to customers to maximize distribution services and improve delivery time. Companies should use this strategy if they have many more customers than suppliers, and the customers are spread out geographically around the market. If the warehouses are closer to the customers, the company can minimize transportation cost with this strategy. Similar to the break bulk warehouse setup, there will likely be FTL shipments coming in from suppliers at a greater distance, and LTL shipments going out shorter distances to customers.

- PRODUCT POSITIONED STRATEGY: Warehouses are set up close to supply sources to collect goods and consolidate before shipping products out to customers. This is basically the reverse of the market positioned strategy. Companies should use this strategy if they have many more suppliers than customers. If the warehouses are closer to the suppliers the company can minimize transportation cost with this strategy. Similar to the consolidation warehouse setup, there will likely be LTL shipments coming in from suppliers at a shorter distance, and consolidated FTL shipments going out longer distances to customers.

- INTERMEDIATELY POSITIONED STRATEGY: Warehouses are set up somewhere midway between the supply sources and the customers to try to balance costs, inventory, and customer service. Companies should use this strategy when distribution requirements are high and product comes from various supply locations.

A warehouse network optimization study may be needed to determine the optimal number and location of warehouses in this strategy. See "Warehouse Network Optimization" which follows.

Warehouse Network Optimization

Companies need to find the balance that will work for their products and markets. There are many consulting companies that offer services to help a company determine the optimal number of warehouses and geographic locations for a given company's situation by using a number of different optimization software programs. The software analyzes the inputs including customer, manufacturer, and supplier locations, then informs the optimal number of warehouses and locations based on all the relevant factors. These programs try to minimize the amount of transportation on both ends—inbound from suppliers and outbound to customers.

LEAN AND GREEN WAREHOUSING ....

Warehouses and distribution centers are continuing to develop their LEAN capabilities. The following are a few ways in which warehousing is adopting and adapting LEAN principles.

Greater Emphasis on Cross Docking

Cross docking is a LEAN concept and it is on the rise in business. Cross docking eliminates the need to store inventory, which is waste, and waste reduction/elimination is the key element of LEAN. Cross docking is a form of consolidation that reduces transportation, which is also waste. The more cross docking a company can do, the "leaner" their operations will be.

Reduced Lot Sizes and Shipping Quantities

Just as small batch scheduling is a LEAN concept, because it drives down costs by reducing inventories and makes the company more flexible to meet customer demand, this same concept can be applied to warehouse operations. By reducing lot sizes and shipping quantities, a company can actually increase the velocity or throughput in the warehouse and get shipments out faster. Smaller lots or orders will take less time to pick and load for shipment, which will keep costs and inventories down. Faster throughput and lower inventories are LEAN concepts.

Increased Automation

Companies are using automated systems like pick to light, voice picking, conveyor systems, automatized guided vehicles (AGVs), and robotics to improve efficiencies and throughput times in the warehouse. Automation can help to speed up the picking process and move products through a warehouse faster and more accurately than manual systems with less resources, again reducing waste.

A Tendency to Be Green

Companies are looking at what green or sustainability programs they can implement in warehousing operations. Companies want to know the size and impact of their carbon footprint. How can they reduce the amount of utilities and resources they use? Smaller, more efficient warehouses take up less physical space and use less energy to operate. One of the more sustainable goals for a green warehouse is to become a net zero energy user. In some cases, net zero buildings are able to sell excess energy back to the power grid, so much so that the cost of generating energy is neutralized by the excess energy sold. Some initiatives in this regard include lighting upgrades to use a more efficient fluorescent system, the use of daylighting, using solar-assisted heat pump or cooling systems, and the type of windows, doors, roofing materials, and insulation that are used, saving significant amounts of energy.

THIRD-PARTY LOGISTICS ....

Third-Party Logistics Company

A third-party logistics (3PL) company is an outsourced provider that manages all or a significant part of an organization's logistics requirements for a fee. Some of the typical services that are offered by 3PLs include but are not limited to inbound transportation, warehousing, pick and pack, outbound transportation, freight forwarding, freight bill auditing/payment, customs brokerage, customs clearance, order taking, billing/invoicing, and inventory auditing.

3PLs are used by large and small business but are particularly favored by small businesses that do not have their own logistics operations. Small business may not want to invest in activities outside their areas of expertise, and the 3PL company can bring their substantial logistics expertise into the engagement.

3PLs are also used to a significant degree for international logistics. A company is more likely to use a 3PL internationally rather than to try and establish an in-house operation in each foreign market themselves. Also, 3PLs likely know more about the logistics in those international markets, and they will have local contacts and local contracts already established. It is potentially much more cost effective and efficient for a company to ship product internationally using the services of a 3PL than to handle this activity internally, unless this is a major part of the business, and the company decides to invest significant resources and manpower into developing this expertise.

MAJOR ADVANTAGES OF USING 3PLs:

There are a number of benefits companies gain by outsourcing logistics activities to a 3PL. Utilizing a 3PL provides businesses with a reliable logistics advantage, and maximizes profitability through a combination of knowledge and resources.

- COST: Eliminates the need for a company to invest in warehouse space, technology, transportation, and staff to execute the logistics process.

- LOGISTICS EXPERTISE: 3PLs are knowledgable of industry best practices, and stay up to date with the latest developments in technology. This is their core competency.

- EFFICIENCY: Improved efficiency by exploiting a 3PL's economies of scale. 3PLs can leverage relationships and volume discounts, which results in lower overhead and the fastest possible service.

- FLEXIBILITY: Ability to rapidly scale space, labor, and transportation according to business needs.

- FOCUS ON CORE COMPETENCY: Outsourcing logistics allows your company to focus on your core competencies.

MAJOR DISADVANTAGES OF USING 3PLs:

There are also some issues and concerns that companies should consider before making a logistics outsourcing decision.

- CONTROL: A company will not have direct control over the logistics operation. They are relying on the 3PL to consistently deliver the promised services. This lack of direct control means that companies are at the mercy of any problems the 3PL faces.

- DEPENDENCY: Outsourcing logistics to a 3PL is a large commitment. When businesses contract with 3PLs it creates a dependency which can be significant. This dependency puts the company in an uncomfortable situation if pricing or service from the 3PL is not as expected. Logistical downtime can translate into large amounts of lost productivity and revenue. Although the free market dictates that a business dissatisfied with its 3PL could switch to another 3PL, the reality is not so simple. Switching logistical support can create great problems in unforeseen costs and higher risks resulting from the transition.

- PRICING: Contracting with a 3PL means that the company is locked into the pricing model specified in the business agreement. By outsourcing logistics to a 3PL, companies are forgoing the possibility that an in-house logistics department could discover a less expensive or more efficient solution.

- LOSS OF EXPERTISE: Companies that outsource in-house logistics to a 3PL may lose their own expertise in logistics by outsourcing.

- RISK: Sharing confidential information with an outside partner such as a 3PL may leave some companies feeling vulnerable.

Fourth-Party Logistics Company

Fourth-party logistics (4PL) is an interface between the client company and multiple logistics service providers. A company will select a lead logistics partner (referred to as a 4PL) that is then charged with managing the activities of all the other 3PLs being used by the company. Ideally, all aspects of the client company's supply chain handled by 3PLs would be managed by the 4PL organization.

TRANSPORTATION ....

Transportation is "the function of planning, scheduling, and controlling activities related to mode, vendor, and movement of inventories into and out of an organization."[1] Transportation attempts to fulfill three of the seven Rs—to get the <u>right</u> product, to the <u>right</u> place, at the <u>right</u> time by ensuring that the product is moved as efficiently and effectively as possible from point of origin to point of destination.

Transportation Objectives

Transportation has three objectives:

1. TO MAXIMIZE THE VALUE TO THE COMPANY THROUGH PRICE NEGOTIATIONS. In simple terms this means that the transportation function adds value by getting the best price to transport goods whether the goods are coming from the supplier or going out to the customer.

2. TO MAKE SURE SERVICE IS PROVIDED EFFECTIVELY. If you move product from a supplier, move product around internally, or move product out to a customer, you want to do it in

as few moves as possible, and making sure the product is not damaged or somehow otherwise negatively affected.

3.   To satisfy customers' needs. Ensure that the product gets to the right place at the right time. If you moved the product efficiently, effectively, and at the lowest possible cost, but it is not at the place where customers want it, when they need it to be there, the transportation function is not actually adding value.

Transportation Company Classifications

Companies transporting freight or cargo regardless of the mode of transportation are classified according to the following categories:

- Common Carrier: A person or company that transports freight for a fee that can be hired by anyone to transport goods. Common carriers transport the majority of the freight shipments that you see on the road, rail, air, among other methods.

- Contract Carriers: A person or company that transports freight under contract to one or a limited number of shippers. These carriers are not bound to serve the general public. Contract carriers establish an agreement with a shipper(s) that spells out the kinds of shipments the carrier will accept, where the carrier will take them, and the shipping fees the shipper will be obligated to pay. Shippers may in turn collect these fees from their customers.

- Exempt Carriers: A person or company specializing in certain services (such as taxi service) or certain commodities (such as farm products or bulk cargo) exempt from regulation by the Interstate Commerce Act. The exempt commodities usually include unprocessed or unmanufactured goods, fruits and vegetables, and other items of little or no value. The exemption under the interstate commerce act is to help the simple service groups such as taxis, farmers, and school bus drivers to operate without any interference from government regulations, as there is no threat of monopolization in these services.

- Private Carriers: A person or company that transports its own cargo, usually as part of a business that produces, uses, sells, and/or buys the cargo that is being hauled. The private carrier's primary business is not transportation, but performing a transportation function to facilitate the primary business. These carriers may refuse to sell their services at their own discretion, whereas common carriers must treat all customers equally.

Carriers, regardless of the classification type, may be prohibited by law from carrying certain types of items, including illegal and dangerous materials.

MAJOR MODES OF TRANSPORTATION ·······························

Mode refers to the way in which goods are transported; **carrier** refers to the company or service provider that actually transports the goods or materials.

There are five major modes of transportation:

- Motor carriers (trucking)

- Rail carriers

- Air carriers

- Water carriers

- Pipeline carriers

Motor Carriers

© Nethuz/Shutterstock.com

Trucking is the most prevalent mode of transportation and the one people are probably most familiar. It is also the most flexible mode of transportation in that it carries the most varied kinds of freight to the most locations. Motor carriers (trucks) are involved in more than 80% of U.S. freight transportation annually. This doesn't mean that the rest of the carriers only transport the remaining 20%. There is actually a significant overlap with other modes of transportation, because most product that is moved by rail, air, or water is also moved by truck to and from the railyard, airport, or seaport. Motor carriers are also heavily involved with what is known as the "last mile" of transportation. The last mile is the final leg of transportation in the supply chain when the product is delivered to its final destination. In the majority of shipments, the last mile is handled by truck.

Motor carriers transport nearly anything from packaged household goods, to building materials, to liquids. Motor carriers compete directly with rail and air for short to medium distance hauls.

There are two major categories of motor carrier: short haul and long haul.

- SHORT HAUL is defined as operating within 200 miles of the driver's home terminal. Drivers operate a day cab unit, and are performing short transportation legs, maybe within the state;

these are small, local type routes, and for the most part, drievers are home every night. Short-haul drivers can make four or more stops per day, loading and unloading at each location. With more stops and local work, short-haul drivers also spend more time driving on smaller streets, with difficult turns, and going to places with challenging loading docks. This requires mastering different driving skills than with long-haul trucking. Driving short haul is not as profitable as long-haul trucking; however, the quality of life is considered to be better than long haul.

- LONG-HAUL is defined as anything over 200 miles from the driver's home terminal. Long-haul truck drivers transport goods over hundreds and even thousands of miles. Long-haul drivers spend a lot of time traveling on large highways and they generally carry loads for two or more days before unloading. They may drive flatbed rigs, which are used for carrying things like steel, or drive tankers, or tractor trailers. They usually drive at night when traffic is light. Long-haul routes are driven by the most experienced drivers because it is challenging work and the cargo can be extremely valuable.

GENERAL FREIGHT CARRIERS AND SPECIALIZED FREIGHT CARRIERS

Motor carriers can be further categorized into general carriers and specialized carriers:

- GENERAL FREIGHT CARRIERS comprise the majority of the trucks you see out on the road-way, carrying most of the goods. These are trucking companies that engage in shipping pack-aged, boxed, and palletized goods that can be transported in standard, enclosed tractor-trailers, generally 40 to 48 feet in length. General freight carriers include common carriers as well as other kinds of carries discussed in this chapter.

- SPECIALIZED FREIGHT CARRIERS transport articles that, because of size, weight, shape, or other inherent characteristics, require specialized equipment for transportation. Some im-portant types of specialized equipment are bulk tankers, dump trucks, refrigerated trucks, and motor vehicle haulers (i.e., car carriers).

Shipments by motor carrier can be divided into either less-than-truckload (LTL) or full-truckload (FTL), generally indicating whether the volume of the shipment fills the truck trailer / container or not. Motor carriers may offer LTL or FTL, or both services.

LESS-THAN-TRUCKLOAD CARRIERS

LTL carriers are those that move small shipments—that is, when you don't have enough to fill a truck. There are many carriers that offer LTL service. Some further specialize in services such as lift gate and residential pickups and deliveries, guaranteed services, and freeze protection, just to name a few.

They stop at depots and transfer locations to match loads to the final locations. What that means for shippers is their cargo is likely going to be combined with other shippers' cargo because the carrier needs to fill up the truck as much as possible to make money. Therefore, multiple shippers' commodities will get loaded onto the same truck, going in the same direction, and there might be multiple handoffs along the way. An individual shipper's product could be picked up at the warehouse, then go to a depot or multiple depots, and be handed off from one carrier to another, making its way from point of origin to the final destination. The shipment will be subject to multiple stops and starts while other product is being picked up and dropped off, and because of that, LTL usually takes longer to get from origin to destination than FTL shipments.

LTL is also more costly in terms of price per unit, or price per weight, than FTL because carriers cannot always guarantee that they will fill the truck up and they may need to spread their fixed costs out over a smaller number of units/weight.

FULL TRUCKLOAD CARRIERS

FTL is used when a shipper has enough volume (or value) to fill the truck. These carriers generally contract an entire trailer out to a single customer. Thus, the carrier actually spreads its fixed costs out over the whole shipment and generally the individual per unit cost of shipping is lower than for LTL shipments.

A shipper may also decide to pay for a full truckload even if the volume being shipped doesn't actually fill up the whole truck. The reason may be to avoid having another shipper's cargo on the same truck for security reasons or for faster delivery. By paying for the full truck even if the shipper's cargo doesn't fill it up, the shipper can probably get a faster delivery time because the shipment won't go to a depot or make other stops along the way. Additionally, the shipper could potentially avoid any cargo mixups or cross contamination by using a dedicated truck.

Rail Carriers

A rail carrier is a company whose business is transporting persons or goods or both by railroad. Rail transportation is best used for very heavy shipments such as building materials, construction equipment, and coal, particularly when the transport distance is long.

© Route55/Shutterstock.com

ADVANTAGES OF RAIL TRANSPORTATION:

- Rail is better structured than any other form of transportation. It has fixed routes and schedules making its service more certain and regular compared to other modes of transport.

- Rail is the most dependable mode of transportation as it is the least affected by weather conditions compared to other modes of transport.

- Rail transport is economical, quicker, and best suited for carrying heavy and bulky goods over long distances.

- Rail has the best speed over long distances except for air transport, but it can carry heavy bulky goods making it more versatile than air.

- Rail is a less expensive mode of transport compared to other modes. It has lower variable costs and most of the operating expenses are fixed costs. Rail is economical in terms of labor as one driver and one crewman can handle a much larger shipping load than other modes of transportation, such as motor carriers.

- The carrying capacity of rail is extremely large and can be easily expanded even further by adding more railcars.

- Rail is also the safest form of transport.

DISADVANTAGES OF RAIL TRANSPORTATION:

Although rail transport has a number of advantages, it has a number of disadvantages as well:

- Rail requires a large capital investment in infrastructure and this investment is fixed, meaning that it is not easily adaptable to changing volume requirements. Construction costs, maintenance, and overhead expenses are very high compared to other modes of transport. Railroad infrastructure and aging equipment in the United States are also problems for the railroads. The rails, bridges, and other aspects are old and deteriorating, and require a lot of upkeep and further capital expenditure. Some of the infrastructure improvements the rail carriers can make themselves; however, other improvements must be handled through local, state, or the federal government.

- Rail transport is inflexible. Trains run on a specific timetable and schedule and therefore must arrive and depart according to their set timetable. Its routes and timings cannot be adjusted to individual requirements.

- Rail transport cannot provide door-to-door service. Instead, rail provides terminal-to-terminal service, which requires loading and reloading of products at stocking points, involving greater cost, more wear and tear, and additional time. Therefore, rail carriers are generally paired with trucks for door-to-door delivery. To overcome this disadvantage, some rail carriers have begun purchasing motor carriers and now offer point-to-point pickup and delivery service.

- Rail is unsuitable and uneconomical for short distance and small volume goods. Rail transport by its nature is considered slow and inflexible and compares unfavorably with motor carriers in terms of transit times and frequency of service in short to medium distance hauls.

- Due to the high capital investment, rail cannot be operated economically in rural areas, creating an inconvenience for this mode of transportation in those areas.

- The time and labor necessary to book and take delivery of goods is unfavorable compared to motor carriers.

- Rail must fully utilize all of its available capacity to operate economically, and it has a very large carrying capacity, which can create a significant financial problem.

- Rail companies use each other's railcars to build a rail transport, so keeping track of railcars and getting them where needed can be problematic.

- The time and cost of terminal operations can also be a great disadvantage.

Some new rail technologies include articulated cars, unit trains, and double-stack cars.

- **Articulated cars** are railcars that share an axle or are suspended by other railcars. They are operated as a single unit, often called a trainset. Articulated cars reduce cost, weight, noise, vibration, and maintenance expenses. However, they reduce flexibility as additional railcars cannot easily be added to the trainset when there is additional volume.

- **Unit trains** transport a single commodity such as coal or steel. A unit train is similar to the concept of a dedicated truck.

- **Double-stack cars** are railcars specially designed to carry intermodal containers, where the intermodal containers are stacked two high on each railcar.

Air Carriers

Air carriers are organizations transporting passengers and cargo by aircraft. Air is the newest transport mode and the least utilized.

Air shipments are relatively expensive compared to the other modes of transportation, partially because the fuel is expensive, they have a limited amount of cargo space, and they have to deal with weight and balance issues on the plane itself.

Air is the fastest mode transportation for medium and long distances. If a company has an item that is urgently needed or being expedited by a customer, air shipment might be the way to go. Many companies use air shipments if they have had a backorder or stockout to try to get the replenishment inventory back into the marketplace or to a customer quickly. Air carriers usually transport high-value goods (i.e., items with a high cost-to-weight ratio). These are very light, high-value goods that need to travel long distances quickly, and include such products as jewelry, fine wines, pharmaceuticals, and racehorses. Air carriers can't transport extremely heavy or bulky cargo because of the weight and balance restrictions. There are also commodities that are restricted from air shipments due to the nature of the product (e.g., some materials that are hazardous, combustible, explosive, even if it is a cargo-only aircraft).

Air transport represents about 5% of the total U.S. air freight. Internationally, according to multiple sources, air cargo represents less than 0.5% of the weight of all international cargo, while at the same time this segment represents around 30% of the total worldwide shipment value. Half of the goods transported by air are carried by cargo-only airlines such as FedEx and UPS, and the other half goes by passenger planes along with passengers and their luggage.

Cargo is loaded on the main deck or in the belly of the airplane by means of nose loading, where the whole nose is opened, or side loading, through a large cargo door. When a package is shipped on a passenger plane, it is usually consolidated with other packages and freight and packed into special containers that fit in the storage area under the passenger compartment (i.e., the belly of the plane). Since there often

FUNDAMENTALS OF SUPPLY CHAIN MANAGEMENT

isn't room to drive a forklift truck into the plane to load the pallets, the load floor is equipped with electric rollers. Once a pallet is pushed through the doorway, the electric rollers are used to move it to the front or rear of the cargo hold.

Similar to rail, air is also paired with trucks for door-to-door delivery.

Water Carriers

Water carriers are organizations transporting goods or people using waterways. Water carriers cover a broad range of water transportation routes including ocean / deep water, coastal and inter-coastal, and in-land waterways such as rivers and lakes. Transportation by water is the oldest form of transport in the United States, dating back to the birth of the nation. Water transport plays an important role in foreign trade.

© Route55/Shutterstock.com

Like rail, transportation by water is slow and inflexible, but is also inexpensive compared to the other modes of transportation. Water transportation is an efficient form of transportation in terms of energy costs per dollar of gross output, or compared to the market value of the goods.

Water transport is primarily used for heavy, bulky, and low-value materials (e.g., coal, grain). However, because transport by water is so comparatively inexpensive, almost any item may be shipped by water, including automobiles, petroleum, containerized cargo, and produce.

Domestic water carriers compete with railroads for the movement of bulk commodities such as grains, coal, ores, and chemicals, and with pipelines for the movement of bulk petroleum, petroleum products, and chemicals.

As with air and rail, water transportation is paired with trucks for door-to-door delivery.

Pipeline Carriers

Most people don't think of a pipeline as a mode of transportation, but any type of pipeline that moves material from one place to the other is a form of transportation. Pipeline costs are extremely low, dependability is very high, and there is limited risk of damage to the product being transported. It is actually the most efficient form of transportation. Once the pipeline is set up, there is very little maintenance, very little additional infrastructure that you have to build around it, and it is a continuous flow. It's also the most reliable form of transportation, not subject to the weather, traffic congestion, or breakdowns along the way.

The pipeline industry is unique in a number of important aspects, including the type of commodity hauled, the ownership, and visibility. The industry is relatively unknown to the general public, which has

© silavsale/Shutterstock.com

little appreciation for the role and importance of pipelines. Pipelines are limited in the markets they serve and very limited in the commodities they can haul. Furthermore, pipelines are the only mode with no backhaul; that is, they are unidirectional with products that only move in one direction through the line.

A major advantage offered by the pipeline industry is low rates. Pipeline transportation can be extremely efficient with large-diameter pipelines operating near capacity. Average revenues for pipeline companies are below one-half of a cent per ton-mile, which is indicative of their low-cost service. Two additional user cost advantages complement the low rates. First, pipelines have a very good loss and damage record. Second, pipelines can provide a warehousing function because their service is slow. Another positive service advantage is dependability. Although the service time is slow, scheduled deliveries can be forecasted very accurately, diminishing the need for safety stock. Additionally, the risk of terrorism is reduced when the pipelines are buried in the ground.

Although the pipeline's slow speed can be considered an advantage due to its use as a free form of warehousing, in some instances the pipeline's slow speed can be considered a disadvantage. Pipelines are also at a disadvantage when it comes to completeness of service, because they offer a fixed route of service that cannot be easily extended into a door-to-door service. That is, they have limited geographic flexibility or accessibility. The use of pipelines is limited to a rather select number of products: crude oil, oil products, natural gas, water, and a limited number of chemicals.

Ranking of Transportation Modes

Figure 9.5 is a chart that compares and ranks the various modes of transportation against key transportation service elements on a scale of 1 (best) to 5 (worst).

- Truck ranks the best overall but only ranks number 1 in the accessibility category.

- Pipeline is the lowest cost and the most reliable.

- Air is the fastest.

- Rail has the most capability.

- Water does not come in first in any category but is widely used for international shipments.

FIGURE 9.5

1 to 5 = Best to Worst

	Lowest Per-unit Cost	Speed	Reliability	Capability (can handle the most diversity of freight)	Accessibility	Total
Truck	4	2	2	2	1	11
Rail	3	3	3	1	2	12
Air	5	1	4	3	3	16
Pipeline	1	4	1	5	5	16
Water Ocean	2	5	5	4	4	20

Lowest overall score = best relative transport method

(McLaury, 2016)

Intermodal

Intermodal is sometimes referred to as the sixth mode of transportation, but it is really the use of multiple modes of transportation to execute a single transport shipment. Intermodal is growing substantially because it is fairly cost efficient and cost effective.

Some of the more common examples include:

- **RAIL AND MOTOR CARRIERS:** Offer point-to-point pickup and delivery service known as trailer-on-flatcar (TOFC).

- **RAIL AND WATER CARRIERS:** Offer point-to-point pickup and delivery service known as container-on-flatcar (COFC).

- **WATER AND MOTOR CARRIERS:** Offer point-to-point pickup and delivery service for overseas manufacturers.

- **ROLL-ON/ROLL-OFF (RO/RO) SHIP:** This is one of the most successful types of cargo ships operating today and its flexibility, ability to integrate with other transport systems, and speed of operation have made it extremely popular on many shipping routes. A RO/RO ship is specifically designed to carry wheeled and tracked vehicles as all or most of its cargo. Vehicles are driven or towed on and off the ship by means of either the ship's own ramps or shore-based ramps. Because it is designed to accommodate cargo that cannot be stacked

FUNDAMENTALS OF SUPPLY CHAIN MANAGEMENT

but varies in height, below-deck space and volume utilization is generally less efficient than on a containership. RO/RO ships are thus commercially viable only in certain specialized trades.

TRANSPORTATION PRICING AND CONSIDERATIONS ....

Since deregulation in the transportation industry, the negotiating of transportation prices is common. The main transportation schemes are as follows:

- COST OF SERVICE PRICING: The setting of a price for a service based on the costs incurred in providing it. The carrier estimates the cost of providing the service and then adds on a percent profit margin. Commonly used for pricing transportation of low value goods or in highly competitive situations.

- VALUE OF SERVICE PRICING: A pricing strategy that sets prices primarily, but not exclusively, in the value, perceived or estimated, to the customer rather than on the cost of the product or historical prices (i.e., "priced at what the market will bear"). Depends on the value of the goods being shipped. Used for high value goods or when no competition exists.

- COMBINATION PRICING: Price setting at a value between cost-of-service minimum and value-of-service maximum. Most carriers use some form of combination pricing. Common in highly volatile markets and changing competitive situations.

- NET-RATE PRICING: Established discounts and accessorial charges are rolled into one all-inclusive price. Pricing is tailored to the individual customer's needs.

Terms of Sale

The delivery and payment terms agreed between a buyer and a seller. In international trade, terms of sale also set out the rights and obligations of buyers and sellers as applicable in the transportation of goods.

EXAMPLES:

- **F.O.B. Origin:**

  - Seller states price at point of origin and agrees to load a carrier.

  - Buyer selects the carrier and pays for the transportation.

  - Title passes to the buyer when the shipment originates.

  - Buyer assumes the risk for in-transit loss or damage.

- **F.O.B. Destination:**

  – Seller arranges for transportation and adds charges to the sales invoice.

  – Seller assumes the risk for in-transit loss or damage.

  – Title does not pass to the buyer until delivery is completed.

Transportation Rate Categories

Price charged by transportation carrier for moving an item or commodity from point A to point B. Actual amount charged varies based on weight of object being moved, type of commodity being moved, and distance traveled. Classified as line haul rates, class rates, exception rates, commodity rates, and miscellaneous rates.

TRANSPORTATION REGULATION ....

The early days of transportation in the United States was like the Wild West. Transportation carriers could charge whatever they wanted for their services and there wasn't much competition to keep the market in check. As a result, there really wasn't good service to the public, so the government began to impose a series of regulations. Some of those major regulations include:

- THE GRANGER LAWS (1870s), which regulated the railroads

- INTERSTATE COMMERCE ACT (1887), which created the Interstate Commerce Commission (ICC)

- TRANSPORTATION ACT (1920), which made changes to the Interstate Commerce Act

- MOTOR CARRIER ACT (1935), which brought motor carriers under the Interstate Commerce Commission control

- TRANSPORTATION ACT (1940), which established ICC control over domestic water transportation

- FEDERAL AVIATION ACT (1958), which created air traffic and safety regulations and the national airport system

- DEPARTMENT OF TRANSPORTATION ACT (1966), which established the U.S. Department of Transportation to coordinate all U.S. transportation-related matters

One of the most important was the 1887 Interstate Commerce Act, which also established the Interstate Commerce Commission (ICC). The main reason for implementing this regulation was due to the monopolies in the railroad industry. The government stepped in to break those monopolies, stop the profiteering in that industry, and improve service offerings to the public.

TRANSPORTATION DEREGULATION

Eventually the pendulum swung back the other way. Transportation regulation became too onerous, and the rest of the world started to catch up in terms of transportation. Foreign transportation companies started to impact the ability of U.S. transportation companies to make money. As a result, the government started to deregulate the industry allowing U.S. companies more freedom so they could become more competitive in the United States as well as in other countries. Some of those major deregulation initiatives include:

- RAILROAD REVITALIZATION AND REGULATORY REFORM ACT (1976), which allowed railroads to change rates without ICC approval

- AIR FREIGHT DEREGULATION (1977)

- MOTOR CARRIERS DEREGULATION (1980), which helped promote competitive, safe, and efficient motor transportation

- SHIPPING ACT (1984), which allowed ocean carriers to pool shipments, assign ports, publish rates, and enter into contracts with shippers

- ICC TERMINATION ACT (1995), which eliminated the ICC

- OCEAN SHIPPING REFORM ACT (1998), which ended the requirement for ocean carriers to file rates

Regulation Pros and Cons

PROS

- Regulation tends to ensure adequate transportation service throughout the country.

- Regulation protects consumers from monopoly pricing, unsafe practices, and liability.

CONS

- Regulation discourages competition.

- Regulation does not allow prices to adjust based on demand or through negotiation.

In contrast, deregulation actually encourages competition and allows prices to be set by the market. Prices are adjusted by demand and an individual's ability to negotiate rates.

Today, the U.S. transportation industry remains mostly deregulated.

OTHER TRANSPORTATION INTERMEDIARIES

- FREIGHT FORWARDERS are the "middle man" between the carrier and the organization shipping the product. They take small shipments (e.g., LTL) from numerous companies and consolidate them to make larger shipments (e.g., FTL). These larger consolidated shipments can take advantage of lower transportation rates associated with volume. Some of these savings can then be passed along to the individual shippers.

- LOAD OR TRANSPORTATION BROKERS find shipments for carriers for a fee. They bring shippers and carriers together.

- SHIPPERS' ASSOCIATIONS are a group of shippers that consolidates or distributes freight on a nonprofit basis for the members of the group to obtain volume rates or service contract rates. Associations will contract for the physical movement of the cargo from members with motor carriers, railroads, ocean carriers, air carriers, and others.

- INTERMODAL MARKETING COMPANIES (IMC) purchase blocks of rail and truck transportation services, utilize equipment from multiple sources, and provide other value added services under a single freight bill to the ultimate shipper. They purchase rail capacity and sell it to shippers. Often, an IMC company will require a minimum number of shipments from a client, to guarantee that shipping equipment will be available.

TECHNOLOGY AND TRENDS IN TRANSPORTATION

As technology has continued to evolve in the trucking sector, it is now essential for companies to remain current with trends. According to a recent report from the *American Journal of Transporta-*

tion, technological trends have disrupted the trucking industry to the extent that early adopters are set to become the most effective and efficient operators.

Everything from driver staffing and recruiting, to driver monitoring and traffic coordination, to safety and communications are now driven exclusively through technology for many companies.

Following are some of the most prominent ways in which companies are now leveraging technologies to improve their operations and logistics.

- DRIVER MONITORING

  With the onset of data sharing technology in the trucking sector, companies are able to keep track of driver and vehicle progress. Mileage, distance routes, and all other behaviors can be monitored remotely now, which gives companies the ability to make real-time changes and improvements.

- TRAFFIC COORDINATION

  With the ability to communicate and access fleet information remotely, companies and drivers are now able to improve delivery times. This is achieved by coordinating driving patterns, delivering real-time traffic reports, updating information on surrounding areas, and even telling a driver about something in his or her blind spot. Traffic coordination technology has resolved many road transport issues for truckers as a result.

- SAFETY TECHNOLOGY

  Safety technology has perhaps been the most significant disrupter in the trucking industry. This facet of the sector is constantly experiencing changes with:

  – Stability control

  – Antilock braking systems

  – Collision avoidance systems

  – Lane departure warning

  – Interior cameras

  – Rearview cameras

  – Blind spot warning devices

  – Side monitor cameras and sensors

Investments in safety technology not only reduce accidents, injuries, and fatalities, but they have been shown to cut costs as well. For instance, according to research cited by TruckingInfo.com, it costs between $100,000 and $200,000 in payouts for property damage, up to $455,000 for accidents with injuries and close to $885,000 and $1.3 million for accidents that end in fatalities. The high costs of accidents have prompted many companies to adapt to new technologies.

The same research showed that just on the adoption of lane departure warning systems alone, there is significant return on investment. The average cost is around $800, which means it generates an ROI of somewhere between $1.37 and $6.55 for each dollar spent (ProDrivers, 2016).

- ## Platooning

Vehicle-to-vehicle communication is tackling two of the trucking industry's largest problems—fuel and safety. By using radar sensors, intelligent braking, video screens, and a wireless link, vehicle-to-vehicle communication makes it possible for two trucks to connect in a "platoon," or "closer together than would normally be safe."

The two trucks are able to get as close as 20 feet from each other

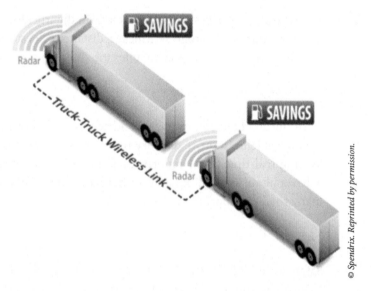

© Spendrix. Reprinted by permission.

while platooning in order to take advantage of fuel-saving aerodynamics. The industry reports fuel savings of 10% for the second truck and 4.5% for the lead truck in a platoon. The trucks are able to get this close thanks to an active safety system that wirelessly links the trucks. The wireless link controls the truck's acceleration and braking, while radar detects potential dangers up ahead. The linked trucks react within a "fraction of a second" whereas a truck driver needs up to two seconds to react to changes in conditions. While the wireless link controls acceleration and braking, drivers still have complete control of the truck (Goldwasser, 2015).

- ## Advanced Vehicle Experience—New Concept Trucking

A collaboration between Peterbilt, Capstone Turbine, and Great Dane Trailer has created a new concept truck—the Walmart Advanced Vehicle Experience, or W.A.V.E.

W.A.V.E. is a means to shake up the way things are done in the trucking industry as it combines many revolutionary ideas in tractor and trailer design.

The advanced concept tractor has a streamlined, aerodynamic body, thanks to the driver's seat placed in the center of the cab. Furthermore, the tractor has a microturbine-powered series hybrid electric drivetrain, programmed to find the most efficient balance between its turbine and electric drivetrains.

The trailer is equally as advanced, made almost entirely of carbon fiber, and weighing 4,000 pounds less than a normal trailer. The sidewalls and roof are single, 53-feet-long pieces, held together with advanced adhesives, eliminating the need for rivets. Finally, the trailer has a convex nose that maintains cargo capacity and improves aerodynamics.

While the W.A.V.E. is still a prototype, Walmart is not only attempting to improve its own fleet efficiency, but also advance the future of the entire trucking industry with this application transportation technology (Goldwasser, 2015).

- **VERTICALLY FOLDING SHIPPING CONTAINERS**

For decades, empty cargo containers have led to inefficiencies at ports.

A new innovation hopes to bring a sustainable alternative to normal, rigid cargo containers through vertically folding, retrofitted containers.

The goal is to reduce the number of container ship movements as well as intrastate truck movements at ports related to empty containers.

These foldable containers will reduce the cost and inefficiencies involved in moving empty intermodal containers. The containers are folded vertically by collapsing the doors of the container and pushing the outer walls of the container in toward each other. With this method, five empty, collapsed containers can fit into the same space as one normal, nonfolding container. Retrofitting old containers to be collapsible rather than designing and building completely new containers is another hallmark of this initiative. With an idea as simple as folding containers, you don't have to build intricate software or design new trucks to have a huge impact on the logistics industry (Goldwasser, 2015).

- ### DRIVERLESS TRUCKS

According to the American Trucking Association, there are some 3.5 million truck drivers in the United States alone. That's 3.5 million people who may be impacted once driverless trucks hit the roads in full force. A convoy of these trucks recently drove across Europe and arrived without incident at their destination at the Port of Rotterdam for 75% cheaper than it would have cost had human beings been driving them.

© Chesky/Shutterstock.com

A large part of the economic efficiency boost will include the fact that driverless trucks never get tired and can drive for 24 hours straight, nonstop, whereas humans obviously need to eat, take breaks, and sleep. Drivers are restricted by law from driving more than 11 hours a day and are required to take breaks each day. That means the technology would effectively double the output of the U.S. transportation network at 25% of the cost. In addition, truck drivers drive faster because they are paid by the mile and they're trying to get more done, a situation that throws fuel efficiency out the window in a way that won't happen with robotrucks, which will drive at a steady, set pace the entire trip (Dykes, 2016).

© Chesky/Shutterstock.com

LOGISTICS MANAGEMENT SOFTWARE APPLICATIONS.....................

Companies that have a lot of inventory and make a lot of shipments may find it necessary to have some type of system(s) in place to manage logistics activities such as warehousing and transportation. The following are the basic logistics systems that companies implement beyond the standard inventory management system or enterprise resource planning (ERP) system.

- WAREHOUSE MANAGEMENT SYSTEMS (WMS): Software application that supports the day-to-day operations in a warehouse. WMS programs enable centralized management of tasks such as tracking inventory levels and stock locations. WMS systems may be standalone applications or part of an enterprise resource planning (ERP) system. The goal of a warehouse management system is to provide management with the information it needs to efficiently control the movement of materials within a warehouse.

- TRANSPORTATION MANAGEMENT SYSTEMS (TMS): Software that facilitate interactions between an organization's order management system (OMS) and its warehouse management system (WMS) or distribution center (DC); it is used to select the best mix of transportation services and pricing. TMS systems may be standalone applications or part of an ERP system. TMS products serve as the logistics management hub in a collaborative network of shippers, carriers, and customers. Common TMS software modules include route planning and optimization, load optimization, execution, freight audit and payment, yard management, advanced shipping, order visibility, and carrier management.

The business value of a fully deployed TMS should achieve:

- Reduced costs through better route planning, load optimization, carrier mix, and mode selection

- Improved accountability with more visibility into the transportation chain

- Greater flexibility to make changes in delivery plans

REVERSE LOGISTICS...

What Is Reverse Logistics?

In supply chain management we are concerned with the efficient, effective, and cost conscious use of resources to move a product from concept to consumer. We must be equally concerned with the reverse flow of products back through the supply chain, known as reverse logistics. **Reverse logistics** involves the process of moving a product from the point of customer receipt back to the point of origin to recapture value or ensure proper disposal.

Keys to Reverse Logistics: Visibility, Efficiency, and Service

Companies must address a diversity of issues when trying to determine "why is there a need for reverse logistics." They must establish return policies, processes for identifying quality issues, ways to handle defective materials, poorly packaged products, shipped errors, and the like. An additional point of importance often overlooked in reverse logistics is the possibility of remanufacturing, refurbishment, and resale of goods.

In today's world of sustainability and green supply chains, questions arise as to the volume and level of waste involved with disposal of both products and packaging materials. There is also a question as to the possibility of the repurpose of products and the reuse of containers and package materials, which of course vary with every company and manufacture. One of an organization's concerns should be what types of material are being used, and if they are recyclable or "green." Additional concerns include which packaging materials can affect pollution, impact energy issues, and require hazardous materials programs?

Product Returns Are on the Rise

It is becoming painfully apparent that reverse logistics is on the rise. All manufacturers and retailers would be more comfortable if all of their products were based on a forward flow only; however, this will never be the case, as there will always be the need for a backward flow. The important questions to be asked are "What are the causes?" and "What can and must be done about it?"

The internet has become a significant contributor to the changing world of reverse logistics. With online shopping, direct sales to stores, along with other internet sale processes, direct to the consumer mistakes can be found at all levels from order taking, to fulfillment, to shipping, all of which have added complexity to the process.

An important factor when discussing reverse logistics is that a majority of errors causing returns is generally attributed to human error and not technological systems; however, the system often becomes the scapegoat for mistakes. One then has to ask the question, "What are these potential errors costing an organization, and in fact are organizations tracking the error data in such a way as to monitor costs and reasons for reverse logistics?"

One of the most important cost factors, which is extremely hard to calculate, is the loss of customer loyalty caused by poor reverse logistics processes and practices. Without a doubt, a poorly developed and managed reverse logistics program can and will have a profound effect on an organization's ROI, bottom line, and certainly customer satisfaction level.

Reverse logistics has not always been at the forefront of enterprise planning. The negative aura that surrounds planning for product distribution failures and/or product rejection is, in itself, off-putting. It is a case where everyone loses—your customer who sends the product back dissatisfied, your supplier who gets your parts back, and the manufacturer who wasted enterprise resources creating and distributing products that are unneeded or unwanted.

To say there is no solution to reverse logistics is no better than saying there is no reverse logistics problem. Reverse logistics is on the rise and it is not going to go away. In fact, it will only get larger as business grows and technology continues to develop.

Reverse Logistics and Returns Are Significant Parts of the Supply Chain

Reverse logistics costs money. It affects the bottom line, which has brought the issue to the forefront where it is beginning to receive significant attention. When organizations begin to truly consider reverse logistics, they will gain significant and direct understanding, control, and rewards from proactively managing the return product flow.

APICS Supply-Chain Council provided an understanding of the benefits of a good reverse/return logistics program. The APICS model suggests eight specific return points:

- Three return points at the supplier level

- Two return points at the manufacturing company level

- Three return points at the customer and the customer's customer level

There is no question the growing importance of returns reflects our changing economy. There is also no question that a strong returns policy should be considered part of an organization's business practices. Historically when times are tough and business is slow, companies tend to search for areas they may have overlooked to increase profits and decrease costs. One such area is product returns and the related manufacturing or distribution errors causing these returns.

An example is the often large return lines (sometimes longer than the checkout lines) following the Christmas season. This is also often indicative of the complexity of the reverse logistics process, including the processing of credit cards and cash returns, returning the wrong item to the wrong place, and so forth. Unfortunately, not all customers are honest, so managing this aspect of the reverse logistics is both critical and sensitive, impacting an organization's reputation. Along with all of this comes the need to be aware that there is often a defective product that requires a significant process for the physical handling to complement the normal product return policy.

Returns affect not only the retail portion of the business community, but also earlier issues with product manufacturing, raw materials use, the suppliers, and potentially how the product was handled and transported domestically and internationally. Returned goods or product can also be returned to suppliers for remanufacture and/or repackaging.

Implications in Today's Business World

In today's marketplace, many retailers treat merchandise returns as individual, singular transactions. Retailers and vendors are challenged to process returns at an effective level that allows quick, efficient, and cost-effective return of merchandise. Today customers demand a high standard of service that includes accuracy and timeliness. It's a company's responsibility to shorten the return cycle and expedite a customer's requirements. By following returns management best practices, retailers can achieve a returns process that addresses both the operational and customer retention issues associated with merchandise returns. Additionally, because of the connection between reverse logistics and customer retention, it has become a key component within service lifecycle management (SLM), a strategy to retain customers through a more efficient overall business operation.

Reverse logistics is more than just returns, it includes all related activities to avoid and those used to protect a company from all aftermarket chain issues. Reverse logistics and return management is well recognized as a significant cause that affects competitive positioning in the marketplace and is an important link between marketing and all logistical issues. Without question a company that improves its internal integration processes will influence customer external factors as applied to its returns management processes. "Studies have shown that an average of 4% to 6% of all retail purchases are returned, costing business and industry about $40 billion per year" (Van Riper, 2005).

Return of Unsold Goods

In some industries, goods are distributed to downstream members in the supply chain with the understanding that the goods may be returned for credit if they are not sold (e.g., newspapers, magazines, even pharmaceuticals). This acts as an incentive for downstream members to carry more stock, because the risk of obsolescence is borne by the upstream supply chain members. However, there is also a distinct risk attached to this logistics concept. The downstream member in the supply chain might exploit the situation by ordering more stock than is required and returning large volumes. In this way, the downstream partner is able to offer a high level of service without carrying the risks associated with large inventories. The supplier effectively finances the inventory for the downstream member. It is therefore important to analyze customers' accounts for hidden costs.

Streamlining the Five Rs of Reverse Logistics

When considering reverse logistics, it pays to improve returns management in five key areas.

1. RETURNS

Returns are typically the first step in the reverse logistics flow. Customers return products for a number of reasons. An item may be defective, damaged, and seasonal; fail to meet expectations; or simply represents excess inventory.

Whatever the reason, the key to handling returns efficiently is having processes in place for receiving, inspecting, and testing products, along with return material authorization (RMA) verification and tracking systems. Some companies find it's more efficient to decouple the return and repair processes completely.

2. Recalls

Another way parts and products are returned is through recalls. A critical reverse logistics category, recalls are more complex than basic returns because they typically involve a product defect or potential hazard and may be subject to government regulations, liability concerns, or reporting requirements.

High-tech devices are typically recalled because of faulty electronics, construction issues, problems with batteries, or potential hazards. The key is to have processes in place to receive, replace, resell, or reclaim failed parts/products—and whenever possible salvage revenues and turn a potentially negative customer experience into a positive one that builds brand trust.

3. Repair (and refurbishment, reuse, and remanufacturing)

Not all products that are returned go directly to landfills. If the faults are not too severe, manufacturers identify the failure and repair, refurbish, or remanufacture the product to like-new condition and return it to stock. Alternately, at end of life, manufacturers may harvest various functional components for reuse.

These practices are becoming more common as manufacturers recognize the value of reusing materials from returned goods. This may be to advance sustainability efforts, recoup costs, or both. Either way, retail shelves are increasingly stocked with both new and reused or remanufactured products.

Without a reverse logistics process in place to streamline the repair, refurbishment and/or remanufacturing of these products—and inventory management processes to go with them—you may invest too much time and money on repair parts or labor. Visibility and tracking are essential to ensuring efficiency.

4. Repackaging (for restock or resale in secondary channels)

There are two scenarios where returned parts and products might be remanufactured. Most products are returned because customers are dissatisfied with them (in the neighborhood of 95%) not because there's something wrong with them. When testing reveals "no trouble found," these products are typically repackaged and returned to inventory as quickly as possible.

Alternately, parts/products with minor flaws may be repaired, reconditioned, and repackaged for re-sale. This is an area where co-locating forward and reverse logistics processes can deliver important returns. With multiline packaging capacity already available for packaging new products, the same facility can be used to repackage returns for resale using secondary channels such as Overstock.com.

5. Recycling, disposal, and disposition

The focus on recycling returned or end-of-life parts, components, and products is driving more sustainable practices in every industry, but particularly so in high-tech industries. When products reach the ends of their useful lives and must be scrapped, electronic manufacturers are increasingly finding safe, cost-effective, and environmentally friendly ways to dispose of them. That might mean engaging third-party recycling companies to collect/reclaim waste and dispose of assets for them.

One area that's seeing a surge in recycling and reclamation efforts is in high-tech devices such as mobile phones or circuit boards, where companies recover rare earth metals of gold, silver, titanium, palladium, or copper. By salvaging, reclaiming, and reusing components, companies can reduce costs and minimize waste.

Setting up or fine-tuning reverse logistics processes can be a complex and time-consuming undertaking—especially if reverse logistics is not a core competency or you don't have the in-house resources to devote to it. As a result, many businesses outsource returns management to experienced third parties that can help them improve quality, cost savings, visibility, inventory management, and the overall customer experience.

Reverse Logistics Add-in

Six Sigma and quality are key parts of the reverse logistics process. When a product is returned to a retailer for any reason, there should be a significant process in place to track backwards what caused the reason if in fact it is a quality problem. The reverse questions of quality have to follow a specific order, starting with (1) was the product damaged when placed upon the shelf for sale by a salesperson or a stock person, (2) was it damaged when put into the stockroom by a delivery person, (3) was it damaged by a shipment from either a public or a private transporter to the retail store, or (4) was it damaged when it arrived at a distribution center?

A further examination has to go backwards again to how it arrived at a distribution center: Was it damaged in shipment? Was it damaged by the manufacturer in packaging? Was it damaged from the manufacturer when loaded onto pallets and sent to a dock for shipment? or Was it damaged when shipped from a port of exit to a port of entry and equally damaged from a port of entry to the central warehouse?

A flow diagram of this nature should be designed and followed by an organization to carefully identify where products are damaged, if it is by the manufacture, by shipping agents, or internally by the retail trade.

SUMMARY

- Logistics is "that part of supply chain management that plans, implements and controls the efficient, effective flow and storage of goods, services and related information from the point of origin to the point of consumption in order to meet customer requirements."

- Logistics is necessary to accomplish three things:

  - To move goods and materials from suppliers to buyers

  - To move goods and materials between sites, either internally, or between internal and external sites

  - To move finished goods out to customers

- Warehousing is all "the activities related to receiving, storing, and shipping materials to and from production or distribution locations."[1]

  - Warehousing is the function that allows a company to store all types of inventory (i.e., raw materials, WIP, and finished goods) that the company may have or need.

  - Decisions driving warehouse management include site selection, the number of warehouse facilities in the network, the layout of the warehouse(s), and the methods of receiving, storing, and retrieving products and materials.

- The basic functions of a warehouse include receiving, storage, picking, packing, and shipping. They can also perform other functions such as consolidation, break bulk, quality inspections, repackaging, and assembly operation.

- There are different types of warehouses that companies must consider: public, contract, private, consolidation, break bulk, and cross docking.

  - A public warehouse is a business that provides storage and related warehouse functions to companies on a short- or long-term basis, generally from month to month.

- A <u>contract warehouse</u> is a variation of public warehousing that handles the shipping, receiving, and storage of goods for a specific client on a contract basis.

- A <u>private warehouse</u> is a storage facility that is owned by the company that owns the goods being stored in the facility.

- A <u>consolidation warehouse</u> receives products from suppliers, sorts them, and then combines them with similar shipments from other suppliers into larger, more economical shipping loads for further distribution.

- A <u>break bulk warehouse</u> is similar to a consolidation warehouse except that the incoming shipments are generally truckloads of homogeneous items from a single plant or supplier.

- <u>Cross docking</u> is the logistics practice of unloading materials from an incoming truck or railcar and loading these materials directly onto outbound trucks or railcars, with little or no storage in between. This is a type of consolidation and/or break bulk warehouse.

- A warehouse network is simply the number of, and the relationship between, the warehouses that a company has in its organizational structure.

- Whether a company determines that it needs one or multiple warehouses, it will also have to determine which location strategy makes the most sense for its business. This strategy decision will be different from one business to another depending on the nature of the business and how many customers and suppliers interact with the company. The three main warehouse network location strategies are:

  - <u>Market Positioned Strategy:</u> Warehouses are set up close to customers to maximize distribution services and improve delivery time.

  - <u>Product Positioned Strategy:</u> Warehouses are set up close to supply sources to collect goods and consolidate before shipping products out to customers.

  - <u>Intermediately Positioned Strategy:</u> Warehouses are set up somewhere midway between the supply sources and the customers to try to balance costs, inventory, and customer service.

- A warehouse network optimization study may be needed to determine the optimal number and location of warehouse in this strategy.

- Warehouses and distribution centers are continuing to develop their LEAN capabilities. The following are a few ways in which warehousing is adopting and adapting LEAN principles.

- Greater emphasis on cross docking, which eliminates the need to store inventory, which is waste, and waste reduction/elimination is the key element of LEAN.

- Reduced lot sizes and shipping quantities. Just as small batch scheduling is a LEAN concept because it drives down costs by reducing inventories, and makes the company more flexible to meet customer demand, this same concept can be applied to warehouse operations.

- Increased automation. Companies are using automated systems like pick to light, voice picking, conveyor systems, automatized guided vehicles (AGVs), and robotics to improve efficiencies and throughput times in the warehouse.

- A tendency to be green. Companies are looking at what green or sustainability programs they can implement in warehousing operations.

- A third-party logistics (3PL) company is an outsourced provider that manages all or a significant part of an organization's logistics requirements for a fee. Some of the typical services that are offered by 3PLs include but are not limited to inbound transportation, warehousing, pick and pack, outbound transportation, freight forwarding, freight bill auditing/payment, customs brokerage, customs clearance, order taking, billing/invoicing, inventory auditing.

  - 3PLs are used by large and small business but are particularly favored by small businesses who do not have their own logistics operations.

  - 3PLs are also used to a significant degree for international logistics. A company is more likely to use a 3PL internationally rather than to try and establish an in-house operation in each foreign market themselves.

- Fourth-party logistics (4PL) is an interface between the client company and multiple logistics service providers. A company will select a lead logistics partner (referred to as a 4PL) that is then charged with managing the activities of all the other 3PLs being used by the company.

- Transportation is "the function of planning, scheduling, and controlling activities related to mode, vendor, and movement of inventories into and out of an organization."[1]

- Transportation has three objectives:

  - To maximize the value to the company through price negotiations

  - To make sure service is provided effectively

  - To satisfy customers' needs

- Companies transporting freight or cargo regardless of the mode of transportation are classified according to the following categories:

  - Common Carrier: A person or company that transports freight for a fee that can be hired by anyone to transport goods

  - Contract Carriers: A person or company that transports freight under contract to one or a limited number of shippers

  - Exempt Carriers: A person or company specializing in certain services (such as taxi service) or certain commodities (such as farm products or bulk cargo) exempt from regulation by the Interstate Commerce Act

  - Private Carriers: A person or company that transports its own cargo, usually as part of a business that produces, uses, sells, and/or buys the cargo that is being hauled

- There are five major modes of transportation:

  - Motor carriers (trucking)

  - Rail carriers

  - Air carriers

  - Water carriers

  - Pipeline carriers

- Motor Carriers (Trucks): The most prevalent mode of transportation and the one people are probably most familiar. It is also the most flexible mode of transportation in that it carries the most different kinds of freight to the most locations.

  - There are two major categories of motor carrier: short haul and long haul.

    - Short haul is defined as operating within 200 miles of the driver's home terminal.

    - Long haul is defined as anything over 200 miles from the driver's home terminal.

  - Motor carriers can be further categorized into general carriers and specialized carriers:

    - General Freight Carriers: Trucking companies that engage in shipping packaged, boxed, and palletized goods that can be transported in standard, enclosed tractor-trailers, generally 40 to 48 feet in length.

- **Specialized Freight Carriers:** Transport articles that, because of size, weight, shape, or other inherent characteristics, require specialized equipment for transportation.

- Shipments by motor carrier can be divided into either less-than-truckload (LTL) or full-truckload (FTL), generally indicating whether the volume of the shipment fills the truck trailer/container or not. Motor carriers may offer LTL or FTL, or both services.

  - **LTL carriers** are those that move small shipments—that is, when you don't have enough to fill a truck.

  - **FTL carriers** generally contract an entire trailer out to a single customer.

- **Rail Carriers:** A company whose business is transporting persons or goods or both by railroad. Rail transportation is best used for very heavy shipments such as building materials, construction equipment, and coal, particularly when the transport distance is long.

- **Air Carriers:** Organizations that transport passengers and cargo by aircraft. Air is the newest transport mode and the least utilized. Air shipments are relatively expensive compared to the other modes of transportation, partially because the fuel is expensive, they have a limited amount of cargo space, and they have to deal with weight and balance issues on the plane itself.

- **Water Carriers:** Organizations that transport goods or people using waterways. Water carriers cover a broad range of water transportation routes including ocean / deep water, coastal and intercoastal, and in-land waterways such as rivers and lakes

- **Pipeline Carriers:** Most people don't think of a pipeline as a mode of transportation, but any type of pipeline that moves material from one place to the other is a form of transportation. Pipeline costs are extremely low, dependability is very high, and there is limited risk of damage to the product being transported. It is actually the most efficient form of transportation.

- **Intermodal** is sometimes referred to as the sixth mode of transportation, but it is really the use of multiple modes of transportation to execute a single transport shipment. Intermodal is growing substantially because it is fairly cost efficient and cost effective.

- **Transportation Pricing and Considerations:** Since deregulation in the transportation industry, negotiating transportation prices is common. The main transportation schemes are as follows:

  - **Cost of Service Pricing:** The setting of a price for a service based on the costs incurred in providing it

- Value of Service Pricing: A pricing strategy that sets prices primarily, but not exclusively, in the value, perceived or estimated, to the customer rather than on the cost of the product or historical prices (i.e., "priced at what the market will bear")

- Combination Pricing: Price setting at a value between cost-of-service minimum and value-of-service maximum.

- Net-Rate Pricing: Established discounts and accessorial charges are rolled into one all-inclusive price

- Terms of Sale: The delivery and payment terms agreed between a buyer and a seller. In international trade, terms of sale also set out the rights and obligations of buyers and sellers as applicable in the transportation of goods.

- Transportation Rate Categories: Price charged by transportation carrier for moving an item or commodity from point A to point B. Classified as line haul rates, class rates, exception rates, commodity rates, and miscellaneous rates.

- Transportation Regulation: The early days of transportation in the United States was like the Wild West. Transportation carriers could charge whatever they wanted for their services and there wasn't much competition to keep the market in check. As a result, there really wasn't good service to the public, so the government started to impose a series of regulations.

- Transportation Deregulation: Eventually the pendulum swung back the other way. Transportation regulation became too onerous, and the rest of the world started to catch up in terms of transportation. Foreign transportation companies started to impact the ability of U.S. transportation companies to make money. As a result, the government began to deregulate the industry allowing U.S. companies more freedom so they could become more competitive in the United States as well as in other countries.

- Other transportation intermediaries include:

  - Freight Forwarders are the "middle man" between the carrier and the organization shipping the product. They take small shipments (e.g., LTL) from numerous companies and consolidate them to make larger shipments (e.g., FTL).

  - Load or Transportation Brokers find shipments for carriers for a fee. They bring shippers and carriers together.

  - Shippers' Associations are a group of shippers that consolidates or distributes freight on a nonprofit basis for the members of the group to obtain volume rates or service contract rates.

- Intermodal Marketing Companies (IMC) purchase blocks of rail and truck transportation services, utilize equipment from multiple sources, and provide other value added services under a single freight bill to the ultimate shipper. In other words, they purchase rail capacity and sell it to shippers.

- As technology has continued to evolve in the trucking sector, it is now essential for companies to remain current with trends. Some of the most prominent ways in which companies are now leveraging technologies to improve their operations and logistics are:

  - Driver monitoring

  - Traffic coordination

  - Safety technology

  - Platooning

  - Advanced vehicle experience, or new concept trucking

  - Vertically folding shipping containers

  - Driverless trucks

- Companies that have a lot of inventory and make a lot of shipments may find it necessary to have some type of logistics management software application in place to manage logistics activities such as warehousing and transportation. The following are the basic logistics systems that companies implement beyond the standard inventory management system or ERP system:

  - Warehouse Management Systems (WMS): Software application that supports the day-to-day operations in a warehouse.

  - Transportation Management Systems (TMS): Software that facilitates interactions between an organization's order management system (OMS) and its warehouse management system (WMS) or distribution center (DC).

- Reverse Logistics: We must be concerned with the reverse flow of products back through the supply chain, known as reverse logistics. It involves the process of moving a product from the point of customer receipt back to the point of origin to recapture value or ensure proper disposal.

  - The keys to reverse logistics are visibility, efficiency, and service.

- Product returns are on the rise.

- Reverse logistics and returns are a significant part of the supply chain.

- When considering reverse logistics, it pays to improve returns management in five key areas:

  1. Returns
  2. Recalls
  3. Repair (and refurbishment, reuse, and remanufacturing)
  4. Repackaging (for restock or resale in secondary channels)
  5. Recycling, disposal, and disposition

REFERENCES

[1] *APICS Dictionary* (14th ed.). (2013). Chicago, IL: APICS. www.apics.org

Ackerman, Ken. (1994). *Warehousing profitably*. Author.

Ackerman, Ken. (1997). *Practical handbook of warehousing*. London: Chapman & Hall.

Bolten Ernst, F. (1997). *Managing time and space in the modern warehouse*. New York, NY: AMACOM, a division of American Management Association.

Dykes, M. (2016). Driverless trucks already being tested; Three million-plus truck drivers to lose their jobs soon. *The Daily Sheeple*. Retrieved from http://www.thedailysheeple.com/driverless-trucks-already-being-tested-three-million-plus-truck-drivers-to-lose-their-jobs-soon_042016

Goldwasser, B. (2015). Trends in transportation technology. UseReload.com. Retrieved from http://blog.usereload.com/trends-in-transportation-technology/

Jenkins, Creed H. (1990). *Complete guide to modern warehouse management*. Upper Saddle River, NJ: Prentice Hall.

Lambert, Douglas M. (1998). *Fundamentals of logistics management*. New York, NY: McGraw-Hill;

ProDrivers. (2016). 4 ways technology is changing the trucking industry. Retrieved from https://www.prodrivers.com/news/2016/4/40121518/4-ways-technology-is-changing-the-trucking-industry

Ryder Exchange. (2014). Reverse logistics, supply chain, sustainability, technology.

Van Riper, T. (2005). Reseller sees many happy returns. *Forbes* (December).

Chapter 10

Global Logistics and International Trade

CHAPTER OUTLINE

Global Locations

Global Facilities—Strategic Roles

Global Location Factors

Global Location Decisions

International Trade Management

Major U.S. International Trade Legislation

U.S. Customs and Border Protection

U.S. Department of Homeland Security

Trade Compliance

Global Logistics Intermediaries

Import Process

Export Process

Penalties for Violations

GLOBAL LOCATIONS ....

Why would a company want to manufacture products outside of their domestic market? There are a number of significant reasons why this might be an attractive strategy, including:

- Reducing costs (direct, indirect, capital, logistics, etc.)

- Reducing taxes, and overcoming tariff barriers

- Access to more customers, and improved customer service

- Mitigating certain risks

- Establishing alternative sources of supply

- Gaining an advantage over competitors

- Obtaining knowledge from foreign suppliers, competitors, customers, and research institutions

- Securing access to global talent

In today's business environment, companies can locate anywhere in the world due to such aspects as increased globalization, advancements in technology, new transportation options, and open markets. Therefore, facility location must be part of the company's supply chain strategy.

Global location decisions involve:

1. Defining each facility's strategic role (i.e., the purpose of each facility)

2. Determining the location for each facility (i.e., where in the world to locate)

3. Identifying the market(s) that each facility will serve (i.e., local, regional, global)

GLOBAL FACILITIES—STRATEGIC ROLES ....

Manufacturing facilities can be categorized based on what they produce, where they are located, how much decision-making authority they have, what technical activities they perform, what markets they serve, and more. Research done by Professor Kasra Ferdows, Georgetown University, identified six specific strategic roles that a manufacturing facility can assume.[6]

1. Offshore Factory

An offshore factory is a very basic factory set up for manufacturing or assembly in a country where labor and/or raw materials are less expensive, typically for import back into the manufacturer's home country. An offshore factory can also be defined as "a plant that imports or acquires locally all components and then exports the finished product."[1]

© AVD_88/Shutterstock.com

OFFSHORE FACTORY CHARACTERISTICS:

- Low cost manufacturer; set up in markets with low labor costs and lower material costs.

- Local management serves in a supervisory role, not in making management decisions.

- Little to no engineering work or technical activities.

- Imports or obtains materials locally, and then exports products to the parent company or directly to customers.

2. Source Factory

A source factory is similar to an offshore factory in that it is generally located in a market with low labor and material costs, but it takes advantage of skilled workers and allows for more managerial input and control. Source factories have a more substantial role than offshore factories and are established to be the main source of specific products or processes.

© The Vectorminator/Shutterstock.com

SOURCE FACTORY CHARACTERISTICS:

- Low cost manufacturer; set up in markets with low labor costs and lower material costs.

- Local management has an expanded role and is involved in making some management decisions regarding procurement, production planning, process changes, and distribution.

- Increased technical and managerial resources.

- Access to a skilled workforce.

- More developed local infrastructure.

3. Server Factory

A server factory is set up to serve a specific market(s). It may also be set up to take advantage of government incentives and/or reduced taxes/tariffs. A server factory can also be defined as "a facility making minor improvements to products; set up primarily to avoid the host country's barriers to trade."[1]

© Nerthuz/Shutterstock.com

SERVER FACTORY CHARACTERISTICS:

- Serves a specific market(s).

- Local management serves primarily in a supervisory role, not in making most management decisions; however, local management may be involved in managing the flow of materials from suppliers, to the factory, and out to customers.

- Takes advantage of government incentives and reduced taxes/tariffs.

- Makes minor improvements to product and processes.

4. Contributor Factory

A contributor factory is set up to serve a specific market(s) similar to a server factory, but the role is expanded to also be the focal point for specific company activities. These factories are given the role to develop and contribute know-how for the company. They provide product development and engineering for products that they manufacturer, and they are typically involved in new product introductions.

© IKuvshinov/Shutterstock.com

Contributor Factory Characteristics:

- Serves a specific market(s).

- Increased technical and managerial resources.

- Involved in supplier, product, and process development including new product introductions.

- Local management involvement in procurement decisions and production planning.

5. Outpost Factory

An outpost factory is set up in an area with an abundance of advanced suppliers, competitors, research facilities (e.g., a business cluster) for the purpose of obtaining knowledge and information.

Outpost Factory Characteristics:

- Established in or near a business cluster.

- Primary purpose is to obtain knowledge and information.

© IKavshinov/Shutterstock.com

6. Lead Factory

A lead factory is the source of product and process innovation and provides a competitive advantage across the entire organization. They are set up to build strategic capabilities in manufacturing, and to develop the ability and knowledge to innovate and create new processes, products, and technologies for the entire company. Lead factories are typically the major producer of the main products of a company for the global market.

Lead Factory Characteristics:

- Major production facility for the company.

- Leader in technologies and innovation.

© VectorPot/Shutterstock.com

- Development of manufacturing capabilities.

- Competitive advantage of the organization.

- The company's "go to" factory.

GLOBAL LOCATION FACTORS ....

Global location factors are used to compare and contrast one potential location against another when making global location decisions. The most common location factors are:

- Access and Proximity to Markets

- Access to Suppliers and Cost

- Business Clusters

- Competitiveness

- Currency Stability

- Environmental Considerations

- Labor Availability and Cost

- Land Availability and Cost

- Quality of Life Factors

- Taxes and Incentives

- Trade Agreements

- Utility Availability and Cost

© Jelica Videnovic/Shutterstock.com

Access and Proximity to Markets

The company's ability to deliver its products and services to customers in a timely and cost-effective manner is not only a goal or objective, but also absolutely critical to the company's long-term survival. When choosing a global location from which to establish operations, the proximity to customers and the access to the markets being served are vitally important, and may be the deciding factors when making the final location selection.

There are some markets around the world that are restrictive, and to be granted access to sell products in those markets, companies may be required to establish local operations within those countries.

Because logistics timelines and costs are significant concerns, the trend in manufacturing is to be within delivery proximity of your customers. This also reinforces the business cluster concept discussed later in the chapter, where manufacturers, suppliers, customers, and service providers all locate near one another generally in places that offer lower cost labor, tax breaks, and lower real estate prices.

In the service industry, proximity to customers is even more critical. A company can't easily or cost effectively service a piece of equipment that they sold to a customer if the technician is thousands of miles away.

Access to Suppliers and Cost

The company's ability to receive materials and services from suppliers in a timely and cost effect manner is also critical to the company both short and long term. If the company wants to source materials and services locally, are those materials and services available, and are they priced competitively in the global locations being considered?

When choosing a global location from which to establish operations, the proximity to suppliers and the ability suppliers have to deliver materials and services to the company will be major factors in determining the effectiveness of the supply chain, and may therefore be deciding factors when making the final location selection.

Business Clusters

A business cluster is a network of manufacturers, suppliers, service organizations, and related businesses and institutions connected to one another within an industry, all located in the same geographical area. These industry concentrations are believed to provide a benefit to all of the co-located businesses and institutions whether they are partners or competitors. The proximity to

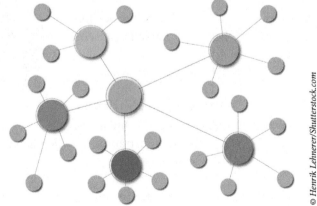

© Henrik Lehnerer/Shutterstock.com

one another provides easy access to talent, knowledge, services, supplies, technology, and even competitive information. Companies located in these business clusters are often able to increase their efficiency and productivity making them more competitive. Research parks and special economic / industrial zones can serve as magnets for business clusters. Examples of business clusters include Silicon Valley (technology), Research Triangle Park (research & development), Wall Street (financial), New Jersey (pharmaceuticals), Singapore (high-tech manufacturing), and India (software).

Reasons for the success of business clusters include:

- Innovation and competition can be geographically concentrated.

- There is close cooperation, coordination, and trust among clustered companies.

- Companies recruit from local skilled workers.

Competitiveness

The World Economic Forum defines competitiveness as the "set of institutions, policies, and factors that determine the level of productivity of a country" and identifies "12 Pillars of Competitiveness" in their Global Competitiveness Report 2014–2015.[2]

These pillars are used to rank and compare country locations. In general, countries that have a higher overall ranking potentially provide a more favorable business environment than lower ranked countries.

The 12 Pillars of Competitiveness are:

© Jelica Videnovic/Shutterstock.com

1. INSTITUTIONS: "Concepts related to property rights, efficiency and transparency of public administration, independence of the judiciary, physical security, business ethics and corporate governance"[2]

2. INFRASTRUCTURE: "Quality and availability of transport, electricity, and communication infrastructures"[2]

3. MACROECONOMIC STABILITY: "Fiscal and monetary indicators, savings rate, and sovereign debt rating"[2]

4. HEALTH AND PRIMARY EDUCATION: "State of public health, quality and quantity of basic education"[2]

5. HIGHER EDUCATION AND TRAINING: "Quality and quantity of higher education, and quality and availability of on-the-job training"[2]

6. GOODS MARKET EFFICIENCY: "Factors that drive the intensity of domestic and foreign competition, and demand conditions"[2]

7. LABOR MARKET EFFICIENCY: "Labor market efficiency and flexibility, meritocracy and gender parity in the workplace"[2]

8. FINANCIAL MARKET SOPHISTICATION: "Efficiency, stability, and trustworthiness of the financial and banking system"[2]

9. TECHNOLOGICAL READINESS: "Adoption of the technology by individuals and businesses"[2]

10. MARKET SIZE: "Size of the domestic and export markets"[2]

11. BUSINESS SOPHISTICATION: "Efficiency and sophistication of the business processes in the country"[2]

12. INNOVATION: "Capacity for, and commitment to, technological innovation"[2]

Currency Stability

Any decision about locating an operation in a particular country must consider currency stability. Fluctuation in currency exchange rates is a reality of international business. An unstable currency market will have a definite impact on determining and managing business costs. A company's purchasing power could be impaired or improved, inventory could be devalued or overvalued, labor and material costs might be unpredictable, among other things.

© Vladnik/Shutterstock.com

- A few years back, Brazil had 1,000% annual inflation rate. It is nearly impossible to determine costs and set prices in that type of currency environment.

Environmental Considerations

Another global location consideration involves understanding and evaluating the environmental situation within each potential location. Companies must consider the local environmental impact on their organization and employees, as well as the impact that their operations may have on the local environment. Countries and specific locations may have differing environmental laws, regulations, and resources which may restrict company operations and impact costs. Air and water quality, carbon emissions, and disposal of waste, among other environmental factors, could be issues a company encounters depending on the global location selected.

© Jemastock/Shutterstock.com

Labor Availability and Cost

Availability of the type of labor, in the volumes needed, and at the desired cost are major drivers for many companies when evaluating one potential global location over another.

When a company is evaluating a global location, it should consider labor factors such as the availability of skilled or unskilled labor, labor productivity, unemployment and underemployment rates, wage rates, turnover rates, and labor force competitors. Depending on the company's needs, one or more of these factors could make or break the decision. Another factor to consider is the long-

© donskarpo/Shutterstock.com

term prognosis for the labor market in a particular global location. Labor costs and availability may be favorable in the short term, but could change significantly over time.

If the company is evaluating locations within the United States, another consideration may be the right to work laws. A **right to work law** guarantees that a person cannot be required to join or not

FUNDAMENTALS OF SUPPLY CHAIN MANAGEMENT

join (or to pay dues to) a labor union, as a condition of employment. There are currently 26 U.S. states that have right to work laws protecting the rights of employees.

Land Availability and Costs

A company considering various global locations may also be considering building a new facility or buying an existing one. In either situation, the availability and cost of land could potentially be an issue, and must be a consideration in the location decision. Many popular areas around the global have scarce land resources available and/or the land prices are extremely high. Companies have expanded their focus beyond the major cities to include some of the more suburban and rural areas where land may be more readily available and at a lower cost, while still being close enough to the urban areas where suppliers, customers, and service providers are located.

© Iconic Bestiary/Shutterstock.com

Quality-of-Life Factors

A higher quality of life in the workplace and also in the surrounding environment leads to higher employee morale, satisfaction, and retention. Companies that establish facilities in various global locations will need people to work at these locations. Some of the workforce will likely be local, and some personnel may transfer from other locations either from inside or from outside the company. In all cases, the quality of life in each global location will be a factor in attracting and retaining skilled and unskilled workers to that location. Companies should therefore understand and evaluate the following quality of life factors in terms of maturity, sophistication, robustness, and so forth, in each location before making a location decision:

© ALMAGAMI/Shutterstock.com

1. Culture

2. Economy

3. Education

4. Government / Politics

5. Healthcare

6. Mobility

7. Natural Environment

8. Public Safety

9. Recreation

10. Social Environment

Taxes and Incentives

Taxes and governmental incentives are significant considerations when comparing potential global locations. From a tax perspective, multiple levels of government must be considered as there may be federal, state/region, and/or local community taxes, any or all of which could impact the business and influence the location decision. Import tariffs, which are designed to generate revenue and/or protect local businesses, may also be imposed in various countries. Countries with high tariffs encourage multinational corporations to produce locally, and discourage importing goods into the country.

© Rawpixel.com/Shutterstock.com

Countries may provide tax incentives (e.g., reductions or deferments) to attract businesses to locate operations within their borders. These incentives may also be tied to the volume of business done within the country, how many local labors are employed, whether materials are purchased from local suppliers or not, among others.

Trade Agreements

Regional trade agreements impact global location decisions. A location may be more favorably viewed if there is one or more trade agreements in place providing a financial incentive and a better business environment than another country location. The following are a few examples of regional trade agreements:

© Iconic Bestiary/Shutterstock.com

- European Union (EU):

    – [1950] Following WWII, consists of 27 members countries in Europe

- North American Free Trade Agreement (NAFTA):

    – [1994] Removed most barriers to trade and investment among United States, Canada, and Mexico

- Southern Common Market (MERCOSUR):

    – [1991] Argentina, Brazil, Paraguay, and Uruguay

- Association of Southeast Asian Nations (ASEAN):

    – [1967] 10 member countries in SE Asia

- Common Market of Eastern and Southern Africa (COMESA):

    – [1993] 19 member countries in East and South Africa

These regional trade agreements, and many more, are monitored by the World Trade Organization (WTO).

"The World Trade Organization (WTO) deals with the global rules of trade between nations. Its main goal is to ensure that trade flows as smoothly, predictably and as freely as possible."[3] The WTO was established in 1995, and is headquartered in Geneva, Switzerland. There are currently 164 member countries (as of July 2016) that use the WTO to facilitate and resolve trade issues with each other.

WTO functions[3] include:

- Administering WTO trade agreements

- Forum for trade negotiations

- Handling trade disputes

- Monitoring national trade policies

- Technical assistance and training for developing countries

- Cooperation with other international organizations

Utility Availability and Cost

The cost and availability of utilities such as water, electricity, natural gas, and telecommunications could be an important consideration for companies making location decisions. The availability of all utilities on a consistent basis, as well as the cost of those utilities, are critical considerations, particularly for companies producing or supplying heavy industrial products such as iron, coal, oil, ships, and machinery. In some parts of the world, the supply of various utilities is not reliable in general, and also not able to meet the demand of local business growth. This has been an issue particularly in emerging markets, where some of the lower cost labor and materials are centered.

GLOBAL LOCATION DECISIONS

Generally, when a company considers various global locations for its operations there is a hierarchy or step-wise approach to narrowing down the possibilities. Companies will first start by dividing the globe into regions, and then hone in on countries that align with the company's vision, mission, and business strategy. From there, the company can begin to look at specific areas within countries, and then finally down to specific communities or sites to evaluate.

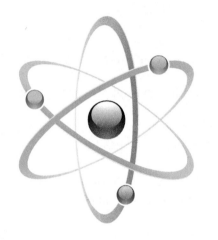

© Alhovik/Shutterstock.com

Some of the decision factors outlined in this chapter are federally controlled or related to the country as a whole, such as competitiveness, currency stability, federal taxes and incentives, and trade agreements. Some of the decision factors are locally controlled or related to the local community or specific site selected, such as land availability and costs, and local taxes and incentives. The balance of the decision factors are related to, or influenced by, all levels (i.e., federal, regional, local) within the country.

Weighted-Factor Rating Model

One method of evaluating the potential global locations is the weighted-factor rating model, which compares the attractiveness of several locations against some or all of the location factors described in this chapter. The process involves:

- Identifying the factors to be considered/evaluated

- Assigning a weight to each factor:

  - The individual factor weights must sum to 1.

  - Equal weight can be applied to all factors, or different individual weights can be applied to factors, with some factors weighing more than others in the decision-making model. This determination is made by companies based on how they value each factor, and it is company specific.

- Determining a score for each factor at each location

- Multiplying the factor score by the weight, and then calculating the sum of the weighted scores

- The location with the highest total weighted score is the recommended location.

INTERNATIONAL TRADE MANAGEMENT

Operating a Global Supply Chain

Operating your supply chain globally can present opportunities and challenges over operating domestically.

OPPORTUNITIES

- Increased customers and revenue. Global business means the opportunity to reach many more potential customers than are available within the domestic market alone.

- Increased sourcing options. Global business means more potential sources of supply from which to choose. These additional sources of supply can bring reduced costs, more alternatives, additional knowledge, and help spread out risk. Additional sourcing options may also lead to additional customers, by opening up previously closed markets.

CHALLENGES

- International trade frequently involves having to pay tariffs or duties (i.e., import taxes) when crossing international borders, and this will obviously increase costs.

- Transporting goods across borders will potentially add distance and time to the transportation activity, and it involves additional steps to clear customs which will also add time. Carriers specializing in international transportation may be needed, which likely means building relationships with new partners.

- Customs, business practices, and regulations vary by country, and are in a constant state of change. Many companies do not have the expertise to ensure compliance with all of the international trade laws, necessitating outsourcing this activity to a specialized third party.

- Not all foreign markets are homogeneous within the country, which can create additional layers of regional and local issues to overcome.

Managing International Trade Activities

Managing international trade activities is a complex process. A typical cross-border shipment involves:

- Accurately completing and filing about 35 documents

- Compliance with over 600 laws and 500 trade agreements, which are constantly changing

- Interfacing with about 25 parties, including customs, carriers, freight forwarders, other government agencies, etc.

Trade regulations and related content are at the heart of international trade management, but staying up-to-date is a major challenge because:

- The information changes frequently.

- It's often made available only in a foreign language.

- It's not always produced in an electronic form.

MAJOR U.S. INTERNATIONAL TRADE LEGISLATION........................

In the 70 years from 1930 to 2000 in the United States, there were seven major laws or acts created to regulate international trade. Most of these regulations were economic based:

1. Tariff Act of 1930 & Subsequent Regulations

2. Anti-Smuggling Act of 1935

3. Public Law 95-410

4. Trade & Tariff Act of 1984

5. Title VI of the NAFTA –"Mod Act" and Subsequent Regulations

6. CAT Audits – Compliance Assessment Team Audit

7. FDA/USDA – Presidential initiatives for safety of imported goods.

In only the two plus years immediately following 9/11 in the United States, there were 10 new major laws or initiatives created to regulate and control international trade. Many, if not all, of these regulations were security based:

1. Focus Assessment – Replacing CAT

2. Container Security Initiative (CSI)

3. Automated Customs Environment (ACE) – Replacing ACS

4. 24-Hour Rule

5. Trade Act of 2002

6. C-TPAT (Customs–Trade Partnership Against Terrorism)

7. TCMP (Trade Compliance Measurement Program)

8. The Bio-Terrorism Act of 2002

9. U.S. Customs and Border Protection

10. Department of Homeland Security established

The major challenge remains, to facilitate the free flow of goods across borders while still being able to secure the borders and prevent terrorism from entering the country through international trade channels.

- Transportation across national boundaries introduces added complexity and challenges security.

- Since 9/11 there has been an increased level of conflict between the U.S. government and industry regarding the adoption of additional security measures and the restrictions on international shipments.

U.S. CUSTOMS AND BORDER PROTECTION

Originally established in 1789 as the U.S. Customs Service, "U.S. Customs and Border Protection, CBP, is one of the world's largest law enforcement organizations and is charged with keeping terrorists and their weapons out of the U.S. while facilitating lawful international travel and trade. As the United States' first unified border entity, CBP takes a comprehensive approach to border management and control, combining customs, immigration, border security, and agricultural protection into one coordinated and supportive activity."[4]

© danielfela/Shutterstock.com

- CBP is the gateway agency for more than 20 other government agencies, each of which has some control over various aspects of international trade.

- CBP's mission is to safeguard America's borders thereby protecting the public from dangerous people and materials, while enhancing the nation's global economic competitiveness by enabling legitimate trade and travel.

- CBP works to secure and facilitate imports arriving in the United States, accommodating the increasing volume and complexities of international trade.

- CBP protects the United States through active inspections at ports of entry. In an effort to "push the border outward," CBP has now expanded operations to review and preclear cargo shipments at foreign ports prior to departing for the U.S. homeland. Many of CPB's programs and initiatives are designed to facilitate this preclearance activity (e.g., CSI, 24 hour rule, Security Filing 10+2).

- CBP has a strong base of industry partnerships and technology to safeguard the American public and promote legitimate international commerce (e.g., C-TPAT).

U.S. DEPARTMENT OF HOMELAND SECURITY

"The Department of Homeland Security combined 22 different federal departments and agencies into a unified, integrated cabinet agency when it was established in 2002."[5]

- DHS is the government agency whose mission is to:

  1. Prevent terrorist attacks within the United States
  2. Reduce America's vulnerability to terrorism
  3. Minimize the damage from potential attacks and natural disasters

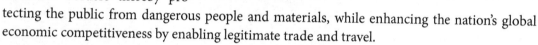

© Mark Van Scyoc/Shutterstock.com

- On March 1, 2003, the U.S. Customs Service was incorporated into DHS, officially becoming U.S. Customs and Border Protection, and thus DHS assumed responsibility for securing U.S. borders and transportation systems, which straddle 300+ official ports of entry and connects the U.S. homeland to the rest of the world.

- The department's first priority is to prevent the entry of terrorists and the instruments of terrorism, while simultaneously ensuring the efficient flow of lawful traffic and commerce.

TRADE COMPLIANCE

Trade compliance is the process by which goods enter a country such as the United States in conformance with all laws and regulations, and it is a major concern of any company conducting international business. There are dozens of laws, regulations, and rules that have to be checked and complied with for every import or export transaction.

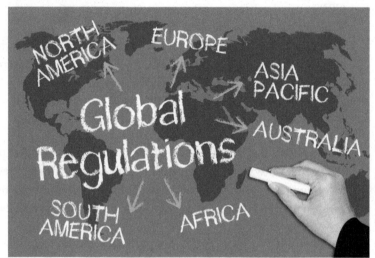

© docstockmedia/Shutterstock.com

Millions of shipments cross into the United States annually, providing the country with goods and services:

- On a typical day, 72,179 truck, rail, and sea containers are arriving at 328 ports across the United States.[4]

- In 2015, CBP processed approximately 33 million imports (entries) valued at more than $2.4 trillion U.S. dollars.[4]

Businesses violating trade regulations face fines of up to 40% of the value of the merchandise for "negligence," which can simply mean failing to keep certain necessary records.

Trade Compliance Systems (or Global Trade Management Systems)

A trade compliance system is a database and software tool for monitoring and processing business activities and transactions in line with international trade laws and regulations enforced by various regulatory agencies.

Because of the complexity of international trade regulations, a trade compliance system has become a vital tool for every major importing and exporting company in the United States, and around the world. It is really the only way to keep current with all of the continuously changing laws, regulations, and procedures. A trade compliance system can automate the process of checking every transaction for commercial and noncommercial products against every legal regulation before import or export.

Trade Compliance Systems Benefits

The benefits of implementing a trade compliance system include:

- Increased level of compliance compared to a manual process

- Decreased number of physical inspections by U.S. Customs and Border Protection

- Faster release of shipments by U.S. Customs and Border Protection

- Avoidance of fines, penalties, and delays

- Opportunity to interface with other systems

GLOBAL LOGISTICS INTERMEDIARIES......................................

The following are a few key global logistics intermediaries that companies may interact with to execute international trade activities.

Customs Broker

"Customs Brokers are private individuals, partnerships, associations or corporations licensed, regulated and empowered by U.S. Customs and Border Protection (CBP) to assist importers and exporters in meeting Federal requirements governing imports and exports."[4]

Customs brokers are also described as "[a] person who manages the paperwork required for international shipping and tracks and moves the shipments through the proper channels."[1]

© one photo/Shutterstock.com

A customs broker is typically the importer's only point of contact with the CBP, and advises the importer of record about the requirements for importing, including preparing and filing entry documents, obtaining the necessary bonds, handling import duties, tracking shipments, securing release of the goods, and arranging delivery to the importer's facility. The broker often consults with CBP to determine the proper rate of duty.

Export Management Companies

Export management companies (EMCs) are agents for domestic companies in foreign markets. An EMC provides a manufacturer immediate access to foreign market knowledge and export know-how. They act as the exclusive export sales department for a manufacturer, and function in foreign markets just like a sales representative functions for a manufacturer in a domestic market.

International Freight Forwarder

© Krunja/Shutterstock.com

An international freight forwarder provides the expert know-how and experience needed to arrange for the movement of cargo from domestic points of origin to foreign destinations with maximum speed and efficiency. They have detailed knowledge of international transportation possibilities and limitations.

As an agent of the exporter, the international freight forwarder advises the exporter about the regulations affecting foreign trade, as well as the import rules of various foreign countries. They prepare shipping documents, arrange for space on ocean vessels, arrange transportation of cargo to shipside, arrange for cargo insurance, and generally orchestrate the entire movement of goods from point of origin to destination in the most cost-efficient manner.

Non-Vessel-Operating Common Carrier

A non-vessel-operating common carrier (NVOCC) is a "carrier that uses ocean liners and works similarly to freight forwarders."[1] An NVOCC does not own or operate any ocean vessels, but they are a shipper in relation to the ocean carrier involved. However, they do function as a common carrier by issuing their own bills of lading and assuming responsibility for the shipments they arrange. NVOCCs specialize in less-than-container load (LCL) shipments and perform many of the same functions as freight forwarders.

Trading Company

"A company that introduces foreign buyers and sellers and arranges all product export/import details, documentation, and transportation."[1] In a strict definition, trading companies purchase and take ownership of products in one country and export these products to sell in another country.

IMPORT PROCESS

An import is an item brought across a national border into a jurisdiction from an external source. The purchaser/owner of the item is the "importer of record." An import into the destination country is also an export from the origination country.

© theromb/Shutterstock.com

Based on information provided by CBP:[7]

- It is the importer of record's responsibility to arrange for examination and release of the goods.

- When a shipment reaches the United States, the importer of record must file entry documents at the port of entry:

  1. Documents necessary to determine whether the item may be released from CBP custody
  2. Documents containing information for duty assessment and statistical purposes

- Following the entry, the shipment may be examined by CBP, or examination may be waived.

- The shipment can then be released by CBP if no legal or regulatory violations have occurred.

- Goods are not legally entered into U.S. commerce until:

    1. The shipment has arrived at the port of entry.

    2. Delivery to the shipping destination has been authorized by CBP (following submission and review of required documentation).

    3. Estimated duties have been paid.

CBP is also concerned with revenue collection (i.e., tariffs and duties). Revenue is determined by such items as:

- Correct valuation (price paid or payable)

- Correct classification

- Country of origin (COO)

- Correct identification of merchandise

- Correct identification of buyer and seller and whether or not they are related

Foreign Trade Zones

Foreign trade zones (FTZs) are "areas supervised by U.S. Customs and Border Protection that are considered to be outside U.S. territory. Material in the zone is not subject to duty taxes, which are payable when the material is moved outside the zone for consumption. There is no limit on the time material may remain in the zone. Internationally, similar areas are called free trade zones."[1]

- FTZs are subject to the laws and regulations of the United States as well as those of the states and communities in which they are located.

- Foreign and domestic merchandise may be moved into FTZs for operations not otherwise prohibited by law, including storage, exhibition, assembly, manufacturing, and processing.

EXPORT PROCESS ....

An export is "An actual shipment or transmission out of the United States, including the sending or taking of an item out of the United States, in any manner"[8]

- When an item/shipment is ready to be exported, the shipper will file export documents for the goods at the port of departure.

- Shipments must conform to export administration regulations.

- In order to complete the documents for filing, the shipper must:

© theromb/Shutterstock.com

  - Know the product or technology being exported

  - Know where it is being produced

  - Know where and to whom it is being sent

  - Know who will use the product

  - Know whether there are any illegal restrictions in the order, L/C, or other document (e.g., boycott clauses)

- The shipper will complete and submit a shippers export declaration (SED), and submit a commercial invoice for the product.

Deemed Exports

A deemed export is "any release in the United States of "technology" or source code to a foreign person is a deemed export to the foreign person's most recent country of citizenship or permanent residency."[8] including <u>within</u> the U.S. borders. Such a release is "deemed" to be an export to the home country of the foreign national.

An export of controlled technology can easily occur even within the walls of a company in the United States, intentionally or unintentionally, if the company has foreign nationals working at the location. Care and formal processes must be in place to prevent this type of disclosure without the proper licenses.

- "Technology" is defined as the specific information necessary for the development, production, or use of a commodity. Usually, the technology is even more strictly controlled than the commodity itself.

- The release can be visual, oral, through on-the-job training, systems access, website download, etc.

- The proper controls are needed to ensure that any such export occurs legally (i.e., with the proper licenses and approvals) and does not expose you or your company to penalties.

PENALTIES FOR VIOLATIONS

The penalties for violating international trade regulations can be substantial and serious. There are criminal and administrative penalties as well as civil penalties for unlawful acts and statutory sanctions.

- **Criminal penalties** can reach 20 years imprisonment and $1 million per violation.

- **Administrative penalties** can reach the greater of $250,000 per violation or twice the amount of the transaction that is the basis of the violation.

- Violators may also be subject to **statutory sanctions**:

  - Seizure and forfeiture of items in violation, including the vessels and aircraft carrying the items

  - Loss of import and/or export privileges for a business unit, division, or for the entire company

  - Detailed inspections of every single shipment, and delayed release by U.S. Customs and Border Protection

REFERENCES

[1] *APICS Dictionary* (14th ed.). (2013). Chicago, IL: APICS. www.apics.org

[2] Global Competitiveness Report 2014–2015. (n.d.). World Economic Forum. Retrieved from http://reports.weforum.org/global-competitiveness-report-2014-2015/

[3] World Trade Organization. (2016). Retrieved from https://www.wto.org/

[4] U.S. Customs and Border Protection. (2016). Retrieved from https://www.cbp.gov/about

[5] U.S. Department of Homeland Security. (2016). Retrieved from https://www.dhs.gov/history

[6] Ferdows, K. (1997). Making the most of foreign factories. *Harvard Business Review* (March–April), 73–88. Retrieved from https://hbr.org/1997/03/making-the-most-of-foreign-factories

[7] US Customs and Border Protection. (n.d.). Importing into the United States, A guide for commercial importers. Retrieved from https://www.cbp.gov/sites/default/files/.../Importing%20into%20the%20U.S.pdf

[8] § 734.13 EXPORT, Export Administration Regulations, Bureau of Industry and Security, September 2016, page 10, retrieved from https://www.bis.doc.gov/index.php/documents/regulation-docs/412-part-734-scope-of-the-export-administration-regulations/file)

Chapter 11
Customer Relationship Management

CHAPTER OUTLINE

Introduction

Why Do Companies Need CRM?

Goals and Benefits of CRM

Focus on Strategically Significant Customers

CRM Limitations

Building and Maintaining Long-Term Relationships

Being Successful

Key Components of CRM

Managing Customer Service

Customer Service—Transaction Elements

Customer Service and the Logistics Function

Call Centers

Additional Components of CRM

Six Steps to a Successful CRM Program

Current Trends in CRM

Summary

INTRODUCTION ....

Customer relationship management (CRM) is the transformation of the people, processes, and technology required to become a customer-centric organization; a philosophy of putting the customer first. It involves acquiring, retaining, and partnering with selective customers to create superior value for both the company and the customer. CRM is about building and maintaining profitable long-term customer relationships beyond the one-off buy and sell transaction. It provides a means and a method to enhance the experience of individual customers so that they will remain customers for life.

WHY DO COMPANIES NEED CRM? ....

Companies need a CRM program in order to (1) acquire new customers, and maybe even more importantly, (2) to retain their existing customers. Loyal customers are the source of most profits, and a relatively small percentage of those customers may generate most of the profits for the company. Companies can expect to lose approximately 50% of their customers every five years (Reichheld, 1996), so any effort to slow the rate of defection will grow the customer base. Satisfied customers tell others about their experiences; unfortunately, so do dissatisfied customers, who tell others about their experiences to an even greater extent. It typically costs five to ten times more to acquire a new customer, while the marketing costs and efforts are relatively low for retaining existing customers. "In general, the longer a customer stays with a company, the more that customer is worth. Long-term customers buy more, take less of a company's time, are less sensitive to price, and bring in new customers. Best of all, they have no acquisition or start-up cost. Good long-standing customers are worth so much that in some industries, reducing customer defections by as little as five points—from, say, 15% to 10% per year—can double profits" (Reichheld, 1996).

Additionally, a CRM program will help companies meet the changing expectations of customers in general due to aspects such as social and demographic factors, economic situations, competitor's products and marketing efforts, and other market experiences.

GOALS AND BENEFITS OF CRM ....

You must have a clear set of goals in order to get the most from your CRM program. Making **customer satisfaction the primary goal of the CRM program** is the best way to improve the bottom line.

A successful well-designed CRM program can provide companies with many improvements and benefits. Some of the most important are:

1. Increased customer satisfaction

2. Increased customer loyalty and retention by offering value and service to encourage repeat business; competing on the service experience in addition to price

3. Better customer service and faster responses to customer inquiries

4. Increased customer revenue

5. Growth of the customer base through referrals

6. A simplified and more cost-effective marketing and sales process

7. Increase sales effectiveness; closing sales faster

8. Increased sales through cross-selling, and/or up-selling

9. Access to updated customer information in a centralized location and personalized customer interactions

10. Automation of repetitive tasks

FOCUS ON STRATEGICALLY SIGNIFICANT CUSTOMERS ....

Not all markets and customers are equally important. Relationships should be built with strategically significant customers that are likely to provide the most value for the effort. Building relationships with customers that provide little value can be counterproductive.

Strategically significant customers fall into one or more of the following categories:

- Customers with high lifetime value (i.e., customers that will constantly buy the product[s] or use the service[s] in the long-term)

- Customers who serve as role models or benchmarks for other customers

- Customers who inspire change in the supplier and/or the supply chain

Companies should pursue developing and building customer relationships with customers who meet any of the abovementioned criteria.

CRM LIMITATIONS

CRM is not feasible for every market and every customer. Some customers don't want to be committed to every brand and/or relationship. CRM is not practical for low-involvement, routine purchasing in B2B or B2C situations. Some markets/customers may have low "personalization potential." Therefore, as noted, companies should only focus their CRM program on strategically significant customers.

© Ribah/Shutterstock.com

BUILDING AND MAINTAINING LONG-TERM RELATIONSHIPS

Of all the components of supply chain management, building and maintaining profitable long-term customer relationships is one of the most critical considering the fact that a company produces products and/or services to sell, and therefore, requires customers who want to buy those products and/or services. The long-term retention of those customers is a critical issue, which must be confronted by every organization that provides a product or service.

When considering the "what" and the "how" of CRM, the first important issue to focus on is, "*What are the customer's requirements for delivering products and services in a manner resulting in a high level of customer satisfaction?*" Customer expectations have been and are likely to continue rising for the foreseeable future, which in turn drives the need for customer satisfaction efforts to go well beyond just the actual on-time delivery and best price. Companies like Amazon help to fuel the escalation in customer expectations and shape customer satisfaction, because they can be thought of as "supply chain disruptors," continuing to challenge the norms and push against the traditional boundaries of the supply chain—setting the bar ever higher.

The "how" in CRM starts with **talking to the customer**, and even more importantly is supported by **listening to the customer**.

Companies won't be able to find out what customers want unless they communicate with them. They may choose to interact with customers directly or indirectly, or both. Companies can speak directly with customers in person or through a phone interview. Some companies may decide to conduct focus groups where small sets of customers are brought in and asked a series of questions to get their input and feedback. Companies may also opt to interact with customers indirectly by sending out a mail or electronic survey. Each of these communication methods has its pros and cons.

Understanding customer behaviors and their requirements is not just about collecting initial data and information; you have to collect that data over the long term, because as the market evolves and the business environment changes, customer behaviors and requirements change over time as well. It is important to analyze the data and information for trends. If you create a product or service and the associated support functions to satisfy customers today and allow it to stagnate, you may find out that somewhere in the not too distant future, your customers are no longer satisfied. CRM is an iterative and ongoing process, not a one-off exercise that you complete and put on the shelf. All elements of CRM should be considered fluid.

BEING SUCCESSFUL ....

A CRM program is both simple and complex. It is simple in that it involves training users in treating customers right, to make them feel valued. It is complex in that it also means finding affordable ways to identify (potentially thousands if not millions of) customers and their needs, and then designing customer contact strategies geared toward creating customer satisfaction and loyalty among segments of customers. If you as the customer are satisfied

with the product, the service, the treatment that you received from that supplier, you are likely to come back over and over again as a customer. Therefore, you become more valuable to that business.

It has been well documented by several significant advertising agencies that one satisfied customer will tell at least five other people of the experience, whereas a dissatisfied customer in turn will tell 50 people about a bad experience.

To be successful, a company must find ways to meet its customer's needs; otherwise, just as any firm would react with a nonperforming supplier, the customer goes elsewhere and takes years' worth of future purchases along. Just as companies must create methods for finding and developing good suppliers, companies must also create methods for becoming and staying a good supplier themselves. Companies should evaluate themselves from their customer's perspective, as a supplier. In that light, you are the supplier to your customers and you need to do all the same things for your customers that you require and expect from your suppliers, if you want to be considered a top-quality, preferred supplier to your customers.

Because many companies do not sell their products directly to the end consumer, companies may also need to train and certify that their intermediate customers are able to adequately represent their company's products. If a company sells their products through a wholesaler, distributor, or retailer, then those entities are representing the company and their products in the marketplace. If they do not do the job adequately or appropriately, it will have a negative impact on the company. It is the manufacturing company's name on the product and their reputation at stake. Therefore, it is in the company's best interest to ensure that any downstream supply chain partners are appropriately informed, trained, and incentivized as necessary to ensure good customer service is provided and customer satisfaction is achieved.

KEY COMPONENTS OF CRM

For a CRM program to be effective there are a number of components that must be developed and implemented as part of the program. The key components of a CRM program are outlined as follows:

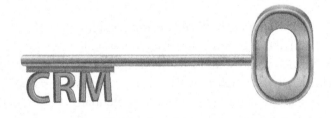

- **PREDICTING CUSTOMER BEHAVIORS:** If a company is in the business of selling products and/or services to customers, they can also collect information from these customers' buying history, preferences, and trends, which could then be used to predict customer buying behaviors going forward. This information could also be used to determine how effective marketing efforts, advertising and promotions, and so forth, have been in the past, and whether these practices should be continued or altered for the future. This predictive information could be used by the company to potentially create a more accurate forecast and a more effective marketing and sales budget.

The current trend is to use predictive customer behavior modeling techniques, instead of just looking at historical data. These models use a mathematical construct to represent the common behaviors observed among segments of customers in order to predict how similar customers will behave under similar circumstances. The models are typically based on customer datamining, and each model is designed to answer one question at one point in time. If a model can be used to predict what a segment of customers will do in response to a particular marketing action, then the company should see that most of the customers in the segment responded as predicted by the model.

- **PERSONALIZING CUSTOMER COMMUNICATIONS:** Effective marketing that makes an impact on the customer is crucial to business success, but marketing is more than just advertising the company's products and services. It is about meeting the needs and expectations of customers through focused, personalized communications. A proven and effective approach involves ensuring that customers feel that their preferences and needs are being taken into consideration when they interact with a company. When a company communicates with their customers they need to use the customer's "language" and communicate with them in a meaningful way. Communication that is personalized sends a message to the customer that the company cares about the customer. It is a powerful way to differentiate the company from its competitors and it helps to build customer loyalty. In today's business environment, customers expect businesses to understand their needs and provide relevant and desirable information. They tend to apply the same principles when evaluating a business relationship as they do when evaluating a personal relationship. If the interaction is pleasing, engaging, and satisfying, then there's a good chance they'll build on that relationship through future interactions. The goal is to reach customers on an emotional level so that they feel a genuine personal connection with the company and their products and services, like a friendship. Once customers are comfortable in the relationship, they tend to remain loyal and even recommend others to the brand.

Considering today's technology and the use of the internet in the buying habits of people through catalogs, etc., it is easy to track how customers navigate a website and the types of things they buy.

"Clickstream" is one way to do that. It is a method to track the parts of the computer screen a user clicks on while web browsing. It can help a company tailor a website's images, ads, or discounts based on past usage of the site. This type of process allows an organization to personalize its communications to the various customers not only to categorize the buying habits of customers in what they buy, but also when they buy, and at what price levels they buy.

- **CUSTOMER SEGMENTATION:** "The practice of dividing a customer base into groups of individuals that are similar in specific ways relevant to marketing. Traditional segmentation focuses on identifying customer groups based on demographics and attributes such as attitude and psychological profiles."[1] In simple terms, it is grouping customers to create specialized communications about products. There are many different ways to group customers (by demographics, income, geography, buying preferences, etc.). Segmenting customers allows a company to zero in on a particular population of customers to sell a specific product, or to define a specific product(s) for a particular segment of customers. If a company can identify different segments of customers, it can potentially be more efficient and effective in the use of its resources by tailoring programs and initiatives for each segment.

- **TARGET MARKETING:** A target market is a segment of customers toward which a company has decided to aim its marketing efforts and ultimately its products and/or services. A well-defined target market is the first element of any marketing strategy. Target marketing is the process of promoting products and services via media that are likely to reach the potential target market (i.e., customer segment), by building a marketing strategy aimed at that specific customer segment. It is usually much more effective than mass marketing, which tends not to focus too deeply on the qualities, preferences, or characteristics of the customer, and allows the company to focus efforts on marketing to those customers most likely to respond. Generally, it is a more efficient use of the company's resources and it reduces the chances of being a nuisance to those potential customers who do not fit the targeted criteria (i.e., the "wrong" customer segment).

- **EVENT-BASED MARKETING:** Event-based marketing is a form of marketing that identifies key events in the customer and business lifecycle. When an event occurs a customer specific marketing activity is undertaken. An event can be something basic and predicted, like the end of a contract, a holiday, a season, or something more detailed and personal, like a birthday, a mar-

© chrupka/Shutterstock.com

riage, or a graduation. Event-based marketing is a more personalized form of marketing, which can help to form personal connections with the customers. A great event-based marketing strategy allows you to respond to your customers at precisely the right moment. It can improve brand recognition and drive profits quickly and efficiently. Many company marketing programs are tied to specific annual events (e.g., Memorial Day, Fourth of July, Halloween, Black Friday, Cyber Monday, Christmas). Many companies also generate a significant amount of their annual revenue associated with these events. Companies such as Toys 'R Us make more than 50% of their annual sales in just the six weeks leading up to Christmas.

- ## CROSS-SELLING AND UP-SELLING

<u>CROSS-SELLING</u>: I am sure that at some point we have all heard the famous cross-selling phrase, "Would you like fries with that?" Cross-selling occurs when a company sells an additional related or complementary product(s) or service(s) to an existing customer after the initial purchase. <u>Example</u>: If you're buying an item on Amazon.com, you may be shown other similar items to the one you are

looking at, or companion products to the item that you are considering. Cross-selling can occur in a number of different ways. It can be blatant as in the examples above or it can be subtle as occurs in some stores. <u>Examples</u>: If you go to a grocery store to buy waffles or pancake mix, you may see the syrup on the shelf right next to it. If you go to a grocery store to buy coffee, you may see coffee filters, coffee creamer, stirrers, cups, and other related items in the same general area next to the coffee. On the one hand, it is a convenience to you because you may in fact have intended to buy some or all of those items anyway, but on the other hand it is still a form of cross-selling.

<u>UP-SELLING</u>: You may have also heard the common up-selling phrase, "Would you like to super-size your order?" Up-selling involves persuading a customer to buy a more expensive item or upgrade a product or service to make the sale more profitable. It also involves selling the customer extra features or add-ons to the product he or she is already buying or considering. Incentives are crucial

features of up-selling, because incentives such as discounts or free shipping give the customer good reasons to purchase something extra right away.

Not attempting to cross-sell or up-sell when the customer is already in a buying frame of mind is a wasted opportunity.

- RELATIONSHIP OR PERMISSION MARKETING: Relationship or permission marketing is an approach to selling products and services in which a customer explicitly agrees in advance to receive marketing information. Example: An "opt-in" e-mail, where a potential customer signs up in advance for information about certain products or services. The customer is giving permission to the company to provide them with marketing and sales information. Permission marketing is about building an ongoing relationship of increasing depth with customers. According to Seth Godin (who coined the term), "permission marketing is the privilege (not the right) of delivering anticipated, personal, and relevant messages to people who actually want them." Permission marketing does not typically create immediate sales, but rather grabs a customer's attention and preserves a business relationship.

  If you've ever accessed a website to buy something, you may have been requested to set up an account. You enter your information and somewhere, probably near the bottom, there is likely a little checkbox that asks your permission for the company to send you additional information, advertising, promotions, and the like, going forward. You can self-select in or out of that particular permission marketing program. Usually the box is already checked, and if you don't want to give permission, you can uncheck the box and self-select out of that marketing program. Some companies may also simultaneously or separately ask for your permission for their partner organizations to send you advertising and promotional information, and you can again self-select in or out of that marketing program as well. These examples are typical of how you can opt-in or opt-out of permission marketing programs. Another way might be for you to choose to use a QR code displayed on a product or on company advertising materials, to voluntarily find out more about the company or a particular product or service by using your smartphone and the internet. In that situation you are actively indicating that you want to find out more information, and you are using a mechanism that the company provided to self-select into (i.e., give your permission for) that marketing program.

- CUSTOMER DEFECTION ANALYSIS AND CHURN REDUCTION: Customer Defection Analysis is the process of analyzing the customers who have stopped buying to determine why. Churn is the process of customers changing their buying preferences because they find better and/or cheaper products and services elsewhere, and Churn Reduction is all of the efforts companies develop to stop losing customers to the competition. Customer defection analysis and churn reduction go hand in hand. It's important to determine why customers leave and then finding ways to retain them.

What is causing your customers to defect to your competitor? Is it because they don't like the quality of your product? Is your price too high? Is there some other service not being offered? Are you having shortages? Determining the root cause of your customer defections and then working to resolve those issues will help you retain customers.

You've already spent time and money identifying customers and getting them to buy. One of the worst things that can happen is to lose them as a customer. If you lose customers, you have to go out and replace them to stay in business. Replacing customers costs a lot of money. Finding a new customer costs on average five times as much as keeping an existing customer. You have to spend more money going out and identifying new customers and then getting those new customers to buy from you. According to *Harvard Business Review* (2006), a 5% improvement in customer retention can result in a 75% increase in profits. The more customers you can retain, the greater the profitability you will have as a result.

- CUSTOMER VALUE DETERMINATION: Determining the customer lifetime value is vital, so that appropriate communications, benefits, services, or policies can be established for each customer segment.

CUSTOMER LIFETIME VALUE (CLV) is a prediction of the net profit attributed to the entire future relationship with a particular customer. Some customers are worth a lot more than others, and identifying your key or top-tier customers can be extremely valuable to your business. CLV is an important metric for determining how much money a company is willing to spend on acquiring new customers and how much repeat business a company can expect from particular customers. The CLV can affect many different areas of the business, because it emphasizes efficient spending to maximize customer acquisition and retention practices.

© nasirkhan/Shuterstock.com

MANAGING CUSTOMER SERVICE

What is customer service? It can have multiple meanings even within the same organization. Generally, customer service is viewed in three different ways:

- CUSTOMER SERVICE AS A PHILOSOPHY: Customer service is a company-wide commitment to providing customer satisfaction through superior customer service by placing emphasis on quality and quality management.

- **Customer Service as an Activity:** Customer service is a particular task that a firm must accomplish to satisfy the customer's needs. Order processing, billing and invoicing, product returns, and claims handling are all typical examples of the customer service activity.

- **Customer Service as Performance Measures:** Customer service is a category of performance measures, such as the percentage of orders delivered on time and complete, and the number of orders processed within acceptable time limits.

For our purposes in CRM, we will define customer service as the process of ensuring customer satisfaction with a product or service. Often, customer service takes place while performing a transaction for the customer, such as making a sale or returning an item. It is the act of taking care of the customer's needs by providing and delivering professional, high-quality service before, during, and after the customer's requirements are met.

Customer service performance measurements are designed around the "Seven Rights Rule":

1. Right **product**

2. Right **quantity**

3. Right **quality**

4. Right **place**

5. Right **time**

6. Right **customer**

7. Right **costs**

8. Right **documentation**

© donskarpo/Shutterstock.com

A newer customer service trend is to add on one more right, the Right documentation, which includes elements such as the right labeling, information, returns instructions, and invoice. This, combined with the other seven rights, is commonly referred to as the "perfect order." If a company can deliver on all eight rights, then it's creating the perfect order. Everything that the customer wants and everything that you as a supplier want to deliver is encompassed in the perfect order. Companies that can do this consistently are deemed to be providing excellent customer service.

These kinds of services only come at a significant cost, with a lot of planning, careful implementation, and appropriate and proper training of all personnel involved.

CUSTOMER SERVICE—TRANSACTION ELEMENTS ....

When you complete a sales transaction, there are three different elements that you must consider as part of the transaction; the pre-transaction, the actual transaction itself, and the post transaction. Each element involves different aspects of customer service.

© iQoncept/Shuterstock.com

- PRE-TRANSACTION ELEMENTS: These are elements of the sales transaction that <u>precede</u> the sale, and include such things as the customer service policies, the company's mission statement, organizational structure, and system flexibility. Before any customer service can take place, the organization must first define its customer service policies. Organizations should have mission, vision, and value statements, and it is from these that its customer service policies are derived. The infrastructure (i.e., people, process, and technology) to support a company's sales must also be in place prior to the sales transaction to achieve the company's customer service goals. As with other aspects of the CRM program, this is not a one-off exercise. Organizations change and so do the needs, desires, and trends of the customer community. Therefore, all processes, customer service policies, and the systems that deliver customer service have to be designed and implemented with flexibility in mind to accommodate those changes as and when they occur.

- TRANSACTION ELEMENTS: These are elements of the sales transaction that occur <u>during</u> the sale, and include such things as the order lead time, order processing capabilities, and the distribution system accuracy. It is during the actual sales transaction where the Seven Rights Rule outlined above is really implemented and measured. Nothing will destroy customer satisfaction faster than customers finding out that they cannot get their order(s) satisfied in an agreed upon length of time, or finding out that their order(s) was not filled accurately. <u>Example</u>: A customer identifies a specific item in the company catalog that spells out color, size, and item number, and then places an order. When the item is delivered the customer discovers that is the wrong color and the wrong size. The item number was correct on both the shipping label and in the catalog, but the item was improperly picked from stock, packaged, and shipped inaccurately.

- POST-TRANSACTION ELEMENTS: These are elements of the sales transaction that occur <u>after</u> the sale, and include such things as warranty repair capabilities, complaint resolution, product returns, and operating information. In the age of e-commerce, post-transaction elements are becoming an even more important part of the CRM process. They must be carefully defined by the company with appropriate instructions for both the customer to understand at the time of the sale, and for the customer representatives within the company to understand at the time the customer contacts the company about an issue.

Hiring of appropriate staff and proper training are key elements in the success of post-transaction issues. A customer service representative has to be able to make judgment calls as to the level of service to be provided. There are times when an item may be out of warranty by only a short time and the customer service representative has to make a decision as to whether to accept or deny the customer's request for warranty. These types of decisions and interactions will have a significant impact on the long-term relationship with the customer.

CUSTOMER SERVICE AND THE LOGISTICS FUNCTION......................

From the point of view of the supply chain management/logistics function, customer service can be described as having four traditional dimensions: time, dependability, communications, and convenience:

- TIME: From the company/seller's perspective, the time dimension is the order cycle time. From the customer/buyer's perspective, the time dimension is the lead time, or replenishment time.

- DEPENDABILITY: Dependability can be more important than lead time. The customer can potentially minimize its inventory levels if lead time is fixed and known.

  - Cycle time: A seller that can assure the buyer of a specific lead time, can differentiate the company and its product(s) from its competitors. A seller that offers a dependable lead time allows the buyer to minimize the total cost of inventory, stockouts, order processing, and production scheduling.

  - Safe delivery: If products arrive damaged or are lost, the customer cannot use the products as intended. A shipment containing damaged products aggravates several customer cost centers (e.g., inventory, production, and marketing) and negatively impacts the long-term relationship.

  - Correct orders: An improperly filled order forces the customer to reorder, assuming that the customer is not angry enough to buy from another supplier. If a customer who is an intermediary in the distribution channel experiences a stockout, the stockout cost also directly affects the seller.

- COMMUNICATIONS: The two logistics activities vital to order-filling are the communication of customer order information to the order-filling function and the actual process of picking the items ordered from inventory. In the order information stage, the use of EDI or internet-enabled communications can reduce errors in transferring order information from the order to the warehouse receipt.

- CONVENIENCE: Convenience is another way of saying that the logistics service level must be flexible. Basically, logistics requirements differ with regard to packaging, the mode of transportation, the carrier the customer requires, routing, and delivery times.

CALL CENTERS

A <u>Call Center</u> is "a facility housing personnel who respond to customer phone queries. These personnel may provide customer service or technical support. Call center services may be in-house or outsourced."[1]

A call center links a customer and an organization together. It gives customers quick access to the information they want and enhances the customer-to-business relationship. Call centers have helped most organizations focus on growing their business and concentrating on customer building. They can eliminate the need to hire and train new staff members to provide customer support, and thereby save money as well. Call centers help to continuously monitor different customer service parameters in an effort to gauge performance and ultimately improve quality and efficiency. Maybe most importantly, by utilizing a call center, the company's internal resources can be freed up to focus on the company's core competencies.

Call centers have become a significant part of the CRM program in many companies. A call center can actually handle a number of different activities/tasks. They handle basic tasks like answering customer's inquiries and resolving customer's issues. They can also categorize the calls (placing orders, information, complaint, question, request for repair, etc.). Data collected by the call center can be used to determine such things as how long it takes to answer a call, how long it takes to resolve an issue, or to track the type and frequency of issues or inquiries. Call centers can use information collected to help determine the root cause of issues that might be occurring on a frequent basis. A properly designed database for gathering the information from a call center can support demand forecasting for future sales as well as manufacturing requirements and resource allocations.

If they are well set up and managed, call centers can increase customer satisfaction levels. One of the most successful customer service call centers is that of the Lands' End Company, where customer service satisfaction levels over the years have been among the highest in the country. They can also decrease customer satisfaction levels if you don't do them well. As positive as good customer satisfaction can be, equally bad customer service can clearly destroy a company's reputation even faster. In today's business world, the internet has provided an immediate source for customers to not only complain but to tell the world through social media how bad service was in a given situation with any company. "There's nothing worse than calling your service provider and finding out you know more than the person on the other end of the line," said Neil Armstrong, marketing director at UK broadband service provider PlusNet.

ADDITIONAL COMPONENS OF CRM ....

Measuring Customer Satisfaction

Measuring customer satisfaction is about customers being given opportunities to provide feedback about product(s), service(s), the organization, and so forth. Depending on the types of products and services offered, there is potentially a significant amount of information to be captured and analyzed. This can be done through surveys, questionnaires, and in many cases direct phone calls to customers asking them their opinions on the service they have been provided. Most companies will need some type of a database to manage the data. Decisions have to be made regarding how to capture the data, and how to analyze the information so you can use it productively going forward. It is of very little value until it can be analyzed and acted upon.

Website Self-Service

Websites act as support mechanisms for call centers. Many companies provide these portals for customers to be able to access their account information, check operating hours, ask questions, see product information, find contact information, check on placed orders, and get shipping information. Customers can not only access this information but in some cases, edit and modify the information accordingly. Customers can put their own customer information into the system, to save on company time and to potentially eliminate errors. These sites also allow for customers to opt out of future emails and information they may not wish to receive, and conversely, it allows the customer to access or opt into future sales, subscriptions, and corporate information if desired.

Field Service Management

Field service management involves setting up the company operations to allow customers to interact directly with the company's service personnel. Customers can call the service people directly and make an appointment with the service person to come out to service the product. Because customers are communicating directly with product specialists for service issues, it is more likely that the right diagnosis can be made quickly, which will help to ensure customer satisfaction.

Sales Force Automation

Sales force automation (SFA) tools are used for documenting field activities, and keeping track and managing what your sales force is doing in the field. These tools provide communication with the home office, and facilitate retrieving sales history out in the field. Depending on the type of product or service, the company may have a huge sales force. There are many different tools and mechanisms that management can use to manage a sales force.

The following are a few examples:

SALES ACTIVITY MANAGEMENT: Tools that offer sales reps a guided sequence of sales activities, in addition to the fact that it provides a stepwise approach on how to sell the company's products and/or services. If there is a series of sales activities that the sales reps have to go through, the tool can help to make sure sales reps take all the steps that are appropriate, including documentation. It can also be used to capture new buying habits from a customer, new customer contact information, new location information, or new phone numbers.

SALES TERRITORY MANAGEMENT: Tools used by sales managers to obtain information on each sales rep's activities. These tools identify which sales reps are productive and which ones are not in terms of generating sales, how many sales calls they make per day/week/month, whether they distributed the sales and product information they were supposed to leave, whether they scheduled a follow-up appointment, and so forth. All that information can be captured and used by sales managers or district managers to manage the sales force. If there is a certain segment of customers that are not being adequately covered, sales managers can use this information to redirect some of the sales force to that customer segment.

LEAD MANAGEMENT: A technique used to help sales reps follow some specific tactics that will help them close the deal. Example: If you are trying to sell a particular commodity and the customer is not ready to make a buying decision, what techniques have worked in similar situations in the past which the sales reps could use to try and close the deal? Do they offer the customer free delivery, extended financing, a discount? There may be many tactics or activities that a sales rep could use to try to close a sale and these may vary by customer segments. Understanding what those tactics are and what tactics work on which customer segments is all part of lead management. This could be a significant amount of information to manage and a tool and database may be needed to be able to provide that information to your sales force.

KNOWLEDGE MANAGEMENT: It is basically a database and software tool to manage all of the above, plus more. This is could be a significant amount of information about your customers, your company's sales policy, warranty information, even things like expense reimbursement. A company may have several different types of software packages that need to be integrated. A knowledge management tool will help to do this, so sales reps and management can have immediate access to all that information. A tool that enables quick decision making, better customer service, and a better-equipped and happy sales staff makes for a much more effective and satisfied sales team.

SIX STEPS TO A SUCCESSFUL CRM PROGRAM................................

Step 1: Creating the CRM Plan

The first step to a successful CRM program is to create the CRM plan itself; that is, do all of the planning. It's important to address the following questions: What are the objectives of the program? What am I trying to achieve? Does it fit with my corporate strategy? It is important for the plan to have flexibility because the market and the customer world will change periodically based on the demographics, the nature of the product, the time of year, and so forth.

© iQoncept/Shuterstock.com

The plan should consider that the CRM program will likely need some type of software application(s) to help manage the program and all the information. The software tools will have to be identified, purchased, developed, and implemented. This may also require that the company's legacy systems are integrated or replaced. It is not unusual for the technology currently being used to change frequently and require upgrades and modifications to meet the needs of an evolving CRM program.

The CRM program, process, policies, and tools should be reviewed on a regular basis and upgraded based on changes to product service requirements, warranties, guarantees, and how these should be managed by a CRM staff.

To implement a CRM program an organization has to understand that there are costs involved in hiring the right people, and that it will take time to train and prepare staff for CRM positions. Equally, it will take time for implementation of any new system(s) and upgrades along with educating new employees on CRM practices, policies, and procedures.

Step 2: Involve CRM Users from the Onset

The second step is to involve the people who are actually going to be working with the CRM system(s) right from the very beginning. It actually might create a lot of controversy within the company if you set up a CRM program and people are not aware of how it could impact their jobs. They may feel threatened and there will likely be some resistance.

Getting the people who are actually going to be working with CRM system(s) involved will help in several ways:

a.   They have the most information and this will most likely help you set up a better system.

b.   They will potentially feel less threatened because they will understand more about what's happening directly.

c.   They will start to take ownership. They will feel it is their system that is being implemented, not something being imposed on them.

d.   You will get some early buy-in upfront and potentially need less training later on.

Many companies will do a pilot or test before doing a full implementation. They don't want to expose the entire company, their entire product line, or all their customers to a new process or untested system, so they do a small test to make sure everything works before they move on to expand it to all their products in their portfolio.

Step 3: Select the Right Application and Provider

The third step is selecting the right application and the right provider. There are lots of different potential applications and software packages out there to pick from. You will have to find an appropriate application and determine the extent of customization. Some of the best ways to get information on what is available, and to begin the evaluation process, is to visit tradeshows, read literature, and/or hire a consultant. It may be wise to have a company team of cross-functional individuals help define not only the requirements for a CRM program, but also to work as a focus group in finding an application that will satisfy the requirements as defined by that focus group. Then identify the potential alternatives out there and do some comparisons based on how well the system performs, security, reporting, capabilities, and system availability, before making a final decision to purchase and implement.

Step 4: Integrate Existing CRM Applications

The fourth step is integrating any existing CRM systems. This can be a major time-consuming undertaking. CRM is generally a collection of various applications implemented over time, both new and legacy. Your existing CRM applications (if any) will already have customer information, product information, and other data that will be needed in any new application that you install. Customer contact mechanisms need to be coordinated so that every CRM user in the firm knows about all of the activity associated with each customer. You may have some centralized database or a data warehouse containing all customer information. You want to be able to take that data, easily access it, synthesize it, and analyze it so that you can use the data to benefit your business going forward. There's no sense collecting a lot of data if you can't use it to actually improve your business.

It would be highly unlikely for the company to buy a new application, customize it to meet its needs, and then immediately implement it and have it work exactly as expected. Checking for errors during implementation and integration and maintaining the current business at the same time is an exceptionally difficult task. Therefore, it is likely to require a significant team of well-trained personnel to integrate any new systems along with support from the provider.

Step 5: Establish Performance Measures

The fifth step is to establish performance measures. This allows the firm to determine if objectives have been met, and to compare actual to plan variances so that corrective actions can be taken if necessary. What are the objectives of the program and are they being achieved?

Step 6: Providing CRM Training for All Users

The sixth step is to provide training for all users of the CRM program and tools. You will need to have the initial training for all users, and you will need to have ongoing training when changes are made, upgrades, etc. Potentially, you will also have new employees over time and they will have to be trained as well. One mistake that companies make is that they do the initial training, but they don't have a budget and program set up for ongoing training. What happens is that the program starts to fail, and they end up blaming the system rather than recognizing that they don't have a key process in place.

You can also use the training to convince key users such as sales, call centers, and others, of the value of the CRM program. The training not only provides information on how to use the program, but it will also show them the value of the system itself. You can use the training to take people who are not early adopters (i.e., those who are resistant to the system) and help them get on board with the system and become productive members of your organization in the new environment.

CURRENT TRENDS IN CRM

Customer Data Privacy

Privacy is one of the current trends in CRM. You may have personally received privacy notices in the mail from some account that you have or from a supplier. They state things like "we collect certain information from you, but we don't share that information outside of our organization or with our trading partners," for example. People and organizations are understandably worried about giving out personal or confidential company information. Protecting customers' data and information is critical. There are rules and laws that companies must follow regarding invasion of privacy. These include the U.S. Patriot Act and EU's Internet Privacy Law. One of the elements to consider when you're looking at an application or a system, may be the security features. What type of security does that system have?

Social Media

Many companies have expanded the use of social media. Creating and cultivating virtual communities around product or brand is a powerful way to engage customers in terms of selling and advertising, in providing information to customers, and also getting information back from customers on their buying preferences and requirements.

Cloud Computing

Cloud computing is basically an alternative to buying the software package. You can actually buy "software as a service" through the cloud instead of purchasing the actual CRM software. Therefore, if there are upgrades, maintenance, and the like, you don't have to go through the expense and exercise of actually doing the upgrades and maintenance yourself. The company that is managing the software in the cloud will actually do those activities. Many companies will start out this way, because it's a way to "dip your toe in the water" without getting fully immersed. You can make sure that the system works for you, performs as you expect it to perform, and gives you the value that you are expecting before making a major investment.

SUMMARY

- Customer relationship management (CRM) is the transformation of people, process, and technology required to become a customer-centric organization; a philosophy of putting the customer first. It involves acquiring, retaining, and partnering with selective customers to create superior value for both the company and the customer.

- Companies need a CRM program in order to (1) acquire new customers, and maybe even more importantly, (2) to retain their existing customers. Loyal customers are the source of most profits, and a relatively small percentage of those customers may generate most of the profits for the company.

- You must have a clear set of goals in order to get the most from your CRM program. Making customer satisfaction the primary goal of the CRM program is the best way to improve the bottom line.

- Relationships should be built with strategically significant customers that are likely to provide the most value for the effort.

- CRM is not feasible for every market and every customer. Some customers don't want to be committed to every brand and/or relationship.

- Of all of the components of supply chain management, building and maintaining profitable long-term customer relationships is one of the most critical considering the fact that a company produces products and/or services to sell, and therefore, requires customers who want to buy those products and/or services. The first important issue to focus on involves the customer's requirements for delivering products and services in a manner resulting in a high level of customer satisfaction. It starts with talking to the customer, and even more importantly listening to the customer.

- CRM involves finding affordable ways to identify customers and their needs, and then designing customer contact strategies geared toward creating customer satisfaction and loyalty among segments of customers. Just as companies must create methods for finding and developing good suppliers, companies must also create methods for becoming and staying a good supplier themselves.

- Key components of CRM:

  - <u>Predicting Customer Behaviors:</u> If a company is in the business of selling products and/or services to customers, it can also collect information from these customers' buying history, preferences, and trends, which could then be used to predict customer buying behaviors going forward.
  - <u>Personalizing Customer Communications:</u> Is about meeting the needs and expectations of customers through focused, personalized communications. A proven and effective approach involves ensuring that customers feel that their preferences and needs are being taken into consideration when they interact with a company.

- Customer Segmentation: Grouping customers to create specialized communications about products.

- Target Marketing: The process of promoting products and services via media that are likely to reach the potential target market (i.e., customer segment). Targeted marketing builds a marketing strategy aimed at that specific customer segment.

- Event-Based Marketing: Is a form of marketing that identifies key events in the customer and business lifecycle. When an event occurs, a customer-specific marketing activity is undertaken.

- Cross-Selling and Up-Selling: Cross-selling occurs when a company sells an additional related or complementary product(s) or service(s) to an existing customer after the initial purchase. Up-selling involves persuading a customer to buy a more expensive item or upgrade a product or service to make the sale more profitable. It also involves selling the customer extra features or add-ons to the product they are already buying or considering.

- Relationship or Permission Marketing: Is an approach to selling products and services in which a customer explicitly agrees in advance to receive marketing information.

- Customer Defection Analysis and Churn Reduction: Customer defection analysis is the process of analyzing the customers who have stopped buying to determine why. Churn reduction is all of the efforts companies develop to stop losing customers to the competition.

- Customer Value Determination: is determining the customer lifetime value so that appropriate communications, benefits, services, or policies can be established for each customer segment. Customer lifetime value (CLV) is a prediction of the net profit attributed to the entire future relationship with a particular customer.

• Customer service is a philosophy, an activity, and a performance measure. Customer service performance measurements are designed around the "Seven Rights Rule": The right product, quantity, quality, place, time, customer, and costs. A newer customer service trend is to add on an eighth right, the right documentation. This, combined with the other seven rights, is referred to as the perfect order.

• When you complete a sales transaction, there are three different elements that you must consider as part of the transaction; the pre-transaction, the actual transaction itself, and the post-transaction. Each element involves different aspects of customer service.

• From the point of view of the supply chain management/logistics function, customer service can be described as having four traditional dimensions: time, dependability, communications, and convenience.

- A call center links a customer and an organization together. It gives customers quick access to the information they want and enhances the customer-to-business relationship. Call centers have helped most organizations focus on growing their business and concentrating on customer building.

- Measuring customer satisfaction is about customers being given opportunities to provide feedback about product(s), service(s), the organization, and so forth.

- Website self-service functions act as support mechanisms for call centers. Many companies provide these portals for customers to be able to access their account information, check operating hours, ask questions, see product information, find contact information, check on placed orders, and get shipping information.

- Field service management operations allow customers to interact directly with service personnel.

- Sales force automation tools are used for documenting field activities, keeping track, and managing what your sales force is doing in the field. These types of tools include sales activity management, sales territory management, lead management, and knowledge management.

- The six steps to a successful CRM program include creating the CRM plan, involving CRM users from the onset, selecting the right application and provider, integrating existing CRM applications, establishing performance measures, and providing CRM training for all users.

- Current trends in CRM involve such aspects as customer data privacy, social media, and cloud computing.

REFERENCES

[1] *APICS Dictionary* (14th ed.). (2013). Chicago, IL: APICS. www.apics.org

Bachelor of Management Studies. (2012). Explain the elements of customer service. *Logistics Management*. Retrieved from http://www.bms.co.in/explain-the-elements-of-customer-service-2/

Burton, Nigel. (2004). Personalizing your customer communications. *Entrepreneur* (March). Retrieved from https://www.entrepreneur.com/article/70084

Carnes, Cassandra. (2010). Best practices for one-to-one marketing. Digital Publishing Solutions. Retrieved from http://www.dpsmagazine.com/Content/ContentCT.asp?P=869

Hopkins, Jeanne. (2011). 60 ways personalization is changing marketing. Hubspot Blog. Retrieved from http://blog.hubspot.com/blog/tabid/6307/bid/13829/60-Ways-Personalization-is-Changing-Marketing.aspx

Reichheld, Frederick F. (1996). Learning from customer defections. *Harvard Business Review* (April). Retrieved from https://hbr.org/1996/03/learning-from-customer-defections

Chapter 12
Supply Chain Management in the Service Industry

CHAPTER OUTLINE

Introduction

Service Supply Chain versus Manufacturing Supply Chain

Types of Services

Service Productivity Challenges

Global Services

Service Strategies

Service Delivery System

Service Response Logistics

Distribution Channels

Service Quality

INTRODUCTION ··

Throughout this text we have been focusing on supply chains that produce a physical product, but supply chains exist in the service industry as well. Service firms offer intangible products, meaning products that do not have physical dimensions. What customers are actually paying for in the service industry is the labor and the intellectual property of the service provider. While the service itself is not tangible, it likely involves use of, or work on, a tangible item. For example, we do not pay a dry cleaner for a shirt; instead, we provide our own shirt and pay the dry cleaner for the service of cleaning the shirt. Examples of service products include insurance, healthcare, entertainment, finance/banking, training/education, transportation, warehousing, and business consulting.

Because the nature of service products is so significantly different from physical products, the supply chain models for service products operate differently from those of physical products. Service products cannot generally be produced in advance or inventoried, and frequently the customer of a service provides the tangible item that will receive the service (e.g., a car for automotive repair, hair for a haircut, carpets for cleaning). Customers play a vital and more involved role in the delivery aspect of the service supply chain than they do in the supply chain for a physical/tangible product. Customers supply clothes to the dry cleaner to be cleaned, their refrigerator to the appliance repair shop to be serviced, and themselves to the healthcare provider to receive checkups and treatment. These types of services are said to provide state utility, meaning that the service is performed on something that is owned by the customer. In this context, without the customer also being a supplier in the service supply chain, the service could not be delivered. Consequently, in the service supply chain, it is much more about managing the relationships between the trading partners than it is about managing the chain of supply.

SERVICE SUPPLY CHAIN VERSUS MANUFACTURING SUPPLY CHAIN

How does supply chain management in the service industry differ from supply chain management in manufacturing?

- TANGIBILITY: Unlike manufactured products, services are <u>not</u> tangible (i.e., they cannot be seen, weighed, or measured, and you can't touch them in the same manner as tangible products that have physical dimensions). Service intangibility also presents the problem of customers not being able to try out and test a service before purchase. Unlike a product innovation, a service innovation cannot be patented, so a new concept must expand rapidly before competitors can copy the new service offering.

- LABOR CONTENT: There is a much higher ratio of labor to materials in the service industry.

- CUSTOMER INVOLVEMENT: Customers are much more directly involved in the service process than with manufactured goods. Services typically require direct interaction with a customer for the service to be completed or delivered. Customer satisfaction happens in real time with the customer witnessing and taking part in the process. Services can be customized to provide "a personal touch" so the customer feels that the service they are receiving is specifically for them. The use of a customer's name is still one of the most significant factors when engaging a customer. Most of us have at one time or another gone to a restaurant and paid with a credit card, but how many times did the wait staff look at your name on the credit card, and thank you by name when returning with the check to be signed? Customization can be simple and leads to customer satisfaction.

- ASSESSMENT OF QUALITY: Quality is assessed differently in the service industry. Each customer and each service provider are different. Services are often unique to the customer (insurance policies, legal services, tax preparation, etc.). Defining service quality can be highly personal, and it can therefore vary from one customer to the next. Services can often change weekly, daily, or even hourly. Goods are generally produced to meet precise specifications and in most cases do not change very often.

- PERISHABILITY: For the most part, services are simultaneously produced and consumed. They cannot be saved, stored, returned, or inventoried. A service company may use inventory management techniques for managing items that facilitate providing the service, but not for the service itself. This also leads to the challenge of planning for services as it is very difficult to ensure a high level of customer satisfaction if you cannot rely at least in part on having an inventory of services available to buffer for variability in demand or supply.

- LOCATION CONSIDERATIONS: Services are decentralized due to the inability to inventory and/or transport service products. Tangible goods are frequently produced in a location that is remote from the customer, whereas in most cases services require a well-designed customer-oriented facility in order to meet a customer's needs. Services are largely provided very near to where the customers are located, and are therefore heavily impacted by location decisions.

TYPES OF SERVICES

Service offerings can typically be categories into three service types:

1. PURE SERVICES: Services offering very few or no tangible products to customers (e.g., consulting, storage facilities, training/education)

2. END PRODUCTS: Services that offer tangible components along with the service component (e.g., restaurants; food along with the dining service)

3. STATE UTILITY: Services that directly involve things owned by the customer (e.g., car repair, dry cleaning, haircut, healthcare)

The Goods–Services Continuum

Almost every product offering is a combination of goods and services. Figure 12.1 illustrates this concept along a continuum spanning from Pure Goods to Pure Services.

- PURE GOODS are generally low-margin commodity businesses that, in order to compete against one another, often add some services (e.g., extended warrantees, consulting).

- CORE GOODS suppliers provide a significant service component (e.g., spare parts, repairs) as part of their businesses.

- CORE SERVICES suppliers must integrate tangible goods (e.g., cars for rental, food at a restaurant, planes for air travel) in order to provide their services.

- PURE SERVICES do not need much in terms of facilitating goods, but what they do use is essential to providing the service, thus facilitating goods (e.g., software, diagnostics tools).

FIGURE 12.1

Pure Goods	Core Goods	Core Services	Pure Services
Food products	Appliances	Hotels	Teaching
Chemicals	Data storage systems	Airlines	Medical advice
Book publishing	Automobiles	Internet service providers	Financial consulting

Goods ◄───► Services

(Anders Gustofsson and Michael D. Johnson, 2003)

SERVICE PRODUCTIVITY CHALLENGES..

In manufacturing, optimization of the supply chain is accomplished primarily by improving the speed of delivery and by reducing costs. Companies work to reduce bottlenecks and inventory, and try to negotiate better pricing on raw materials. The main way to speed production is to find a faster way to move or manipulate the component materials.

A research paper published by Eastern Illinois University points out that the main drivers of optimization in a service model are relationships and information flow. By eliminating bottlenecks caused by duplicate approvals or other intangible delays, a service company may be able to realize the same goal as the manufacturing company: a lower-cost product, delivered to the customer more quickly.

The following are some of the challenges encountered when attempting to improve productivity in the service industry.

1. HIGH LABOR CONTENT

   Most service offerings are almost entirely labor with very little, if any, materials. As a result, it may be more difficult to make improvements in productivity because the labor component is harder to improve than a material component. There may also be more people involved in providing the labor effort, each with their own knowledge and expertise. A significant part of service quality is predicated on the skill and ability of the person who's providing the service, rather than on the quality of the material and the design of the product, as in a manufacturing supply chain. Each person providing a service is unique and will likely bring different skills and experiences into the process. Not all lawyers, doctors, dry cleaners, service repair technicians, for example, are equal, and some may perform better than others.

2. INDIVIDUAL CUSTOMIZED SERVICES

   Because many service offerings are unique and customized for a specific customer (tax returns, legal services, healthcare, etc.), a service provider may not be easily able to improve beyond the standard approach simply by using knowledge and information gained over time, and best practices. While small incremental improvements can be made to the basic service, the customized nature of many service offerings limit improvement efforts. What worked before may not necessarily work with the next customer.

3. DIFFICULTY OF AUTOMATING SERVICES

   It is also difficult to improve productivity through automation in the service industry. In manufacturing, significant productivity improvements can be made by using automation to increase speed and reduce throughput times and costs. These opportunities are limited when providing many of the services being offered, partially due to the high level of customization in the service industry. For instance, how does a service provider automate customized legal services, or financial consulting?

In some cases, a service provider may be able to automate parts of a service such as making/taking reservations or appointments, or by the use of more technology and automation in supporting functions and facilitating goods used to help provide a service. These measures will certainly help, but may not appreciably improve the productivity.

4. PROBLEM OF ASSESSING SERVICE QUALITY

Because services are often unique to the customer (insurance policies, legal services, tax preparation, etc.), service quality can be very subjective, creating problems assessing the quality of the service. Defining service quality can be highly personal, and vary from one customer to the next. If the service provider can't determine what service is good and what service is not good, until it is delivered to the customer, it makes it difficult to identify where improvements are needed.

Another problem in assessing service quality is getting the customer to respond to feedback requests. Offering some form of additional benefit may help to entice a response from the customer. There are also customers that are afraid to respond to bad service because of an attitude presented by the service provider or representative. It is imperative that personnel in the service industry are properly trained and educated on both the service they are offering and how to properly and professionally interact with customers. Appropriate to this situation, Warren Buffett has been quoted as saying, "It takes 20 years to build a reputation and five minutes to ruin it."

GLOBAL SERVICES

Historically, most services were unique to the local market. Recently, the industry has seen the growth of services occurring worldwide, opening up new markets and challenging companies to manage services in a global environment. Many companies that were providing services in one market are now expanding and providing those services in other markets as well. This creates challenges as markets vary significantly. A manufacturer is likely to be able to offer the same exact product in every market it serves, but a service provider may not be able to offer the same exact service in every market.

Some of the reasons for this challenge are:

- **COMPETITION:** Service providers expanding into global markets must be aware of local competition and the services the competition is already offering. Can the expanding service provider offer a competitive advantage over these domestic companies? On what components of the service offering will they compete; price, quality, speed, capabilities? What is the business environment around the specific service(s) that will be provided in that market? Are there rules of engagement or business practices that a service provider needs to understand when moving into a new global market? There may be formal and informal ways of doing business in various countries. Competition in the service industry is significant, and customers looking for service will readily compare one organization to another. For an organization to survive it is important to be fully cognizant of what the competition is doing and what capabilities they have to offer.

- **CUSTOMERS:** A service provider needs to identify where potential global customers are before deciding to expand the business globally. Customers for a particular service may not necessarily be in every market, or in large enough numbers to sustain the global expansion. An overextension to weaker markets can be a huge drain on resources. Being selective will help to use resources wisely. Service offerings may also need to be modified or customized for specific markets and customer segments.

- **GOVERNMENT:** Expanding globally means understanding local regulations and legal requirements. Some markets are more open than others, and some are very restrictive. Governments may adopt a protectionist strategy and erect barriers such as taxes and tariffs on foreign companies in order to maintain an advantage for local companies. These barriers may discourage foreign companies from entering the market, or if they do enter the market, provide the government with additional revenue. Some countries may require foreign companies to partner with a local company, or even with the government itself, in order to do business in that market. This could be a hindrance, or it may be a benefit if the foreign service provider is not familiar with the local market.

- **INFRASTRUCTURE:** Infrastructure varies by country. Markets have differing qualities and types of suppliers, facilities, transportation, communications, and institutions available to support a service provider. The variances can be so significant that it precludes the quality of service response needed to maintain a significant economic position in that market. A service provider may need to modify its service offerings according to the resources available.

Franchising

Franchising is an arrangement where one party (the franchiser) grants another party (the franchisee) the right to use its trademark or trade name as well as certain business systems and processes, to produce and market a good or service according to certain specifications. It can provide an easy way to develop and grow an organization particularly when expanding internationally:

- "Allows services to expand quickly into dispersed geographic markets"[2]

- "Protects existing markets"[2]

- "Builds market share"[2]

- Facilitates expansion when the owners have limited financial resources[2]

SERVICE STRATEGIES

A company providing services, just like a company manufacturing a product, must adopt a strategy that it believes will lead to success. A sound strategy enables a service provider to consistently outperform competitive alternatives over time, across business cycles, industry disruptions, and changes in leadership.

In order to select the best strategy, a company should explore some key strategic questions, including:

- What markets will be served, and what is the opportunity in those markets?

- What are the potential customers' wants and needs?

- How does a company's current service capabilities align to customer needs?

- What service solutions will deliver the highest customer value and loyalty?

- What role does the company want to play in this market with these customers?

- What strategies are required to capture a leadership position and achieve goals?

- What services and delivery processes should be deployed?

- What systems and support processes should be implemented?

- What factors will determine success or failure?

Companies in the service industry may choose to adopt a version of one of the following three strategy types.[2]

Differentiation Strategy

A differentiation strategy calls for the development of a service(s) that is unique from that of the competition. Approaches to differentiation include developing unique brand images, unique technology, unique features, unique channels, unique customer service, and the like. In other words, the key to differentiation is obtaining an advantage over your competitors that is perceived by the customer as valuable. Collecting feedback and input from the customer base is generally the best way to identify a differentiating aspect of the service offering that customers will value. If the differentiating aspect of the service is truly valuable, customers will be more willing to pay for it. Example: Sunday car servicing. Most car servicing facilities are only open Monday through Saturday. Offering car servicing on a day that competitors aren't may help serve customers that couldn't otherwise take advantage of that service, because they are not available to bring the car in for servicing during the regular work week. This differentiation strategy sets the service provider apart from competitors and potentially increases business as a result.

Leadership Strategy

A leadership strategy involves establishing the company as the market leader by providing the best service at the lowest cost. This strategy may require a large capital investment in state-of-the art equipment, the newest and most efficient technologies, and significant efforts to control and reduce costs. Example: Auto diagnostics software. If the service provided is auto repair, and the service provider has a leadership strategy, the company will need to use less labor and complete repairs faster to be able to keep costs low. One way of doing this might be through the use of some automated equipment and software to help speed up the process of diagnosing the issue before repair, leading to less labor used, less chance of an error in diagnosing the issue, less delay, which leads to faster repairs and lower cost.

Niche Strategy

The niche strategy involves focusing the service offering on a narrow area and customer base in order to become extremely proficient at providing that particular service. An organization that wants to succeed in service response has to be strong in its market expertise and be better and more responsive than the competition. This strategy allows for high customization and personalized service, where the service provider may be the only company providing that service in that area. Example: A mechanic who specializes in repairing just one type of automobile, usually a high-end model. It is a service offered only to customers that have that type of automobile. The mechanic focuses all effort and expertise on this niche area and becomes extremely proficient at it.

SERVICE DELIVERY SYSTEMS...

The delivery of services can be expressed as a continuum with mass produced, low-customer contact systems such as a ticket kiosk, vending machine, or ATM, at one end, and highly customized, high-customer-contact systems such as a personal shopper, hair stylist, or financial manager at the other end. See figure 12.2.

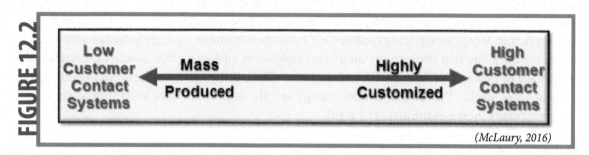

FIGURE 12.2

(McLaury, 2016)

Every service offering falls somewhere along the continuum; however, some service offerings have components of both ends of the continuum blended together.

- **Example:** Restaurant

    - Front of the house staff (e.g., hostess, waiter) are high customer contact.

    - Back of the house staff (e.g., chef, dishwasher) are low customer contact.

- Service delivery systems may be designed to keep these separate in order to use various and different management techniques to maximize performance in each area.

Regardless of where on the continuum a service offering falls, the service delivery system should be audited often to assess performance and make improvements.

Bundle of Service Attributes

The bundling of service attributes such as explicit and implicit services, along with facilitating goods and supporting infrastructure, can help to enhance customer satisfaction. An example of commonly bundled services is in the banking industry.

- SUPPORTING INFRASTRUCTURE: Includes location, decoration, layout, architectural appropriateness, equipment, etc.

    - Banking Industry Examples: drive-up tellers, ATMs

- FACILITATING GOODS: Tangible elements that are used or consumed by the customer, or the service provider, along with the service provided.

  - Banking Industry Examples: cash and coins, deposit forms, statements

- EXPLICIT SERVICES: includes the availability and access to the service, consistency of service performance, comprehensiveness of the service, and training of service personnel.

  - Banking Industry Examples: check cashing, safe deposit boxes, loans

- IMPLICIT SERVICES: includes the attitude of the servers, atmosphere, waiting time, and convenience.

  - Banking Industry Examples: security, privacy

Service Location Strategy and Layout Strategy

LOCATION STRATEGY

There is an old adage in real estate: "location, location, location." In the context of the service industry it means that the business might thrive or fail based on the location. Many services, as described in this chapter, are heavily dependent on proximity to customers and are therefore highly susceptible to location issues. The "right" location can make or break a service business. An example of a company that has done a good job of this is McDonald's. They spend a great deal of time and money to research the right location for a new franchise to ensure success. Aspects considered include population, demographics, income levels, vehicle traffic, pedestrian traffic, number and type of competitors in the area, and proximity of competitors. Service providers should make it easy for customers to find the facility.

When considering a location it may be important to know what support services are in the immediate area such as fire, police, and medical facilities, as well as support services from the local city operations departments.

LAYOUT STRATEGIES

Once customers arrive, service providers should also make it easy for customers to find what they are looking for, or to find what the service provider wants them to find. The layout of the facility should be designed to reduce the distance traveled by the customer within the facility.

For example, a doctor's office waiting room usually has a receptionist where patients (i.e., customers) check in when they arrive, and generally, immediately adjacent to the waiting room are the examining rooms. The doctor's office wants the patients to arrive, check in with the receptionist, sit in the waiting room, and then wait to be called to go into the examining room where they can be examined. Once the meeting with the doctor is concluded, the process is reversed to exit.

Another example is a service center such as a car dealership, a pet grooming facility, or a car wash. The customer can enter, check in, and then watch the service personnel working on their possession while sitting in the waiting room waiting for the service to be completed. This is also a way to occupy the customer's time while waiting. It's provides something to do that interests the customer and distracts them from consciously being aware of how long it might be taking to complete the service.

Transportation and Warehousing in Services

Services may require the use of facilitating goods which are tangible elements that are used or consumed by the customer, or the service provider, along with the service provided (computers, furniture, office supplies, medical supplies, repair parts, equipment, etc.).

- These facilitating goods need to be transported and warehoused in order to provide the service activity.

- Generally these transportation and warehousing activities occur behind the scenes (i.e., out of view of the service customer).

- Customers may have no idea how these facilitating goods actually get to the destination but they are likely to notice if they are not available as expected.

SERVICE RESPONSE LOGISTICS ....

A primary concern of service response logistics is the management and coordination of the organization's service activities.

The four primary activities of service response logistics are:

- Managing service capacity

- Managing waiting times

- Distribution channels

- Service quality

Managing Service Capacity

SERVICE CAPACITY

Service capacity can be expressed as the number of customers per day, per shift, per hour, per month, or per year that the company's service system is designed to serve. Regardless of the specific breakdown, it's the number of customers that the service provider can service at any one time. It is the planned capacity for the service environment.

Not Enough Capacity:

If the **demand exceeds capacity**, and the service provider does not currently have the capacity to serve all of the customers, there are three basic alternatives:

1. Turn customers away and not service them

2. Make customers wait until service is available for them

3. Increase service capacity (i.e., the number of service personnel and the associated infrastructure to provide the service)

Since most services are accomplished by service personnel, the service provider will likely need to hire more people to respond to the increased demand. Hiring, training, supervising, and equipping personnel is costly and can account for approximately 75% of the service provider's operating costs. This situation makes forecasting service demand critically important, particularly because services cannot be inventoried or carried out in advance.

To minimize the cost of hiring and laying off employees, the following strategies may help handle periods of **high demand:**

- Sharing employees who have been cross-trained so that they can help on the task that is busy at the moment

- Using part-time employees (e.g., during the holiday season)

- Using customers—"hidden employees" (e.g., self check out)

- Using technology (e.g., scanning documents in the insurance industry for use in multiple departments as necessary)

- Using employee scheduling policies (e.g., nurses have to work alternating holidays)

<u>Too Much Capacity</u>:

If the **capacity exceeds demand**, and the service provider does not have enough work, instead of disposing of excess capacity (e.g., laying off personnel), find other uses for the available capacity:

- Do other jobs when it's not busy. Example: in a restaurant you might have workers clean the bathrooms, prep for the dinner rush, and other various tasks.

- Do training or cross training.

- Use demand management techniques to shift demand from peak demand periods into non-peak periods by offing incentives like discounts and special sales (e.g., early bird specials, 20% off from 9 am to noon).

SERVICE CAPACITY PLANNING CHALLENGES

Service providers are 100% reliant on the customer to create the flow of demand, which has a direct impact on their ability to fully utilize capacity. Some of the challenges are:

- Customer arrivals fluctuate, and service demands can also vary by customer.

- Idle capacity is a reality for services for which service providers must plan.

- Customers are participants in the service, and the level of congestion can impact on perceived quality.

SERVICE CAPACITY DECISIONS

- **LONG-RANGE:** Capacity can be used as a preemptive strike where the market is too small for two competitors to coexist. Example: the first to build a luxury hotel in a midsized city may capture all the business.

  - A strategy of building ahead of the demand is often taken to avoid losing customers.

- **SHORT-RANGE:** The lack of short-term capacity can generate customers for the competition. Example: If restaurant staffing is inadequate to handle the volume of customers arriving at the restaurant, the customer will likely go elsewhere.

- **BALANCE:** Capacity decisions must be balanced against the costs of lost sales if capacity is inadequate, or against operating losses if demand does not reach expectations.

Service Capacity Utilization

Service capacity utilization is calculated as the number of actual customers served per time period, divided by the available capacity.

Examples:

1. A hotel has 80 rooms booked out of a total of 100 rooms available. Utilization = 80%

   – This is pretty straightforward in that there are a fixed number of rooms and they are either booked or not booked. (80 / 100 = 0.8 or 80% utilization)

2. On average, a doctor can see X patients per hour. But, if the doctor takes longer with each patient than the average, the patient wait time starts to get backed up and some patients wait longer.

   – The doctor's office is not going to call in a temporary doctor for the rest of the day to catch up.

Demand Strategy

Similar to planning for manufacturing supply, planning for service capacity follows the level demand strategy, or the chase demand strategy.

Level Demand Strategy

Service capacity is set to remain constant regardless of demand. When demand exceeds capacity, queue management tactics are used to handle the excess customers.

Examples:

- The use of one queueing line (instead of many lines) at a bank or at a McDonald's to provide first-come-first-serve priority.

- The use of numbers at the deli. Note: This technique does not work well in all settings, such as a hospital emergency room.

Chase Demand Strategy

Service capacity is set to vary along with demand. The company hires and lays off workers to match the fluctuating demand. The company must take appropriate actions in advance to have available options for this strategy to work.

Examples:

- Grocery store opening up additional checkout line(s) with additional cashiers as volume in the checkout queue starts to grow.

- Restaurant calls in additional off-shift wait staff to meet increased demand following a local sporting event.

Managing Waiting Time

Managing waiting time involves managing both the actual waiting time and the perceived waiting time. The perceived waiting time by the customer is just as important as the actual waiting time, and may even be more impactful. In order to develop an effective waiting time management strategy, some basic information needs to be determined.

- "What is the average arrival rate of the customers?"[2]

- "In what order will customers be served?"[2]

- "What is the average service rate of the providers?"[2]

- "How are customer arrival and service times distributed?"[2]

- "How long will customers wait before they either leave or lower their perceptions of service quality?"[2]

- "How can customers wait even longer without lowering their perceptions of service quality?"[2]

Having this information will allow the service provider to develop a waiting time strategy specific for their business and location that will minimize the impact to the customers and on the business in general.

QUEUING SYSTEMS

A queue management system is used to help control the flow and prioritization of people expecting to receive a service. Often referred to as "crowd control," queues can be utilized for almost any situation where large numbers of people are gathering, or waiting in line to purchase tickets, enter a facility, etc. Queues are common in airports, amusement parks, and retail stores.

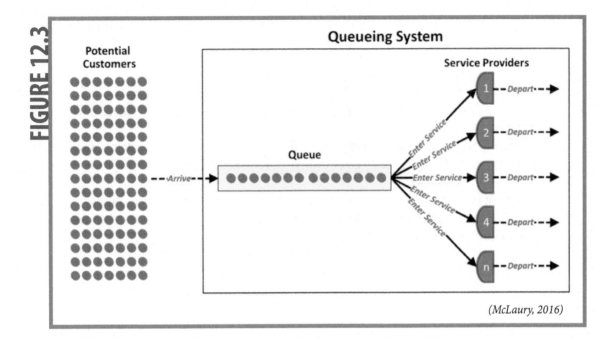

FIGURE 12.3

Potential Customers

Queueing System

Service Providers

Queue

Arrive

Enter Service
Enter Service
Enter Service
Enter Service
Enter Service

1 — Depart —
2 — Depart —
3 — Depart —
4 — Depart —
n — Depart —

(McLaury, 2016)

QUEUE TYPES:

- **Structured queues:** See figure 12.3. These queues are set in a fixed position such as a supermarket checkout line, airport, or bank. Queue management systems can be structure with or without customers being assigned a number and waiting for that number to be called after all previous numbers have been served in order of assignment (i.e., "take-a-number"). This option will allow customers to temporarily leave the queue and walk around while waiting for their number to be called.

- **Unstructured queues:** When people form queues somewhat informally in various directions and locations. These types of queues are seen in retail stores, at an airport waiting for a taxi, and people waiting for an ATM machine, for example.

- **Mobile queues:** Queues formed virtually with technology. Customers can use technology such as a smartphone to place their name in a real-time electronic queue such as at a restaurant. This type of queuing has provided a great deal of flexibility.

QUEUING SYSTEM INPUT:

- Customers are the demand source for services, and their arrival triggers the start of the service experience.

- Customers generally appear in predictable arrival patterns (e.g., the dinner rush at a restaurant).

- There are mathematical models available to help predict customer arrivals for planning purposes, such as the Poisson distribution model.

QUEUING SYSTEM ASSUMPTIONS:

- Most queuing models assume that customers enter the queue, and stay in the queue until served.

    - **Balking** is when customers refuse to join the queue. They arrive and determine that the queue is too long and decide to go elsewhere or return later.

    - **Reneging** is when customers decide to leave the queue. They are already in the queue and then decide that it is taking too long, or they change their mind about the service, and decide to leave the queue.

- Queuing models, for the purposes of calculations, assume an infinite length of a queue.

QUEUE SYSTEM DESIGN:

- Queue discipline describes the order in which customers are served. Examples: first-come-first-served, greatest need such as in a hospital emergency room.

- Queuing configurations can be comprised of single or multiple queueing lines.

- Queue lines can be serviced by either a single server or multiple servers.

- Multiple servers can also act in series or in parallel.

Choosing the correct design and queueing layout is a matter of individual service provider or organization design. Depending on the nature of the service and the desired flow of people, an organization will create and change the flow as needed.

The following gives a brief idea of several types of layouts:

- Single channel, single phase, single server (figure 12.4)

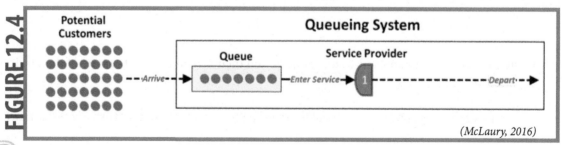

FIGURE 12.4

(McLaury, 2016)

- Single channel, multiple phase, acting in series (figure 12.5)

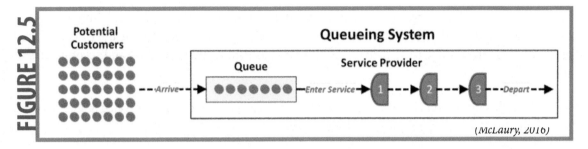

(McLaury, 2016)

- Multiple channel, single phase (figure 12.6)

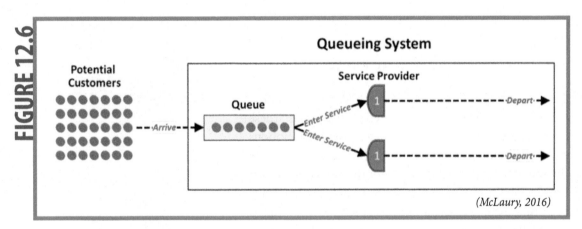

(McLaury, 2016)

- Multiple channel, multiple phase, acting in parallel (figure 12.7)

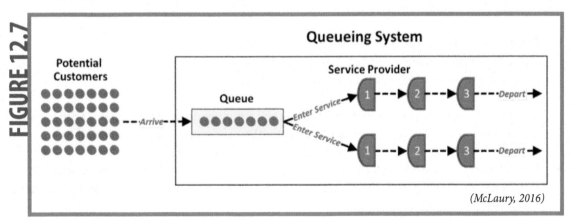

(McLaury, 2016)

MANAGING PERCEIVED WAITING TIMES

Waiting time has a huge impact on customer satisfaction, whether that is the actual time that customers must wait for the service to be delivered, or what customers perceive as the time that they are waiting for the service to be delivered. This issue leads directly to the first and second rules of service:

1. Customer satisfaction is achieved when the customer's perception of the service is at least equal to if not better than the customer's expectation.

2. It is hard to play catchup. A company may only get one chance to get it right in the eyes of the customer before losing that customer permanently, and also risk receiving a bad public review.

WAITING TIME MANAGEMENT TECHNIQUES

No one likes to wait in line; however, it is a reality, and even a necessary evil, for many service offerings.

There are mathematical formulas (which we will not explore in this text) used to help predict wait times. These formulas are based on certain predetermined assumptions and probabilities. There are also techniques for reducing the actual time spent waiting and/or the perception of the time spent waiting for the service to be delivered. Disney and other theme parks, for example, use these techniques. The answer is to keep the customers' minds off of waiting.

© fluidworkshop/Shutterstock.com

The following are some of the more common waiting time management techniques in use:

- **Keep customers occupied** during the wait time, and distracted from watching the time pass. Consider adding some form of entertainment to the waiting process to keep peoples' minds off of the wait. Examples: video programs, reading materials, games and activities, information boards with facts and history, viewing windows/areas to see the service they are waiting on, related exhibits[2]

- **Start the service quickly**. Don't make the customer wait again. Example: Once seated in the restaurant, <u>don't</u> make customers wait again before seeing the wait staff, receiving the menu, and starting the ordering process.[2]

- **Relieve customer anxiety**. Communicate. Let them know that there is no issue, everything is normal. The service will start soon or is progressing as expected.[2]

- **Keep customers informed.** Examples: "The wait time from this point is…," "The ride is stopped but will resume in 6 minutes."[2]

- **Group customers together in the queue**. Customers will often talk with one another, which occupies them and distracts them from watching the time.[2]

- **Design a fair waiting system.** Examples: first-come-first-serve, single file / single queue, take-a-ticket numbers, pre-arranged reservation or appointment[2]

DISTRIBUTION CHANNELS

There are a variety of traditional and contemporary ways that services can be delivered. Some of the more common ways are through:

- Facilities

- Retail stores

- Mail order

- Telephone

- Door to door

- Television

- Seminars and classrooms

- Automated equipment (ATM, kiosk, etc.)

- Mobile units

© KAMONRAT/Shutterstock.com

The following are some relatively new and unique ways that services are being distributed:

- **"Eatertainment"**[2] is a combination of food (restaurant service) and entertainment—that is, dinner and a show. Examples: Medieval Times, Rainforest Café, Dave & Buster's

- **"Entertailing"**[2] is a combination of the retail business with entertainment elements. Examples: shopping mall with children's play area, rides, fashion show

- **"Edutainment"**[2] is a combination of learning activities to go along with entertainment elements. Examples: Epcot Center, Liberty Science Center

- **Internet,** as a distribution channel for services, offers convenient and immediate access to information in real time. Customers, whether individuals or businesses, can use the tools on the internet to search for information, find suppliers, make appointments, do comparison shopping, buy things, sell things, provide feedback or reviews, and much more. Waiting times can be virtually eliminated. There are companies that offer products and services exclusively via the internet. This is referred to as a **pure strategy.**[2]

© Mmaxer/Shutterstock.com

Other companies offer products and services both in a physical store or facility location and via the internet. This is referred to as a **mixed strategy.**[2]

SERVICE QUALITY...

Identifying the quality of services is more difficult than identifying the quality of a physical product. This is largely because perceptions and expectations are subjective. What one customer versus another customer might think is good quality service, might be significantly different for the exact same service. This has much to do with expectations. To have excellent customer service all the time, the service provider needs to consistently exceed the customer's expectations, which may mean helping to form the customers' expectations. One example of forming the customers' expectations are the greeters at Walt Disney World. When new arrivals come onto the park, the greeters' job is to "make them happy" and they are trained to do just that. Another example is a service provider promising to deliver a service in 4 hours knowing that he or she can actually complete the service in 3.5 hours.

Service quality also depends significantly on the service provider's employees due to the ratio of labor to materials in service products and the expertise and professionalism of those individuals providing the service. Even an exceptional service provider can have a bad day.

In their research, Parasuraman, Zeithaml, and Berry[3] identified five dimensions typically used by customers to rate service quality.

1. RELIABILITY: Consistently performing the service correctly and dependably. This dimension was consistently identified by customers as the most important of the five dimensions.

2. RESPONSIVENESS: Providing prompt and timely service.

3. ASSURANCE: The ability to convey trust and confidence to customers.

4. EMPATHY: Providing caring attention to customers.

5. TANGIBLES: The physical characteristics of the service, including facilities, servers, equipment, and associated goods

There is no excuse for poor service. It does happen for any number of reasons, and when it does, the immediate issue is to recover from the situation such that it will not leave a lasting impression in the mind of the person who just faced what he or she considers to be bad service. People who have received great service on average are likely to tell at least five other people, whereas people who feel that they received what they consider to be bad service are likely to tell ten times that many.

To recover from poor service quality consider the following:

- Develop recovery procedures that are thought out prior to the bad event happening.

- Train employees in these procedures prior to the event, and practice them.

- Empower employees to remedy customer problems, and recognize them publicly when they do, to encourage others to do the same.

REFERENCES ··

[1] Gustofsson, A., & Johnson, M. D. (2003). *Competing in a service economy*. San Francisco, CA: Jossey-Bass, p. 7.

[2] Wisner, J., Tan, K. C., & Leong, G. K. (2016). *Principles of supply chain management, A balanced approach*. Boston, MA: Cengage Learning.

[3] Parasuraman, A., Zeithaml, V. A., & Berry, L. L. (1988). SERVQUAL: A multiple-item scale for measuring consumer perceptions of service quality. *Journal of Retailing, 64*(1), 12–40; Parasuraman, A., Zeithaml, V. A., & Berry, L. L. (1985). Conceptual model of service quality and its implications for future research. *Journal of Marketing, 49*(Fall), 41–50; Wisner et al., *Principles of supply chain management*.

ENABLE

Chapter 13
Project Management

CHAPTER OUTLINE

Introduction

Project Planning

Manage and Control

Manage Risk

Manage Issues

Conclusions

Project Management Definitions

Project Management Tools and Templates

INTRODUCTION ....

Project management processes, guidelines, and leadership techniques are becoming a predominant factor in the way organizations are conducting business and coordinating supply chain management resources to achieve desired and agreed upon results. All projects (and organizations), large or small, to some degree can utilize the processes project management offers. The question whether projects will be managed reactively or proactively is dependent upon the culture of an organization, its belief and support of supply chain management, project management, and the quality of management and leadership skills provided by the project manager. This being said, it is critical that a practical set of project management guidelines is agreed upon and adapted as a way of conducting project business. To better understand project management, consider the following questions:

- Projects encounter unexpected problems and issues throughout their lifecycle. Are those problems and issues resolved proactively using previously agreed upon guidelines, or is there hesitation when problems arise—questioning who to communicate with, who has the ownership and authority to resolve them?

- Projects can affect a large number of people and are cross-functional throughout the supply chain. This type of structure creates an uncertainty of risk causing planned tasks or activities not to happen as planned, and delivers less than agreed upon results, late schedules, and budgets over estimates. Are risks proactively managed, controlled with resolution before their occurrence, or after they occur with consequences resulting in changes to time, cost, resource reallocation, and cause and effects to other projects?

- Projects have stakeholders each of whom has specific benefits they want satisfied at the project's completion. Will the project scope (tasks and activities) be discussed and managed through an agreed upon change management process proactively with measurability and verifiability, or will there be a void in the process before reality dictates the project is over budget, off schedule, and will not deliver agreed upon results?

History tells us a great percentage of projects, especially large ones, do not end successfully. It has also been said by some organizations that they would be happy just to have their projects finish with some degree of success. This last statement is not true, because today's organizations expect projects to be completed faster, cheaper, and with the highest level of quality possible. The most successful way to meet project objectives is utilization of practical and effective project processes and guidelines led by a qualified manager with strong people skills and an involved and committed project team. Considering size, complexity, and other characteristics of project complexities, successful projects can only come from the utilization of guidelines to conduct business throughout the supply chain and education of the project team to those guidelines. Asking the team for involvement and commitment of tasks supported by measurability and verifiability is a winning combination for project success.

There is an old saying applicable to project management: "Plan the work and work the plan." Clearly, this is the key to successful project management. You must first plan the project, then monitor and control the execution of defined tasks and activities. The following is an overview of the project process to support successful results.

PROJECT PLANNING ....

A fear striking the hearts of many supply chain project managers and team members is the perceived inaccuracies of stated project objectives, time frames, and costs as handed down from on high. To eliminate this fear, the following two points of reference are being made: (1) In most cases persons initiating the project are using past experiences, knowledge, and current issues being faced to generate said information; and (2) project managers and teams who do not complete a Phase One "Concept and Feasibility" to accurately determine both best and worst case scenarios are not fulfilling a professional responsibility to the project owners. By providing proper business information to the project conceptors, they are then in a position to make informed business decisions. It cannot be overstated how important proper planning of a project is. The two most significant factors causing project failure are "poorly defined objectives and a lack of communication," which point to something lacking in the planning process.

There are three major deliverables from the project planning process: (1) a project objective definition or statement, (2) the work plan consisting of tasks and activities, and (3) the project management procedures or guidelines to conduct supply chain project business.

Project Definition

Plan the Work by First Utilizing a Requirements Document

Two tendencies that often occur during the planning portion of projects are to (1) shortcut the initial planning process by jumping into the performance of project work immediately upon receipt of the project, and (2) spend too much time planning excess detail for the project's lifecycle. These can be major mistakes. First, not to plan is a self-explanatory error on everyone's part and requires no further discussion. Second, to plan excessive detail for a period of time far down the line requires something greater than a crystal ball, because no one can predict the future. As an example, something heavily detailed today, called task B, but scheduled to happen several months from now could, and often does, become adversely affected by changes from other activities. These changes will ultimately cause a redesign of task B and all tasks linked thereafter. Even though a significant amount of project planning must take place up front, it should first be completed at the summary level with a detail level extended only out to a logical time frame such as 30, 60, or 90 days ahead. This provides a rolling wave effect of adding a new week as the current week is completed, allowing for detailed planning but with less chance of change.

As a project progresses, changes occur. As each change occurs the plan from that date forward will also change, thus the need for an ongoing project planning process. Time spent properly planning a project results in reduced cost, and duration of time, better utilization of resources, and increased quality over the life of the project. The project definition is the primary deliverable (agreed upon result) and is generated from the project's planning process. The project plan describes all aspects of project work starting at a high (summary) level including appropriate phases and guidelines on how to conduct project business. Once approved by the customer, relevant stakeholders and management, it becomes the basis for project work (tasks and activities) to be performed and the processes by which to conduct project business. The project definition and requirement document should include the following:

- PROJECT OVERVIEW: Describes the background context for the project and why it is being undertaken; it speaks to the business value of the work being performed.

- OBJECTIVE STATEMENT: Provides a summary of the project. This contains a high-level explanation of the project deliverables, scope, timeline, approach, and organization.

- SCOPE: Clearly defines the logical parameters of the project. This is the area to define what is to be included (in scope) and what is to be excluded (out of scope). Lack of clarity here is what often leads to "scope creep," excessive changes and dissatisfied customers.

- DELIVERABLES PRODUCED: It is important to describe agreed upon deliverables of the project. Provide enough explanation and detail (measurability and verifiability) allowing the reader to understand what has been agreed upon and understood as the final product.

- ASSUMPTIONS AND RISKS: What events are being taking for granted (assumptions), and what risks are circumstances or events exist outside the control of the project team?

- APPROACH: How will the project conduct business? Describe the use of business processes (project management guidelines) to be utilized.

- ORGANIZATION: Show the significant roles (and responsibilities) of the project team. Identifying the project manager is easy, but who is the sponsor? Who is on the project team? Are any of the stakeholders represented? Completion of a RACI chart provides a strong picture of responsibility, accountability, consultative support, and information flow. Use of a RACI chart helps provide a picture of who has what level of authority.

- INITIAL EFFORT, COST, AND DURATION ESTIMATES: These estimates must start as best effort estimates to reflect actual performance time (duration estimates are the start-to-finish calendar dates to complete effort estimates) multiplied by the cost per hour of doing business per functional area, then revised as required when changes take place throughout the project lifecycle.

- SIGNATURE PAGE: Ask for sponsor and stakeholders' approval. Their signature signifies they agree to the plan.

Project Work Plan

After the initial project definition has been prepared, the work plan (also called the "scope of work") can be defined. The work plan is derived by conducting a work breakdown structure (WBS) process and provides a step-by-step outlined list of activities (tasks) for completing project deliverables. The results of the WBS task list provides a vehicle for managing and tracking progress—providing that measurability and verifiability have been accurately identified to appropriate tasks. When available, use a prior work plan from a similar project as a template. Use of a task planning worksheet expedites development of a logic diagram by defining predecessors and successors for each task.

CREATE A PLANNING HORIZON

In addition to summary level tasks, create a detailed work plan, including assigning resources (identifying skill requirements) with effort estimates for each task as far ahead as you feel comfortable. Because objectives and tasks change throughout the life of a project, utilize the 30-, 60-, or 90-day outlook mentioned earlier. This allows for better ongoing planning without mass destruction to time schedules and planned resources. This becomes your planning horizon.

Project Management Procedures

DEFINE PROJECT MANAGEMENT PROCEDURES (UPFRONT GUIDELINES)

The project management procedures (guidelines) include sections on how the team will manage issues, scope, change, risk, quality, communication, and so on. It will also include resource utilization and effort and elapsed time estimating. It is important to be able to manage the project proactively, ensuring the project team and all stakeholders have a common understanding of how to conduct business within the project environment. If procedures (guidelines) have previously been established by an organization (corporate culture), then utilize them; however, carefully review them for each project to ensure they are current and accurate for that environment.

MANAGE AND CONTROL ....

Once the project has been accurately planned at the high (summary) level, execution of the tasks can begin. In theory, since you have agreement (requirements document with inclusions and exclusions) on the project definition (agreed upon results) and a work plan and project management procedures (guidelines) are in place, the next challenge is to execute your plans and processes correctly. Most projects do not proceed exactly as estimated and planned. Herein lies the prime reason for task measurability and verifiability and it is the responsibility of the project manager to exercise leadership skills to proactively track project tasks. The project manager must exercise course correction, when and if required, utilizing change management procedures stipulated in the project guidelines to get the project back on track or in line with newly agreed upon deliverables.

Manage the Work Plan

Regularly reviewing the work plan determines progress in terms of schedule and budget. If the project is small (short in terms of duration), weekly tracking of the schedule and daily monitoring of work tasks (measurability and verifiability are essential here) are sufficient. Larger projects may require a more rigorous effort of daily monitoring of tasks and schedules. Using a scheduling program such as Microsoft Project helps with schedule tracking.

- Monitor the schedule. Identify activities that have been completed during the previous time period and update the work plan to show they are finished. Determine whether there are any other activities that should be completed but have not been. After the work plan has been updated, determine if the project will be completed within original estimated effort, cost, and duration. If not, determine the critical path and look for ways to expedite these activities to get back on track.

- Monitor the budget. In today's business environment, cash flow is critical; therefore, monitoring the budget for cash flow is of prime concern. Look at the original budget against current spending; identify variances and determine whether spending is more than or less than originally estimated. This information must be based on the work completed to date and if there is a deviation from budget plan always identify the exact variance and reason for that variance documenting it by specific tasks.

Look for Project Trouble Signs:

- A small variance exists in the schedule or the budget is beginning to increase, especially early in the project.

- Tasks that are considered complete are still being performed.

- There is a need to rely on unscheduled overtime to meet deadlines.

- Team morale is fading fast.

- The quality of service and/or process is starting to deteriorate.

- Quality-control steps and project management time begin to be cut back.

Manage Scope and Change

Along with managing a schedule, managing scope is critical to control a project. Projects often fail not through problems with estimating or resource skills but with team members working on deliverables not part of the original project definition or agreed upon result. Even with good change management procedures in place, two major areas of change management must be understood and in place for a project to be successful. They are understanding who the customer is and the fact there will be scope creep.

Ensure the Sponsor Approves Change Requests

The project sponsor is the person funding the project (internal or external to the organization). Although there is usually only one sponsor, a project could (and almost often does) have many stakeholders or people who are impacted by the project. Requests for scope change often come from stakeholders, many of whom may be managers of functional support units. It doesn't matter how important a change is to a stakeholder, they cannot make scope-change decisions alone, and cannot give a team approval to make a change. In proper scope-change management, the sponsor (or their designate) must give the approval and accept the impact of changes, as they are the only ones who can authorize additional funding to cover cost, schedule, resource relocation, and domino effect to other projects.

Guard Against Scope Creep

Projects must utilize an agreed upon change management procedure as defined in the project management guidelines; however, sometimes small scope changes are not recognized and these add up over time. Scope creep is a term defining a series of small changes made to a project without change management procedures being utilized. Projects can easily fail because of scope creep; therefore, the project manager and team need to be ever alert for scope creep and guard against them.

MANAGE RISK

Risks refer to potential events, issues, or circumstances outside the project team's control, which usually have an adverse impact on project tasks and overall agreed upon results (deliverables and objective).

Identify Risks Up Front

During project planning the project team should identify any and all known risks (utilizing a database of past project variances and their reasons is invaluable). For each risk, determine the probability of occurrence (identify reasons as well as percentage), the impact it will have on the project, and what the impact will affect (i.e., cost, time, quality, and agreed upon results). Then place them in a priority order. Events and issues with high risk should have specific plans put in place at once to ensure nonoccurrence. Medium risks must also be evaluated to help proactively manage them. Low-level risks must also be identified as assumptions, because these can always turn into higher level risks at a later date. Once a project begins, periodically perform a risk assessment to determine if other risks may surface within the next window of time being tracked. Refer to figure 13.1.

MANAGE ISSUES

All projects will have issues arise that must be dealt with even when strong risk management procedures are in place. The opportunity for risk occurrence is far greater if project tasks are not monitored regularly (through measurability and verifiability) and a change and risk management process is not in place and agreed upon as part of the project management guidelines.

Resolve Issues as Quickly as Possible

The project manager must manage open issues (problems) promptly and thoroughly, ensuring their resolution. If there is no urgency to resolve an issue then it may not really be an issue. It may be a potential problem (risk), or it may be an action item that needs resolution at a later point in time.

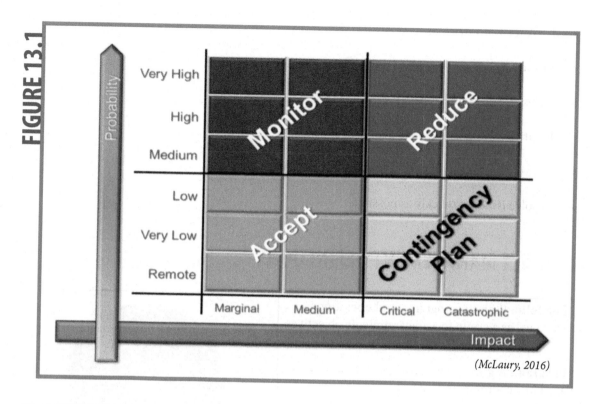

FIGURE 13.1

(McLaury, 2016)

CONCLUSIONS

Projects can be lengthy and costly to an organization. There are always complexities dealing with new technology, systems, processes, and products. There are also challenges to implementing a project with as little adverse impact on the customer as possible. All these challenges can be met and overcome through a well-defined process of planning, monitoring, controlling, and executing. The planning, monitoring, and controlling aspects are where project management guidelines, processes, and techniques are important. Resist the urge to jump right into the project execution. Proper planning and management of the project will take more time up front but will be rewarded with efficiencies and savings throughout the life of the project. Remember project management best practices include:

- Plan the work by utilizing a project definition (requirements) document.

- Create a planning horizon.

- Define project management (guidelines) procedures up front.

- Look for warning signs.

- Ensure the sponsor approves scope-change requests.

- Guard against scope creep.

- Identify risks up front.

- Continue to assess potential risks throughout the project.

- Resolve issues as quickly as possible.

PROJECT MANAGEMENT DEFINITIONS ....

Portfolio: Projects, programs, and operations managed as a group to achieve strategic objectives **Program:** A group of projects and activities managed in a coordinated way **Project:** A temporary endeavor undertaken to create a unique product, service, or result	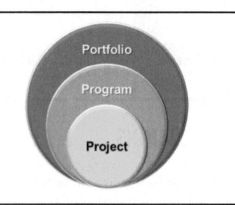
Project Management: The application of knowledge, skills, tools, and techniques to project activities to meet project requirements	
Project Manager: The person authorized by the organization to direct the team accountable for realizing the project objectives	
Project Stakeholders: Includes all project team members, and anyone impacted by, or anyone impacting, the project	
Triple Constraint: the foundation of project management is balancing the triple constraint of scope, time, and cost, with quality at the center	

(McLaury, 2016)

PROJECT MANAGEMENT TOOLS AND TEMPLATES......................

As described earlier in this chapter, project management is a process that is best achieved when managed in a systematic way. The following pages describe a basic process, and tools which may be used to help manage the project management process as described earlier.

FIRST A DECISION TO HAVE A PROJECT. The decision to have a project is often determined by management usually at a senior level, and often presented in a verbal format. It is best when a project request is made that it be supported by a preliminary requirements document (e.g., SCM PM 01A). This document provides a baseline for the PM to communicate with those supply chain functional managers who will participate in confirming the accuracy of the project's objective, high-level timeline, and budget.

THE ABC CORPORATION - - - - SUPPLY CHAIN MANAGEMENT	
Project Title:	
Preliminary Project Requirements Document	**Date:**

General Information			
Company:		**Location:**	
Contact Person:		**Date:**	
Phone No.:		**Email:**	

Preliminary Project Overview Statement (Project Specifics and Focus Statement)
Provide as specifically as possible an overview statement of the projects objective(s) and agreed results.

Project Assumptions:
What high-level assumptions have already been made about the project?

Approval and Authority to Proceed to a Requirements Document Using Project Process Approach		
We approve the project as described above, and authorize the team to proceed.		
Name	**Title**	**Date**

Item	Add Attachments As Needed
1	
2	

SCM PM 01A

The Project Requirements Document

The project requirements document contains greater detail as defined by the project manager and team of supply chain functional members. This document is presented to the stakeholder for approval (prior to the actual start of a project) but is often rejected for modification prior to its final signed approval.

THE ABC CORPORATION - - - - SUPPLY CHAIN MANAGEMENT			
Project Title:			
Project Requirements Document		**Date:**	

General Information			
Created by:		Date:	
Phone No.:		Email:	

Project Overview Statement (Project Title and Focus Statement)
Answer the question, Why is it important to achieve the project objective? What do you hope to achieve by executing this project?

Project Scope (List Inclusions)

Project Scope (List Exclusions)

Project Agreed Results (Expressed with Measurability and Verifiability)
What will the project actually produce?

Project Assumptions:
What high-level assumptions have already been mad about the project?

Project Approach (Project Management Guidelines, PMG) **Include: communication, risk management, and reporting plans.**

List the Project Stakeholders			
Name	**Title**	**Name**	**Title**

Approval(s) and Authority to Proceed		
We approve the project as described above, and authorize the team to proceed.		
Name	**Title**	**Date**

Item	**Attachments**
1	

SCM – PM 01

The Project Phase Approach

To better manage a project, divide it into several phases providing better management control and appropriate ways to measure and verify accuracy of the project performance and progress.

THE ABC CORPORATION - - - - SUPPLY CHAIN MANAGEMENT				
Project Title:			Chart Project Phase	
Phase Number One: Title:	**Phase Number Two:** Title:	**Phase Number Three:** Title:	**Phase Number Four:** Title:	**Phase Number Five:** Title:
Phase Statement:	Phase Statement:	Phase Statement:	Phase Statement:	Phase Statement:
Summary Level Task List	**Summary Level Task List**	**Summary Level Task List**	**Summary Level Task List**	**Summary Level Task List**
Phase agreed results are:	**Phase agreed results are:**	**Phase agreed results are:**	**Phase agreed results are:**	**Phase agreed results are:**
Buy off this phase: Yes No Buy in to next phase: Yes No	Buy off this phase: Yes No Buy in to next phase: Yes No	Buy off this phase: Yes No Buy in to next phase: Yes No	Buy off this phase: Yes No Buy in to next phase: Yes No	Buy off this phase: Yes No Buy in to next phase: Yes No

Senior Phase Review Committee			
Signatures			
Title:	Date:	Title:	Date
Title:	Date:	Title:	Date:

SCM – PM 09

CHARACTERISTICS OF PROJECT PHASES are identified at completion with "agreed results" on the deliverables. The deliverables should be tangible and marked with measurability and verifiability confirming accuracy and timeliness. Each phase should culminate in a review meeting where an agreement is made to progress to the next phase or if needed to detect errors and correct before moving ahead.

Control of each phase is often referred to as a "buy-off" on a current phase and a "buy-in" to the next. A phase can include both summary and sublevel tasks and the following diagram provides an example of what might be included in a given phase.

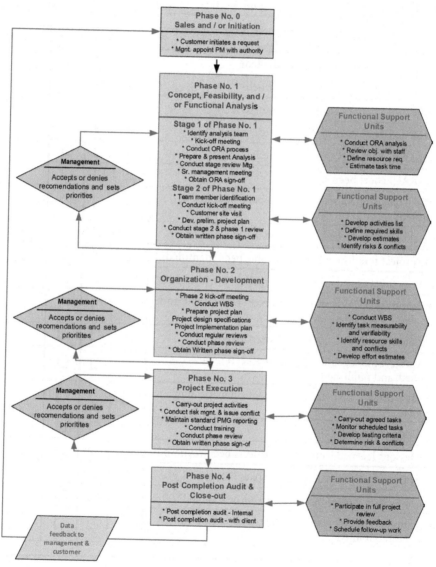

The following provides an example of what might be designed as a checklist for each of the phases. This checklist will be dependent upon the nature and make of both the project and specifics of the individual phases.

THE ABC CORPORATION - - - - SUPPLY CHAIN MANAGEMENT					
Project Title:					
Phase One (1) Checklist:	**Date:**		**Completed by:**		

Item	Description	Yes	No	N/A	Comments
1	Was a phase kick-off meeting conducted?	❏	❏	❏	
2	Has the project manager been identified?	❏	❏	❏	
3	Has the project sponsor(s) been defined?	❏	❏	❏	
4	Have all necessary stakeholders been identified?	❏	❏	❏	
5	Has the project team been established?	❏	❏	❏	
6	Has a RACI chart been started?	❏	❏	❏	
7	Has all background documentation been obtained and identified?	❏	❏	❏	
8	Have all issues, risks been discussed and documented?	❏	❏	❏	
9	Is the project mission, vision, and value been identified?	❏	❏	❏	
10	Has the projects agreed results (deliverables) been identified?	❏	❏	❏	
11	Are the project objectives (deliverables) measurable and verifiable?	❏	❏	❏	
12	Have any major project constraints been identified?	❏	❏	❏	
13	Have project management guidelines been reviewed, modified, and published?	❏	❏	❏	
14	Does this project have necessary senior management support?	❏	❏	❏	
15	Is the project feasible?	❏	❏	❏	
16	Have lessons learned from other projects been reviewed?	❏	❏	❏	
17	Is the project ready to proceed to the planning phase?	❏	❏	❏	
18	Is a phase review meeting planned and/or initiated?	❏	❏	❏	
19	Has a buy-off on this phase and a buy-in to the next phase been obtained?	❏	❏	❏	

Additional Comments or Phase Exceptions Noted:

TASK PLANNING WORKSHEET

The task planning worksheet is designed to help the project manager and team more accurately define the tasks to be performed including both the task predecessors and successors along with an effort to estimate for the performance of the tasks. The TPW is also designed to aid in identifying additional requirement for each of the tasks as seen here.

THE ABC CORPORATION - - - - SUPPLY CHAIN MANAGEMENT				
Project Title:				
Task Planning Worksheet – Summary Level			**Date:**	
General Information				
Department:		**Manager:**		
Created by:		**Date:**		
Phone No.:		**Email:**		

2. Preceding Task(s) Title and Agreed Results Required in Order to Start Next Task(s)?	**1. Summary Level Task(s)** Required to Support Successful Completion of This Project	**Task(s)** Effort Estimate	**3. Succeeding Task(s)** Title and Agreed Results Required in Order to Start Next Task(s)?

4. State Quality Issues Related to These Tasks	**5. Unit or Person(s) Responsible for Quality**

6. Required Performance Skills	**7. Perceived Task Risks**	**8. Solutions for Risks**

9. Required Checklist(s)	**10. Required Task Form(s)**	**11. Key Milestones**

SCM – PM 05

BASIC PROJECT FORMS

When managing projects, it is always better to develop a standard way of conducting business and in so doing the following forms, "Meeting and Agenda, "Change Request," and "Risk Management" should be considered as critical and standards for running projects.

Meeting and Agenda From

THE ABC CORPORATION - - - - SUPPLY CHAIN MANAGEMENT		
Project Title:		
Agenda / Minutes for Project Meeting Number:	Date:	Time:

General Information		
Location		
Participants	**Meeting Chair:**	

Item	Time	Topic
1		
2		
3		
4		
5		

Item	Due By	Responsible	Topic Details
1			
2			
3			
4			
5			

Item	Results / Resolutions / Action Steps
1	
2	
3	
4	

Item	Attachments
1	
2	

SCM – PM 04

CHANGE REQUEST FORM

THE ABC CORPORATION - - - - SUPPLY CHAIN MANAGEMENT		
Project Title:		
Change Request Form Number: Date: Completed by:		

Additional and/or Support Materials Attached: Yes: No:		
Current Condition / Situation:		

Proposed Change(s):

Justification:

Change Management Information		
Change Control Number:	**Priority(s):** High: Medium: Low:	
1	**Cost Impact:**	
2	**Timing Impact:**	
3	**Schedule Impact:**	
4	**Quality Impact:**	
5	**Scope Impact:**	
6	**Deliverable Impact**	
7	**Other Impact(s):**	

Change Review Committee Information	
Disposition:	Approval: Disapproved:

Signatures		
Title:	Title:	Title:
Title:	Title:	Title:

	Follow Up	
Documentation Updated	Yes: No :	**Change Implemented:** Yes: No:

SCM – PM 06

RISK MANAGEMENT FORM

THE ABC CORPORATION - - - - SUPPLY CHAIN MANAGEMENT

Project Title:

Risk Management Format: Date: Completed by:

Step No. 1: Define in writing a clear statement of the task and/or problem:

Step No. 2: Identify the probability of this occurrence:

Step No. 3: Identify the impact of this occurrence (on time, cost, and resource reallocations):

Step No. 4: Will there be an effect on other projects and if so what?

Step No. 5: Identify, list, and explain possible preventative plan(s):

Step No. 6: List appropriate contingency plan(s) and trigger points to imitate them:

Additional and/or Support Materials Attached: Yes: No:		
Risk Management Plan Authorizations		
Signatures		
Title:	Title:	Title:
Title:	Title:	Title:

SCM – PM 07

TEAM MEMBER EVALUATION

The ABC Corporation - - - - Supply Chain Management							
Project Title: Team Member Evaluation Form							
Team Member: Date: Completed by:							

Item	Description	5	4	3	2	1	N/A	Comments
1	Completes task on time							
2	Defines task(s) agreed results with measurability and verifiability							
3	Attends team meetings on time and stays until the end							
4	Makes positive contribution to the project and team							
5	Displays technical competence							
6	Takes responsibility appropriately							
7	Contributes fair share of the work							
8	Easy and cooperative to work with							
9	Works well under pressure							
10	Communicates well when speaking							
11	Assists other team members when needed							
12	Demonstrates good problem-solving skills							
13	Works well with customer(s)							
14	Listens well							
15	Coaches less experienced individuals well							
16	Learns quickly							
17	Works well by themselves							
18	Takes the initiative							
19	Reliable							
20	Produces high-quality work							
21	Handles conflict well							
22	Accepts feedback well							
23	Well organized							
24	Has a professional demeanor							
25	I look forward to working with this person in the future on another project							

Additional Comments:

SCM - PM 08

CPSIA information can be obtained
at www.ICGtesting.com
Printed in the USA
LVOW02s0009250117
522044LV00001B/1/P